EU ENERGY LAW AND POLICY

EU Energy Law and Policy

A Critical Account

KIM TALUS
Inspired by Thomas Wälde

OXFORD
UNIVERSITY PRESS

OXFORD
UNIVERSITY PRESS

Great Clarendon Street, Oxford, OX2 6DP,
United Kingdom

Oxford University Press is a department of the University of Oxford.
It furthers the University's objective of excellence in research, scholarship,
and education by publishing worldwide. Oxford is a registered trade mark of
Oxford University Press in the UK and in certain other countries

Published in the United States of America by Oxford University Press
198 Madison Avenue, New York, NY 10016, United States of America

British Library Cataloguing in Publication Data
Data available

Library of Congress Control Number: 2013938586

ISBN 978–0–19–968639–1

Printed and bound in Great Britain by
CPI Group (UK) Ltd, Croydon, CR0 4YY

Table of Contents

Background for this Book

I ended up working on European and international energy law issues more or less by coincidence. Having embarked on a career in general EU law, I worked on the first merchant infrastructure case under the (then) new EU regulatory frameworks for electricity and gas. Thinking that this was an interesting project, I decided to write an article explaining the regulatory considerations to be taken into account in applying for a merchant exemption in an electricity internconnector project. Shortly after finishing this article, the European Court of Justice gave its decision in a case involving electricity interconnectors. Again, I decided to write something on that case. Both articles were published in an international energy law journal then headed by the late Professor Thomas W. Wälde.

Thomas later contacted me and suggested that we should cooperate, given that we had similar interests and he liked my articles. So we did. We published two more articles together on electricity markets and Thomas introduced me to the academic energy and investment law community in Europe and internationally. At some point in 2006, Thomas told me that he had an old manuscript which he had started to write at his summer place in France but had never finished. He was a person who always had too much to do, but usually managed to get it all done. This particular project had slipped due to his many other commitments. He suggested that we complete the book project together. Given that this was Professor Thomas Wälde asking, I accepted without hesitation. We agreed that I would work simultaneously on my PhD and this book, plus many other projects. This turned out to be too much and, given that the book project was the least urgent of the various tasks to be done, it got pushed further and further into the future. At some point it became clear that the EU would roll out yet another legislative package. Given that it made little sense to write a book when the legislative framework was about to change, we decided to put the project on hold and wait for that package to come out.

In 2008, the International Bar Association annual meeting was held in Buenos Aires. As is customary, the IBA awarded scholarships to attend the meeting. That year, the topic for the writing competition for the scholarship was 'How to ensure security of supply in fully liberalised energy markets'. I had written several papers on related topics. When the information about the topic was published I was a visiting researcher at the University of Houston trying to understand the system of regulation used in the US natural gas market. Thomas suggested I enter the competition, despite already having too many things to do while in Houston. So I did, and got lucky. I told Thomas that I had been awarded the scholarship and he wrote back with a suggestion: 'Try lomito with mendoza wine.' I did.

During the conference we received the sad news of his passing, and OGELFORUM, the global discussion forum initiated by Thomas, was flooded with emails about his life and significance. One IBA session held a moment of silence for Thomas.

Having promised to write the book, I decided to continue with the project. I intended to complete the book to a certain timetable, but intervening events meant I had to push back the deadlines I had set. In 2011 I finally came to the conclusion that this situation could not continue and began to set aside time for the book each week. By this stage, over ten years had passed since Thomas wrote the first incomplete draft of the manuscript. Needless to say, a great deal had happened since then: Enron had collapsed, the California power crises had taken place, the rise of China and India had gathered pace, oil prices had continued to rise, unconventionals (shale gas being but one example), and, of course, a complete overhaul of EU energy law had occurred. These factual, real world changes, together with the regulatory changes that had taken place after Thomas had written his manuscript, meant that a lot had to be rewritten, a lot had to be taken out, and even more had to be added. As Thomas never saw the end-result and had not given his blessing to the project, we decided to publish the book under my name with the addition, 'Inspired by Professor Thomas W. Wälde'. The word 'inspired' is, however, an understatement. Thomas is behind large sections of the book, although they have been modified to fit the present-day factual and regulatory context. In addition to the text itself, I have tried to maintain the style of Thomas W. Wälde throughout the book: argumentative, critical, yet well-informed about international and EU energy policies. I hope that I have succeeded.

I would like to thank Angus Johnston for his valuable comments and insights into the first draft of the book. I would also like to thank Kaisa Huhta for her help in editing the final version of the book. Finally, I would like to thank my family, Anu, Bea, and Cilla, for their continuing love and support.

I dedicate this book to Thomas W. Wälde. Thank you for your help, support, and friendship.

Table of Cases

GENERAL COURT

COMMISSION (ANTITRUST) DECISIONS

Table of Legislation

DIRECTIVES

DECISIONS (EXCLUDING ANTITRUST DECISIONS)

NOTICES, GUIDELINES, RECOMMENDATIONS, PRESS RELEASES, ETC.

1

Introduction

EU Energy Law and the Approach Taken in this Study

Is there such a thing as 'EU Energy Law'? Or is what we call EU energy law nothing but a special colouring acquired by the elements of general EU law when applied to the energy sector? Such elements comprise EU rules on the internal market: on freedom of establishment, movement of goods and services, competition, state aid, the environment, climate change, and the international treaties of the EU as they affect economic activities in particular economic sectors. The answer one might give to this question depends on the specificity of the particular problems experienced by the energy industries in relation to EU law, the level of interest—public, professional, academic, and commercial—in these problems, EU law's response to them, and distinctive, significant features which permit focus on the economic regulation of energy by the EU and in the EU with some degree of insulation from other industries. In common with the late Thomas Wälde, I believe the issue is sufficiently specific to warrant separate treatment, as do many academics and other professionals who have chosen to concentrate on this particular subject.

There are hundreds of different industries, and only a few have, so far, given rise to a particular professional and academic sub-discipline.[1] The energy industries have been among the most dominant industries of the 20th century—the lifeblood of modern economies, fuelling both industrial and private consumption.[2] They encompass:

- the 'upstream' exploration and extraction of oil and gas (but also hard minerals like coal and uranium and unconventional sources of oil and gas including shale gas or shale oil);

- the generation of electricity using a number of primary fuel sources (oil, gas, coal, uranium, hydropower, unconventional sources);

- sea and overland transport, storage and final distribution to power companies, industrial and household consumers of oil and gas through pipelines or LNG ships;

---

[1] Behind the emergence of such sub-disciplines is the interest and strategy of legal practitioners to market their often quite generalized expertise presented as special to significant segments of client groups, and the equal interest of academics to develop a recognized specialized niche.

[2] The role of oil for the industrial world has been excellently captured by Daniel Yergin in his, now notorious, book, D. Yergin, *The Prize* (New York: Free Press 1991).

- the transportation of electricity through transmission and distribution networks, and access and utilization by electricity generators and large and small consumers.

The energy industries are big and heavy. They require massive investment of capital, involving large finance packages stretching over many years. They are closely linked with domestic, regional, and national politics—'geopolitics' as some call it. Their financial support is frequently an important issue for for political parties, as is political control over them. As large-scale employers, they are important to trade unions and in particular to regional politics. If the energy industries work smoothly—which in developed market economies they tend to do—they form a large, but quite innocuous part of the political and economic landscape. This changes dramatically if supply problems occur—such as the gasoline shortages due to price- and tax-inspired blockades in 2000 in the UK, the Californian power crisis in the summer of the same year,[3] the home-grown power crisis in Japan in 2003 due to a shortage of reliable reprocessing facilities,[4] a semi-crisis in Germany caused by exceptional heat that led to a scarcity of coolants for nuclear power stations,[5] or the spot market deteriorations in New Zealand caused by severe water shortages and lack of reserve capacity,[6] similar difficulties faced by Norway, or the unprecedented 2009 supply cut resulting from contractual disputes between Russian company, Gazprom, and its Ukranian trading partner, which left parts of south-eastern Europe in major difficulties.[7] In addition, one should not forget the series of blackouts that happened in 2003 in northeastern America, southeastern Canada, Italy, London and the southeast of England, and Sweden and Denmark. These seemed to point to the organizational and technical vulnerability of interconnected systems to unforeseen events (as in the case of Italy and Sweden), or to human error (as in London), or to a combination of both (as in the US).[8] In these situations, society realizes its complete dependence on a regular supply of energy, which is of more critical importance than, say, telecommunications and internet services.

Until quite recently, the electricity and gas industries (as distinct from upstream oil and gas production) were, by dint of their technical features, licensing, and regulation, and through the political control exercised over them, domestic industries

---

[3] *Financial Times*, Californian power suppliers face market overhaul (1.11.2000).

[4] *The Economist*, Japan's Energy Crisis—Darkness falls on Tokyo, (19.7.2003), p. 53.

[5] *Frankfurter Allgemeine Zeitung*, Hitze treibt Strompreise, (12.8.2003), p. 9; *Frankfurter Allgemeine Zeitung*, Hitze stellt Stromversorgung auf die Probe, (13.8.2003), p.9. Prices peaked at €185 per MWh.

[6] Electricity Commission Will Deliver Supply Security (Pete Hodgson, 20 May 2003). New Assessment of Electricity Supply Security (Pete Hodgson 20 December 2002). NZ Electricity Outlook, Dry Year Risk, 2003/2004–2006/2007, Energy Link Study for The Ministry of Economic Development, 18/12/2002. Government Policy Statement on Electricity Financial Transmission Rights, Released (11 December 2002).

[7] S. Pirani, J. Stern, and K. Yafimava, 'The Russo-Ukrainian Gas Dispute of January 2009: A Comprehensive Assessment', NG 27 (Oxford Institute for Energy Studies, February 2009) and A. Kovacevis, 'The Impact of the Russia-Ukraine Gas Crisis in South Eastern Europe', NG 29 (Oxford Institute for Energy Studies, March 2009).

[8] *Frankfurter Allgemeine Zeitung*, An Fehlerquellen herrscht kein Mangel, (7.10.2003) (deals with a wrong fuse terminating supplies in London; breakdowns of generation capacity in Sweden; a Swiss tree causing one of two interconnectors to be closed whereby the Italian grid became unstable; and a lack of network capacity, mis-handling of balancing services and failing communications in the US).

with few if any transnational activities.[9] Having been built up mainly through entrepreneurial activity with state support in the 19th century, in the 20th century they became state-owned or largely state-controlled.[10] From 1882 onwards, private investors created isolated central station electricity systems. The interconnections were completed by the 1920s. In the early days, electricity undertakings were used to facing ongoing competition from gas lighting. In the aftermath of the 1929 Wall Street Crash, public utility regulation was introduced.[11] Public management of the 'National Grid' in England and Wales was established with effect from 1930. Large-scale public investment made following the end of World War II reflected the paradigm of state involvement with the sector. Contrary to the present state of technology, consideration of economies of scale took precedence over everything else: the larger the investment, the lower the expenditure per kW generated. Economically, gas and electricity in particular constituted natural, and legally supported, monopolies. As a result of these features, energy law emerged as a package of economic law rules governing the licensing, establishment, and operations—in particular, generation, transport, and supply—of electricity and gas, with public control exercised through either public ownership or a system of control over licensing and tariff rules. Energy law was exclusively national public-administrative law. It reflected a number of economic and political objectives, but primarily the generally shared expectation was that the state had the ultimate responsibility to ensure the provision of a proper energy supply.

Energy, in this perspective, was seen as a highly politicized 'strategic' industry, for the functioning of which the political system was held responsible. This system, comprising the energy industries themselves, trade unions, governmental regulators, and professional and academic communities, has been breaking down in virtually all EU countries under the onslaught of technological, economic, attitudinal and, finally, also political changes. Privatization—necessarily followed by new forms of economic regulation focusing on the natural monopoly segments of the industries and proactive steering towards competitive markets, the emergence of competitive markets encompassing more and more components of the energy industry, some degree of inter-fuel competition, at least in the investment stage, and internationalization of investment, ownership, finance, production, and trade—is exerting strong pressure on long-established and quite inward-looking national energy law systems.

EU energy law is a prime reflection of such influences coming from global markets and global realities, but also a major contributor to the patterns of change. Energy law has thus advanced quite far in its transition from either regulating relationships between public energy entities (i.e. the mercantilist system) or establishing a degree of state supervision among corporate cartel structures (i.e. the

---

[9] In electricity, cross-border connections where mainly for security of supply purposes. In gas, cross-border connections where often necessary to accommodate the imports of natural gas from production points.

[10] Here, see the interesting survey authored by W. Patterson, *Transforming Electricity* (London: Earthscan 1999) p. 10, Ch. 3, pp. 41–7, 52, 54.

[11] For example, U.S. Public Utility Holding Companies Act of 1934, German Energy Industry Act of 13.12.1935 (EnWG).

German tradition) to a new function of public supervision of energy markets, with the objective of creating and safeguarding the functioning of competitive energy markets and exercising political responsibility for ensuring the effective supply of energy with both economic and (sometimes, and rather camouflaged) political objectives in mind.

This book has been written with several types of user in mind. It is intended to serve as an overall introduction to the economic, institutional, and energy policy background, the key aspects of primary and secondary EU law of relevance to the energy industries. However, the book is not an *introductory* book on EU energy law and policy. It should be of interest to any professional or academic, whether or not a lawyer, with an interest in understanding EU energy law beyond the level of written law. Similarly, it should be of use to students, especially graduate students, with a special interest in the economic and, in particular, energy law of the EU. The book should also serve as an introduction to special issues with sufficient context, guidance, and references to develop the ramifications of such special issues, though it does not purport to constitute an exhaustive manual or compendium dealing with every conceivable aspect of EU energy law.

The book covers the developments which have taken place, and examines the progress made, from the 1950s to the current status quo. It examines the process for changing the long-established national structures under the impact of market forces and the drivers of liberalization. It also examines the gradual expansion of the EU energy *acquis* to non-EU countries through various steps and mechanisms. As such, it takes account of the external dimension of EU energy law, with a focus on the Energy Charter Treaty and the more recent European Community Treaty.

This study is also driven by a wider ambition. There are numerous books, law firm manuals, official documents, and articles on most of the special issues of EU energy law. These cover the old and amended directives, the constantly evolving state of play in EU energy law and policy, special legal problems caused by the application of primary law, problems caused by the application of the directives—or their implementation in domestic law—to situations which often vary markedly between Member States. However, the increasingly detailed nature of EU energy law is gradually eroding these differences. While much of the general, descriptive discussion has tended to date fairly rapidly—especially since the enactment of the 1996/98 electricity and gas directives or the adoption of the Acceleration Package in 2003 and the Third Package in 2009—the discussion of special problems, in particular those connected with primary EU law (competition law, state aid, or free movement provisions) is still relevant. But given the progress through the three energy law packages and the progress in the application of general EU law (especially competition law), which has led to the breaking-up of energy companies and forced change in pre-liberalization structures, now is an opportune moment to present EU energy law as a whole, in terms of a coherent narrative, based on the context and history of the black letter law. It is also intended to be more comprehensive and to have a more consistent internal narrative than tends to be the case with books on EU energy law based on the many, regularly organized conferences.

The book is not an attempt to emulate the 'law firm manual' type of survey[12] with an emphasis of textual summary and description of the key legal instruments and court cases, nor the official documents produced by the departments of the European Commission. These—essential—official documents are by necessity, and due to their political and administrative orientation, presented in a very low-key, non-analytic, descriptive style, intentionally devoid of critical, conceptual, or systematic analysis and very much controlled by political and institutional taboos. By contrast, this book aims to be an independent scholarly study which analyses the legal documents, identifies their institutional, economic, and political setting and evolution, and which is not dependent on the particular bias and perspective of a major player. Given that EU energy law and policy is a specialized, niche subject, much of the writing necessarily comes directly (e.g. staff of organizations) or indirectly (i.e. from professionals and academics with considerable practical linkages and dependencies) from the major actors. These actors all possess considerable know-how, including access to public and non-public information and experience. However, given that they are continuously involved in national and EU-wide negotiation and lobbying/persuasion processes in order to defend their vested interests or to advocate openings to develop new business opportunities, such writings are often not truly scholarly in the sense that expertise, rational analysis and at least relative independence are combined.

One of the aims of this study is to illustrate the evolution and context of economic regulation in the energy sector. One sometimes gets the impression from black letter legal analysis that law is like a glacier: frozen at the point of observation, without history and without much connection to anything else. But the analysis of EU energy law illustrates that much law (e.g. primary EU law) existed for decades without application to a number of national energy industries which were insulated from EU law. The actual relevance of EU law was only revived under the impact of global competition, the advent of market-oriented economic philosophies, and the push that came from the EU single market programme in the 1980s.[13] Legal concepts and pressure to apply the law on the books in a specific way come (and go) depending on outside events, market forces, and political feasibility. Law functions in a context, not independently of it. When analysing the law as it stands today, one needs to treat older precedents with care—they may no longer be relevant and may have been replaced by new precedents and emerging concepts in tune with economic and political philosophy and the contemporary direction of the markets. Comparison of the Commission's approach to capacity reservations in electricity markets and downstream gas contracts before and after the new millennium illustrates this paradigm shift, as does comparison of the legal reasoning applied by the ECJ in *Campus Oil* (1984) and *Commission v Greece* (1998).[14] The proportionality

---

[12] See R. Tudway (ed.), *Energy Law and Regulation in the EU* (London: Sweet & Maxwell 1999).

[13] See Council Resolution of 16 September 1986 concerning new Community energy policy objectives for 1995 and the convergence of the policies of the Member States (OJ C 241, 25. 9.1986, p. 1).

[14] Case C-72/83, *Campus Oil v Minister for Industry* [1984] ECR 2727 (Ireland) and ECJ Case 347/88, *Commission v Greece* [1990] ECR I 4747.

test regarding the justification of trade restrictions on the grounds of security of supply under Article 36 TFEU could hardly make the difference any greater.

Similarly, it is hard in practice to distinguish in analysis between 'policy' (energy policy, competition policy), which is used to design institutional arrangements, and law used to focus enforcement efforts and to underlie new concepts of interpretation for old law and the law itself. Apart from issues of great detail, energy and competition *policy* and energy and competition *law* seem therefore almost identical at the level of practice, though not at the level of theory. As a result, this book illustrates both the changing policy and institutional context of EU energy law and incorporates academic analyses from non-legal disciplines. It is quite surprising how little the various academic disciplines working on the same subject take note of each other's work—for reasons of professional jealousy, mere ignorance, or absence of academic incentive to look beyond one's own discipline.[15] Much of the work done by lawyers (both academics and practitioners) writing on EU energy law largely amounts to a careful re-paraphrasing of very complicated and dense EU legislative documents, presented as accurate and detailed accounts of complex legal texts. This may serve to protect a reputation for legal meticulousness and correctness, but it is not always very illuminating. There are obvious exceptions, but this type of close rephrasing of the law is nevertheless the main content of much legal writing. Admittedly, it may be difficult to write a complete narrative of EU energy law without boring most readers to death. Nevertheless, this book at least aims to present EU energy law as something that can provoke intellectual, political, and professional curiosity about the slowly moving train of economic regulation under the typical pressures and contradictions of countries and the EU in the global economy.

As will be seen throughout the chapters of this book, energy law and policy constitute a constantly changing area of study: a 'moving target'. Of course, patterns of technological development may change, as has happened with the emergence of unconventional sources of natural gas. Consequently, the consistent application of economic doctrines, such as the notion of 'natural monopoly', to specific network industries cannot be taken for granted. Similarly, global issues and pressures impact upon law, climate change being but one example of this. Contemporary approaches to energy governance undergo change. The current market-based approach is already showing signs of fatigue and a return to greater state and public sector involvement seems likely. Clearly, energy law will continue to be subject to frequent adaptations caused by further technological, economic, and societal advances, transitions, or fallbacks.

'Energy law' is inextricably linked to 'energy policy'. The law on the books is a frozen form of energy policy at a certain moment—but policy evolves and hence is bound to change the meaning and implication of the words. Rules relying on policy standards—e.g. natural monopoly, security of supply, or public service—can

---

[15] This was also noted by Professor Jonathan Stern in his foreword in Kim Talus, *Vertical Natural Gas Transportation Capacity, Upstream Commodity Contracts and EU Competition Law* (Alphen aan den Rijn: Kluwer Law International 2011).

change dramatically if such concepts undergo evolution or if their meaning and general acceptance collapses. The legal structure, format, details, and intricacies function to make 'policy' more than a set of specific intentions—that is, they translate policy into rules so that it is more likely to work as intended, can be relied upon by the users of the law, and gives predictability to commercial transactions. But the two are related: there is law on the books (e.g. the four freedoms of the EU Treaty) that was earlier, neither relevant to the energy sector nor applied to it. But with a change of policy pervading the European institutions, the law on the books sprung back to life. This close interrelationship between law and policy is nowhere clearer than in EU law and in the energy sector. Significant policy standards, such as 'security of supply', 'public service', 'economic interest', 'competitiveness', 'sustainable development', and even the more technical notions such as 'vertical integration' or 'third party access', influence the interpretation of EU law, which in any case is dominated by broad, policy-oriented, teleological-purposive interpretation.[16] So black letter law can only be properly applied, complied with, and predicted if the user has a reasonable understanding of the policies behind the law—and of the historical evolution, internal contradictions, and current role of both law and policy. Law only functions in its proper context, not independent of it. In EU energy law, policy is law—much to the distress of proponents of traditional formalistic traditions of civil law, though such policy-law is inevitably open-ended and, albeit with considerable difficulty, accessible to traditional linguistic and formal interpretation methods.[17] Any analysis and presentation of EU economic and energy law which serves to explain, but also to guide the reader to a realistic understanding of how the text of the law is likely to be applied and work, will therefore show the interaction between policy and law, and the relevance (and manipulability) of policy standards in the process of applying the law. EU law formulae have been known to go into hibernation, only to spring back to life when they suit the policy consensus of the moment.[18] For a legal scholar or author, this means that it is necessary not to present law as a monolithic facade of a certain time, but as the result of changing policies and forces—i.e. bring together the history and the policy underpinning the analysis of law. However, as distinct from the approach taken by a political scientist, it must also mean that the rules must be analysed and systematically presented to give a consistent picture of the law as it exists at the time of writing, and to give guidance on how the law is likely to be applied by its users (courts, EU institutions, legal advisers, and companies). Such analysis should also involve making some proposal, particularly in relation to areas of ambiguity and controversy, as to how the law should be applied—and a consideration of how both policy and the application of the law may evolve in the future.

---

[16] J. Usher, *General Principles of EC Law* (London: Longman 1998).

[17] In a discussion some years ago, a senior Commission energy official put it well: Energy law is what the current political consensus is, and it will be transported into the text whatever the text seems to say.

[18] Consider the *Campus Oil v Greek Oil* case and *Sacchi v Manghera and Corbeau*. These cases are discussed further in various sections of this book.

This is a 'European' book on EU energy law. It is surprising that the extant literature on what should be a common EU subject is often largely national in focus—written in the national language, examining EU law and policy developments on the basis of their relevance to the specific Member State in question, and largely using analytical methods prevalent in that Member State. Even where issues of common EU interest are concerned, the treatment used is often national rather than international in scope. This may be attributed to the peculiarly domestic character of law as an academic discipline (even EU and international law), to linguistic constraints, to the availability of research materials, and the segregation of legal publishing into national markets—even if discussing the internal European market. Of course, there are exceptions to this as well.

Finally, this book is also marked by a strong 'law-in-context' approach. While there are many excellent books on various areas of EU energy law (in particular, those of P. Cameron and C. Jones, the latter being an edited work[19]), these focus purely on the legal aspects of EU energy regulation. As such, they largely omit the political, historical, and economic aspects of energy markets and energy regulation. This book takes a different approach, attempting to place EU energy law in its context and examine the relevant legal regimes through the prism of non-legal factors. It explains the context and background for various policy approaches and legal instruments. The basis of this approach is that law does not function in a vacuum but is affected by a multitude of factors. This impact of extra-legal factors should not be hidden, but rather openly admitted and considered as a part of academic research in this area. A narrow focus on the legal aspects of EU energy law and policy only gives a partial picture of the application of law in the EU energy sector. Examples of this impact will be apparent in various chapters of the book.

1.1 Sources of Information on EU Energy Law

The main sources of EU energy law are:

- primary EU law with particular relevance for the energy industries: the EURATOM Treaty[20] and the Treaty on the Functioning of the European Union in its current form.[21] As far as the TFEU is concerned, the articles on free movement, competition, public monopolies and undertakings entrusted with services in the general economic interest, and state aid are of particular relevance.

---

[19] P.D. Cameron, *Competition in Energy Markets – Law and Regulation in the European Union* (Oxford: OUP 2007); C. Jones (ed.), *EU Energy Law: The Internal Energy Market,* (Leuven: Claeys & Casteels 2010); and C. Jones (ed.), *EU Energy Law: EU Competition Law and Energy Markets* (Leuven: Claeys & Casteels 2011).
[20] Treaty Establishing a European Atomic Community of 25.3.1957.
[21] Of course, there was also the now obsolete Treaty establishing the European Coal and Steel Community.

The most recent addition—the likely effect of which is as yet unclear—is the energy-specific article in the Lisbon Treaty;

- secondary EU law, mainly the directives aimed at creating an internal energy market (from the first price transparency[22] and international transit[23] directives, to hydrocarbons licensing[24] public procurement by utilities,[25] to the line of electricity[26] and gas[27] directives and regulations,[28] to the security of supply directives[29] and regulations[30]) and for the environmental aspect of energy law (from renewable energy and biofuels[31] to the EU emission trading scheme,[32]

[22] Council Directive 1990/377/EEC of 29 June 1990 concerning a Community procedure to improve the transparency of gas and electricity prices charged to industrial end-users OJ L 185, 17.7.1990, p. 16. See also Council Recommendation 1983/230/EEC of 21 April 1983 on the methods of forming natural gas prices and tariffs in the Community, OJ L 123, 11.5.1983, pp. 40–1.

[23] Council Directive 1990/547/EEC of 29 October 1990 on the transit of electricity through transmission grids, OJ L 313, 13.11.1990, p. 30. Council Directive 1991/296/EEC of 31 May 1991 on the transit of natural gas through grids, OJ L 147, 12.6.1991, p. 37.

[24] Directive 1994/22/EC of the European Parliament and of the Council of 30 May 1994 on the conditions for granting and using authorizations for the prospection exploration and production of hydrocarbons, OJ L 164, 30.6.1994, p. 3.

[25] Directive 2004/17/EC of the European Parliament and of the Council of 31 March 2004 coordinating the procurement procedures of entities operating in the water, energy, transport and postal services sectors, OJ L 134, 30.4.2004, pp. 1–113.

[26] Directive 1996/92/EC of the European Parliament and of the Council of 19 December 1996 concerning common rules for the internal market in electricity, OJ L 027, 30.1.1997, pp. 20–9, Directive 2003/54/EC of the European Parliament and of the Council of 26 June 2003 concerning common rules for the internal market in electricity and repealing Directive 96/92/EC—Statements made with regard to decommissioning and waste management activities, OJ L 176, 15.7.2003, p. 37, Directive 2009/72/EC of the European Parliament and of the Council of 13 July 2009 concerning common rules for the internal market in electricity and repealing Directive 2003/54/EC, OJ L 211, 14.8.2009, pp. 55–93.

[27] Directive 1998/30/EC of the European Parliament and of the Council of 22 June 1998 concerning common rules for the internal market in natural gas, OJ L 204, 21.7.1998, p. 1, Directive 2003/55/EC of the European Parliament and of the Council Concerning common Rules for the Internal Market in Natural Gas and Repealing Directive 98/30/EC, OJ L 176, 15.7.2003, p. 57, Directive 2009/73/EC of the European Parliament and of the Council of 13 July 2009 concerning common rules for the internal market in natural gas and repealing Directive 2003/55/EC.

[28] Most recently, Regulation (EC) No. 714/2009 of the European Parliament and of the Council of 13 July 2009 on conditions for access to the network for cross-border exchanges in electricity and repealing Regulation (EC) No. 1228/2003, Regulation (EC) No. 715/2009 of the European Parliament and of the Council of 13 July 2009 on conditions for access to the natural gas transmission networks and repealing Regulation (EC) No. 1775/2005.

[29] Directive 2005/89/EC of the European Parliament and of the Council of 18 January 2006 concerning measures to safeguard security of electricity supply and infrastructure investment, OJ L 33, 4.2.2006, pp. 22–7 and the new repealed Directive 2004/67/EC concerning measures to safeguard security of natural gas supply.

[30] Regulation (EU) No 994/2010 of the European Parliament and of the Council of 20 October 2010 concerning measures to safeguard security of gas supply and repealing Council Directive 2004/67/EC, OJ L 295, 12.11.2010, pp. 1–22.

[31] Directive 2009/28/EC of the European Parliament and of the Council of 23 April 2009 on the promotion of the use of energy from renewable sources and amending and subsequently repealing Directives 2001/77/EC and 2003/30/EC, OJ L 140, 5.6.2009, pp. 16–62.

[32] Directive 2003/87/EC of the European Parliament and of the Council of 13 October 2003 establishing a scheme for greenhouse gas emission allowance trading within the Community and amending Council Directive 96/61/EC, OJ L 275, 25.10.2003, p. 32 and Directive 2009/29/EC of the European Parliament and of the Council of 23 April 2009 amending Directive 2003/87/EC so as to improve and extend the greenhouse gas emission allowance trading scheme of the Community, OJ L 140, 5.6.2009, pp. 63–87.

energy savings,[33] and carbon capture and storage[34]). A large number of very specialized instruments, such as those on oil stocks,[35] measures promoting trans-European energy networks[36] and various additional instruments are also of relevance:

- external treaties of the EU like the Partnership & Co-operation Agreements (PCA) with Countries of Eastern Europe and Central Asia, the Euro-Mediterranean partnership programmes, the European Neighbourhood Policy, the EU-Russia Energy Dialogue and the Common Strategy with Russia and the Energy Charter Treaty, the Energy Community Treaty, but also bilateral economic and trade collaboration agreements, as well as various climate-change-related agreements to which the EU is a party;

- the judgments of the Court of Justice of the European Union (CJEU) and the General Court (GC);

- the administrative decisions of the European Commission, in particular in competition and state aid cases; and

- academic and professional literature.

Very little academic and professional writing on EU energy law existed before the 1990s,[37] basically because the subject itself did not exist either in terms of its practical relevance or as an academic sub-discipline. With the efforts led by the Commission to move towards more integrated energy markets, starting around 1985 and first advanced by the 1996/98 energy directives, then accelerated by the 2003 and 2009 directives, academic and professional literature (and pertinent conferences) started to emerge. Several books describing electricity and gas regulation in Member States and the first steps taken by the European Commission

---

[33] Directive 2010/31/EU on the energy performance of buildings; Directive 2010/30/EU on the indication, by labelling and standard product information, of the consumption of energy and other resources by energy-related products; Regulation (EC) No 1222/2009 on the labelling of tyres with respect to fuel efficiency and other essential parameters; Regulation (EC) No 106/2008 on a Community energy-efficiency labelling programme for office equipment; Regulation (EU) No 1015/2010 implementing Directive 2009/125/EC with regard to ecodesign requirements for household washing machines, OJ L 293/21; Regulation (EC) No 859/2009 amending Regulation (EC) No 244/2009 as regards the ecodesign requirements in respect of ultraviolet radiation for non-directional household lamps, OJ L 247/3.

[34] Directive 2009/31/EC of the European Parliament and of the Council of 23 April 2009 on the geological storage of carbon dioxide and amending Council Directive 85/337/EEC, European Parliament and Council Directives 2000/60/EC, 2001/80/EC, 2004/35/EC, 2006/12/EC, 2008/1/EC and Regulation (EC) No 1013/2006, OJ L 140, 5.6.2009, pp. 114–35.

[35] Directive 2009/119/EC of 14 September 2009 imposing an obligation on Member States to maintain minimum stocks of crude oil and/or petroleum products, OJ L 265, 9.10.2009, pp. 9–23.

[36] Decision No. 1364/2006/EC of the European Parliament and of the Council of 6 Sep. 2006 laying down guidelines for trans-European energy networks and repealing Decision 96/391/EC and Decision No. 1229/2003/EC, OJ L 262, 22.9.2006, 1–23 and the new Proposal for a Regulation on guidelines for trans-European energy infrastructure and repealing Decision No 1364/2006/EC (COM(2011)658).

[37] But see: T. Daintith and L. Hancher, *Energy Strategy in Europe: The Legal Framework* (Berlin: de Gruyter 1986).

were published in the early 1990s.[38] Several edited books dealing with a number of issues particularly relevant at the time came out of conferences.[39] A German book,[40] commissioned as a legal opinion, surveyed the then new directives and reviewed the compatibility of the energy directives (then in draft form) with constitutional law (positively), while other German publications took a critical view.[41] Some monographs compared energy law and energy law reform in major EU countries against the background of the energy directives (by then enacted).[42] In the post-2000 era, a number of more detailed books emerged, some as monographs dedicated either to specific areas of EU law or taking a more general approach,[43] others as edited works.[44] Throughout the 1990s a large number of professional and academic articles dealing with the requirements of the internal market and the reform of both EU and Member States energy regimes emerged. A number of these appeared in energy law journals, but some were also published in European Law journals and in national journals devoted solely to energy law or to administrative/ EU law in general.[45] Some of these works focused on a particular issue (e.g. EU competition law and 'essential facilities' in the energy sector, an issue that has raised questions from the early 1990s all the way through to post-2010). Others examined the impact of both primary and new directive-based EU law on the process of national energy law reform, often accompanied by privatization, liberalization, and the opening-up of energy industries to competition.[46] This trend was reinforced in the first decade of the 2000s, with an increasing scholarly focus on EU energy law,

---

[30] L. Hancher, *EC Electricity Law* (London: Chancery 1992), P. Cameron, *Gas Regulation in Europe* (London: FT Reports 1996), E. Cross, *Electric Utility Regulation in the European Union: A Country by Country Guide* (Chichester: Wiley, 1996), F. Burchard and L. Eckert, *Natural Gas and EU Energy Law* (Baden-Baden: Nomos 1995).

[39] E. J. Mestmaecker (ed.) *Natural Gas in the Internal Market* (London: Graham/Nomos 1993), T. Wälde and D. MacDougall, *European Community Energy Law* (London: Kluwer 1994), T. Wälde, 'Die Regelung der Britischen Energiewirtschaft nach der Privatisierung', in P. Tettinger (ed.), *Strukturen der Versorgungswirtschaft in Europa* (Stuttgart: Boorberg 1996), pp. 59–95.

[40] H. Jarass, *Europaeisches Energierecht* (Berlin: Duncker & Humblot 1996).

[41] U. Hueffer, K. Ipsen, and P. Tettinger, *Die Transitrichtlinien für Gas und Elektrizität* (Stuttgart: Boorberg 1991), another commissioned legal opinion.

[42] P. Cameron, *Competition in Energy Markets: Law and Regulation in the European Union* (Oxford: OUP 2001), M. Roggenkamp et al. (eds), *Energy Law in Europe* (Oxford: OUP 2001), J. Schneider and C. Theobald (eds), *Handbuch zum Recht der Energiewirtschaft* (München: Beck 2003), J. Schneider, *Liberalisierung der Stromwirtschaft durch Regulative Marktorganisation* (Baden-Baden: Nomos 1999).

[43] C. Jones, *EU Energy Law, Volume I—The Internal Energy Market* (Leuven: Claeys & Casteels 2004 and subsequent editions), C. Jones, *EU Energy Law*—Volume II—EU Competition Law and Energy Markets (Leuven: Claeys & Casteels 2005 and subsequent editions), P. Cameron, *Legal Aspects of Energy Regulation: Implementing the New Directives of Electricity and Gas Across Europe* (Oxford: OUP 2005), and P. Cameron, *Competition in Energy Markets: Law and Regulation in the European Union* (Oxford: OUP 2002 and 2007).

[44] Like the annual publication *EU Energy Law and Policy Issues*, most recently: B. Delvaux, M. Hunt, and K. Talus (eds), *EU Energy Law and Policy Issues* (Cambridge: Intersentia 2011).

[45] Such as Recht der Energie, Zeitschrift für Neues Energierecht or Energiewirtschaftliche Tagesfragen in Germany; Cahiers du Droit de l'Energie in France. Other include Utilities Law Review, Competition and Regulation in Network Industries, OGEL. The most recent and rapidly growing journal being the Journal of World Energy Law and Business, though this journal focuses on international energy law.

[46] G. Gentile (ed.), *La Privatissazione nel Settore Elettrico* (Milano: Giuffre 1995).

attested to by the appearance of new journals focusing on this area, new publishing houses specializing in EU energy law, and annual conferences on the subject. Interest in the topic also became apparent in the widening scope of the writings relating to the area, which ranged from competition to environmental and sustainability issues and, following the level of detail of the regulatory framework for EU energy, which progressed from basic and general questions to increasingly focused and narrow questions. In a similar vein, energy matters are now reflected more than before in relevant commentaries on general EU law and in the literature on state aid, state monopolies, and EU competition law.[47] The EU Commission, with its annual reports on the energy industry in Europe, the papers initiating consultation processes, policy proposals intended to be developed into formal directives or regulations, and communications on its policy intentions and on the status of policy implementations, is evidently a major source of information. Major law firms with an energy specialization, particularly in London but increasingly in Brussels, have started—for marketing reasons—to produce specialized newsletters.[48] These often report on the firm's experience in the energy field and summarize new developments, including Commission policies, new directives, and new EU-level and Member State-level cases relevant to the energy industries. The professional literature—where law firm marketing is engineered through presentation of recent developments by the firm's lawyers—also uses the professional journals for special issues on EU energy law. Up-to-date information on recent events in EU energy policy is available from a variety of European energy and business intelligence services, albeit sometimes at considerable expense.[49]

An increasingly important recent source of information is the internet. The advantage of internet-based research is the extensive availability of primary regulatory materials (treaties, directives, administrative and judicial case law) and some secondary material (speeches by senior Commission staff, technical reports, and updates on activity) from, in particular, the European Commission's various directorates that deal with energy, the Energy Charter Secretariat and the Secretariat for Energy Community Treaty. But one needs to treat the information found with some care. While there are various internet fora dealing with EU law and policy, the focus and quality varies. Some, like OGEL, only contain refereed and carefully considered and checked information, while others are open to all contributors. While the energy policy blogs focus on specific areas, OGEL examines both EU

---

[47] But this happened also in the earlier days. See F. Blum and A. Logue, *State Monopolies under EC Law* (Chichester: Wiley 1998) or B. Devlin and C. Levasseur, 'Energy', in J. Faull and A. Nikpay (eds), *The EC Law of Competition* (Oxford: OUP 1999), L. Hancher, T. Ottervanger, and P. Slot, *EC State Aids* (London: Chancery 1993).

[48] Perhaps the most comprehensive being that of Herbert Smith's *European Energy Handbook*, edited by Silke Goldberg.

[49] In the past, we have seen several *Financial Times* newsletters dealing with European Energy, East European Energy, gas and electricity complementing a series of FT business reports summarizing, in a well-edited and clear format of presentation, the essentials of specific developments, e.g. electricity, gas regulation in Europe. Other commercial newsletters—e.g. Petroleum Economist, Petroleum Review plus internet-based information services digest as well recent developments, e.g. reports on EU meetings, relevant ECJ cases, Commission communications, and national legislative developments.

energy and the energy law and policy developments in various national, regional and international contexts.[50]

1.2 Overview of the Book

This book is organized into seven chapters and a conclusion.

This first chapter explains the background, rationale, and focus of the book. The second chapter then moves into the substantive issues of EU energy law and policy, focusing on the regulatory developments in EU energy law from 1957 onwards, up to the adoption of the first electricity and gas directives. It examines both the regulatory initiatives and previous legal instruments employed to change the way in which EU energy business was done, and also looks at the related case law. As the chapter clearly shows, both mechanisms had their role to play.

Chapter 3 looks at the evolution and status quo of sector-specific regulation. The chapter covers the development of the rules on power generation, third party access, unbundling, various derogations and exemptions and security of supply. While the chapter clearly focuses on the general energy market directives, other EU energy law instruments are also discussed.

The fourth chapter focuses on the application of Treaty law to energy markets. It covers the progressively intrusive application of EU competition law to force changes in market structures, and recognizes the failings of this approach. The chapter examines the application of EU rules on state aid in areas most central to energy markets: renewables, stranded costs and preferential tariffs. It also discusses issues relating to the free movement of goods in energy markets and focuses on the exemptions granted in the name of security of supply and environmental protection. It also examines the application of case law in today's world.

Chapter 5 examines the environmental aspects of EU energy law and policy. After a general discussion of the conflicting policy considerations and the inherent weaknesses of the sustainability goal of EU energy policy, the chapter looks at environmental issues as they present themselves at various stages of the energy value chain, from production to transport and utilization. The chapter also assesses the key areas for the '20–20–20' by 2020 objective: energy savings, renewable energy, emission reductions, and climate change. The chapter also discusses the conflicts between various EU energy policy objectives as well as their interaction with the internal market objective. Finally, certain future directions for EU energy policy in this area are examined.

Chapter 6 looks at the international aspects of EU energy law and policy, by reference to the players and interest groups involved in the external aspects of EU energy policy. It examines the bilateral relations and legal instruments in this area and discusses various aspects of the association agreements, energy dialogues and the Cotonou Agreement. Multilateral cooperation is then examined, focusing on

---

[50] <http://www.ogel.org>.

the Energy Charter Treaty and the Energy Community Treaty, in respect of which both new developments and their current roles are discussed. Finally, space is given to certain sensitivities in the relationship between EU law and international law.

Chapter 7 focuses on the changes in the ideological approach to energy. It first examines the movement from a state-driven to a market-driven system, followed by discussion of the partial return to a more public sector and state-involved system. The changing energy paradigms are illustrated through various examples and the role of the EU institutions in the new regulatory set-up is highlighted. Chapter 8 then offers some concluding thoughts.

2

The Regulatory History of EU Energy

The Evolution of EU Energy Law from 1957 Onwards

2.1 The First 30 Years of Hibernation

The 1951 Paris Treaty establishing the European Coal and Steel Community (ECSC) laid the foundations for the EU. Its apparent aim was to develop a common market in the two most strategically important industries—it is important to remember that this took place in the largely *dirigiste* environment of the years immediately following World War II. But in reality it was conceived by its architects, Robert Schuman, Jean Monnet, Walter Hallstein, and others, to bring about economic collaboration in a field at that time (although no longer) considered crucial, in order to put a final end to Franco-German hostility and create political unity out of joint economic reconstruction. So energy—predominantly in the form of coal, which was then much fought over—was the key driver of a political process which developed into the 1957 EURATOM Treaty (which focused on the source of energy then considered most relevant for the future) and the Treaty of Rome establishing the European Economic Community. Three decades after the legal ratification of the EEC Treaty's core principle of freedom of movement of goods, the Community's energy sector (apart from oil and coal) was still nationally segregated, dominated by publicly-owned or publicly-supported energy monopolies, with little if any cross-border trade in gas and electricity. As Terence Daintith and Leigh Hancher noted in their 1984 study,[1] 'the Community's performance in this field has been inadequate'. The authors referred to a Commission statement deploring the inadequacy and inconsistency of the action taken.[2] On reviewing the decades since the Treaty of Rome, one finds that no progress was made in the creation of a single market in energy, despite the fact that this was the original intention of its architects, who had no desire to exclude energy from other areas of economic integration.[3] Periodic Commission reports raised the pressing energy

---

[1] T. Daintith and L. Hancher, 'The Management of Diversity: Community Law as an Instrument of Energy and Other Sectorial Policies', 4(1) *Yearbook of European Law* (1984), pp. 123–67.

[2] The development of an energy strategy for the Community (COM (81) 540 final), para. 1.

[3] Daintith and Hancher note that there is 'no indication in the Treaty that the basic range of rules should not be applicable in the energy sector as in all others covered by the Treaty'. T. Daintith and L. Hancher, 'The Management of Diversity: Community Law as an Instrument of Energy and Other Sectorial Policies', 4(1) *Yearbook of European Law* (1984), pp. 123–67, pp. 15–16. See also the notorious Spaak Report.

issues of the time, which were quite similar to those being grappled with in the US following the realization that oil supplies were vulnerable due to the political volatility of the Middle East. These included security of supply, the management of scarcity, reducing energy import dependency, and increasing energy efficiency. Most of the targets then set were not achieved and are still on the agendas of many consuming states and regions today, much like in the US. There was a flurry of activity during the oil crises of 1973 and 1981, mainly comprising attempts by the Commission to develop an EU-wide emergency system.[4] This followed concerns about oil scarcity triggered by the Yom Kippur War, growing dependency on oil imports, and rapid increases in oil prices on two occasions during the period from 1973 to 1981. Such initiatives were ultimately displaced by the founding of the Paris-based International Energy Agency, the brainchild of Secretary of State Henry Kissinger and the US leadership. Due to fears about the exhaustion of supplies of natural gas—which later proved unfounded—the one major EU directive of 1975 limited the use of natural gas by power stations, a prohibition that was based on erroneous forecasts and which has now been lifted.[5] Otherwise, EU energy law then amounted to a requirement that governments notify statistical information about energy consumption and import, investment projects relating to the oil, gas and electricity sectors (nuclear projects were subject to earlier notification requirements), and prices.[6] Following spikes in oil prices, various initiatives aimed at reducing energy dependency and—on the flipside—enhancing energy efficiency came to nothing as the market worked and high oil prices regularly collapsed (for instance, the 1981 peak was followed by the trough of 1985, with another cycle down to the bottom in 1998/99).

Surveys of EU energy policy from 1957 to 1985 ('energy policy' being taken to encompass reflections, recommendations, policies and, sometimes, directives and regulations)[7] indicate that while some—in particular the mercantilist 'planning' countries, had conscious, explicit, and comprehensive national energy policies[8]—and

---

[4] Directive 68/414 of 20.12.1968 about minimum storage requirements for oil and oil products, OJ 1968, L 308, p. 14, Regulation concerning notification of import of hydrocarbons, OJ 1972, L 120, p. 3, Directive concerning measures to weaken the impact of difficulties of supply with oil and oil products, OJ 1973, L 228. For more see T. Daintith and L. Hancher, The Management of Diversity: Community Law as an Instrument of Energy and Other Sectorial Policies, 4(1) *Yearbook of European Law* (1984), 123–67, p. 22. This was basically a translation of OECD initiatives into binding EC measures, such as emergency stock requirements and obligations on Member States to develop powers to deal with an energy crisis.

[5] Council Directive 75/404 on restriction of use of natural gas in power stations, OJ 1975, L 178/24.

[6] Regulation (EEC) No 1056/72 of the Council of 18 May 1972 on notifying the Commission of investment projects of interest to the Community in the petroleum, natural gas and electricity sectors, OJ L 120, 25.5.1972, pp. 7–10.

[7] T. Daintith and L. Hancher: *Energy Strategy in Europe: the Legal Framework* (Berlin: Walter de Gruyter & Co. 1986) and T. Daintith and L. Hancher, The Management of Diversity: Community Law as an Instrument of Energy and Other Sectorial Policies, 4(1) *Yearbook of European Law* (1984), pp. 123–67.

[8] T. Daintith and L. Hancher: *Energy Strategy in Europe: the Legal Framework* (Berlin: Walter de Gruyter & Co. 1986) and T. Daintith and L. Hancher, The Management of Diversity: Community Law as an Instrument of Energy and Other Sectorial Policies, 4(1) *Yearbook of European Law* (1984), pp. 123–67.

while the Commission consistently pushed for a similar explicit policy to be anchored in a specific Directorate General and in an energy chapter for the Treaty exploiting, in particular, the energy crises and anxieties of the 1970s—Member States were simply unwilling to delegate such powers and surrender their 'energy sovereignty' to the Commission. This was neither for lack of effort on the part of the Commission, nor for lack of opportunities which the 1970s energy crises—which engendered anxiety sometimes bordering on hysteria—provided.[9] At that time, shortly after the two World Wars, energy was still regarded as being too bound up with national sovereignty and national survival, and the national energy endowments between Member States (e.g. between close to 100 per cent self-sufficiency in the UK in 1975 as against close to 100 per cent import dependency in the case of Italy) too different, to envisage a common policy. In addition, the methods of organizing domestic industry and external supply were fundamentally different. Northern European countries mainly relied on corporately linked private companies, while southern European countries, led by France, were traditionally mercantilist. Daintith and Hancher[10] speak here of the 'structural stiffness' of the institutional arrangements for energy supply in the Member States, which made an integrated approach difficult to achieve. It is therefore not surprising that the EC Treaty's single-market obligations remained a dead letter in the face of such formidable impediments. While the law theoretically existed, neither the Commission—which undoubtedly calculated the relative balance of political power—nor corporate claimants, were able to enforce it.[11] Almost all energy companies were involved in some sort of inward-looking monopoly and had no interest in breaking out of their boundaries and entering a counterpart-colleague's territory. US companies, which later became the newcomer maverick boundary-breakers, were at that time equally locked into their own monopoly structures.

2.1.1 The Transformation

Why did this comfortable system, which provided energy for everybody, ample employment, extensive privileges for managers and owners, and cosy patronage for local, regional and national politicians throughout the EU[12] start to break

---

[9] The scenario of 'resource wars' was then prevalent and the EU, with less political and military muscle, seemed destined to be a loser in the race for resources with the US.

[10] T. Daintith and L. Hancher: *Energy Strategy in Europe: The Legal Framework* (Berlin: Walter de Gruyter & Co. 1986), pp. 148 and 149.

[11] Daintith and Hancher, 1986, remark on the absence of plaintiffs using their rights of freedom of energy investment and trade under the Treaty.

[12] In all European countries the relationship between state-owned, or privately-owned but cartel-organized utilities and both the trade union and the public sector was highly corrupt. The Italian '*mane pulite*', but also French or German press and prosecutors' campaigns illustrated that the energy monopolies, and their legal protection by the state, constituted huge and safe corruption machines (D. Porch, *The French Secret Services* (Oxford: OUP 1997), *Le Nouvel Observateur*, 12 March 1998 pp. 64–5; Les comptes extraordinaires de la Maison Elf; Elf and German party corruption are linked with the Leuna-Affair, *Figaro*, 12 July 2000, 'L'Elysee de Mitterand au coeur du systeme Elf'). One can safely assume that such relationships existed in all EU countries, based less on national culture prone to corruption as on the close linkage between state-protected monopolies and the financial needs and greed of politicians in control of state support.

down under the onslaught of both markets and the Commission in the late 1980s? Daintith and Hancher, the main commentators on EU energy law before the transformation, noted a great deal of disparity between countries, little success for the many attempts made by the Commission to introduce EU-wide energy law, and full insulation of the national energy industries from the theoretically mandated application of the internal market principles. They had, in 1984,[13] no particular reason to believe that the 'entrenchment of instrumental divergences in Member States' might be changed, or to forecast either 'imaginative and effective employment of the Commission's legal competences of its responsibility to protect the integrative achievements of the Community'. But then things started to move, slowly.

The existing literature neither provides any forecasts of these developments, nor adequate explanation as to why this paradigmatic change of policy happened and why the dormant features of the EC Treaty were suddenly revived—apart from the explicit or implicit assumption that the Delors Presidency's drive towards a single market did not intend to leave out energy. But this explanation is not enough. It would have been possible to leave out the energy sector. However, another explanation seems more likely: the system of energy monopolies, which served European countries well in the phase of (re-)building their economies after World War II, had by the 1980s lost its purpose and its political, and moral, legitimacy. The idea that energy could be run privately via competitive markets (as it once was) was inconceivable—except in the works of economic theoreticians—up until the late 1980s. It became a realistic alternative, free from scaremongering about collapse of the energy system, once the UK and several US states had proven that privatization and competitive energy markets would work. With this fear being taken care of, the *raison d'être* of the energy monopolies was gone. Consumers—i.e. the people—realized that the monopolies charged them much higher tariffs than were necessary and that the surplus from the higher tariffs—the monopoly rent—was not used for public purposes but, as in the case of all private or public monopolies, was eaten up by the privileged employees and managers of the utilities and by the politicians providing political and legal support for the maintenance of the monopolies. With the widespread investigations into corruption in Italy, France, and Germany, it became public knowledge that there was a large, mutually profitable symbiosis between the state-owned or state-licensed monopolies and the political classes. The energy monopolies were in some cases close to large corruption machines, not due to bad culture or bad people, but simply due to the logic of a state-licensed monopoly over an essential service for a captive market. With the gradual realization of these connections in the late 1980s and early 1990s, the moral and political legitimacy of energy monopolies faded. As a result, the political credibility of the 'public service through monopoly' argument lost persuasiveness, in particular due

---

[13] T. Daintith and L. Hancher, 'The Management of Diversity: Community Law as an Instrument of Energy and Other Sectorial Policies', 4(1) *Yearbook of European Law* (1984), 123–67, pp. 155 and 156.

to the fact that a simple comparison of energy policies demonstrated that proper and universal energy supply could be provided in more market-based regimes. The Commission, as initiator of the liberalizing energy directives, appears in this narrative as the one institution able to exploit these opportunities and move, aligned with the development of innovation in national markets (the UK in particular), parallel to the development of both market forces and political consciousness in Europe.

The fine detail of the long and complex negotiations that led from a mandate from the Council of Ministers to the three phases of directives and a comprehensive overhaul of EU energy markets may safely be left to historians. From our perspective, it is primarily the results which count. They now contribute to the growing body of 'EU energy law'. These negotiations were influenced by a number of issues which—having been discussed elsewhere in great detail[14]—are only briefly discussed here.

First, the Commission's internal energy market proposals should be viewed in the overall context of its ongoing internal market programme, with telecommunications leading the way and postal services following energy. Similarly, the 1990s were not characterized by supply concerns (high oil prices, the prospect of shortages), but were instead a time of sustained economic prosperity with great enthusiasm over the collapse of communism and the anticipated rapid transition of post-Soviet economies to the structure of the market economy.[15] Completion of the internal market remained a priority for the Commission (although this has still not yet been successfully completed), in particular to link the outlying Member States (Greece, Ireland) to the EU core. The Commission pursued the goal of reducing state aid (in particular in the case of the massive German coal subsidies), which maintained the most inefficient European energy fuel production, and pursued several energy programmes with an environmental dimension, such as SAVE (aimed at reducing CO^2 emissions) and ALTENER (aimed at increasing renewable energy production). On the environmental front, the Commission promoted a 'carbon tax' on hydrocarbon emissions, although that proved to be, on an EU-wide basis, too difficult to enforce.

Early debate on the internal energy market directives focused on the introduction of third-party access (TPA). TPA is necessary in order to open up energy monopolies principally based on control over gas and electricity transmission. The French energy monopolies, in particular Électricité de France (EDF), more or less dictated the French position on this topic and promoted the 'single buyer' alternative,

---

[14] For the background of the more recent developments, see for example B. Delvaux, *EU Law and the Development of a Sustainable, Competitive and Secure Energy Policy: Opportunities and Shortcomings* (Cambridge: Intersentia 2012). Delvaux focuses in particular on the negotiating history for the Agency for the Cooperation of Energy Regulators (ACER).

[15] With early caution only raised by very few commentators: T. Wälde, 'Developing a Framework for Russian Oil&Gas Legislation: Will a Russian Model Emerge?' 3(2) *Butterworths Central & East European Business Law* (March 1993), pp. 19–24; T. Wälde, The Russian Oil & Gas Industry and Foreign Investment, Opec-Bulletin, 25 (July 1994) 16–21 Bulletin, Vol. 3, No.2, March 1993, pp. 19–24, T. Wälde and J. Gunderson, Legislative Reform in Transition Economies, 43 *International & Comparative Law Quarterly* (1994), pp. 347–79, T. Wälde and C. von Hirschhausen (eds), Legislative Reform in the Energy Industry of Post-Soviet Societies, in R. Seidman, A. Seidman, and T. Wälde, *Making Development Work: Legislative Reform for Good Governance* (London: Kluwer 1999).

whereby EDF would have to be the exclusive agent of any energy imports into France, which would greatly hamper arm's length negotiations between large-scale consumers and foreign suppliers. The German monopolies relied on the problematic notion that, through the protection it afforded to property, German constitutional law (reflected in the fundamental principles of EU law implied by the ECJ into the Treaty)[16] would guarantee the immunity of the pipeline/transmission grid monopoly from economic regulation aimed at promoting greater competition.

The result was that an accommodation was made for both French and German opposition, but in a form that in effect obliged a transmission facility owner to provide non-discriminatory access to third parties: i.e. more of a nominal than a substantial incorporation of the opposition's arguments. This was undoubtedly facilitated by the decline of political legitimacy of the energy monopolies, the grow-ing enthusiasm of consumers and their political representatives (including in the European Parliament) for the benefits of energy competition, and moves within Member States, for example in Germany, to foster competition in the provision of natural gas by the—legally authorized—building of new, competing overland pipelines.[17] As energy law reform—inevitably towards privatization, liberalization, and competition—advanced in many EU member countries and other benchmark countries (UK, Germany, the Netherlands, Sweden, Finland, Norway, the US, Australia, Canada), opposition gradually declined. The federal (as opposed to cen-tralized) character of the EU allowed the more advanced Member States (typically in the north) to experiment with the new-economy energy law reforms. As these did seem to work, it became increasingly difficult to maintain the standard defences in this debate. These involved arguing that gas or electricity was different from oil; that the situation in country X was different from other countries (which had its own, or more or different types of energy supply); that long-term contracts necessary for new investment required the maintenance of the monopoly; that large investment was made with confidence on the basis of the continuity of a closed regulatory structure and would become 'stranded' as liberalization advanced; and, if no other arguments proved persuasive, then even senior spokesmen from major companies did not hesitate to climb aboard a socialist or fundamental environmentalist bandwagon by claiming that 'the market could and should not decide everything'. Presumably, in such very profitable, very comfortable cases with wide political patronage and benefit, competitive markets were too disruptive for the quiet and the very pleasant life key players were enjoying.

The EU had by then become subject to increasing pressure from the much more open and competitive economy of the US, which enjoyed much greater

---

[16] J. Usher, *General Principles of EC Law* (London: Longman 1998), for the German argument: U. Hüffer, K. Ipsen, and P. Tettinger (eds), *Die Transitrichtlinien für Gas und Elektrizität* (Stuttgart: Boorberg 1991), and the counter argument by: H. Jarass, *Europäisches Energierecht* (Berlin: Duncker & Humblo 1996), pp. 46–58.

[17] Although litigation before German courts to get direct access to natural gas customers by using Ruhrgas access pipelines by its newcomer competitor Wintershall/Wingas was not that successful, on the court decision, see (Weissenborn): K. U. Pritzsche and A. Meier, 'Third Party Access in Germany after the VNC Decision', 13(307) *OGTLR* (1995).

productivity and leadership in almost all 'new economy' technologies being adopted worldwide, so that the 'logic of global markets' exerted constant pressure on European policy makers to adapt or fall behind. With the push from these new economic forces, and with resistance getting weaker and weaker, the internal energy market made its—slow, gradual, and incremental—appearance, with only France, with its tireless resistance to Anglo-Saxon models and its perceptions of the dangers of the global economy to the established French ways of life (and interests), manning the rearguard.

Sections 2.1.2–2.7 focus on the development of sector-specific energy regulation in the EU. They examine the rationale, context, and content of various early instruments and look at certain more general issues of EU law in order to provide the background to various seemingly independent developments in the regulation of EU energy markets.

2.1.2 The Shaping of EU Energy Law by 'Harmonization Legislation'

The streamlining of the application of primary EU law to the energy sector as a whole was to be achieved using a multiple and multi-staged approach. The Commission was keen on completing the internal energy market programme as envisaged in the Single European Act (SEA). In order to push through its agenda for the promotion of intra-EU trade in goods and services and the strengthening of the competitiveness of Member States' economies and industries as a whole, it had to overcome strong opposition from network-bound energy industries.

One has to bear in mind that until the late 1980s common European energy policy was virtually non-existent. This is true despite the fact that two of the three Communities then in existence obviously dealt with energy matters (ECSC and EURATOM) and despite the setting-up of certain EC instruments with a view to maintaining minimum standards for the security of oil and gas supplies.

First, the now obsolete ECSC constituted a supranational common market for coal and steel. Since these industries had long since lost the strategic importance they had enjoyed in the decades immediately following the end of World War II and supplies on the global market were both abundant and cheap, the ECSC degraded into a system of stabilization and defence measures against cheap foreign supplies. As the Treaty itself did not explicitly grant powers to the Commission to take such measures, it relied on a comprehensive clause backed by a broad and purposive interpretation of general Treaty rules.[18]

Secondly, the EURATOM Treaty is basically limited to a joint effort on research, technological development and demonstration of nuclear power as well as safety aspects of nuclear production. Consequently, energy policy and the organization of the energy sectors were largely left to the Member States: the basic freedoms of

---

[18] Article 95 (2–5) ECSC; e.g. Recitals of Commission Decision 528/76/ECSC of 25 February 1976 regarding the Community system of measures taken by the Member States to assist the coal-mining industry, OJ L 063, 11.3.1976, p. 1 (effective from 1.1.1976–31.12.1985). This approach was first used by High Authority Decision 1965/3/ECSC. Afterwards, it became common sense.

the Treaty were dormant and the notion of undue 'super-subsidiarity' prevailed, in practice giving supremacy to national legislation.[19]

In its quest for competitive energy product markets of European rather than national or regional scope, the Commission based its framework strategy on Commission directives, actions for failure to fulfil an obligation, and harmonization legislation. In the end, it was not so much rationale but rather coincidence, or a sign of the ongoing constitutional reform that characterized the times, which explained the success of this protracted approach: the legislation was based on Article 95 of the EC Treaty (now 114 TFEU). Following the entry into force of the SEA in 1987, this article entitled the Commission to propose directives designed to approximate domestic laws. This could be done by taking advantage of majority voting in the Council, albeit maximizing the say of the European Parliament by means of a cooperation procedure. With effect from 1993, the Treaty of the European Union further expanded the European Parliament's powers on harmonization issues, by providing that the Parliament was to co-decide instead (now called the ordinary legislative procedure under Article 294 TFEU). Before going into the details of the long march to success, this study will attempt to explain why the energy industries were exempted from EU law in factual terms for so long.

2.2 The Early Days of EU Energy Law:
The First Steps Towards an Internal Market

Who was responsible for the unduly cautious application of primary EU law to the energy sector up to the mid-1990s? Many commentators have noted that the EC Treaty was not applied to the energy industries in an effective way,[20] while noting at the same time that the Treaty covers general energy matters and therefore confers on the EU institutions the competence to pursue common energy policies.

The rise of such once-contentious views may have been inspired by the triumph of the so-called Washington Consensus in the 1980s.[21] Inspired by the end of the Cold War, in the years from 1988 onwards there was widespread and intensive debate about the 'end of history'. As a consequence of this debate, and backed by several years of falling prices for primary fuels during a period of stable economic growth with only modest increases of primary fuel consumption in industrialized countries, the strategic relevance of the energy industries took a serious blow. Nevertheless, the agents for change proved fairly weak, as demonstrated by the discussion below of the lengthy negotiations on harmonization legislation.

A more precise diagnosis of the enduring failure to effectively apply primary law to the energy industries prior to the mid-1990s would be that its interpretation

---

[19] Basically, the doctrine of supremacy of EU law (*Costa-ENEL* doctrine: Case 6/64, *Costa v ENEL* [1964] ECR 1251) was turned on its head.

[20] E. Cross, L. Hancher, and P. Slot, 'EC Energy Law', in M. Roggenkamp et al. (eds), *Energy Law in Europe* (Oxford: OUP 2001), p. 215.

[21] The Washington Consensus is essentially about privatization, liberalization, convertibility of currencies, and tight monetary policy.

by the European Court of Justice (ECJ) and, to a lesser extent, the Commission, and the resistance on the part of 'vested interests' (i.e. existing energy monopolies and companies, their industry associations and political supporters in central and local government and trade unions and their academic cohorts) to a broader and more liberal interpretation aimed at freeing up segregated national markets had prevented the ideal—i.e. the achievement of an open, integrated, and competitive energy market—from being achieved through application of the Treaty alone. The Court, as the principal controller of the legal value of the Treaty, declined to take on tasks that it considered 'regulatory' in character. These tasks involved making changes (and supervizing such changes) to industry structure requiring a vast amount of economic analysis, political, and industry-wide negotiation and the risk of liability for failure.[22] Such a cautious line of action was possibly and implicitly based on an understanding of the close relationship between energy and sovereignty—i.e. the need to respond to future conflicts and to deal with major supply crises—as was underlined by Iraq's aggression in 1990, the collapse of the Soviet Union, Yugoslavia, and the built-in shortcomings of the EU's Common Foreign and Security Policy.

2.2.1 Draft Regulation on Investment Notification (1989–1996)

The first victim in the Commission's quest for liberalization was a proposal for a new regulation on notification to the Commission of investments in energy infrastructure. The draft faced stiff opposition from national governments and, as a consequence, was shelved for a period of seven years.[23] As late as 1996 and just before the Council endorsed a common position on the electricity directive of 1996, new common rules for the notification of investments in petroleum, natural gas and electricity infrastructure were adopted on the basis of a second Commission proposal.[24]

2.2.2 Commission Directives under Article 106(3) TFEU (1991–1996)

Article 90(3) EEC (which then became 86(3) EC and now 106(3) TFEU), provided an effective tool for the Commission's internal market agenda for the utilities sector

---

[22] Foremost articulate analysis by ECJ Judge Edward, D.A.O. (with M. Hoskins), 'Article 90: Deregulation and EC Law', 32(159) *CMLR* (1995), an article that precedes and effectively allows prediction of the 1997 energy judgments (Liberalization Cases): Case C-157/94, *Commission v Netherlands* [1997] ECR I-5699, Case C-158/94, *Commission v Italy* [1997] ECR I-5789, Case C-159/94, *Commission v France* [1997] ECR I-5815, Case C-160/94, *Commission v Spain* [1997] ECR I-5851.

[23] Draft Regulation on the notification of investment projects in the Petroleum, Natural Gas & Electricity sectors (COM (1989) 335). See P. Cameron, *Competition in Energy Markets* (Oxford: OUP 2001), p. 99.

[24] Council Regulation 1996/736/EC of 22 April 1996 on notifying the Commission of investment projects of interest to the Community in the petroleum, natural gas and electricity sectors, OJ L 102, 25.4.1996, p. 1. It replaced the old Regulation 1972/1056/EEC; Commission Proposal: OJ No C 346, 23.12.1995, p. 10.

in the late 1980s, starting with the liberalization of markets for telecommunications terminal equipment.[25] According to the Commission, this trick should have been repeated in the early 1990s in the energy sector. Unfortunately, the adoption of draft Commission directives did not work out in the end.

Article 106(1) TFEU obliges Member States not to exempt public undertakings, or those to which they grant exclusive or special rights, from Treaty rules. In this regard, it is irrelevant whether such measures are established prior to the adoption of the Treaty or later, nor does it matter if the measures are non-binding.[26] The term 'public undertaking'[27] is characterized in European law as a market player established either under public law or under domestic corporate law but which is nevertheless influenced by public authorities by means of significant shareholdings, financial participation, or through articles of association or other company rules. Exclusive rights assign specific product markets to one player or a limited number of players,[28] whereas special rights assign such markets to a limited number of undertakings or merely improve the competitive position of the recipient on a given and otherwise unrestricted market.[29] However, the distinction is somewhat vague.[30] In a somewhat related fashion, for the purposes of this discussion, Article 37(1) TFEU obliges Member States to adapt existing state monopolies of a commercial character, with a view to ensuring compliance with the rules on the free movement of goods and to avoiding any discrimination between national undertakings and those set up in other Member States.

2.2.3 The Exceptions: Article 106(2) EU

The second paragraph of Article 106 TFEU reminds Member States that undertakings are not exempt from competition and general Treaty rules, even if the latter are made subject to obligations to provide services in the general economic interest

---

[25] Utilities sector legislation based on Article 106(3): the Commission Directive 1988/301/EEC of 16.5.1988 on Competition in the Markets in Telecommunications Terminal Equipment, OJ L 131, 27.5.1988, p. 73; Commission Directive 1990/388/EEC of 28.6.1990 on comp in the markets for telecommunications services, OJ L 192, 24.7.1990, p. 10. However, the relation between Member States and domestic public undertakings is—as far as transparency of financial relations is concerned—addressed by a Commission Directive: Directive 1980/723. N.B. Article 4 of said piece of legislation exempted the utilities sector: WETTP (water, energy, transport, telecommunications, and postal services).

[26] For this, see R. Whish, *Competition Law* (Oxford: OUP 2009), p. 224.

[27] See the Opinion of AG Reischl in Joined Cases 188 to 190/80, *France et al. v Commission*, delivered 4.5.1982, p. 2,596.

[28] Joined Cases C-271, 281 and 289/90, *Spain, Belgium and Italy v Commission* [1992] ECR I-5833, paras. 28–32; Case C-202/8, *France v Commmission* [1991] ECR I-1270, paras. 45–47. However, both the ECJ and the Commission once treated both phenomena as being identical: Case 66/86, *Ahmed Saeed Flugreisen and Silver Line Reisebüro GmbH v Zentrale zur Bekämpfung Unlauteren Wettbewerbs e.V.* [1989] ECR 803.

[29] Arts. 1I(b) and 2(1)(a)(ii) Commission Directive 1994/46/EC amending Directive 1988/301/EEC and Directive 1990/388/EEC in particular with regard to satellite communications, OJ L 268, 1994, p. 15. For a detailed discussion: J. Buendia-Sierra, *Exclusive Rights and State Monopolies under EC Law* (Oxford: OUP 1999) at 1.04 and 2.04.

[30] For several undertakings being granted exclusive rights to the same market, see Case C-209/98, *Entreprenørforeningens Affalds/Miljøsektion (FFAD) v Københavns Kommune* [2000] ECR I-3743.

(or have the character of revenue-producing monopolies). However, derogations from Treaty rules under national laws or regulations, where these are necessary in order to ensure that these public service obligations are met either in law or in fact, are permissible. Such a derogation is to be restricted to the least distorting but still effective measure. Under no circumstances can trade between Member States be affected to an extent contrary to the interests of the EU.

As Article 106(2) TFEU permits derogation from general Treaty rules, it has to be interpreted restrictively. In this respect it resembles well-established concepts curtailing the use of basic freedoms: i.e. justifications under Article 36 TFEU (public safety and health, life and health of humans, animals and plants, cultural heritage and property) and the mandatory requirements under the *Cassis de Dijon*[31] formula. Since the preliminary ruling in the *Dassonville*[32] case, it has been widely acknowledged that, for the sake of the promotion of free trade in goods, the meaning of 'measures having equivalent effect' to quantitative restrictions on free trade must be interpreted broadly. Nevertheless, the Court jeopardized cross-border commerce by ruling that certain types of measures, while falling within the ambit of that concept, might not qualify as measures of equivalent effect: EU law shall ignore measures of a non-discriminatory nature insofar as they pursue coercive public ends, which take precedence over a curtailment of the free movement of goods on a case-by-case basis, and do not go beyond what is necessary.[33] Clearly, a narrow interpretation of this barrier to free trade is of the essence. Similarly, the reasoning in the case of *Keck*[34] again reduced the initial scope of the *Dassonville* judgment by excluding selling arrangements.

What makes Article 106(3) so special then? It is the most interesting playing field for the beauty contests of dogmatic science. According to the present scoreboard—which is, *inter alia*, set by the 'energy judgments' of 1997—and discounting the antagonistic reasoning adopted in *Franzén* and earlier landmark cases like *Sacchi*—it is the extraordinary power to justify interferences with primary law that go beyond the scope of other exceptions from Treaty rules.[35] It entrusts the Commission with

---

[31] Case 120/78, *Rewe-Zentral AG v Bundesmonopolverwaltung für Branntwein* 1979 [ECR], p. 649.

[32] Case 8/74, *Procureur du Roi v. Benoît and Gustave Dassonville* [1974] ECR 837.

[33] The case law evolved with respect to German provisions ruling out sales of certain spirits not complying with minimum specifications as to the contents of alcohol: Case C-120/78, *REWE v Bundesmonopolverwaltung für Branntwein* [1979] ECR 649.

[34] Joined cases C-267/91 and C-268/91, *Criminal proceedings against Bernard Keck and Daniel Mithouard* [1993] ECR I-6097

[35] Case C-157/94, *Commission v Netherlands* [1997] ECR I-5699, Case C-158/94, *Commission v Italy* [1997] ECR I-5789, Case C-159/94, *Commission v France* [1997] ECR I-5815, Case C-160/94, *Commission v Spain* [1997] ECR I-5851. Also Case C-202/88, *France v Commmission* [1991] ECR I-1223, Case 260/89, *ERT v DEP* [1991] ECR I-2951, Case C-320/91, *Corbeau* [1993] ECR I-2533. For the Commission: most explicit Recital 12 of Directive 1990/38/EEC. See also Case C-189/95 *Franzén* [1997] ECR I-5909, Case C-41/90, *Klaus Höfner and Fritz Elser v Macrotron GmbH* [1991] ECR I-1979, Case C-18/88, *RTT v SA-GB* [1991] ECR I-5973, Case C-72/83, *Campus Oil v Minister for Industry* [1984] ECR 2727, Case 155/1973 *Sacchi* [1974] ECR 409. The grant of exclusive rights by a Member State was as such deemed compatible with EU law—as long as it served public ends. Article 106(1) TFEU reference 'shall neither enact … any measure contrary to the rules contained in this treaty', e.g. the basic freedoms, was virtually ignored. Only the entity's behaviour had to be monitored under said freedoms and Article 102 TFEU (Rec. 14: 'prohibitions of discrimination') unless the attainment of Public Service Obligation would be frustrated in terms of Article 106(2).

powers to police the application of paragraphs 1 and 2 of Article 106 TFEU and grants the power 'where necessary, to address appropriate directives or decisions to Member States'.

Here, it is hard to establish any democratic link between the electorates and the Commission's powers. There is talk of 'administrative self-restraint' and perhaps the potential that the latter element of Article 106(3) is nowadays inconsistent with the democratic principle enshrined in various articles of the TEU, since the impact EU law has on peoples' lives today is far greater than was the case at the time the EEC was founded.

2.2.4 Directives 80/723/EEC and 88/301/EEC

In 1980, the Commission addressed a directive to Member States dedicated to clarifying the transparency of financial relations between Member States and domestic public undertakings.[36] This directive was challenged by France, Italy, and the UK but the Court's ruling of 1982 was in favour of the Commission, which enjoyed support from the governments of the Netherlands and Germany. The Court ruled that one could not derive any principle from the Treaty that limited the powers the Commission enjoyed under Article 106(3) TFEU—on an *a priori* basis—to a mere specification of existing duties.[37] Despite the fact that the Commission's competences are primarily of an administrative nature, that its law-making powers are often limited to implementing the Council's acts of secondary legislation, and that the principle of separation of powers is commonplace in constitutions throughout Europe and goes back at least as far as Montesquieu's *De l'esprit des lois*, the applicants failed to establish such a principle.

Eight years later, the Commission addressed a small piece of utility liberalization legislation to Member States. Issued in May 1988, Directive 88/301/EEC was intended to liberalize European markets for telecommunications terminal equipment and ancillary services.

In brief, 'liberalization' may be understood as any reform of regulatory patterns moving away from either hierarchical or association-based mechanisms towards market-based solutions.[38] The price mechanism was based on the publication of verifiable criteria to achieve a situation of perfect competition, involving the maximization of the number both of suppliers and of willing and able consumers, and the removal of barriers to entering and exiting the markets in question.

The directive was carefully crafted to fall within the scope of Article 106(3) and, as such, it stood its ground in the forthcoming judicial review. Member States were obliged to put a stop to the granting of exclusive rights to undertakings active in importation and marketing in connection with such equipment, including

---

[36] Commission Directive 80/723/EEC of 25 June 1980 on the transparency of financial relations between Member States and public undertakings, OJ L 195, 29.7.1980, pp. 35–7.

[37] Joined Cases 188–190/80, *France, Italy, UK v Commission* [1982] ECR 2545, Recital 1.

[38] M. Arentsen and R. Künneke, 'Economic Organization and Liberalization of the Electricity Industry', *Energy Policy* (1996), p. 547.

ancillary services (Articles 1–3 of the Directive), to specify access to connection points, and to communicate technical specifications and type-approval procedures (Articles 3–4 of the Directive). Moreover, Member States were obliged to ensure that 'undertakings' terminated long-term contracts, leases, or maintenance agreements for equipment (Article 7).

Before drawing profound conclusions from this directive with a view to applying them to network-bound elements of the energy sector, one has to bear in mind that the equipment in question mainly comprises handy, small, and valuable gadgets which can be bought and sold independently from networks and require little servicing. So, the most important preliminary lesson is that the wasp may well upset the monopoly by stinging its tail—but never confuse the tiger's tail with the tiger itself. Therefore, it is interesting to note that the directive was part of a comprehensive framework, which also included other measures. Originally, the tigers were to be captured not only by a wasp but also with the support of a horde of elephants. The role of the elephant-rider was performed by the Council Resolution of 30/06/1988, which called for the definition of a common telecommunications policy. Such policy was to be based upon the opening-up of telecommunications services markets, primarily by virtue of Council legislation defining technical conditions, conditions of use, and principles governing charges for an open network provision (ONP) and thereby harmonizing standards.[39]

Not surprisingly, Directive 1988/301 was subject to an action for annulment brought by France, which attracted widespread support from Belgium, Germany, Greece, and Italy.[40] After almost four years of deliberation, the Court eventually dismissed much of the application. First, it implicitly abandoned large parts of the *Sacchi* reasoning. It clarified that EU law does not presume it to be compatible with the Treaty if Member States enact or maintain measures relating to undertakings enjoying exclusive or special rights (e.g. the setting up of monopolies by virtue of legislation or regulation). No such finding can be derived simply from the acknowledgement of such undertakings in Article 106(1) TFEU and, accordingly, the Court assessed the exclusive rights in question under the provisions governing the free movement of goods.[41] It applied the *Dassonville* test and found such rights to be in breach of Article 34 TFEU: i.e. as having equivalent effect to quantitative restrictions.

Secondly, the path chosen in the court's judgments in Joined Cases 188–190/1980 was exposed again and broadened. Taking advantage of the *lex specialis derogat legi generali* doctrine, the scope of Commission directives was defended against any notion of supremacy of Council legislation. This remained true even in the light

---

[39] It seems that the elephant horde got lost somewhere in the urban jungle of Brussels' suburbs. Therefore, the Commission took charge and issued Commission Directive 90/388/EEC of 28 June 1990 on competition in the markets for telecommunications services, OJ L 192, 24.7.1990, pp. 10–16 (See Recital 32 of there).

[40] Case 202/88, *France v Commission* [1991] ECR I-1223.

[41] Case 202/88, *France v Commission* [1991] ECR I-1223, paras. 22, 33–39. Surprisingly, Article 31 (EC) was not mentioned even if France challenged that the directive was wrong to assume any breach of that provision (q.v. para. 29).

of Council directives under what is now Article 103 TFEU or the constitutional reform embarked upon in 1986. The Commission's competences were narrowed neither by the SEA's new legal basis for harmonization legislation (then Article 100a EEC, which then became Article 95 EC and now Article 114 TFEU) nor by the strong backing for the European Parliament's legislative role under cooperation procedures[42] (and later for co-decision powers, since the EU Treaty was ratified in November 1993). Nothing obliges the Commission to initiate actions for failure to fulfil an obligation first before relying on its own directives.[43]

However, the applicant and interveners gained two victories. First, the Court found that the Commission had included 'special rights' in the scope of the law, but had failed to attribute any specific meaning to that term in contrast to exclusive rights. In that respect, Article 2 lacked legal justification and was declared void to that extent.[44] This gain was of a purely academic nature.

However, the second victory really mattered. The Court found that a Commission directive exceeds its legitimate legal base if it obliges Member States to transpose rules that regulate agreements and concerted practices between normal players and undertakings holding exclusive rights or pursuing services in the general economic interest, which are nevertheless based on the free determination of the players. Such conduct must be an exclusive subject of the competition policy based on the implementation of Articles 101 and 102 TFEU[45] (or of Council legislation especially under Article 103 TFEU). Consequently, the Court annulled Article 7 of Commission Directive 88/301/EEC. That provision obliged Member States to implement provisions requiring undertakings enjoying exclusive rights, *inter alia*, for the importation, marketing, or servicing of telecommunications terminal equipment (Article 1) to terminate *long-term* leases and maintenance agreements. However, the duration of such agreements was not regulated by the monopoly in question so it was an exclusive matter to be addressed by proceedings relating to Articles 101 and 102 TFEU.

---

[42] Case 202/88 *France v Commission* [1991] ECR I-1223, paras. 24–26.

[43] Case 202/88 *France v Commission* [1991] ECR I-1223, para. 16.

[44] Case 202/88 *France v Commission* [1991] ECR I-1223, paras. 45–47. This situation was remedied by Commission Directive 94/46/EC of 13 October 1994 amending Directive 88/301/EEC and Directive 90/388/EEC in particular with regard to satellite communications, OJ L 268, 19.10.1994, pp. 15–21. Recital 6 defines special rights as an three fold concept: 'rights granted by a Member State to a limited number of undertakings, through any legislative, regulatory or administrative instirument which, within a given (…) area, limits to two or more the number of such undertaking, otherwise than according to objective, proportional and non-discriminatory criteria, *or* designates, otherwise to such criteria, (..) undertakings, *or* confers on any undertaking (…), otherwise than according to such criteria, legal or regulatory advantages which substantially affect' competition in relevant markets. For a detailed discussion: J. Buendia-Sierra, *Exclusive Rights and State Monopolies under EC Law* (Oxford: OUP 1999), at 1.04 and 2.04.

[45] Case 202/88, *France v Commission* [1991] ECR I 1223, paras. 55–57.

2.2.5 Telecommunications Liberalization Continued: Directive 90/377/EEC versus the Burden of Special Rights and the Competition Policy Barrier

It seems that the elephant horde briefly alluded to in 2.2.4 and driven by the Council Resolution of 30/06/1988 got lost somewhere in the urban jungle of the Brussels suburbs, and never actually reached the Rue de la Loi. Therefore, the Commission took charge and issued Directive 90/388/EEC.[46] Various similarities to the energy sectors emerge if one studies its recitals.[47] The recitals took note of ongoing technological advances and various restrictions imposed by network operators on both innovative service providers and users. These restrictions impeded, *inter alia*:

- network access;
- the introduction of new protocols increasing the speed of networks (in energy terms, we would draw an analogy with congestion management); and
- the commercialization of revolutionary information services, being remote access to databases, data-processing, telemetry, e-mail, and of course the Internet.

The Commission duly concluded that those practices were inconsistent with the Treaty. Insofar as the practices were connected to exclusive or special rights of telecommunications undertakings, they were contrary to Article 106(1) TFEU because they hindered intra-Community trade in services, in particular, since it was established that any restriction from private access of providers and users to networks as such qualified neither for the public safety and policy defences under Article 52 TFEU[48] nor for the *Van Binsbergen* doctrine of essential requirements in the general interest, unless the integrity and security of the network, inter-operability and data protection were at stake.[49]

Translating these safeguards into the modern 'eurospeak' of the energy sector leaves one with a list of services regarded as being in the general economic interest, which Member States may oblige the undertaking to honour on the basis of either Article 106(2) TFEU or Article 3 of the 2009 electricity and gas directives. Such obligations may address security—i.e. security of supply and technical safety, regularity, quality, pricing, environmental protection (e.g. efficiency and climate protection)—and 'universal service obligations' by suppliers of last resort (for electricity).

The Commission approach, however, was not limited to that. It permitted the dedication of Public Service Obligation (PSO) to the requirements of the nascent telecommunications services markets, a concept which preceded a later and prominent derogation from the Energy Market Directive: the so-called derogations for emergent and isolated systems.[50]

---

[46] See its Recital 32–33.

[47] Recital 6. The directive is no longer in force. It was once amended by Commission Directive 1994/46/EC, OJ L 268, 19.10.1994, p. 15.

[48] Recitals 7–10.

[49] Case C-33/74, *van Binsbergen* [1974] ECR 1291. On that base, essential requirements are defined in Article 1 I of Directive 1990/388/EEC. Save these requirements, exclusive rights as to telecommunications services and networks were to be abandoned (Articles 1 II, 2 I-II, 4 I).

[50] These are examined further in Chapter 3.

Directive 90/388/EEC also dealt with the legal separation of the operation of telecommunications networks and the licensing of telecommunications services that Member States had been accustomed to entrusting to operators (Recitals 28–29). This need to separate network activities (governmental or commercial) from other commercial functions is well known in the energy sector, where the Member States are required to implement provisions obliging network operators to be set up as separate legal entities distinct from other activities (legal unbundling) and subject to standards relating to independence of management and transparency of accounts. Consequently, there is a requirement to publish technical conditions for access to networks, and third party access is to be given on the basis of tariffs, which are at least approved by a regulator.[51]

For our purposes, it is not appropriate to engage in a more comprehensive discussion of the provisions of the Telecommunications Directive. Having been amended in 1994, the wave of telecommunications liberalization washed it away.[52] In short, it is the Court's reasoning that is noteworthy. This time, Belgium, Italy, and Spain asked the Court for annulment. Spain joined in as it was no longer protected by its accession agreements. It was supported by—no surprise—France; but at least Germany and Greece had digested the lessons learned from the 1988 case. The Court reiterated the reasoning it used in respect of the first Commission Directive 88/301/EEC and dismissed the bulk of the applicants' claims.[53] It again annulled those parts of the law which failed to establish a specific definition and regime for 'special rights' or which sought to oblige Member States to regulate the *mere conduct* of undertakings entrusted with exclusive rights, which is not addressed as such by the monopoly itself (i.e. providing further assurance as to what might be termed the implicit 'competition policy barrier' faced by any directive adopted under Article 106(3) TFEU in relation to Articles 101–102 TFEU). It concluded that legal extensions of exclusive rights covering networks to related up-, or downstream markets are not permissible in the absence of specific justification.[54]

---

[51] These are examined further in Chapter 3.

[52] See Commission Directive 1994/46/EC amending Directive 1988/301/EEC and Directive 1990/388/EEC in particular with regard to satellite communications, OJ L 268, 1994, p. 15.

[53] Joined Cases C-271, 281 and 289/90, *Spain, Belgium and Italy v Commission* [1992] ECR I-5866.

[54] Joined Cases C-271, 281 and 289/90, *Spain, Belgium and Italy v Commission* [1992] ECR I-5866, para. 36. However, by that time the legal reasoning was rather vague as it was left open which approach is to be taken to assess any grant of exclusive rights under 106(1) TFEU: Under the first option, Article 102 TFEU shall not apply to it (Case C-179/90, *Porto di Genoa* [1991] ECR I-1979, para. 16). Secondly the Court cited a contravening judgment held that the extension of service monopolies to trade in ancillary equipment and services was indeed subject to a combined analysis under Articles 106(1) and 102 TFEU (Case C-18/88, *RTT v GB-Inno-BM* [1991] ECR I-5941, para. 24). The first view is definitely persuasive, as public decrees cannot constitute behaviour of undertakings in terms of competition law. For the treatment of special rights: Rec. 11 of Directive 1994/46/EC.

2.3 Draft Commission Directives on Internal Markets for Electricity and Natural Gas

In the final years of the 1980s and the early 1990s, the Commission considered introducing something akin to the US concepts of 'common carriage' to oil pipelines and 'open access' to gas in relation to European power and gas lines, with a view to completing the internal market programme and improving the global competitiveness of European industrial and commercial players. The intention was to bring an end to a period of decades during which the basic freedoms under the Treaty had been hostage to the '*Sacchi* doctrine' of supremacy of grants of exclusive rights to electricity and gas undertakings. The Commission also hoped to close loopholes in national competition legislation with regard to exclusive concessions and vertical and horizontal demarcation agreements. To this end, it relied on several external studies, set up stakeholder committees—which achieved little in the way of verifiable results—and decided to circulate and introduce, in 1989 and the summer of 1991 respectively, proposals for Commission directives on competition in the markets for electricity and natural gas.[55]

The scope of these proposal directives was fairly limited and they would have been subject to complementary measures under the aegis of approximation of laws anyway, since—owing to the approach taken by the Court in respect of telecommunications—it did not seem wise to add any provisions which would have obliged Member States to regulate the conduct of national players in a manner that did not form an integrated part of the grant or maintenance of exclusive or special rights.

To exemplify this scenario, consider how the current energy market directives would look, and whether they would service any useful purpose, if they did not address such issues as:

- authorization procedures or tendering for new capacities;
- unbundling;
- system access;
- regulatory authorities; and
- derogations.

Any such piece of legislation would hardly be sustainable, at any rate if it honoured the findings of the Court's telecommunications judgments.[56] It was therefore mandatory to back up any Commission directive with approximation legislation, which is indeed what the Commission had planned.[57]

---

[55] Completion of the Internal Market in Electricity and Gas (COM (1989) 332 final and 334 final; COM (1991) 548 final). For a detailed discussion of proposals, studies, and counter-studies commissioned on behalf of major players: P. Cameron, *Competition in Energy Markets* (Oxford: OUP 2002) 3.51 et seq.

[56] However, the potential of Article 106(3) TFEU was nevertheless defended: A. Cardoso e Cunha, 'The Internal Energy Market', 9(290) *Journal of Energy and Natural Resources Law* (1991), p. 292.

[57] P. Cameron, *Competition in Energy Markets* (Oxford: OUP 2002) at 3.61.

However, one should not overlook the large-scale temporal drawbacks of the alternative strategy. This was based on enacting legislation aimed at approximating national laws in order to implement basic freedoms, with a view to completing the internal market by removing exclusive rights. Even worse, it was hardly commonplace by that time—i.e. the late 1980s—to seek to arrive at anything resembling a comprehensive common energy policy from the starting-point of harmonization legislation dedicated to removing barriers to cross-border trade. Based on high-flown constitutional dogmatics, it was argued that the introduction of TPA was beyond the EU competences, since TPA would interfere with domestic property rights—a matter deliberately left to the Member States under what is the new Article 345 TFEU.[58] A closer look at that provision, though, makes it more sensible to argue that a 'system of property ownership' is affected by the expropriation of assets or the outright nationalization of industries rather than by mere interference in the question of how one must exercise existing property rights. The objective of this provision is to regulate the division of competence between the EU and the Member States, without granting property rights absolute immunity against the application of EU law. A certain degree of unification of property law is unavoidable due to the process of economic integration taking place within the EU.[59] Moreover, the purpose of Article 345 TFEU is not to evade the enforceability of the fundamental rules of the Treaty with regard to national systems of property ownership.[60] This means, first, that to some extent the EU has competence to deal with issues involving property rights and, secondly, that national legislators have to take into account the general principles and interest of the EU in regulating the means of acquisition and enjoyment of property. The logic of this second consideration tends to dictate that the more difficult it is to duplicate an asset, the more vital that asset is to the community as a whole; and therefore the more equitable it becomes to open up access to that asset beyond the owner to anybody willing and able to pay fair compensation—thus addressing the long-term average incremental costs of replacing the asset in question.

The ratification of the Treaty on the European Union in 1993, however, brought decisive relief for the camp of lobbyists in favour of energy liberalization by virtue of approximation legislation. Since 'energy' as a whole was added to the catalogue of EU competences (EC competences at that time), the mandate for common energy policy internal market harmonization legislation became crystal clear and Article 106(3) TFEU was laid to rest for a while.

---

[58] For discussion of TPA in general and in the light of the Commission's proposals which led to the first 'wave' of EC legislation on energy liberalization, see: J. Schwarze, 'European Energy Policy in Community Law' and J.P. Stern, 'The Prospects for Third Party Access in European Gas Markets', Chs. 10 and 11 in E. Mestmäcker (ed.), *Natural Gas in the Internal Market—A Review of Energy Policy*, (London: Graham & Trotman 1993), J. R. Salter, 'Third Party Access to Gas and Electricity Transmission Systems in the Community: Third Party Access—Your Flexible Friend?', Ch. 6 in D. MacDougall and T. Wälde (eds), *European Community Energy Law—Selected Topics* (London: Graham & Trotman/M. Nijhoff 1994).

[59] F. Campbell-White, 'Property Rights: A Forgotten Issue Under the Union' in N. A. Neuwhal and A. Rosas (eds), *The European Union and Human Rights* (The Hague: M Nijhoff 1995), p. 249.

[60] Case C-302/97, *Konle* [1999] ECR I-3099, para. 38, Case C-300/01, *Salzmann* [2003] ECR I-4899, para. 39, Case C-452/01, *Ospelt* [2003] ECR I-9743, para. 24.

Finally, it should be noted that the golden tale of Article 106(3) TFEU– also referred to as a 'Draconian Threat'[61]—has come to neither a good nor a bad end. History sometimes tends to repeat itself if appropriate conclusions are not drawn in time. During the period from 1999 to 2003, when the consensus-based approach to the regulation of the energy sector, as applied by the Florence and Madrid Fora, needed fresh impetus, the Commission, albeit in a far more modest form than might have been feared, threatened to address directives to Member States under this provision. In the end, this credible threat or ingenious pretext—depending on one's view of the telecommunications judgments—to issue a Commission directive not only hastened the adoption of Regulation 2003/1228/EC on cross-border exchanges of electricity—based on what is now Article 114(1) TFEU—but also contributed to the strengthening of the mandate of proactive negotiators in the forum.

2.3.1 Dismissed Actions for Failure to Fulfil Obligations under Article 258 TFEU (1994–1997)

In a manner in no way coincidental to its 1991 proposals for liberalization directives, the Commission initiated action against nine out of 12 Member States for failure to fulfil obligations under the Treaty. It first sent out administrative letters alleging that the addressees maintained exclusive rights, for instance, with regard to imports, storage and supply of natural gas, and/or imports or exports of electricity. It found those exclusive rights to be contrary to what is now Article 37 TFEU, a provision which had long obliged Member States to phase out trade monopolies of a commercial character. This step was met with harsh responses. The Commission received widespread criticism that either Article 37 TFEU was not applicable to power—a finding hardly compatible with the Court's reasoning[62]—or that at least public safety or policy defences would justify the exclusive rights in question (Articles 36 or 106(2) TFEU).

Some progress was nevertheless achieved. The government of the UK promised to abandon the exclusive rights that the Northern Irish Electricity Supply Board enjoyed for imports and exports of power. Following evaluation of the responses, it was at least clarified that no such exclusive rights existed in Belgium and Greece. Six reasoned opinions were distributed to the remaining countries late in 1992. Denmark complied with the reasoned opinion in 1994 by revoking exclusive import rights granted to Dansk Naturgas. This act was accompanied by a conditional opening up of markets for the transport, storage, and trade of natural gas.[63] With respect to the Republic of Ireland, the Commission suspended its action when it was established that the domestic rules in question did not conflict with general

---

[61] P. Cameron, *Competition in Energy Markets* (London: OUP 2002) at 6.09.

[62] Case 6/64, *Costa v ENEL* [1964] ECR 1253: An Italian law concerning the organization of the domestic power sector implicitly assessed under the free movement provisions. Also Case C-393/92, *Almelo v NV Energiebedrijf Ijsselmij* [1994] ECR I-1477.

[63] See P. Cameron, *Competition in Energy Markets* (Oxford: OUP 2002) at 3.86.

legal principles—e.g. the idea of free circulation of goods and services—as they merely 'enabled' the incumbent utility to import power but did not render such rights exclusive or special.[64]

2.3.1.1　*Case C-157/94, Commission v Netherlands*

Although the Commission had granted a sort of 'sabbatical year' to the six original recipients of its reasoned opinions and thus gave them due time to consider the urgency of the case for the opening-up of their network-bound energy markets—at least if they were to be organized in line with primary EU law under the aegis of the principle of its supremacy—and to increase the standing of pro-liberalization agents in the ongoing negotiations with an eye to the adoption of approximation legislation (as discussed below), this was to no avail. As a consequence, and with support from the UK, proceedings were issued in June 1994.

The first of these opposed the exclusive right, which a Dutch law of 1989 had granted to NV Samenwerkende Elektriciteitsproducktiebberijven (SEP) for the import of electricity using voltages equal to or exceeding 500 volts with a view to distribution to consumers, notwithstanding auto-imports of any scale or low-voltage commercial imports (the latter hardly being an economic venture).

The defendant was supported by France and, interestingly, Ireland. The latter's participation provided a vivid illustration of the fact that its famous domestic 'enabling legislation' was, in fact, rather a virtual spearhead of liberalization of the electricity sector.

The Commission based its argumentation on (alleged) violations of the principle of free trade in goods under Article 34 TFEU and the Dutch failure to abolish existing monopolies or to avoid granting new monopolies to state trading enterprises under Article 37. The Dutch government sought to rely on a public policy defence (security of power supplies) allegedly embedded in Article 36 or at least derived from Article 106(2) TFEU.

Since the Advocate General argued in favour of reasoning while avoiding addressing key issues by denying that import monopolies interfered with free trade in goods, we will turn to the judgment immediately. The Court held that SEP enjoyed a commercial monopoly as the law vested it with the ability to prevent imports within its mandate. It found that existing trade monopolies should have been phased out, since the transitional periods had ended long ago, and that the creation of new ones was illegal in principle under Article 37 TFEU. Since the monopoly in question resulted from a 1989 law, SEP's status was in principle unsustainable. The Court rejected the Dutch government's argument, which was based on the assumption that the creation of a commercial monopoly by means of a governmental act was presupposed under Article 37(1) TFEU, and that the Court could only assess whether the implementation of a given monopoly through SEP was subject to controls relating to abusive behaviour—i.e. whether it was discriminatory under

---

[64] B. Devlin and C. Levasseur, 'Energy', in J. Faull and A. Nikpay (eds), *The EC Law of Competition* (Oxford: OUP 1999) at 10.115.

Article 102 or not.[65] The government's approach lacked a literal foundation in Article 37(1), since it is always helpful to use the predicate 'shall adjust' if one is to derive the meaning of a direct object 'any state monopolies of a commercial character so as to … ' (principle of non-discrimination). Moreover, the second sentence points to the idea that the principle of non-discrimination involves accepting that Member States must not create or maintain any commercial entity which 'in law or in fact, directly or indirectly … appreciably influences imports … between Member States' (i.e. the principle of inclusiveness of non-discriminatory barriers). This extension is vital, as it once provided the textual, systemic, and purposive backbone of the famous *Dassonville* formula in the context of quotas and measures having equivalent effect. That is to say that if Member States are prevented from conferring on state trading enterprises either with commercial monopolies (discrimination) or to enabling them to determine imports (non-discriminatory interferences with free trade), it is, by the same token, true that neither domestic legislation nor government agencies may discriminate against imported goods (by virtue of quotas). Furthermore, measures which place similar limits on domestic and foreign products, but actually entail trade restriction either in law or in fact, in a direct or an indirect manner (analogy to Article 37(1)) cannot be deemed permissible. Moreover, it would not be conducive to the promotion of free trade if Member States were able to compromise trade in goods to a greater extent by virtue either of quotas or licensing and declaration procedures under Article 34, or commercial monopolies under Article 37.

To the Commission's advantage, the Court denied the Netherlands any potential to reject the conclusion that a commercial monopoly was in place by using the argument that SEP merely performed the functions of a public planning authority, or to justify such a monopoly by way of a public policy defence under Article 36 TFEU (i.e. based on 'security of supply considerations').

Nevertheless, the Court went on to examine whether a trade monopoly was justifiable under the PSO defence of Article 106(2). Although the Commission had contested the admissibility of such a defence in the context of trade in goods,[66] the Court clarified that Article 106(2) TFEU was indeed suitable to justify interferences with free trade in goods. Article 106(1) sanctions the existence of service monopolies provided that their creation does not interfere with Treaty rules, (or if that is indeed the case, any such interference is justified by virtue of Article 106(2)).[67] This article could be used as a basis on which to evade such Treaty rules if goods-related aspects of service monopolies were not to be assessed under Articles 34–37 TFEU. It is therefore of consequence explicitly to include trade monopolies in Article 106(1) TFEU.[68] Thus, the paragraph amounts to *lex generalis*

---

[65] Paras. 21–23 with reference to Case 59/75, *Publico Ministero v Manghera* [1976] ECR 91, paras. 9–10.

[66] Para. 26.

[67] Paras. 26–32; see ECJ Case C-158/94 *Commission v Italy* [1997] ECR I-5789.

[68] Paras. 30–31; see ECJ Case C-158/94 *Commission v Italy* [1997] ECR I-5789.

compared with Article 37 TFEU, whereas the second paragraph of Article 106 becomes the chief exception.

As Article 106(2) TFEU is a curtailment of basic freedoms, the Court found it necessary to apply it strictly and to place a (general) burden of proof on the Member State relying on it.[69] So far so good, since the Court's earlier judgments had indicated that it was up to the Member State to show that the absence of the exclusive right in question would endanger the commercial viability of the undertaking in question (financial equilibrium at risk).[70]

However, since the Netherlands argued that the exclusive import right was indeed vital for SEP in order to obtain security of domestic power supplies, being a service entrusted to it in the general economic interest, the Court had to decide whether such a modest substantiation of the exclusive right satisfied the proportionality test built into that provision. Instead of requiring the Netherlands to prove the precise economic link between exclusive rights and advances in security of supply with a view to relying on the derogation, the Court took the view that in order to succeed in its application the Commission had to provide exhaustive data to support the conclusion that—even without exclusive rights or, at least, with lesser ones—the services claimed as being in the general economic interest could be provided on an enduring economic basis.[71]

As the Commission did propose such an analysis in its application, it lost. A pessimist would suggest that the Court here was 'inventing fresh options for joggling and shifting the burden of proof as it suits the forum most'—only to be overturned in a couple of years when the next landmark case is decided and public opinion turns around. For the sake of brevity, we will ignore the Court's complementary findings, the reasoning behind which is derived from the decisive function played by the Commission's pre-litigation procedure in respect of actions for failure to fulfil obligations under the Treaty.

2.3.1.2 Case C-158/94, Commission v Italy

With an eye to avoiding duplication of results, the discussion in this section is restricted to findings complementary to the Dutch case. To that end, the Court extended its reasoning to monopolies on the export of electricity, which were a part of the relevant laws shielding ENEL from competition and making cross-border trade subject to licence.[72] With regard to the Italian double defence that power was primarily not a good in terms of Articles 28–37 TFEU, but only secondarily a good ancillary to services to such a large extent that the Treaty's provisions on

---

[69] Para. 37.
[70] Para. 35 with reference to Case C-320/91, *Corbeau* [1993] ECR I-2533, para. 16, Case C-393/92, *Almelo and Others v Energiebedrijf Ijsselmij* [1994] ECR I-1477, para. 49.
[71] Paras. 45, 58–59.
[72] Italian Law No 1643 of 6 December 1962 (GURI No 316 of 12 December 1962) in combination with Article 20 of the Legislative Decree No 342 of 18 March 1965 (GURI No 104 of 26 April 1965). Article 133 of the Consolidated Law No 1755 of 11 December 1933 on water and electrical installations, as amended by Law No 606 of 19 July 1959; export monopolies: at 24.

services must legally prevail (and exclude any basis on which to apply Article 37), the Court reiterated the *Costa-ENEL* judgment addressing power as a good[73] and drew a distinction between sales of power and sales of goods ancillary to services. The provision of electricity was found not to be an activity ancillary to services.[74] This finding is indeed beneficial, as an electricity provider does not deal with any downstream services—i.e. it is not concerned with what the power actually does in the consumer's appliances (such as lighting, heating, cooking, washing, and cooling). Another approach might be appropriate for forms of single or multi-utility 'energy contracting': that is to say, utilities providing grid connections, power/gas/water/heat appliances, maintenance and servicing on an enduring basis freeing up decentralized industrial and commercial users' valuable managerial capacities and allowing them to focus on core competences.

It is important to stress that the application did not address the exclusive nature of ENEL's rights as to transmission of power on behalf of others;[75] and again it is hardly viable for every major consumer (on an aggregated site basis) to operate its own transmission lines with a view to transmitting to widespread premises. Based on the Dutch case discussed at 2.3.1.1, it is hardly a surprise to see who supported the Commission and who backed Italy.

2.3.1.3 *Case C-159/94, Commission v France*

Based on the preceding analyses, we will cut short our stay in the country where the once most active laggards of power, natural gas, and agricultural liberalization usually celebrate the successes achieved by persistent lobbying in Paris or Brussels. In that respect, it is noteworthy that the Court extended its findings to exclusive import and export rights concerning natural gas.[76]

2.3.1.4 *Case C-160/94, Commission v Spain*

This case deserves to be ignored, since the application claiming that Spain maintained exclusive rights for exports and imports of power lacked legal substantiation. Transmission of power through grids was a public service in Spain under Article 1(1) of a law dating from 1984.[77] Management by a state company which has to operate interconnectors and engage in international trade does not amount to an exclusive or special right to export power from or import it to Spain.[78]

---

[73] Para. 16; backed by ECJ, Case C-393/92 *Almelo and Others v Energiebedrijf IJsselmij* [1994] ECR I-1477, para. 28 supported by the Community's tariff nomenclature (Code CN 27.16); Case 6/64 *Costa v ENEL* [1964] ECR 585.

[74] Paras. 19 and 30.

[75] Para. 67.

[76] Articles 1–2 of Law No 46–628 of 8 April 1946 on the nationalization of electricity and gas (JORF of 9 April 1946) granting exclusive rights to production, transport, distribution, import, and export of power to EDF and of natural gas to GDF (albeit sometimes in combination with long-term exclusive concession agreements for the transmission of power and gas, eventually subject to certain exceptions).

[77] Law No. 49/84 of 26 December 1984 on the unified operation of the national electricity system (BOE No 312 of 29 December 1984). The incumbent entity is REDESA.

[78] Paras. 13–15.

2.3.2 Some Observations

To sum up, the energy judgments of 1997 share a hybrid nature. First, they can be regarded as the dim shining of four glow worms at dawn, inevitably and quickly to be overtaken by the forthcoming morning of approximation legislation. Secondly, they represent a *semi-final*—the scarcely glorious victory of unchecked national sovereignty and state intervention over the growing forces of globalization, which had widely prospered under the aegis of the 'Washington Consensus' and had begun to call into question the traditional national fiefdoms over public undertakings or at least industries exempt from cartel laws. It was no longer assumed that the traditional paradigm served either strategic interests or national economies as a whole. This was especially true because economic growth was no longer tied to proportionate increases in energy consumption, which meant that units—designed with a view to maximizing competitiveness—no longer needed to be on a giant scale. Massive investment plans—commonplace in the 1960s—were rendered obsolete.[79]

In order to understand what constituted the final success of state monopolies of commercial character, one should travel to Sweden, crossing the Baltic Sea by ferry. Once on board, do not refrain from buying strong beer, wine, or spirits in bulk pursuant to the *Alkohollag*.[80] Having landed safely, spontaneously decide to set up a retail outlet to dispose of your on-ship purchases to enthusiastic locals in the marinas of Gothenburg, Ystad, or Malmö, for instance. However, it is also recommended that you have the number of a prestigious defence lawyer number stored in your mobile phone's memory.

In *Franzén*, the Court ruled, in line with the traditional *Sacchi* principles established for service monopolies, that any commercial monopoly for retail trade in goods should be consistent with the Treaty, taking this principle from Article 37 TFEU (presupposition of monopolies doctrine).[81] Any grassroots interpretation of Article 37 reveals that it is designed to outlaw monopolies, not to balance achievements for public health with bans on monopolies. However, the Court took the view that the diverging needs of public health and free trade should be reconciled before the provision could be safely applied.

Clearly, it is not the final viability of the retail monopoly as such that is puzzling, but the failure to support it by reference to an 'application' of a provision dedicated to combat any kind of commercial monopoly on trade in goods by virtue of its wording, system, and teleological rationale. Following the well-established *Corbeau* principles for service monopolies would lead to the unavoidable conclusion that any commercial monopoly is in principle in breach of the Treaty, albeit with the potential for justification on the basis of the tests enshrined in either Article 36 or under Article 106(2) TFEU, since it has long been established that services in the general interest also include trade in goods.[82]

---

[79] W. Patterson, *Transforming Electricity* (London: Earthscan, 1999), pp. 60–4 and 112–6.
[80] Swedish Law on Alcohol: Alkohollag (1994:1738) of 16 December 1994. The situation and the applicable laws in Finland are similar.
[81] Case C-189/95, *Franzén* [1997] ECR I-5909.
[82] Case 82/71, *Pubblico Minstero v SAIL* [1972] ECR 119.

2.4 Draft Harmonization Directives: Obvious Misnomers (1991–1995)

Nothing would be further from the truth than tying together 'harmonization' as an end and the first proposals for measures dedicated to achieve approximation in the energy sector. Hardly any 'harmonization proposal', since the SEA had entered into force in July 1987, was bound to trigger as many political rows between (and within) institutions of the EU and the Member States as the draft harmonization directives. They were proposed in their original form in 1991 and were followed by various successors—the gas draft was even suspended owing to additional complexities attributed to the sector: external supplies and take-or-pay contracts. Both areas continue to be complicated to this day.

Having witnessed the failure of both Commission directives under Article 106(2) TFEU and the mixed and tentative results of its attempt for regulation by action for failure to fulfil an obligation under the Treaty (under Article 258 TFEU), the Commission neither gave in nor abandoned its schedule.

It then naturally fell to the EU's instrument of choice for achieving the single market; i.e. approximation legislation under Article 114 TFEU though the use of directives. As distinct from the Treaty and its application in specific cases by the Commission and the Court, directives can be based on careful preparation, intensive information-gathering, economic analysis by the Commission and its specialist consultants, lengthy consultation and at least implicit negotiation with the main actors, and finally explicit negotiation in the Council. The use of such a procedure means that the outcome may not be perfect in terms of an idealistic view of what the Treaty theoretically commands, but it may be more practical, and suitable for application, voluntary acceptance, and compliance. Directives are not an automatic response to problems in applying the Treaty. The Commission will only invest effort and political capital into their formulation if the time appears ripe—i.e. if the strategy underlying the directive in question is aligned with the directions of markets, if there is at least the likelihood of aligning major actors in Member States in a coalition powerful enough to ensure the enactment, and later acceptance, of the directive,[83] and if it serves its current political and institutional interest and perspective. The process of European integration, involving an increasing role for the Commission usually serves the Commission's interest, particularly if it can achieve political success and appears to be moving within the mainstream of the current paradigm—globalization, liberalization, and competition, all with a human face.

The EU had issued directives on particular energy matters in the past, but they were of minor significance, addressed specific issues (e.g. oil emergency planning

---

[83] R. Putnam, 'Diplomacy and Domestic Politics: The Logic of Two-Level Games', 42 *International Organization* (1988), 427–60.

in the 1970s), and had little effect.[84] The sequence of internal market directives started with relatively innocuous issues (transparency and cross-border transit) and then moved to core issues of discriminatory practices hindering the internal market (utilities' procurement and upstream licensing). The first proper energy *market* directives—the Electricity Market Directive in 1996[85], followed by the Gas Market Directive in 1998[86]—then appeared. These two legislative instruments were later followed by two more energy law packages in 2003 and 2009, and a range of security of supply directives and regulations and green energy packages (emissions trading, renewable energy, carbon capture and storage, energy savings, and so on).

These instruments attempt to codify the application of the Treaty, especially to the energy industries, by providing detailed rules, which—largely—record the state of play of the Treaty since the mid-1990s to the post-2010 period. They also, especially in the early days, interacted with external developments, in particular the negotiation of and EU accession to the main international economic treaties of the 1990s, the 1994 Marrakech GATT/WTO agreements with the General Procurement Agreement and the 1991 European Energy Charter Declaration leading to the 1994 Energy Charter Treaty. These international influences partly influenced and in fact committed the EU to issue implementing legislation (e.g. the Utilities Directive and also the Transit Directives of 1990/1991). To some extent, EU policies have also provided an impetus and a model for treaty language (e.g. the Energy Charter Treaty's articles on non-discrimination, transit and licensing).

The legal relationship between the directives and primary law—the Treaty—is difficult. Theoretically, based on the recognized hierarchy of norms, the Treaty should prevail over directives and where they seem to include a diluted, modified, delayed, and exemption-rife version of the Treaty, such contradictions with the purer commands of the Treaty should simply be regarded as void. The former ECJ judge, Sir David Edward,[87] in his discussion of Treaty versus directive, recognized the Commission's power to *develop* rather than simply restate EU law. His reluctance to get involved in matters of far-reaching economic regulation suggests that the Court would be reluctant to strike a blow in favour of the Treaty and against a regulatory directive if the superiority of the Treaty would involve the Court in economic policy-making.[88] The directives will therefore be seen as a formal expression of the EU interest and as accepted standards for defining the many open-ended standards of the Treaty relating to this EU interest, to general economic interest, subsidiarity and to the implicit standards developed by the Court such as proportionality,

---

[84] Such as the now lifted restriction on gas-fired power stations: Council Directive 1975/404/EEC of 13 February 1975 on the Restriction of the Use of Natural Gas in Power Stations, OJ L 178, 9.7.1977, p. 24; repealed by Article 1 of Council Directive 1991/148/EEC of 18 March 1991 Revoking Directive 1975/404/EEC, OJ L 75, 21.3.1991, p. 52.

[85] Directive 96/92/EC of the European Parliament and of the Council of 19 December 1996 concerning common rules for the internal market in electricity OJ L 27, 30 January 1997, 20–29.

[86] Directive 98/30/EC of the European Parliament and of the Council of 22 June 1998 concerning common rules for the internal market in natural gas OJ L 204, 21 July 1998, 1–12.

[87] D. Edward and M. Hoskins, 'Article 90: Deregulation and EC Law', 32(159) *CMLR* (1995).

[88] In complex economic situations the discretionary powers of the Commission are great. See Case 138/79, *Roquette Frères* [1980] ECR 3333, Case C-4/96, *Northern Ireland Fish Producers' Organisation Ltd* [1998] ECR I-681, Case C-179/95, *Kingdom of Spain v EU Council* [1999] ECR I-6475.

necessity, and the least-restrictive method of regulation available. This does not freeze the text of the directives forever. As the Treaty from now on will be interpreted for maximum conformity with the directives,[89] so the directives will be interpreted for maximum consistency with the Treaty—and both evolve as practice develops with implementation, open-ended and contradictory language is interpreted and clarified, and as markets and attitudes evolve. The steps back from the theoretical and purist demands of the Treaty taken by the first energy market directives were predictably regained in 2003 and 2009 once the time—economically, politically, institutionally, and legally—was again ripe to accelerate the integration of the energy markets. Further impetus for the opening-up of the markets may be drawn from the TFEU, as it introduced a new Title (XXI) on energy which under Article 194 TFEU expressly provides for EU action for, among others, the functioning of the internal energy market and integration of national markets.

The 1996 and 1998 energy market directives could only achieve so much. After all, the Treaty commanded free movement in 1957 and was still interpreted in 1997 as allowing national energy monopolies to erect legal walls between the national markets. They were the first serious step towards the Treaty's goals in this sector, helped by markets and a changing paradigm with an eye to the fora of Florence and Madrid to breaking ground for the 2003 amendments and cross-border trade regulation. They helped to identify legal obstacles and provide legal procedures for facilitating market integration, but encountered much more difficulty in dealing with the invisible discrimination and protectionism inherent in national culture, and the commercial, financial, and institutional set-up. Eliminating legal and formal discrimination is much easier than equalizing cross-border trade with internal trading cost. But then Rome was not built in a day. The US took 200 years to achieve a satisfactory measure of economic integration, and facilitating the creation of an EU energy market will also take time.

Section 2.4.1–2.4.4 examines the 'early birds' of energy liberalization:

- Price Transparency Directive;
- Electricity Transit Directive;
- Gas Transit Directive;
- Utilities' Procurement and Remedies Directives;
- Hydrocarbons Licensing Directive;

2.4.1 Price Transparency Directive

The first step taken by the Commission was to get the Council to enact the Transparency Directive.[90] Based on the EU's competence to ask Member States for

---

[89] See Case C-379/98, *PreussenElektra* [2001] ECR 2099.

[90] Council Directive 1990/377/EEC of 29 June 1990 concerning a Community procedure to improve the transparency of gas and electricity prices charged to industrial end-users, OJ L 185, 17.7.1990, p. 16. For a summary with general observations on transparency obligations as regulatory instruments: E. Cross, L. Hancher, and P. Slot, 'EC Energy Law', in M. Roggenkamp et al. (eds), *Energy Law in Europe* (Oxford: OUP 2001), at 5.179 et seq.

information relevant to the tasks entrusted to the Commission, the Directive aims to provide, through the EU statistical office (Eurostat), aggregated information on prices, terms, and volumes of gas and electricity sales to specified groups of major industrial final consumers (Article 1).

Domestic utilities are obliged to provide such information biannually, but the disclosure format protects commercial confidentiality, as transactions are exempt unless a minimum of three like transactions occurs. It is important to note that nothing in the directive obliges Member States to require large utilities, selling power or gas to regional utilities, the latter supplying the public with power or gas, to submit any information.[91] The directive includes a fairly elaborate system, with extensive industry consultation, on the format in which information must be provided, in order to ensure both reasonable accuracy and confidentiality. According to the recitals to the directive, its purpose is to obtain price transparency to the extent necessary for the functioning of competition on the common market by helping to identify market imperfections as regards the prices and terms of network-bound energy supplies to undertakings. Price transparency is seen as a tool to increase freedom of choice for industrial consumers (or, more realistically, create awareness about the lack of such freedom). To this end, it contributes to the 'achievement and smooth functioning of the internal energy market'.

Later the directive notes that 'with the prospect of the achievement of the internal energy market', the pricing surveillance mechanism should operate as soon as possible. Sometimes it is argued that this reference to the internal energy market is not very logical. How should transparency have helped the functioning of an internal energy market, which did not yet exist, and how could it have brought about freedom of choice for consumers, which did not have that freedom at that time since competition was largely excluded? In line with the legal basis of Article 337 TFEU, one may argue that this directive sets the scene for the internal energy market since it allows the Commission to access reliable data, which again enables it to table sound proposals for the creation of an internal market for network-bound energy industries.

Moreover, one should challenge the official view[92] that the Transparency Directive would help to identify instances of the grant of state aid (such as preferential pricing raised in the Dutch horticultural cases) or discriminatory practices, since the process of data collection and its subsequent analysis and publication by Eurostat produces widely aggregate information but does not reveal pricing data from individual companies. At most, certain patterns inviting further scrutiny may be revealed. However, there seems to be no indication that information produced pursuant to the directive had led to investigation with respect to state aid or discrimination. As a rule, information about discrimination or the provision of state

---

[91] Since supply of power and gas to the public does not involve industrial end-users, the same applies to gas sales with a view to generating power for the public: see Article 1 and Annex 16 (a) Directive 1990/377/EEC.

[92] European Commission, *Transparency of Consumer Energy Prices* (COM (1989) 123 final) 7.3.1989, at 4.1, sustained by: E. Cross, L. Hancher, and P. Slot, 'EC Energy Law', in M. Roggenkamp et al. (eds), *Energy Law in Europe* (Oxford: OUP 2001), at 5.182.

aid comes to light when an affected competitor complains or when a state proves willing to disclose such information, rather than on the basis of aggregated statistical analysis. Comparison of national pricing information thus obtained has always been difficult, even when aggregated, due to differences in taxes, in quasi-taxes (e.g. municipal concession fees), in costs and rules relevant to cost (e.g. treatment of nuclear decommissioning), and locational differences (e.g. between oil and gas producers and non-producers in the EU). Also, and in particular in monopolistic markets, many of the real terms may deviate from the formal tariffs communicated as there may be hidden *quid pro quos*—e.g. a lower price for a longer-term commitment or lower tariffs given in exchange for equity participation. It would be unusual for a public agency to provide information on such commercial terms in a market economy. Here, one would expect price information to be available through quotation on formal exchanges or commercially available specialist providers. It may therefore perhaps be better to interpret the Transparency Directive as the first shot fired by the Commission in order to focus public attention on the great diversity of prices across the EU. Subsequent Eurostat publications in fact demonstrated that Member States which lacked a competitive energy market (e.g. Germany) had prices far above Member States, which had a competitive energy market (e.g. the UK). The reasons for this were still disputed and disputable,[93] but they highlighted the fact that the non-competitive and segregated structures of the EU energy markets were not favourable to consumers, and in particular to large industrial consumers exposed to global cost competition. Highlighting this disadvantage of closed energy systems may have been the real intention, and was probably the main contribution, of the Transparency Directive and its follow-up. The directive was politically easier to achieve as it did not aim at changing market structure per se or at affecting the interests of the energy companies, but it did help to soften up national resistance and undermine the defensive efforts of the energy monopolies by bringing the excessively high prices in protected energy markets to the fore—a fact that is nothing more than an empirical illustration of the fundamental economic logic that monopolies extract monopoly rent from their captive consumers.[94]

2.4.2 Electricity and Gas Transit Directives

The second steps were the two Transit Directives for electricity and gas, which were subsequently repealed with effect from 1 July 2004.[95] There had been cross-border

[93] T. Wälde, 'Die Regelung der Britischen Energiewirtschaft nach der Privatisierung', in P. Tettinger (ed.), *Strukturen der Versorgungswirtschaft in Europa* (Stuttgart: Boorberg 1996) pp. 59–95; Eurostat, *Rapid Reports: Energy and Industry* (1995), No.8.

[94] There is also a periodically updated regulation requiring Member States to provide information on planned investment projects in the energy sector—Commission Regulation (EC) No 2386/96 of 16 December 1996 applying Council Regulation (EC) No 736/96 of 22 April 1996 on notifying the Commission of investment projects of interest to the Community in the petroleum, natural gas and electricity sectors, OJ L 326/13.

[95] Council Directive 1990/547/EEC of 29 October 1990 on the transit of electricity through transmission grids, OJ L 313, 13.11.1990, p. 30; and Council Directive 1991/296/EEC of 31 May 1991 on the transit of natural gas through grids OJ L 147, 12.6.1991, p. 37. Both repealed by the 2003 electricity and gas market directives.

exchanges of electricity and transport of gas among the core EU countries for a long time, though the volumes may not have been particularly large. It is only more recently that the more outlying areas are gradually being connected to the European gas and electricity network through interconnectors.[96] But the problem for the Commission's objective of an internal energy market lay in the transit aspect, where the existence of transport monopolies, natural or rather legally constituted and protected, presented a significant obstacle. While even such monopolies should in principle have a commercial interest in greater, well-remunerated utilization of their transportation networks, their commercial strategies often prevail over simple shipping-fee interests. As a rule, they will exploit their transit leverage to prevent actual or prospective competitors from gaining access to a new market where the transit company has, or might want, to act as supplier. Such hindrance could be achieved through sheer refusal to transport, usually citing capacity constraints and capacity commitments (take-or-pay obligations), or the charging of excessive fees reflecting monopoly rent rather than full cost recovery, or camouflaged by protracted negotiation from a position of defensive strength controlling access. Commercial alliances between companies—frequent, for example, in the natural gas field—might keep a transit operator from letting the competitor of a 'friend' enter into the 'friend's' market, with invisible compensation from the 'friend'. Even the very normal conduct of a transit operator to maximize fee income from its transport utilities will, in the absence of tariff regulation, lead to obstruction of transit, since the transit monopolist will, following economic logic, set the price to maximize its own profit, and not to maximize throughput and utilization of the transit networks.

The very existence of this major stumbling block impeding EU energy integration, implicit in the coexistence of a transit monopoly with supply and trading interest, invited the Commission to do something about it. The logical course of action would have been to create a third-party access obligation for all network operators controlling a natural or legal monopoly, with an EU body operating alone or in conjunction with independent national authority, exercising the role of access, price, and utilization regulator. But this far-reaching objective foundered in the early 1990s due to the determined resistance both of governments and of the domestically influential energy network monopolies—with similar opposition also present in the parallel issues negotiated for the ECT.[97] Even with the subsequent formation of the Council of European Energy Regulators, and now the ACER, this objective is yet to be achieved.

---

[96] For the difficulties in this process, see K. Talus and T. Wälde, 'Electricity Interconnectors—A Serious Challenge for EC Competition Law', 3 *Competition and Regulation in Network Industries* (2006), pp. 355–90.

[97] See the ECT Understanding stating that no 'third-party access' (whatever this may mean) is to be introduced under the Treaty: Final Act of the Energy Charter Treaty Conference, Understandings IV (1)(b)(i). The Treaty's non-discrimination provisions applicable to state monopolies and enterprises with special/exclusive privileges can be read as to imply an obligation to provide access on stable, fair and non-discriminatory conditions (Article 22); T. Wälde, 'International Investment under the 1994 Energy Charter Treaty', 29 *Journal of World Trade* (1995), pp. 5–72.

The Transit Directives should, therefore, be understood as the much-diluted result of the Commission's attempt to introduce at least some form of regulated access to energy transport. Its key points are as follows:[98]

- in lieu of an obligation of Member States to transpose statutory access to grids, Member States must oblige transit and relevant transmission operators to negotiate fair network access and usage agreements—i.e. avoiding conditions that are unfair, unduly restrictive and discriminatory—and to submit to a legally non-binding conciliation procedure with Commission involvement.[99] The latter may give rise to ordinary Commission action (e.g. investigations for abuse of dominant positions contrary to Article 102 TFEU) under the implementing Regulation 01/2003/EC;[100]

- in lieu of setting up a logical EU system of access and tariff regulation, the directives provide for the Commission to be involved on a notification basis: transit requests, transit contracts and failure of negotiations must be notified, and the Commission chairs the conciliation body;[101]

- in lieu of full transparency of access terms and tariffs—which would provide evidence on questions of discrimination, unfairness and restrictive terms—the Commission is only allowed to know of transit requests, contract conclusion (but not specific terms) and failure of negotiations; and

- in lieu of application to all types of contracts and transportation contracts to large-scale consumers, the directives only cover high-voltage electricity transmission, high-pressure gas pipelines and longer-term (electricity transit) contracts.[102]

With these limitations, one might view the directives as doing 'little more than formalizing existing arrangements to manage exchanges between existing utilities'[103] or as being ineffectual for lack of legal obligations of transit and lack of sanctions.[104]

---

[98] On the transit directives: R. Tudway (ed.), *Energy Law and Regulation in the EU* (London: Sweet & Maxwell 1999) part 1, at 2–04, E. Cross, L. Hancher, and P. Slot, 'EC Energy Law', in M. Roggenkamp et al. (eds), *Energy Law in Europe* (Oxford: OUP 2001), at 5.185–5.190, critical: R. Lukes, 'Energierecht', in M. Dauses (ed.), *Handbuch des EU-Wirtschaftsrechts* (München: CH Beck 1999); Vol. 2, para.77.

[99] Recitals and Article 3(1) and (2) and 4 of Directive 1990/547/EEC and 1991/296/EEC. Committees of experts for gas and electricity transit have been set up.

[100] Council Regulation (EC) No 1/2003 of 16 December 2002 on the implementation of the rules on competition laid down in Articles 81 and 82 of the Treaty, OJ L 1, 4.1.2003, pp. 1–25.

[101] See Commission Decision 1992/167/EEC of 4 March 1992 setting up a Committee of Experts on the Transit of Electricity between Grids, OJ L 074, 20.3.1992, p. 43 (repealed with effect from 17.2004). Commission Decision 95/539/EC of 8 December 1995 setting up a committee of experts on the transit of natural gas through grids, OJ L 304, 16.12.1995, p. 57.

[102] One should note that 'transit' is defined in the directives more widely than in international instruments, e.g. the Barcelona transit conventions; Article 5 GATT and Article 7 Energy Charter Treaty. In international law, transit means as a rule that two borders are crossed, while under the directive—Article 2(1)(c) —only one intra-Community border needs to be crossed, see R. Liesen, 'Transit Under the Energy Charter Treaty', 17 *JENRL* (1999), p. 56.

[103] E. Cross, L. Hancher, and P. Slot, 'EC Energy Law', in M. Roggenkamp et al. (eds), *Energy Law in Europe* (Oxford: OUP 2001), at 5.189.

[104] R. Lukes, 'Energierecht', in M. Dauses, *Handbuch des EU-Wirtschaftsrechts* (München: CH Beck 1999); Vol. 2, para.77; also: Festschrift H.J. Mestmaecker (1996) p. 643.

Since the mid-1990s, views have been articulated that the transit directives have been largely superseded by both the subsequent Energy Market Directive and Article 7 of the ECT. For a long period, it remained difficult to judge such rather negative views. It might have been suggested that both the negative view and a much more positive view could have been argued. There is no benefit in putting forward a closely reasoned argument, however, as both directives were repealed in July 2004.[105]

It may be that these directives were nothing more than a face-saving exercise on the part of the Commission, designed to give the impression of taking action. However, the directives may also be seen as initial steps in a dynamic process whereby a transit obligation on reasonable terms is gradually imposed on network operators (the infant form of a negotiated TPA). Using the mechanisms contained in the directives, the Commission has opened a window into the negotiations between transit operators and transit customers. It could encourage transit requestors to complain about the uncooperative way in which network owners conduct negotiations, with a view to bringing competition law instruments into play—in particular the essential facilities doctrine under Article 102 TFEU.[106] The very prospect of greater light being shed on such negotiations and the terms concluded as a result of them, and of intervention by the Commission, might well make network operators negotiate with less reliance on monopoly power 'under the shadow' of EU competition law and the 'soft law' provisions of the directives. Although it seems that this did not happen to a great extent, only a comparison of transit contract terms between 1990 and 2003 would shed more light on the relative effectiveness of the directives. Finally, one should not forget that the obligation to negotiate 'fairly, without discrimination and without unjustified restrictions' under Article 3(2) was not a legally not binding *pactum de contrahendo*, as a common law lawyer might interpret it to be, but in terms of the civil law systems which probably govern the interpretation of the directives it may be regarded as a legally binding and judicially enforceable obligation to conduct negotiations in good faith.

2.4.3 Utilities' Procurement Directive

The enactment of more specific rules translating the general principles of freedom of movement of goods, services, and establishment by way of a directive may be

---

[105] For the continuing impact of the gas transit directive, see K. Talus, *Vertical Natural Gas Transportation Capacity, Upstream Commodity Contracts and EU Competition Law* (Alphen aan den Rijn: Kluwer Law International 2011).

[106] Contrary to what could have been expected at that time, the essential facilities doctrine continues to be one of the chief methods of the Commission in its battle against ex-monopoly companies. For this, see K. Talus, 'Just What is the Scope of the Essential Facilities Doctrine in the Energy Sector: Third Party Access-friendly Interpretation in the EU v. Contractual Freedom in the US', 48(5) *Common Market Law Review* (2011), A. Hauteclocque, F. Marty, and J. Pillot, 'The Essential Facilities Doctrine in European Competition Policy: The Case of the Energy Markets', in J.M. Glachant, D. Finon, and A. Hauteclocque (eds), *Competition, Contracts and Electricity Markets: A New Perspective* (Cheltenham: Edward Elgar 2011). For electricity, the French nuclear in particular, see C. Defeuilley and A. Hauteclocque, 'De la Production d'Electricité est-elle une Facilité Essentielle?', *LARSEN Working Paper* (2010).

regarded as the next area of EU progress towards the creation of an internal energy market. Such actions were relatively easy in the area of procurement where there was both a pre-existing body of EU procurement rules (though not applicable to utilities) as well as the EU's international obligations, including GATT and later WTO-based international obligations. The same applies to the Licensing Directive, which is in essence directed at giving substance and specificity to the general non-discrimination and freedom of establishment principle of the Treaty. Both directives—while seen by states as cumbersome and disruptive to existing ways of conducting business—did not immediately threaten the existing industrial, social and political structure, and vested interests in Member States. For these reasons, the directives were politically easier to achieve in comparison to the much more protracted and tortuous path of the subsequent energy directives of 1996/1998.

2.4.3.1 Why Do We Need EU-wide Procurement Rules—Why Do We Need Specific Rules for Utilities?

Public procurement is a massive business.[107] Billions are spent by public authorities and utilities on goods and services each year. This is essentially taxpayers' money, apart from the utilities procurement which is generated through utility charges in markets, which in the past were mostly captive, and sometimes still are, at least *de facto*. Procurement by the state tends to be much more subject to political influences, to patronage, favouritism for national (and local) suppliers and corruption than procurement by private, commercially-oriented companies subject to the discipline of capital markets. Public procurement is as much an activity to discharge public functions as it is a way of placing well-connected snouts into the financial troughs offered by public authorities. There is often a close connection between procurement activities and the national and local suppliers. Technical standards are skewed to the benefit of favoured suppliers. National and local industrial, professional, political, and social associations, and other linkages of class, religion, background, and education create networks which overcome the force of public procurement rules while remaining able to conform to their form. The same applies in the case of state-owned energy utilities, or those, which are strongly influenced by and dependent upon the state machinery for licences, economic regulation, and other forms of legal, financial, and political support. The incestuous character and natural protectionist inclination of much of public and utility procurement

---

[107] For earlier writings, see L. Hancher and P. Trepte, 'An Overview of Public Procurement in the EC', 14(4) *OGTLR* (1996), J. Flynn and J. Langan, 'Procurement Licensing and Utilities in the UK North Sea', 14(60) *OGTLR* (1996), H. Dundas, 'The Impact of EC Law on the UK Oil and Gas Industry: Directives on Services and Licensing', in D. MacDougall and T. Wälde (eds), *European Community Energy Law* (London: Kluwer 1994) p. 51, J. Armstrong, 'The EC Remedies Directive', in D. MacDougall and T. Wälde (eds), *European Community Energy Law* (London: Kluwer 1994), p. 77 and E. Cross, L. Hancher, and P. Slot, 'EC Energy Law', in M. Roggenkamp et al. (eds), *Energy Law in Europe* (Oxford: OUP 2001), at 5.204–5.232, S. Arrowsmith, *The Law of Public and Utilities Procurement* (London: Sweet & Maxwell 2005), Christopher Bovis, *EC Public Procurement: Case Law and Regulation* (Oxford: OUP 2006), C. Bovis, 'The New Public Procurement Regime: A Different Perspective on the Integration of Public Market on the European Union', 12(1) *European Public Law* (2006), pp. 73–109 and C. Bovis, *EU Public Procurement Law* (Cheltenham: Edward Elgar 2007).

does not produce efficient results for the taxpayer: competition is reduced, since possible competitors are either integrated into the system or refrain from making costly tenders when the procurement systems are rigged for local favourites. Prices for delivering the state services (and consequently the tax burden) are higher than they have to be. These are costs that a society has to bear and which national procurement regulation tries, with mixed success, to combat. From an EU perspective, these disadvantages weigh twice. Since the Commission's main task is to promote an internal market, the existence of public procurement that is not open means that an important part of the overall market is effectively closed. In addition, since the Commission has to be concerned about European competitiveness in relation to more dynamic and less statist economies such as the US, or lower-cost regions like the Far East, inefficient and uncompetitive public procurement means suffering from another competitive disadvantage on global markets. This disadvantage is both direct, since lack of competitiveness is caused by the existence of protected national suppliers, and indirect, through the need to maintain a tax system that taxes and thereby disadvantages its companies and people more than, for example, the US.

The internal logic of EU integration—the internal market—and the external logic of competition in a global economy, therefore, compel the EU to seek to bring about better procurement practices—more transparent, more competitive, and less protectionist and discriminatory. That is far from easy. 'Trading costs' are seen as the major reason why trade is so much greater within a national economy than with its neighbours, even accounting for geographical distances.[108] Systemic public procurement preferences—'discrimination' would be a blunter word for them—are a significant component of cross-border trading costs.

The construction of a legal framework for the global economy, therefore, requires a system of rules to deal with public procurement. Negotiations conducted in the context of the GATT, now WTO, have resulted in considerable progress over the last 20 years. The Government Procurement Agreement of 1994 is as yet a 'plurilateral' agreement—i.e. only certain countries and regional blocs are members. This includes the EU, US, and Japan, but excludes China[109] and India. The three signatory countries have promised to open each other's markets for public procurement (including with limitations by subnational authorities) in exchange for reciprocal access.[110] So EU procurement law can also be seen as a response to the EU's participation in the global economy and its emerging rules.

The key elements of all procurement rules are transparency, competition, and non-discrimination. Competition is fostered by an obligation to look towards the market rather than one, or a number or group of favoured suppliers. This is mainly done by tendering or less formal ways of getting the market to make competing offers. Transparency is necessary to force the procurement process into

---

[108] Evaluation Report: Impact and Effectiveness of EU Public Procurement Legislation (SEC (2011) 853 final Parts 1 and 2). Section 6 of the Report focuses on cross-border procurement.

[109] Except Chinese Taipei.

[110] M. Footer, 'External Aspects of the Community's Public Procurement Policy in the Utilities Sectors', *Public Procurement Law Review* (1994), p. 187; M. Footer, 'Remedies under the New GATT Agreement on Government Procurement Public', *Procurement Law Review* (1995), p. 80.

the open, since favouritism—and the breach or manipulation of rules—thrives in obscurity. Non-discrimination is, finally, the key standard for regulating the overall decision-making process since it forbids the application of standards or procedures (with respect to the use of time limits or provision of information) which put into practice and formalize protectionist sentiment. The relatively simple essence of procurement law is to institute legal rules applicable to the procurement process (rather than internal guidelines and recommendations) which can be enforced, including by those who lose in public tenders. This involves:

- having a clearly prescribed sequence of actions—invitation, qualification, information to competing suppliers, submission of offer, assessment, award of contract, and subsequent contract implementation;

- ensuring that the process receives wide publicity, by publication and other provision of information;

- establishing a system of standard conditions and assessment criteria which are known from the outset, adhered to, and later documented for accountability; and

- minimizing, wherever possible, the use of procedures and criteria which give the procurement authority scope to use non-accountable discretion.

None of these methods is foolproof and every method can be manipulated. Some flexibility and account of the transaction cost (time, preparation of competing offers, and assessment of offers) are necessary—and such flexibility can easily become the entry-point for manipulation. These methods are—with lots of detailed rules, exceptions, derogations, and annexes—what the procurement directives require Member States to enact.

This section now examines some of the provisions of the first Utilities Procurement Directive.[111] Going further than the WTO Government Procurement Agreement (GPA), which covers state (including subnational) authorities and some utilities, the first Utilities Directive 93/38 included both public and private organizations (agencies, contracting entities, undertakings, companies). The directive has two defining features. First, the authorities in question must be either under direct or indirect state control or operate on the basis of 'special or exclusive rights' granted by the state.[112] Secondly, they must carry out relevant activities, which for our purposes principally comprise the operation of electricity, gas, and heat transmission (both large scale and local distribution); the exploration and development of oil, gas, and other energy fuels (mainly coal) are also covered.[113]

---

[111] The new Procurement Directives: Directive 2004/18/EC of the European Parliament and of the Council of 31 March 2004 on the coordination of procedures for the award of public works contracts, public supply contracts and public service contracts (OJ L 134, 30.4.2004, pp. 114–240) and Directive 2004/17/EC of the European Parliament and of the Council of 31 March 2004 coordinating the procurement procedures of entities operating in the water, energy, transport and postal services sectors (OJ L 134, 30.4.2004, pp. 1–113). These have been amended by Regulation (EC) 1177/2009 of 30 November 2009 amending Directives 2004/17/EC, 2004/18/EC and 2009/81/EC of the European Parliament and of the Council in respect of their application thresholds for the procedures for the award of contracts.

[112] The terminology used is more complex, see Articles 1 and 3.

[113] There are some limitations, Article 2 (5)—mainly self-supply.

2.4.3.2 The Procurement Rules

Article 3 of the directive contains a special, Commission-sanctioned opt-out for enterprises engaged in upstream oil and gas development.[114] In brief, the Commission can exempt upstream oil and gas development from the scope of the Utilities Directive if licensing for such development is done in a transparent, non-discriminatory, and competitive way. Compliance with the later Licensing Directive suggests that this is the case. This derogation is balanced by the need to comply with the general principle of competition and non-discrimination in procurement. Reportedly, most upstream oil and gas companies, even if operating in the UK—which now has the benefit of an exemption—still apply procurement practices in line with the principles of the Utilities and Remedies Directives. We are here at the threshold of imposing procurement rules on commercially operating private companies. International oil companies tend to be under strong pressure from capital markets to perform efficiently and commercially—so international and national disciplines are much less necessary than they are for state-owned or heavily state-influenced and regulated energy (i.e. electricity and gas) companies. Nevertheless, the great value of obtaining a licence or concession for upstream oil and gas development, and the element of governmental discretion in licensing that still remains following the entry into force of the Licensing Directive, suggest that there is room for some procurement discipline even on the part of this type of private company. The experience of the UK, where licensing was in effect made conditional upon a verified policy of 'buying British', suggests the linkage between licensing and procurement.[115]

The case of companies (and products) from outside the EU is also a special issue. First, EU procurement rules must properly implement the rules of the WTO General Procurement Agreement. Directive 98/4[116] aligns the Utilities Directives with the subsequent WTO/GPA to which the EU acceded. Article 36 of the Utilities Directive provides for an EU preference clause: tenders with over 50 per cent of goods (not services) from outside the EU can be rejected—except for goods from countries with which an international agreement (e.g. Association Agreements or WTO GPA) exists. Article 37 (the reciprocity Article) provides for restrictions on tenders emanating from countries to which EU companies do not enjoy equivalent access. The procurement issue is particularly sensitive in the EU–US relationship, where trade, investment, and procurement protectionism exist on both sides.

---

[114] Article 3 of the Utilities Directive, amended by Article 12 of the Licensing Directive (*infra*, 94/22), with a derogation accepted for the UK upstream oil and gas sector, Commission Decision 97/367—the 'Remedies' directive though still applies.

[115] T. Daintith and A. Willoughby, *UK Oil & Gas Law* (London: Sweet and Maxwell 1997), at para. 1–835 on the now abandoned OSO–UKOOA memorandum on a voluntary procedure to be followed by UKCS operators to implement UK supplies. The Commission investigation of these UK policies (which may not be that different from similar policies pursued, e.g. in Denmark and in Norway) is probably the background for the linking of the Article 3 exemption to compliance with the Licensing Directive.

[116] Directive 98/4/EC of the European Parliament and of the Council of 16 February 1998 amending Directive 93/38/EEC coordinating the procurement procedures of entities operating in the water, energy, transport and telecommunications sectors, OJ L 101, 1.4.1998, pp. 1–16.

There is insufficient space here to detail the mandated procedures for utility procurement. There is a minimum contract threshold, which has been subject to several modifications over time, and some highly individualized contract types are exempted. The procedures are fairly standard for modern procurement. Contracting agencies have the choice between competitive tendering in various forms (open and accessible to anybody or limited to a shortlist of prequalified suppliers), with direct negotiation only in exceptional cases. Contracts must be advertised in the Official Journal with sufficient notice. Contracting agencies must give early notice of their supply requirements. Tender invitations must identify the relevant standards for assessing bids—which must then also be respected; in practice, this is difficult to enforce, since the existence of multiple standards makes it relatively easy to claim that the preferred bidder scored highest on a particular criterion, which is then held to be of paramount importance. Unsuccessful bidders must be advised and given reasons. In lieu of national technical standards—which would favour national bidders—European standards must be used, and their development is promoted by the Commission. Post-tender negotiations—a favoured way of enhancing the value of a previously preferred tender—must be kept to a minimum, aimed rather at clarifying than modifying the substance (in particular the price–performance ratio) of a tender. To allow 'modern' forms of tendering with reduced transaction costs, 'framework' agreements and qualification systems are allowed. A framework agreement allows a tender for the framework contract; specific individual contracts are then executed under the framework terms without further bidding. A qualification system provides for bidding for entry into a pool of bidders, from which tenders for specific projects are then chosen. Both methods are an attempt to reduce the massive transaction costs involved in tendering. The bulk of such transaction costs are borne by tenderers (who have to absorb the cost of making both successful and—depending on their strike rate—unsuccessful bids alike). However, the tendering agency—which has to go through the various motions of pre-selection, calls for tenders, formal evaluations, often including 'beauty contests' with several higher-ranked tenders, and conclusion of the contracts—also bears significant costs. Contracting agencies need to retain the documentation on the tendering process, in order to facilitate judicial review of a tendering decision if necessary.

While the 2004 consolidation of the EU rules on public procurement[117] modernized and simplified the previous regime, it did not change the fundamental aspects of the pre-existing regulatory regime. Despite this, it did introduce significant changes on the procedural side and in terms of detail.

The Remedies Directive 92/13/EC complemented the Utilities Directive and foreshadowed the obligations of the EU and Member States under the subsequent WTO General Procurement Agreement. Member States had to set up a 'review

---

[117] Directive 2004/17/EC of the European Parliament and of the Council of 31 March 2004 coordinating the procurement procedures of entities operating in the water, energy, transport and postal services sectors, OJ L 134, 30.4.2004, pp. 1–113.

body' which had to have the power to: enforce the procurement rules by eliminating improper specifications and standards, suspending the award of a contract; order 'dissuasive payments'; and award damages.[118] The 2007 amendments[119] to this legal instrument were quite substantial and introduced two innovations that are highly relevant in practice: (1) the 'standstill period'; giving unsuccessful bidders time to make a decision on whether to launch an appeal before the contract is actually signed, resulting in automatic suspension of the process pending the decision of the review body; and (2) increasingly stringent rules on illegal direct awards of public contracts, allowing national courts to declare illegal contracts void.

The final point to be made is that under Article 30(1) of Directive 2004/17/EC (the new Procurement Directive), a Member State in which activity falling under the utilities procurement rules is directly exposed to competition on markets to which access is unrestricted can notify the Commission that it considers that the Utilities Directive does not apply to these activities. The Commission can confirm this by a decision addressed to that Member State. Article 30(2) of the Directive provides that the question of whether an activity is directly exposed to competition is to be decided on the basis of criteria in conformity with the Treaty provisions on competition, such as the characteristics of the goods or services concerned, the existence of alternative goods or services, the prices and the actual or potential presence of more than one supplier of the goods or services in question. For example, Finland requested an exemption under Article 30(4) of Directive 2004/17/EC on 20 February 2006. The request concerned production, including co-generation, as well as the sale (wholesale and retail) of electricity. The Commission gave its decision on 19 June 2006.[120] As far as the electricity generation activities were concerned, the Commission's decision referred to its earlier communication,[121] noting that in respect of electricity generation one indicator for the degree of competition on national markets is the total market share of the biggest three producers. It concluded that during significant parts of the year there is competitive pressure on the Finnish market due to the potential to obtain electricity from outside Finnish territory, particularly since no transmission fee is charged between the Nordic countries. The Commission stated this to indicate a direct exposure to competition. The Commission also considered the workings of the balancing markets as an indicator in respect of electricity production. As such, Article 1 of the Commission's decision provides that Directive 2004/17/EC does not apply to contracts awarded

---

[118] J. Armstrong, 'The EC Remedies Directive', in D. MacDougall and T. Wälde (eds), *European Community Energy Law* (London: Kluwer 1994), pp. 78–84.

[119] Directive 2007/66/EC amending Council Directives 89/665/EEC and 92/13/EEC with regard to improving the effectiveness of review procedures concerning the award of public contracts, OJ L335, 20.12.2007, pp. 31–46.

[120] Commission Decision of 19 June 2006 establishing that Article 30(1) of Directive 2004/17/EC of the European Parliament and of the Council coordinating the procurement procedures of entities operating in the water, energy, transport and postal services sectors applies to the production and sale of electricity in Finland, excluding the Åland Islands, (2006/422/EC). OJ No L 168, 21.6.2006, pp. 33–6.

[121] Communication from the Commission to the Council and the European Parliament: Report on progress in creating the internal gas and electricity market, COM(2005) 568 final of 15.11.2005.

by contracting entities which are intended to enable them to carry out electricity generation or the sale of electricity in Finland.

2.4.4 Hydrocarbons Licensing Directive

One of the most natural aspects of national protectionism is to reserve the mineral wealth provided by the accidents of nature and history to nationals, and exclude or at least restrict foreigners' access to them. The (universal) sentiment is that the natural resources of a country, in particular if seen as scarce and valuable, should not be shared with companies from abroad. A counter-reaction stressing the priority of a national, regional (as in case of EU), or global community over the sharp delimitation entailed by distinct nations and states has therefore always been an assertion of community-wide rights over natural resources, be it within a federal state against federated states,[122] within the EU against Member States or within the global community as 'heritage of mankind' or 'global commons'.[123] These contradictions between an inward-looking and nation-centred and an outward-looking and community-centred tendency can also be observed in EU law. Until the 1990s, mineral resources (and in particular valuable offshore oil and gas resources) could only be developed under protectionist regimes favouring national and in particular state-owned companies. There were domestic procurement preferences: sometimes, as in the UK, engineered under the shadow of the government's licensing and licence-extension powers;[124] sometimes, as in the case of Denmark, by the grant of an exclusive long-term concession for the whole of the Danish offshore to Danish company A. P. Møller; or, as the case in Norway or Italy, by mandatory inclusion of the national state oil company in all licences combined with a licensing policy favouring the state company.[125] Such resource protectionism runs counter to the Treaty's fundamental economic freedoms—in particular, the freedom of establishment and the prohibition on discrimination between EU nationals. It also obstructs the achievement of a single market if access to national resources by other EU nationals is prevented or restricted, or if national control over such resources provides the leverage for other restrictive policies in the areas of procurement or trade, in particular export by national landing requirements. Under the Treaty,

---

[122] P. von Wilmowsky, 'Zugang zu den Boden und Sonstigen Naturschaetzen anderer Mitgliedsstaaten: EWG-Vertrag und US Verfassung im Vergleich', 54 *Rabelz Z* (1990), pp. 693–732 with English summary: Access to Natural Resources in other Member States: A Comparison of the EEC Treaty with the US Constitution.

[123] The latter concept led to the recognition, in the 1982 Law of the Sea Convention, of the minerals in the deep sea outside national jurisdiction (including exclusive economic zone), as common property of man kind, Chapter XI UNCLOS, for a comment: E. Brown, *The International Law of the Sea*, Vol. I (Aldershot: Dartmouth 1994) 448–74.

[124] T. Daintith and S. Williams, 'The Legal Integration of Energy Markets', in M. Cappelletti, M. Seccombe, and J. Weiler (eds), *Integration Through Law: Europe and the American Federal Experience* (Florence: European University Institute—Series A 2/5, 1987), p. 95.

[125] T. Daintith and S. Williams, 'The Legal Integration of Energy Markets', in M. Cappelletti, M. Seccombe and J. Weiler (eds), *Integration Through Law: Europe and the American Federal Experience* (European University Institute—Series A 2/5, 1987), p. 95.

discrimination—in law or in actual licensing practice—is of course illegal, but nonetheless continued throughout the 1980s, mainly because no claimant was able to bring proceedings. Companies which failed to obtain concessions felt there was little benefit in alienating the licensing government, while other governments refrained from complaining because aspects of protectionism were present in most licensing regimes. It was only in the 1980s that the Court started to interpret the principle of freedom of establishment in Article 49 TFEU to cover more than explicit discrimination and focused on the role played by regulatory restrictions in limiting investment by nationals of Member States in other EU countries.[126] But such integrating and liberalizing tendencies are limited by the recognition of different systems of property regimes (in Article 345 TFEU), though this principle tends to lose its strength under the influence of liberalization, privatization and movement towards an internal market. What it currently means is that, while access to and operation of natural resources must be open to EU investors without discrimination, the governments still retain two essential elements of ownership and sovereignty. First, governments have the power to levy general and specific taxes in relation to the extraction of mineral resources (the economic equivalent of selling the resources). Secondly, they retain certain fundamental powers of ownership, namely opening or closing areas in which oil and gas are present[127] to development in principle, and regulating operations from a resource policy, conservation, environmental, safety, and efficiency perspective. Such fine distinctions are hard to develop and operate on the strength of the general economic freedoms contained in the Treaty, in particular since, in the absence of effective complaints, the Court has not been able to develop any finely-tuned principles by way of developing case law. The Licensing Directive[128] is therefore the major EU legal instrument to be used in order to divide, from the overall bundle of property rights in subsoil minerals, those remaining with Member States from those, which are now outside the exclusive regulatory power of governments. The Licensing Directive has no precedent in international trade law (GATT/WTO; bilateral investment treaties), although Article 18(4) of the ECT echoes its leitmotif of non-discrimination and transparency.[129]

---

[126] P. von Wilmowsky, 'Zugang zu den Boden und Sonstigen Naturschaetzen anderer Mitgliedsstaaten: EWG-Vertrag und US Verfassung im Vergleich', 54 *Rabelz Z* (1990), pp. 699–700 with further references.

[127] Oil and gas acreage: a US technical term in petroleum law, which signifies the subsurface rights beneath land relating to the exploration and extraction of oil and gas.

[128] Directive 94/22/EC of the European Parliament and of the Council of 30 May 1994 on the conditions for granting and using authorisations for the prospection, exploration and production of hydrocarbons, OJ L 164, 30.6.1994. See also S. Hankey, B. Westbrook, and P. Warne, 'The EU Hydrocarbons Licensing Directive', 12 *Oil & Gas Law & Taxation Review* (1994), pp. 283–6. There is little discussion of the Licensing Directive in Member States without a significant oil and gas industry, undoubtedly because it has little practical relevance there. Here the emergence of shale gas may change things.

[129] 'The contracting parties undertake to facilitate access to energy resources by allocating in a non-discriminatory manner on the basis of published criteria authorisations, licences, concessions and contracts to prospect and explore for or to exploit or extract energy resources.' The US tried to get an open access to oil and gas acreage included in the NAFTA, but failed as Mexico insisted on keeping its traditional upstream oil and gas state monopoly, E. Smith and D. Cluchey, 'GATT, NAFTA and the Trade in Energy', 12(27) *Journal of Energy & Natural Resources Law* (1994).

The Licensing Directive covers the process of awarding authorizations ('licences'[130]) for hydrocarbons (i.e. mainly oil and gas). It does not affect existing licences—although many of them have an excessive duration or area (e.g. the whole of the Danish offshore area), are not actively explored or developed, and were allocated mainly with protectionist motives. The Commission tried to compel governments to cancel or modify such existing concession rights, against compensation, in order to make a large enough geographical area available for its new transparent licensing regime, but such commendable efforts were successfully resisted by governments, concessionaires of problematic concession rights, and even industry players opposed to what seemed to be a retroactive interference in existing rights.[131] The Licensing Directive's effectiveness therefore suffered from the fact that it imposed a modern licensing regime to a great extent after most of the relevant territory had been already allocated. It would have been logical to impose the licensing regime also on the disposal of territory by state-run or similar enterprises, as happens, in particular, in the course of privatization and restructuring processes. No such obligation has been explicitly spelled out but one can read such an obligation into Articles 1 and 2 if a state enterprise has been entrusted in effect with a licensing or on-licensing function and contracts with risk contractors to develop its oil and gas acreage. Contracting in relation to unexploited territory by state enterprises, such as Statoil, in Norway, could therefore be covered by the Licensing Directive if Statoil were to be considered as a 'competent authority' under Article 1 as opposed to a commercial company.

The Licensing Directive contains state-of-the-art techniques for licensing oil and gas development rights. Without formally requiring a full and formal tendering process through bidding rounds, it comes very close to it in practice. Governments have to announce the opening up of territory and details in public (Article 3(2)), with some reasonable exceptions in Article 3(3). The essential rule is that the licensing authority can choose between competing offers and companies only on the basis of a limited number of technical and financial criteria (Article 5). This rule is intended to reduce the amount of governmental discretion—through which protectionist and other improper influences usually enter. The specific criteria must be formulated in advance and be communicated to the prospective bidders. They cannot be changed without notice to interested parties. The control of the crucial selection criteria includes a prohibition on excessively long terms or large areas (Article 5) and an enumeration of which criteria (apart from technical quality and

---

[130] These are, depending on the Member State called concessions, licenses, or other. The legal effect is largely the same regardless of the name. K. Talus, 'Public–Private Partnerships in Energy—Termination of Public Service Concessions and Administrative Acts in Europe', 2(1) *Journal of World Energy Law and Business* (2009).

[131] For a discussion: H. Dundas, 'The Impact of EC Law on the UK oil and gas industry: Directives on services and licensing', in D. MacDougall and T. Wälde (eds), *European Community Energy Law* (London: Kluwer 1994) p. 51, J. Armstrong, 'The EC Remedies Directive', in D. MacDougall and T. Wälde (eds), *European Community Energy Law* (London: Kluwer 1994). It is suggested that such cancellation has no element of retroactivity if existing, but not effectively utilized concession rights were affected; principles of property protection are sufficiently safeguarded by adding a compensation element. The international oil industry would have benefited much more if passive holdings of oil and gas acreage had been opened to competition.

financial payment for the right to extract (i.e. sales price for extracted minerals))
are acceptable (Article 6(2)). No criteria other than those listed may be used. This
means, in particular, that criteria which refer to such matters as previous or
projected domestic procurement and employment, or (which is even less acceptable)
the popularity, domestic political support, and political strength of the applicant
company are—at least in theory—prohibited. The unsuccessful applicant is
entitled (Article 5(5)) to a reasoned rejection. This is, again, a procedural requirement intended to make non-objective selection more difficult to engineer and to
increase the accountability of the licensing authority towards the informed public,
unsuccessful applicants, and the Commission. The Licensing Directive thus seeks
to set up a system based on a technical and professional assessment of the applicant's
competence and work programme. It also permits selection of a bidder on the
strength of its financial offer (e.g. royalty, front-end bonus payment, or governmental
profit equity shares).

This process is an improvement in terms of greater transparency and accountability,
at least in formal terms. It reduces discretion and the scope for discrimination—but
it does not do away with them altogether. If there is a clear will to choose a favourite,
this can be still be achieved provided that the paperwork is managed smoothly.
The recognition of multiple standards allows the assignment of greatest weight
and priority to the one standard where the preferred applicant can be presented as
ranking highest. A less imperfect selection process would create a shortlist of qualified candidates, and then operate an automatic selection procedure transparently,
mainly by reference to one easily quantifiable criterion (e.g. minimum exploration
commitments or bonus tendered). A more discretionary, but still transparent vari-
ant would assign a specific weight ('points') to each criterion and then organize a
transparent voting process by the selection committee members on each criterion
so that the highest number of points would automatically produce a selection—
as is the case in international dancing or singing contests. The Directive has not
gone that far, nor could it probably go that far. One needs perhaps to see its role
as imposing the requirement to produce a 'paper trail' of formal compliance and at
least a pretension to transparency and objectivity, with the expectation that over
time such procedural rules may be taken more seriously and become an instrument
in the hands of those national forces that favour, if only for reasons of efficiency, an
objective and professional selection process.

Two issues have caused specific problems in relation to the non-discrimination
requirement. First, national state enterprises have, for legal and practical reasons,
an inbuilt institutional, psychological, and political advantage over foreign
competitors. This is dealt with by a complicated set of countervailing rules (Article 6),
which in essence impose a separation between the role of the state or state enterprise
as a licensor or regulator and its role as a participant in a commercial operation—
usually through a joint venture agreement. Similarly, the Directive requires the
state or state enterprise managing the state share to abstain from voting on procurement matters and not to exercise a majority voting control. The intention is that,
through such rules, an operating venture with mandatory state participation will act
commercially, and not be influenced by protectionist sentiment often transmitted

through domestic political pressures and linkages. The intention is commendable, though it is unrealistic to expect that an effective 'Chinese wall' between the commercial and the regulatory arm of the state can be created in practice. All evidence (e.g. on Statoil) indicates that the operations, the appointment of management, and all company policies are subject to intense political scrutiny, debate, and lobbying. Once the state becomes involved in operations, it can in formal terms pretend to act like a commercial owner, but it cannot realistically do so in practice. The Directive is long on commendable intentions, but short on results when it comes to the issue of state participation on both sides of the licensing process. One can only wait for a combination of the application of the formal rules of the Directive, increased pressure by global financial markets to fulfil the 'good governance' principles implicit in the Directive, and the formation of an attitude based more on market considerations than on nation-based consciousness on the part of each country's political, financial, and public opinion classes in order to achieve effective change in governmental licensing policy.

A second issue is the prospect of foreign companies benefiting from the Licensing Directive's non-discrimination rules. The Directive does not limit the application of its rules, including the non-discrimination principle, to companies, which are EU-incorporated and substantially controlled from within the EU. This means that the traditionally leading US oil companies fully benefit from its opening-up effect. To this extent, the Directive can be seen as the EU's offer to non-EU countries to introduce reciprocal and equivalent liberalization measures—much in the spirit of the GATT/WTO process. On the other hand, through Article 8 the Commission has a mandate to negotiate equivalent reciprocal access with other countries (e.g. the US, the Arab oil producers, Russia) and can initiate a process to refuse the award of licences to countries which do not offer equivalent reciprocal access.[132]

The Licensing Directive, like all EU directives, is far from perfect in its contribution to an internal energy market. It leaves considerable gaps in terms of remaining governmental discretion, residual obstacles for external companies in competition against, and negotiations with, state-owned petroleum companies, and the possibility of a Member State cutting an informal deal with a non-Member State on terms of reciprocal access, thereby excluding companies from other Member States. Nevertheless, it is an important step forward in providing specific rules largely consistent with the state-of-the-art method of offshore oil and gas licensing. Their acceptance by governments and industry probably heralds an alignment of both governmental regulation and corporate practices along the lines of the Directive. In time, real compliance, as opposed to mere paper-trail-based compliance, is therefore likely to increase.

---

[132] The Directive (Article 8(4)) does not seem to go so far as to give the Council or Commission the power to *compel* a Member State to refuse licences to a company from such country, which would be the logical solution. The Directive merely allows the Commission and a Member State to refuse licensing. The situation that one Member State (e.g. the UK) continues to grant licences to US companies even after the Commission has found no reciprocal equivalent access exists is, at least under Article 8 of the Directive, still possible.

A final point here is that of direct effect and Member State damages liability. Most of the rules (e.g. Article 5(5)) appear to bestow specific and precise rights on individual companies—mainly applicants engaged in competitive licensing processes. Their effect would be greatly enhanced if the rules could be enforced directly by competitors losing out in the various forms of competitive licensing processes allowed under the Directive. It appears therefore logical to assume that the Licensing Directive has direct effect, and consequently individuals have the right to damages from the state where the Directive is not properly enacted by domestic legislation or where domestic legislation is not properly implemented in administrative practice. Under the rule of the Court deriving from the *Francovich* case,[133] a disappointed applicant should be entitled to rely on the fact that duties are laid down under the Directive before national courts and have the right to damages on this basis. If by all accounts the applicant made a manifestly better offer, it should be entitled to the profit from the licence or the licence itself. If a court cannot determine this, then the applicant should be entitled at least to the cost of putting forward its tender, and possibly also a share of the profit reflecting an averaged probability of winning a tender and to an injunction against completion of the licensing process. These remedies—which are very similar to the remedies provided for in the Utilities and Remedies Directive—require attention, and judicial testing by claimants.

This last point is not purely theoretical, as the proceedings brought by the Commission against Poland in December 2010 show.[134] In this ongoing case, the Commission argues that Poland has failed to comply with certain provisions of the Hydrocarbon Licensing Directive because the Polish legislation on 'Geological Work and Mining' and its implementing regulations set out requirements with which any interested undertaking must comply at the time when it applies for an authorization for the prospection, exploration, and production of hydrocarbons. These requirements place a number of undertakings already operating within Polish territory in a more favourable position than other undertakings, thereby infringing the principle of equal access to those activities. It also argues that the Polish legislation does not subject the whole of the procedure governing the granting of authorization for the prospection, exploration, and production of hydrocarbons to the adjudication procedure required under Article 3(2) of the Licensing Directive. Polish law makes the prospection, exploration, and production of hydrocarbons subject to the acquisition of a mining permit and a concession. The acquisition of a mining permit alone is, as a rule, preceded by a prior adjudication procedure. This is, however, subject to the reservation of a two-year right of priority for an undertaking, which has identified and documented a deposit of hydrocarbons and has prepared geological documentation with the precision required for the purpose of obtaining a concession to extract such hydrocarbons. In addition, the Commission

---

[133] Joined Cases C-6/90 and C-9/90 and C-9/90, *Andrea Francovich and Others v Italian Republic* [1991] ECR I-5357.
[134] Case C-569/10, *European Commission v Republic of Poland*, action brought on 3 December 2010 (pending).

argues that the adjudication of applications submitted for the purpose of acquiring an authorization is not conducted exclusively on the basis of the criteria set out in Article 5(1) of the Licensing Directive and that not all of the criteria governing the appraisal of an application are generally accessible—that is to say, published in the Official Journal of the European Union.

2.5 First Set of Drafts for Stand-Alone Approximation Directives

In the summer of 1991, the Commission adopted informal first drafts for stand-alone harmonization directives under what is now Article 114 TFEU. Facing strong opposition to the legal basis of these drafts, the Commission felt obliged to speedily implement serious amendments. The regime, it was argued, ignored the limits of 'harmonization legislation', interfered with both the subsidiarity and proportionality principles, and dared to reign over domestic systems of property ownership. This last issue was held to be contrary to Article 345 TFEU.

The Commission narrowed the scope of its proposals by introducing a gradual opening-up of markets, placing even more restrictive limits on the number of consumers who are eligible to choose their suppliers—i.e. large industrial users and large distributors.[135] The Commission went on to stipulate:

- transparent and non-discriminatory licensing systems for generation and transmission or distribution system operation;
- management unbundling: that is, the obligation of vertically integrated undertakings or conglomerates to separate the managerial functions of operating transmission and distribution grids—the natural monopolies—from ordinary commercial activities like generation, supply and non-energy related engagements; and
- regulated third-party access: power utilities were to appoint network managers; the incumbents would have been legally obliged to award capacity on the basis of a merit order and to rule out intra-utility cross subsidization as unduly high grid access fees would be to the detriment of independent network users.

In February 1992, the Commission formally introduced its proposals.[136] Various reservations and suggestions to table amendments stalled the initiatives.[137] For

---

[135] I.e. Users consuming ≥ 100 GW of power per annum and site or distributors with a demand equalling at least 3 per cent of the national power market; users consuming ≥ 25 million m³of natural gas per annum and site and distributors whose demands is greater than 1 per cent of the national market.

[136] Commission, Proposal for a Council Directive concerning common rules for the internal market in electricity (COM/91/548 FINAL, SYN 384); OJ C 065, 14.3.1992, p. 4; Commission, Proposal for a Council Directive concerning common rules for the internal market in natural gas (COM/91/548 FINAL, SYN 384).

[137] E.g. Opinion of the Economic and Social Committe on the proposal for a Council Directive concerning common rules for the internal market in electricity; Council Resolution of 30.11.1992, OJ C 073, 15.3.1993, p. 31.

instance, the European Parliament's Committee of Energy, Research & Technology (CERT) argued in November 1993 that exclusive rights, where they existed, should be maintained by Member States except for new capacities.[138] The latter should be awarded by virtue of tendering, and distributors should be made subject to concession systems. Management unbundling was seen as disproportionate, since it was deemed sufficient to separate the system operator's annual accounts from other economic functions carried out by integrated undertakings. The argument that both further harmonization of fiscal regimes and environmental rules are recognized as crucial elements in the creation of a level playing field is noteworthy, even in the context of current discussion regarding the promotion of renewables. However, the Committee went too far in arguing that those elements were *conditiones sine qua non* for pursuing the liberalization of energy markets.

2.6 The Second Set of Drafts for Harmonization Directives

Taking the criticisms discussed in this chapter into account, the Commission made a fresh start and issued a second set of proposals in 1993–1994.[139] The key differences from the first set of proposals included a section on 'general rules for the organisation of the sector'. This was to stipulate that, besides the objective of opening up of national energy markets, nothing would prevent Member States from entrusting undertakings with 'public service obligations' with an eye to sustaining the general economic interest, these comprised security (i.e. security of supply and technical safety); quality and regularity of supply; cost-reflective pricing; consumer protection; and environmental protection.

Instead of obliging Member States to implement regulated TPA, giving applicants a statutory right to access grids unless the operator showed either that the technical standards were incompatible or capacity was lacking, the envisaged directive would enable Member States to transpose a weaker regime into national laws: that is, negotiated third party access (NTPA). Under its aegis, operators are obliged to respond to reasonable applications for grid access with a view to entering into timely and good-faith negotiations.

Pursuant to the findings of the CERT report quoted in Section 2.5, the Commission (provisionally) dropped any common rules for the unbundling of managerial resources. The *acquis communautaire* would limit itself to requiring undertakings to separate the accounts on transmission and distribution from other

---

[138] Legislative resolution embodying the opinion of the European Parliament on the Commission proposal for a European Parliament and Council directive concerning common rules for the internal market in electricity (COM(91)0548—C3–0442/93) (Codecision procedure: first reading), OJ C 329, 6.12.1993, p. 150.

[139] Amended proposal for a European Parliament and Council Directive concerning common rules for the internal market in electricity, (COM/93/643 FINAL)—COD 384, OJ C 123, 4.5.1994, p. 1; Amended proposal for a European Parliament and Council Directive concerning common rules for the internal market in natural gas, (COM/93/643FINAL)—COD 385.

commercial activities within each utility's annual accounts.[140] This policy was of course not sufficient to remove commercial incentives within vertically integrated companies to discriminate against competing suppliers.

As the Council, to which the drafts had been submitted as early as February 1994, could not agree on a common position until November that year, it decided to concentrate on the electricity sector first and to put the envisaged gas market directive on hold.

The Council reached a consensus fairly quickly on the main areas of general rules for the organization of the electricity sector: generation, systems operation, and unbundling of accounts. Nevertheless, the debate went on for approximately two years. It centred on the grid access regime, since the most ambitious defender of the old energy paradigm, France, advocated a third model, in which it was proposed that Member States designate a 'single buyer' responsible for a kind of 'virtual third party grid access'. A single buyer is an entity, which operates separately from generation and supply; it is obliged to buy any power offered to it by generators or traders under the terms agreed on between generators/traders and consumers. The single buyer has the right to deduct a published tariff for grid use from the contracted price; it then resells the power to the consumers under the terms agreed between producers and consumers.[141] A modified 'single buyer' made its way into the electricity market directive of 1996, serving both as one of three admissible regimes for domestic regimes for access to power grids—making the possibility that the European power market would become a level playing field rather remote—and as an elegant pretext for delaying the whole process whilst allowing its supporters at least to look like active promoters—rather flatterers—of energy liberalization.

To advance the game of give and take, the Santer Commission had also strengthened the common rules for generation and direct lines. In part, it supported and to some extent replaced tendering procedures by arguing in favour of authorization procedures both for new capacities and for direct lines, providing that the latter were operated either by generators or by eligible consumers.[142] As late as the middle of 1996, the Council was able to endorse a common position, which was submitted to the European Parliament for a second reading.[143] What the European Parliament received, however, was less a powerful and comprehensive draft directive designed to increase the pace and coherence of the liberalization of energy markets within the EU, but rather a flawed, wounded system plagued with deliberately added loopholes. Owing to well-targeted subsidiarity shots, the 1996 directive was not

---

[140] In the end, management unbundling was re-introduced for transmission system operator (TSO) as it made its way into Article 7(6) of the1996 electricity market Directive 96/92/EC.

[141] See also Commission, The Organisation of the Internal Electricity Market (SEC (1995) 464 final) 22.3.1995.

[142] Commission, The Organisation of the Internal Electricity Market, SEC (1995) 464 final (22/03/1995). q.v. Aricles 6 (6) and 21 (2) of 1996 electricity market directive.

[143] Common Position (EC) No 56/96 adopted by the Council on 25 July 1996 with a view to adopting Directive 96/ … /EC of the European Parliament and of the Council, of …, concerning common rules for the internal market in electricity, OJ C 315, 24.10.1996, p. 18.

born to become a sprinter but rather a long-distance walker, achieving little at the beginning but gaining powerful momentum as a result of both the ongoing Florence Forum and the later European Council and European Parliament resolutions encouraging the Commission to table proposals for amending legislation.[144]

2.7 Findings: Advocating Liberalization but Heading Towards European Command and Control?

The negotiations really turned on just one issue: the opening-up of access to the 'gatekeepers' of electricity and, in particular, gas transmission.[145] These gatekeepers, supported by their political constituencies (in particular Germany) and trade union constituencies (in particular France), have managed to delay the process by exercising political leverage through their home governments, industrial leverage through their influence in industry associations, and 'expertise' leverage through consultative committees and academics. Jonathan Stern, in his excellent survey, has called them the 'ultimate liberalisation refuseniks'.[146] In Germany, an intense debate raged over the assertion that mandatory third-party access without compensation amounted to unconstitutional expropriation,[147] an argument that would be mirrored in a similar assertion under the then 'unwritten' constitutional principles of EU law once derived from the common constitutional law of the Member States, as now enshrined in the Charter of Fundamental Rights of the European Union. Lack of EU competence,[148] the categorization of energy supply as a 'service' rather than the movement of a 'good' and an alleged invisible exclusion of energy from the single market principles, supposedly implicit in the absence of a specific reference to energy in the Treaty of Rome, were other arguments then used.[149]

---

[144] E.g. EP Resolution of 6.7.2000 obliging the Commission to adopt a timetable for the attainment of clearly defined objectives to gradual complete market opening.

[145] The main positions concerning the gas directive, though filtered by a UK perspective with both large gas reserves and the successful achievement of a competitive gas market following 12 years after privatization, are well presented in: Select Committee on the European Communities, House of Lords, Session 1997–98, 7th report (Adviser: M. Brothwood).

[146] J. Stern, *Competition and Liberalization of European Gas Markets* (London: RIIA 1998), pp. 90–5, quote at p. 91.

[147] Equitably arguing in favour of a justifiable re-definition of property rights ('Inhalts & Schrankenbestimmung'): H. Papier, *Durchleitungen und Eigentum* (BB 1997), p. 1213. Decisively in favour of an unjustified (re-)definition of property rights (but still without any scope for claiming compensation; as only lawful expropriation shall trigger compensation under the present state of the art dogmatics, as set by a landmark ruling of the constitutional court): U. Hüffer, K. Ipsen, and P. Tettinger (eds), *Die Transitrichtlinien für Gas und Elektrizität* (Stuttgart: Boorberg 1991) pp. 327 and 334 against the background of rather insignificant Transit Directives 1990/547/EEC and 1991/296/EC. For a summary of the discussion: J. Schneider, *Liberalisierung der Stromwirtschaft durch Regulative Marktorganisation* (Baden-Baden: Nomos 1999), p. 416 and H. Jarass, *Europäisches Energierecht* (Berlin: Dunker & Humblot,1996), pp. 98 et seq. and p. 117.

[148] J. Schneider, *Liberalisierung der Stromwirtschaft durch Regulative Marktorganisation* (Baden-Baden: Nomos 1999), p. 433.

[149] V. F. Burchard and L. Eckert, *Natural Gas and EU Energy Law* (Baden-Baden: Nomos 1995), J. Schwarze, 'European Energy Policy in Community Law', in E. Mestmäcker (ed.), *Natural Gas in the Internal Market* (London: Graham & Trotman 1994) p. 165.

Since these 'gatekeepers' enjoyed, on occasion, both the (threat to obtain) expropriation of land and the monopoly rent for long depreciated natural monopoly assets, their resistance was and is natural. That a rentier does not wish to give up his rent and engage in the unpleasant business of genuine competition requires no further explanation. The issue is very similar to the negotiation history of the European Energy Charter/ECT.[150] The original Charter declaration, strongly influenced by the concurrent first draft of the EEC's energy directives, strongly emphasized third-party access. The ECT contains no explicit mention of the matter—although it is implicit in the obligation of enterprises with 'special and exclusive privileges' mentioned in Articles 22 and 23 ECT to provide 'national treatment' under Article 10 ECT. However, an interpretative memorandum attached to the Final Act asserts that the Treaty is not intended to introduce 'mandatory third-party access'.[151]

'Security of supply', the ever-present and Janus-faced mantra of EU energy policy, was much used by defenders of the status quo, who argued that long-term contracts and firmly-established supply structures were necessary in order to negotiate with external suppliers of, in particular, gas—on which the EU is indeed dependent.[152] The phrase was, however, equally used by advocates of liberalization, who argued that greater diversity of supply forms, suppliers, and supply sources would be fostered by liberalization, and that a more integrated market would steer energy supply to those Member States where it was most needed.[153] In view of such resistance, from parties with strong links to their governments (in particular in France, then in Germany and currently still in Russia), it is in fact surprising that the directives were in the end forthcoming.

Ultimately, the negotiations ended with a result thanks to tactical concessions made by the Commission. It overcame French resistance by accepting French insistence on the 'single buyer' alternative to third-party access, by recognising 'public service obligations', the introduction of 'negotiated' as well as 'regulated' TPA (as was originally proposed), and by the introduction of a 'tender procedure' for new energy generation capacity. It is rather ironic that none of these four, then much-debated, vigorously opposed, and grudgingly accepted concessions has proved to have had any lasting impact. Even French energy companies, now pulling their government along with them, seem to live more happily with the standard access procedure. The tender procedure has fallen into disuse.

The public service obligation to be formulated by Member States and monitored by the Commission, at least initially, seemed to be not much more than a public relations exercise. It was accepted at face value, with full understanding of its limited legal value, by virtually all actors, including governments, companies, and even

---

[150] See contributions by J. Dore and T. Wälde in T. Wälde (ed.), *The Energy Charter Treaty* (London: Kluwer 1996).

[151] Final Act of the Energy Charter Treaty Conference, Understandings IV (1)(b)(i).

[152] See Commission Green Paper on a European strategy for the security of energy supply (COM 2000, 769 final) 29.11.2000 and Report on the Green Paper towards a European Strategy for the security of energy supply (COM (2002) 321 final) 29.6.2002.

[153] Commission, Green Paper on a European strategy for the security of energy supply (COM (2000) 769 final) 29.11.2000, pp. 58–9.

the publicly concerned European Parliament and its consumer and trade union constituencies. Developments at the turn of the millennium, however, proved this finding to be premature, as the Commission was slowly sharpening its arsenal of weapons under various Treaty provisions, mainly Articles 106 and 107 TFEU. The Commission elaborated detailed policies on 'services in the general economic interest', of which security of energy supplies is just one of several sub-categories.[154] This was necessary as '[t]he European Union does not yet have all the means to change the international market'.[155]

2.8 Concluding Thoughts: The First Steps Towards an Internal Market in Energy

The history of the negotiations described in this chapter[156] is not only of a purely explanatory value. The directives create secondary law on the EU level, and possibly (in particular as certain Member States—e.g. France and Germany—did not implement the directives promptly and correctly)[157] gave rise to direct effect at national level. Consequently, there is a great deal of leeway for the use of discretion, in which respect the compromise-based, open-ended formulations are especially at stake. The *travaux preparatoires* should therefore be referred to for interpretative purposes. Given the purposive and integration-friendly approach of the Court, they should, in particular, be relevant if they contain indications of the particular policies and intentions underlying particular provisions. Such constructive use of the negotiating history is, however, of limited use. Much of the wording was formulated explicitly with a view to papering over continuing disagreements so that the drafting history often reveals the existence of carefully maintained, contradictory positions by the main actors. In all likelihood, interpretation will benefit most from an effort to develop maximum consistency with the *acquis communautaire*—in particular the prevailing understanding of primary EU law—and from incorporation of evolving majority attitudes and subsequent negotiations, such as the Madrid and Florence processes of regulators' coordination and consultation with industry.

---

[154] Commission, Communication on services in the general economic interest, OJ C 281, 26.9.1996, p. 3; Commission, (COM 2001/C17/04)—Services of General Interest in Europe, OJ C 17, 19.1.2001, p. 4; Green Paper on services of general interest, (COM (2003) 270 final) 21.5.2003, p. 67; Green Paper on a European strategy for the security of energy supply, (COM (2000) 769 final) 29.11.2000; Final Report on the Green Paper towards a European Strategy for the security of energy supply (COM (2002) 321 final) 29.6.2002.

[155] Commission, Green Paper on a European strategy for the security of energy supply, (COM (2000) 769 final) 29.11.2000, p. 2.

[156] For an account, see J. Stern, *Competition and Liberalization of European Gas Markets* (London: RIIA 1998) or P. Cameron, *Competition in Energy Markets* (Oxford: OUP 2002).

[157] Commission Staff Working Paper, 1st Benchmarking Report on the implementation of the internal electricity and gas market, (SEC (2001) 1957) 3.12.2001, p. 5.

The starting point for energy liberalization back in the early days of the European Community did not allow for any substantial harmonization measures to take place. The energy sector was effectively shielded from the impact of EC law. Only very slowly, and first very cautiously through small steps in the right direction, did EC law start to influence the energy sector. Only when the time was right did the first energy market directives appear, but with little firepower to change the ways in which the energy business had been run for decades.

It was probably clear that the first legislative instruments in this area would not cause significant changes. Instead, these must be viewed as instruments testing the waters and introducing the idea of regulating the energy sector at EU level. Even the first electricity and gas market directives from 1996 and 1998 were largely toothless. As such, they can hardly be considered as real 'internal market directives'. However, this type of cautious approach was probably necessary to give the Member States time to adapt both to the idea of EU-driven liberalization of the energy sector and the concrete changes that this new approach would cause. The movement from state and monopoly to markets and contracts is not easy.

From those early days onwards, the Commission has made use of its dual role within the institutional set-up of the EU. As the initiator of new EU legislation, it has proposed new sector-specific rules and regulations. When this route has failed or proved to be too slow, it has used its powers under EU competition laws and imposed changes, or has challenged existing and established structures and ways to conduct business directly or through the Luxembourg Courts. As will be seen in Chapters 3 and 4, this same approach has been applied through out the ongoing liberalization process.

It is interesting and useful to compare the history of EU energy liberalization with the liberalization recommended (in particular, by the EU), introduced, and to some extent implemented, in the post-socialist societies (essentially the EU–25). EU–10/12/15 liberalization was first articulated in 1988 and enacted in 1996–1998, with a first timetable for effective opening of less than 50 per cent extending until 2006–2008, later to be speeded up by the 2003 Directives (the 'acceleration package') to 2004–2007. The post-socialist economies were frequently urged to pursue a policy of rapid 'shock' liberalization, and were certainly not supposed to proceed at the very measured pace of the EU. It is always easier to recommend measures to others than to take them oneself.

3

The Evolution of the Sector-Specific Regulatory Framework

The essence of both the electricity and gas market directives is the introduction of freedom of choice to engage in the business of and trade in energy—the choice to build power plants and pipelines, the choice to export and import, the choice to select and negotiate with suppliers, shippers, and customers. In order to introduce freedom of choice it was necessary first to eliminate legal obstacles such as, and in particular, exclusive rights. This is a *sine qua non* condition for competition to emerge, but does not guarantee that it will emerge. A much more difficult task, therefore, is the elimination of commercial obstacles and the creation of a commercial environment where freedom of choice can effectively be exercised and result in competition. The example of the UK gas market in the 1980s demonstrated that the elimination of legal obstacles to competition did not bring about competition naturally. The UK gas regulatory authorities had to take a very proactive approach in order to move from the legal possibility of competition to its commercial reality. It was therefore always clear that 'market opening' could not be achieved overnight but would take place gradually. Another question, of course, is whether it has happened or should have happened by now—over 16 years since the first directives.

Both internal market directives are based on the same model, and approach, and use—largely—similar language. Some differences exist. The role of 'gatekeepers', dependence on non-EU suppliers (Russia, Norway, Algeria), and the existence (or at least the successful advocacy) of pre-existing long-term commitments as a temporary impediment to introducing competition have been much more pronounced within the gas industry than within the electricity industry, and are therefore reflected in the gas directives. For example, the management of pre-existing 'take-or-pay contracts' has, rightly or wrongly, played a much greater role in the derogations than might have been expected. Although, as discussed in this chapter, the main thrust of development has sought to minimize the importance of these differences. Today, the differences between both directives are minor. However, this does not suggest that the two markets should be regulated under the same principles or that the same regulatory choices should apply to both electricity and gas. On the contrary, there are considerable differences between the electricity and gas markets and the sector-specific regulatory framework should be sensitive to this. Currently, the differences are most visible in the application of certain provisions in various regulatory instruments (for instance, the exemptions granted under Article 17 of the Regulation (EC) No. 714/2009 and Article 36 of the Directive 73/2009, discussed below). One of the most crucial and significant differences between these two markets is that electricity is generated within the EU in various locations, the choice of which is based on a number of factors, such as availability of sufficient transmission capacity and the proximity of a consumption centre. There are also generating facilities, which are mainly used as a back-up system. This is not the case for natural gas, although gas storage plays a somewhat similar role. Here, the EU is dependent on a very small number of external suppliers. Natural gas is only located in gas fields in areas geologically suitable for natural gas reserves to develop. Unlike electricity, natural gas is also a commodity that will be depleted at some point in time. These factors cannot be affected by any human measures, although technology can push the date of final depletion further into the future, as has been seen with the advent of unconventional gas. The impossibility of storing electricity is also a differentiating factor.[1]

These issues affect the optimal regulatory framework to be used and the application of the law itself. For example, in comparing the exemptions granted under Article 17 of Regulation (EC) No. 714/2009 and Article 36 of Directive 73/2009,[2] it is of paramount significance to heed the need to attract alternative sources of natural gas. Therefore, it seems quite natural that a very lenient approach to the exemption conditions is adopted where they concern regasification plants.[3] Similarly, as the pipeline gas is largely controlled by the dominant players, LNG represents a very significant alternative and an opportunity for new suppliers to enter the market. Shale gas could have a similar effect. This has to be taken into consideration. These considerations are not as relevant for electricity. New competition can be introduced through interconnectors, but also through new generation capacity. Furthermore, the dependence on a limited number of supply sources and the control of the existing import infrastructure by ex-monopolists has to be considered in cases relating to strategic under-investment. It is no surprise that all of the cases on strategic under-investment under Article 102 of the Treaty on the Functioning of the European Union (TFEU) relate to the natural gas markets. While the issue is of significance to the electricity markets, it is much more important for natural gas markets.

The key obligations under the regulatory frameworks for electricity and gas are:

- Member States must ensure that new facilities for production, transport, and distribution of energy (electricity and gas) are licensed on a non-discriminatory

---

[1] This was also discussed in K. Talus, *Vertical Natural Gas Transportation Capacity, Upstream Commodity Contracts and EU Competition Law* (Alphen aan den Rijn: Kluwer Law International 2011).

[2] Directive 2009/73/EC of the European Parliament and of the Council of 13 July 2009 concerning common rules for the internal market in natural gas and repealing Directive 2003/55/EC, OJ L 211, 14.8.2009, 94–136.

[3] The US approach seems to be very similar, though more pragmatic and efficient. For this, see K. Talus, 'Access to Gas Markets: A Comparative Study on Access to LNG Terminals in the European Union and the United States', 31(2) *Houston Journal of International Law* (2009), pp. 343–76. The article argues that the similar approach on both sides of the Atlantic is due to competition over supplies and investment in the LNG supply chain. The recent progress in US shale gas has obviously changed the situation in this regard.

basis: i.e. there are no preferential or exclusive rights for established and/or state-owned companies, earlier monopolies, and 'gate-keepers';

- third party access (TPA) provisions, necessary due to the 'natural monopoly' character of the transportation segment of the electricity and gas markets, require effective (in law and practice) and non-discriminatory access for competitors. Over the years there has been progress in the right direction, away from a single buyer model in electricity (though not in gas); and from negotiated TPA finally to regulated TPA (as the only option);

- similarly to TPA, due to the 'natural monopoly' character of the transportation markets and transmission operators also acting as producers/buyers, traders, and distributors of energy, there is an inherent conflict of interest between their supposedly 'neutral' role as network operators open to all companies and their privileged position with respect to their competitors without control over transmission networks. There is an immanent temptation for them to capitalize in their competitive business on their control of the transmission networks: e.g. by cross-subsidizing their competitive business with monopoly rent. This can be done through a very natural favouritism in network transmission towards their own business over the demands of their competitors, and by using the confidential insight into the business of competitors gained by the network operator to help its divisions engaged in competition. The response to this contained in the directives has been to require different degrees of unbundling, ranging from the unbundling of accounts between the 'neutral transmission' and the other, competitive, activities of the transmission operators (i.e. a 'Chinese wall') to ownership unbundling, although this option has so far not been imposed on Member States;

- the transmission/network operators are given special responsibility for managing the system. This both affirms their current role and the perhaps greater need for such formal responsibility in an open system involving diverse actors in a diversified market;

- the directives do not directly impose 'public service' obligations, but encourage Member States to do so, with the proviso that these are verifiable, non-discriminatory, and transparent. The Commission reserves an oversight role to itself;

- with integrated monopoly and public ownership, the state's role was oversight of the operations of the monopoly. This role needed to be changed as a competitive market developed, with the problematic elements of still-existent or unavoidable natural monopolies. The crucial issue of access requires the presence of a regulatory authority to ensure that access is undermined neither in law nor practice by obstructive actions taken by the network operator to try to use its control over the vital network to thwart competitors. Initially, the directives fell short of requiring an independent energy regulator, but this has subsequently been rectified.

In addition to these elements in the directives, an initial key obligation was also to allow 'eligible customers' to choose their supplier and have access to the transport networks. Eligibility criteria were formulated so as to increase the number of eligible customers in phases, basically by lowering the minimum threshold of annual consumption to define eligibility to achieve a specified, phased increasing minimum market opening, which was finally completed on 1 July 2007.

Sections 3.1–3.5 focus on the developments and individual merits and drawbacks of sector-specific regulation in the areas of generation, third party access, unbundling, derogations and exemptions (including public service obligation and merchant exemption), and security of supply.

3.1 Generation

Articles 7 and 8 of the Electricity Market Directive allow Member States to choose between an authorization procedure and a tender procedure.[4] The authorization procedure obliges governments to apply a limited number of objective criteria when authorizing new generation facilities, to make the decision in a transparent way and to provide reasons and an appeals mechanism for refusals (to be notified to the Commission). It would seem that under these provisions, new entrants therefore must have a legal right to authorization, provided that they comply with the criteria set forth. This interpretation of Article 5 has a bearing on energy investors' rights under national law: if Member States do not explicitly establish such a legal right, the directive may generate one by 'direct effect' or by 'indirect effect': i.e. by a reading of national law in conformity with the directive. The procedure does not depend (unlike the tender procedure) on long-term forward state planning of required capacities put out to tender, but lets the market forecast future demand, supply competition, and commercial feasibility in a competitive context. In principle, it facilitates the establishment of technologically, commercially, and environmentally superior power plants to out-compete existing operations. The devil is in the detail of the criteria listed. These are very general and can easily be manipulated to undermine the policy of this 'freedom to build new capacity'. But if such manipulation takes place—which can be identified through its having a discriminatory effect, through lack of transparency and failure to comply with the criteria as used in practice, or through a visible attempt by state agencies to replace the new entrants' judgement of future energy needs with their own and thereby protect existing national producers from competition—a case of non-compliance will exist and can be challenged under international and EU law. The problem for a new investor, then, is not so much obtaining authorization to build a plant, but securing access to customers and transmission capacity.

While open in nature, the criteria laid down in both Articles plainly allow for discrimination in favour of generation of green electricity. This is clearly illustrated by Article 7, which refers explicitly to the protection of the environment, the

---

[4] For a very detailed analysis, see H. Bjørnebye, *Investing in EU Energy Security: Exploring the Regulatory Approach to Tomorrow's Electricity Production* (Alphen aan den Rijn: Kluwer Law International 2010).

nature of the primary sources (here security considerations might also come into play), contribution to the EU targets for renewable energy, and the contribution of generating capacity to reducing emissions.

The tender procedure is only meant as a backup, to be used when markets fail and security of supply is at stake. One might assume that a state would use long-term power purchase contracts as 'carrots'. It seems, however, that this option has not been used by Member States (including, surprisingly, France).

A final point is that, as the rationale of the provision is to allow market access under non-discriminatory conditions, there is no need actually to have a formal authorization procedure. For example, in principle there are no general energy-related authorization procedures for the construction and operation of power plants in Finland and, as such, power production is not subject to a specific licence or authorization. (Obviously, general concession procedures, which are linked to land-use planning and environmental protection, still apply.) A special licensing procedure applies for nuclear power stations under the Nuclear Energy Act of 1987 and for the exploitation of hydropower under the Water Act of 1961.[5]

3.2 Third Party Access

The EU electricity and gas markets are both network-bound markets, with the obvious exception of LNG markets in which large LNG ships can take the cargo wherever the best price can be obtained.[6] This means that the success or failure of a competitive market depends to a significant extent on the TPA provisions. Unless access to the transmission networks—usually natural monopolies in the hands of incumbents mostly acting as producers, importers, and suppliers, and sometimes distributors as well—both the freedom to produce and the freedom to purchase are pointless. TPA is therefore the pivot around which the push towards open and competitive markets turns. It is recognized that purely voluntary access—on the theory that the network owners might want to develop more of a profitable transport business—did not work and does not work. TPA means that the owner and operator of infrastructure must provide access to the capacity, either total capacity or only unused capacity, for eligible third parties on non-discriminatory conditions. As long as the network is in the hands of a vertically integrated company—that is, where full ownership unbundling has not taken place—the legislator has to take positive action in order to guarantee TPA, often against the will of the owner. The legislator has two main options to regulate TPA: negotiated access or regulated access. In addition, a single buyer model is possible.

As far as electricity is concerned, the first (1996) directive offered a choice between three options. The first of these was the single-buyer model (included on

---

[5] See, K. Talus et al., *Energy Law of Finland* (Alphen aan den Rijn: Kluwer Law International 2010).

[6] For example, see K. Talus, 'Access to Gas Markets: A Comparative Study on the Access to LNG Terminals in EU and US', 31(2) *Houston Journal of International Law* (2009).

French insistence), which was quickly recognized as not workable, and not adopted even in France. The second was the regulated access model. The third was negotiated access where, supposedly, the terms are freely negotiated but some pressure is exerted to push the recalcitrant network operator in the right direction if need be. As per Article 17(3) of the first electricity directive, negotiated access did not require 'tariffs', but 'indicative prices'. However, it is not practical to consider that any transmission might be based on separate detailed negotiations.

The 1998 gas directive did not include the single-buyer model. Where gas was concerned, Member States were able to choose between negotiated access and regulated access (under Articles 14–16). These access regimes were, in both cases, accompanied by the demands of objective, transparent, and non-discriminatory operating criteria. A mixed regime was also possible.[7] Denmark and the Netherlands, for example, applied a mixed system in which they opted for negotiated access for the transmission grid and regulated access for the distribution grid.[8]

As with electricity, under the negotiated access regime the gas companies were obliged to negotiate access to the gas network with the eligible customers in good faith and to publish the main commercial conditions for access.[9] Under the regulated access regime, the gas companies were obliged to provide access on the basis of published tariffs and other possible terms and conditions for use of the system.[10]

As distinct from the first electricity directive, the 1998 gas directive already mentioned the Member States' right to oblige gas TSOs to expand transport capacity if the customer is willing to pay for it. The gas directive also included access to 'storage', but this had very little practical effect.

To understand the TPA system prescribed by the first internal energy market directives from 1996 and 1998, one should envisage the first step as a legal right (of producers and consumers) of access against the network operator (and sometimes the distributor). This right of access is nothing but the transposition into the directive (and from there into national law) of the duty of the owner of an essential facility under Article 102 TFEU to deal with prospective users on reasonable and non-discriminatory terms. But this legal entitlement is then almost prohibitively limited in all sorts of ways. The main excuse for refusing access was (and is) lack of capacity. A refusal must be substantiated and the reasons given verifiable. The lack of capacity objection is a most malleable excuse. Since the network operator has control over technology, management, contractual commitments, capacity, and information, it is not difficult for them to formulate such an objection.[11]

---

[7] Article 14 of the first gas market directive. See also the Commission explanatory information at: <http://ec.europa.eu/energy/gas/legislation/historical_documents.htm>.
[8] M. Roggenkamp et al. (eds), *Energy Law in Europe* (Oxford: OUP 2008), p. 1305.
[9] Article 15 of the first gas market directive.
[10] Article 16 of the first gas market directive.
[11] This provision is examined in great detail in K.B. Moen and S. Dyrland, *EUs Gassmarkedsdirektiv* (Bergen: Fagbokforlaget Vigmostad & Bjorke AS 2002), pp.188–302. The authors discuss, among many other issues, the meaning of 'serious' and 'threat' and the role of the provision as a safety-valve for companies. They conclude that the effect of the provision will depend on the market trends and the approach of the Member States and the Commission.

The next set of excuses (which may overlap with the no-capacity excuse) were the pre-existing contractual arrangements (including those created by the network operator's own or affiliated competitive electricity sales operations), technical constraints (under the control of the network operator), and priority to be given to renewable energy sources and energy produced from indigenous fuel (e.g. German coal; Dutch gas, with 15 per cent of the total ceiling).

The last set of excuses (both from the network operator and Member State) lies in the public service obligation, if Member States can prove that such access would essentially undermine the feasibility of providing a mandatory public service and there is no less restrictive alternative available.

The logical strategy of the recalcitrant network operator keen to exclude newcomer competitors from the market it already serves is to rely on technical and environmental constraints in order to interpret capacity very narrowly and then to fill such capacity with its own, affiliates' and friendly companies' contractual deliveries (which may be secretly conditional). If access is requested and negotiated, the counter-strategy is to fill the network with 'friendly' capacity before the negotiations advance to detail. Proving that discrimination has taken place represents a very difficult, costly, uncertain, and protracted battle for any company seeking access.

Clearly, the first internal energy market directives can only be considered as having been a first step towards a regulatory regime able to enhance and support free EU-wide competition, instead of national and tightly regulated and controlled markets. A stronger and more clear-cut access regime was simply not a possibility at that time. The political compromise resulted in a choice of three different access regimes, to be selected by the Member States. However, even given the well-known shortcomings of these first directives, they represent an important start in the road towards a competitive EU-wide markets.

The second energy market package[12] pushed the energy *acquis* towards a regulatory system able to accomodate the emergence of a further degree of competition, and went considerably further in 'regulating for competition'.[13] The two new directives and accompanying regulations sought, with mixed success,[14] to rectify the failures

---

[12] Directive 2003/55/EC of the European Parliament and of the Council of 26 June 2003 concerning common rules for the internal market in natural gas and repealing Directive 98/30/EC, OJ L 176, 15.7.2003, pp. 57–78; Directive 2003/54/EC of the European Parliament and of the Council of 26 June 2003 concerning common rules for the internal market in electricity and repealing Directive 96/92/EC, OJ L 176, 15.7.2003, pp. 37–56; Regulation (EC) No. 1228/2003 of the European Parliament and of the Council of 26 Jun. 2003 on conditions for access to the network for cross-border exchanges in electricity, OJ L 176, 15.7.2003, pp. 1–10; Regulation (EC) No. 1775/2005 of the European Parliament and of the Council of 28 September 2005 on conditions for access to the natural gas transmission networks, OJ L 289, 3.11. 2005, pp. 1–13.

[13] P. Cameron, *Competition in Energy Markets: Law and Regulation in the European Union* (Oxford: OUP 2007), 30.

[14] Prospects for the internal gas and electricity market (COM(2006)0841); Progress in creating the internal gas and electricity market (COM(2008)0192); Progress in creating the internal gas and electricity market (COM(2009)0115). For the early effects of the new regime, see the national reports in P. Cameron, *Legal Aspects of Energy Regulation: Implementing the New Directives of Electricity and Gas Across Europe* (Oxford: OUP 2005). However, it must be noted that the legislative situation described in the book represents the situation in October 2004. Needless to say, a lot has happened since then—especially since a large number of Member States had not yet implemented this regulatory package.

and shortcomings of the previous regulatory regime. As far as TPA is concerned, the new regime eliminated the negotiated access regimes from electricity and limited its application to specific parts of the gas supply chain such as storage or linepack.[15] As such, the access regime relating to most of the supply chain in gas and electricity was now based on a regulated access regime. Tariffs had to apply to all eligible customers, including supply undertakings, and had to be applied objectively and without discrimination as between system users.[16] According to the ECJ, non-discriminatory TPA concerns both the potential supply undertakings and the eligible customers.[17]

The latest step along the way to competitive markets is the third energy package. The new regulatory framework extends the application of the TPA rules to new areas and pushes the obligations of the TSO to a new level by, for example, highlighting investments and the need to ensure the long-term viability of the system. Clearly, the visible trend throughout this development from the first to the second and third package is a move towards a more comprehensive regulation of TPA and towards shorter-term capacity reservations.

3.2.1 Regulation of TPA under the EU Energy *Acquis*

In general terms, TPA in the sector-specific regulation relating to EU electricity and gas markets is developed through three levels of regulation with very different levels of detail. The general framework was established in the general internal market directives,[18] which lay down the basic rules and principles of TPA. The content of these rules and principles are then further elaborated in the two access regulations (715/2009 (gas) and 714/2009 (electricity)), which specifically focus on access issues and complement the more general directives. However, the third and most detailed level of regulation are the network codes and guidelines which can be adopted on the basis of the regulations.[19]

At a general level, the access rules under the third energy market directives are not very different from those of the previous 2003 regime. In simple terms, the new directives require that the regulated TPA regime is based on published and

---

[15] The TPA regime of the gas market directive also includes the appointment of the operator and designation of certain tasks and duties. These issues will not be examined here. Instead, the focus will be on the substantial and directly TPA-related provisions.

[16] The exception was the TPA regime for upstream pipeline systems within EU.

[17] Case C-239/07, *Julius Sabatauskas and Others* [2008] ECR I-7523.

[18] Directive 2009/72/EC of the European Parliament and of the Council of 13 July 2009 concerning common rules for the internal market in electricity and repealing Directive 2003/54/EC, OJ L 211, 14.8.2009, pp. 55–93 and Directive 2009/73/EC of the European Parliament and of the Council of 13 July 2009 concerning common rules for the internal market in natural gas and repealing Directive 2003/55/EC, OJ L 211, 14.8.2009, pp. 94–136.

[19] Framework Guidelines on Capacity Allocation and Congestion Management for Electricity (FG-2011-E-002) 29 July 2011 and Framework Guidelines on Capacity Allocation Mechanisms for the European Gas Transmission Network (FG-2011-G-001) 3 August 2011. For comments and analysis, see A. de Hauteclocque and K. Talus, 'Capacity to Compete: Recent Trends in Access Regimes in Electricity and Natural Gas Networks', in B. Delvaux, M. Hunt, and K. Talus (eds), *EU Energy Law and Policy Issues* (Cambridge: Intersentia 2011).

pre-approved tariffs, which are applied in a transparent and non-discriminatory way. In addition, there are provisions addressing many related issues such as balancing, publishing requirements (though most elements are left for the national regulators to decide), and on fixing or approving the tariffs or the methodologies for their calculations (though, again, most of the details, including return on risk or investment incentives, are left for the national regulatory authorities), etc.

Access tariffs payable by shippers vary from Member State to Member State. However, the directives require that the tariffs or the methodologies underlying their calculation be approved by the national regulatory authorities and then published before entering into force. Therefore, renegotiation with particular customers is not possible. In particular, no rebates or special schemes may be offered to group companies.

The situations where access might be denied largely follow the old regime. Access may be refused where there is: (i) lack of capacity; (ii) a public service obligation imposed by the Member States; and (iii) a 'sudden crisis' under Article 46 for gas, and Article 42 for electricity (essentially a *force majeure* provision). In addition, access to the gas transportation network can be refused on the basis of serious economic and financial difficulties with a take-or-pay contract. Access refusal must be reasoned and Member States may choose to ensure that the TSO/Distribution System Operator (DSO) makes the necessary enhancements to the system when it is economical to do so, or when the customer is willing to pay for such enhancements in capacity or connection (Article 35 for gas and Article 32 for electricity). The case law of the ECJ indicates that this possibility to refuse access to the system must be assessed on a case-by-case basis. It does not give Member States the right to lay down derogations in a general manner without assessing the technical capacity of the system to meet third parties' access demands.[20]

Where gas is concerned, the upstream pipeline network is one major exception. This is not a novelty introduced through the third gas directive. On the contrary, all three regimes, from the first to the third Gas Market Directive, regulated access to upstream pipelines. Access to this section of the gas supply chain was organized and regulated separately from the general TPA provisions—an access regime in line with practice in the North Sea area. On discovery of new gas fields, access to the existing pipeline system was negotiated between the producer and the pipeline company or operator. However, the governmental control brought about by formal regulation of the access regime in upstream gas is a welcome addition.[21] Article 34 of the third gas market directive stipulates that natural gas undertakings and eligible customers must be able to obtain access to upstream pipeline networks, including facilities supplying technical services incidental to such access. The parts of the upstream networks and facilities used for local production operations at the site of a field where the gas is produced constitute an exception to the TPA

---

[20] Case C-439/06, *Citiworks AG Flughafen Leipzig v Halle GmbH, Bundesnetzagentur* [2008] ECR I-3913, para. 57.

[21] For more details, see M. Roggenkamp et al. (eds), *Energy Law in Europe* (Oxford: OUP 2008), p. 1305.

obligations contained in Article 34. This access must be provided in accordance with the objectives of fair and open access, achieving a competitive market in natural gas and avoiding any abuse of a dominant position, taking into account security and regularity of supply, the amount of capacity, which can reasonably be made available, and environmental protection. Access can only be refused under the conditions listed in the directive, although it must be noted that these conditions are sufficiently broad to enable a fairly broad recourse to such refusal. One condition, for example, is the reasonable needs of the owner, operator, or other users. To strengthen this upstream access regime, a dispute settlement mechanism must be put in place. This exception from the general TPA regimes seems logical, considering the many differences between upstream and downstream pipelines and the number of Member States where upstream pipelines actually exist (arguably, this market segment could have been left to subsidiarity).

Much like the 2003 directives, the new regime leaves Member States with considerably less discretion as to implementation.[22] However, this does not mean that differences cannot persist. Neither does it mean that the access regime is complete and perfectly functioning.[23]

To complement these basic rules on TPA, the EU energy *acquis* also includes access-specific regulation, which takes these basic provisions as a starting point and develops the access regime further by regulating the allocation of capacity where demand exceeds supply.

The two central issues raised by the transmission of electricity and transportation of gas in the context of the liberalization of the EU energy market are access to the network and the availability of capacity on the network. Initially, EU energy market regulation focused primarily on access issues.[24] The question of availability was only addressed later. For electricity, these questions were largely addressed in the 2003 regulation on conditions for access to the network for cross-border exchanges in electricity and the related guidelines.[25] Again, much as with the first energy market directives from 1996 (electricity) and 1998 (gas), gas regulation lagged two years behind and these issues were addressed in 2005 through Regulation (EC) No. 1775/2005 on conditions for access to the natural gas transmission networks. These regimes were then repealed and replaced by Regulation (EC) No. 715/2009 (gas) and No. 714/2009 (electricity). The objectives of these two regulations include: the setting of rules for cross-border trade and harmonized

---

[22] Many of the 46 (25 for electricity and 21 for gas) infringement proceedings initiated by the Commission in June 2009 related to access issues (lack of transparency, insufficient coordination efforts by transmission system operators to make maximum interconnection capacity available, absence of regional cooperation, and others). See the press releases IP/09/1035 and IP/09/1490.

[23] See, for example, Commission press release, 'Energy infringements': Country fact sheets (MEMO/09/296, 25 June 2009) and Commission press release, 'Q&A: the infringement exercise concerning cross-border energy network access and regulated prices' (MEMO/09/297, 25 June 2009).

[24] U. Hammer, 'The Relationship between Capacity Markets and Spot Market in the Gas Sector', in M. Roggenkamp and U. Hammer (eds), *European Energy Law Report II* (Cambridge: Intersentia, 2005), 230–1.

[25] Regulation (EC) No. 1228/2003 of the European Parliament and of the Council of 26 June 2003 on conditions for access to the network for cross-border exchanges in electricity, OJ L 176, 15.7.2003, 1–10.

principles for capacity allocation and congestion management; the determination of transparency requirements;[26] the facilitation of capacity trading; and the emergence of well-functioning wholesale markets.

Various methods—both market-based and others—are available to allocate the available transfer capacity. A market-based capacity allocation mechanism involves auctioning, where the capacity is auctioned and the highest price is the price paid for the capacity. An explicit auction will start at a minimum price and, depending on the demand, will rise until the entire capacity is used. While market-based allocation methods are used in some Member States' gas markets, they are much more extensively used in the electricity markets. There is no obvious reason for this differentiation. It also seems, as discussed below, that the approach used in the two markets is converging and that auctions will also become the method of choice in natural gas markets. Other mechanisms used include *pro rata* allocation, where the capacity is divided further on request of the market participants until all capacity has been allocated. Where demand exceeds maximum capacity, the market participants' requests are denied, using a specific mechanism. The obvious risk of this allocation mechanism is that a shipper's capacity is restricted to the point where it is no longer commercially attractive. Another risk is that the shipper anticipates high demand and requests more capacity than it needs. The first-come, first-served mechanism, in which capacity request orders are fulfilled in the order received, is another possible approach. The hoarding of capacity is the obvious risk here, where an undertaking books more capacity than is actually necessary, in order to block competitors from accessing the network. In all cases, a high degree of transparency can obviously alleviate these problems.

At a general level, Articles 37(6) (electricity) and 41(6) (gas) of the energy market directives require that the national regulatory authorities draft the procedures for the allocation of cross-border capacity and congestion management. However, in practice, the details of this requirement are largely left to the more detailed rules. At a basic level, Regulations (EC) No. 715/2009 and No. 714/2009 require that the capacity allocation must facilitate new investment and be market-based. Explicit and implicit auctions are the market-based methods compatible with these regulations. As in all parts of the energy *acquis* dealing with access issues, the requirements of non-discrimination and transparency accompany the more detailed provisions.[27]

On the request of the Commission and on the basis of Articles 6 of Regulation (EC) No 713/2009 and of Regulation (EC) No 715/2009 (for gas) and Regulation (EC) No 714/2009 (for electricity), the ACER has developed framework guidelines to deal with these issues (capacity allocation and congestion management).[28]

---

[26] Transparency is one of the most crucial issues for a functioning market both in terms of capacity reservations and capacity allocation. Essentially, the operations of the network must be so transparent that in practice—not just in theory—outsiders face no *de facto* handicaps in using the network as compared to insiders.

[27] Article 13 of Regulation (EC) No. 715/2009.

[28] Framework Guidelines on Capacity Allocation and Congestion Management for Electricity (FG-2011-E-002) 29 July 2011 and Framework Guidelines on Capacity Allocation Mechanisms for the European Gas Transmission Network (FG-2011-G-001) 3 August 2011.

Without going into the detail, these guidelines[29] require, in line with the directives and regulations, that TSOs offer both firm and interruptible and both short-term and long-term TPA, and they provide detailed guidance in this regard. Existing contracts also need to be adapted to the new guidelines (also for gas).[30]

The objectives of the TPA provisions of both the electricity and natural gas regulations are very similar: to create capacity to compete. However, the specific features and development stage of these two commodities result in different routes towards this common goal. For electricity, the development of market-coupling initiatives creates new regulatory challenges, although prices are increasingly converging. For gas, progress has been slower and efficiently-functioning spot markets have yet to emerge. However, the rapid and fundamental changes brought about in world LNG markets have caused a significant change in this respect and have created favourable conditions for short-term trading. In addition to the significant increase of available volumes and decreases in LNG prices, there is also an important regulatory dimension to this development. The introduction of TPA along with ownership unbundling, driven by both regulatory changes and antitrust enforcement, has combined with elimination of destination clauses (and other historical elements of the market structure) completely to transform the regulatory context in which natural gas companies operate. These fundamental changes have had a significant impact on the markets and spot trading in the EU natural gas markets has taken off.

One issue with respect to TPA is that the access regimes for electricity and gas are very similar, despite significant differences in the ways in which the markets are organized. The sector-specific regulatory regime in the internal market directives creates a market design in both sectors based as much as possible on short-term capacity allocation with liquid secondary trading platforms. The right portfolio of capacity periods is crucial to achieve a functioning energy system. Periods of long duration—far exceeding three years—are needed to facilitate investment in both sectors, but the optimal mix of short- and longer-term contracts is likely to differ greatly between the sectors.[31]

3.3 Unbundling

Due to the natural monopoly character of both electricity and gas networks explained in the introductory section of this chapter, this segment of the energy industry is a non-competitive market and needs to be separated from competitive

---

[29] These have been examined in detail in A. de Hauteclocque and K. Talus, 'Capacity to Compete: Recent Trends in Access Regimes in Electricity and Natural Gas Networks', in B. Delvaux, M. Hunt, and K. Talus (eds), *EU Energy Law and Policy Issues* (Cambridge: Intersentia 2011).

[30] This issue is discussed in detail in K. Talus, *Vertical Natural Gas Transportation Capacity, Upstream Commodity Contracts and EU Competition Law* (Alphen aan den Rijn: Kluwer Law International 2011).

[31] A. de Hauteclocque and K. Talus, 'Capacity to Compete: Recent Trends in Access Regimes in Electricity and Natural Gas Networks', in B. Delvaux, M. Hunt, and K. Talus (eds), *EU Energy Law and Policy Issues* (Cambridge: Intersentia 2011).

segments such as production and supply. This is the underlying objective of unbundling: to separate the competitive from the non-competitive segment in order to prevent misuse through control of the latter. This objective underpins the current regulation of the energy market: all unbundling obligations concern the separation of network activities from other possible activities. An undertaking may therefore engage in different activities as long as it stays out of the network business.

In the most basic terms, unbundling is necessary because there is an internal conflict of interest within a vertically integrated company: by allowing access to the network, the transmission/distribution branch of the company creates competition for the supply arm, which will have a negative impact on the company's overall return.[32] Logically speaking, a company will strive to maximize group revenue (the management also has this obligation to the shareholders). This idea conflicts with the idea of market liberalization: taken to the extreme, it will eliminate any and all competition and prevent market entry.

3.3.1 The Status Quo—From Account Unbundling to Legal Unbundling and Ownership

Clearly, if the logic of regulation of a natural monopoly were to be pursued to its conclusion, network (transmission system) operators would have to be divested from integrated energy companies and fulfil the independent public service of transporting natural gas or electricity,[33] their business interest being aligned with the interest of maximizing transport revenues. This end result, achieved for example in the UK, Spain, and the Netherlands,[34] has so far been diluted in EU energy market regulation. Interestingly, this was never done in the US, where liberalization of the gas markets started much earlier than in the EU. In the US, the method of choice has been conduct-related rules coupled with heavy supervision by the Federal Energy Regulation Commission (FERC).

The first internal market directives contained mere 'management unbundling'— i.e. transmission must be organized as a separate division with separate accounts within a corporate system. This mandatory building of 'glass walls' or 'Chinese walls', designed to insulate the transmission business from the same company's business competing with new entrants requiring grid access, could only be of limited practical

---

[32] DG Competition Report on Energy Sector Inquiry of 10 January 2007 (SEC(2006) 1724) 10.1.2007, p. 14. See also a speech by the Competition Commissioner Neelie Kroes, 'A new European energy policy; reaping the benefits of open and competitive markets' (SPEECH/07/63, Essen, 5 February 2007).

[33] The concept 'third party access' is distinct from the concept 'common carriage' used in connection with oil pipelines. The latter concept cannot be used in connection to natural gas. See J. Stern, 'The Prospects for Third Party Access in European Gas Markets', Chs. 10 and 11 in E. Mestmäcker (ed.), *Natural Gas in the Internal Market—A Review of Energy Policy* (London-Dordrecht-Boston: Graham & Trotman 1993), pp. 184–5.

[34] For a detailed overview of the Dutch situation, see M. Roggenkamp, 'Full Transparency Through Ownership Unbundling: Ownership Unbundling of Transmission and Distribution Grids in the Netherlands', in M. Roggenkamp and U. Hammer, *European Energy Law Report VI* (Antwerp: Intersentia 2009), pp. 61–76.

value. Such artificial structures may, at best, result in a kind of quasi-independence.[35] Admittedly, there were also rules to strengthen it, such as a report on affiliate transactions, but it was naturally unrealistic to expect the management of a corporate division to neglect their own career and collegiality in order to favour competitors threatening the incumbent firm's livelihood.

The 2003 directives marked a significant and necessary improvement over the previous regime.[36] In essence, they provided for both legal and functional unbundling for both transmission system operators and larger distribution system operators.[37] This meant that where the TSO or a DSO was a part of a vertically integrated undertaking, the ownership had to be legally separate from other activities of the group. The TSO or the DSO had to be independent 'at least in terms of its legal form, organisation and decision making from other activities not relating to' transmission or distribution. These provisions were further strengthened by rules relating to the conduct of the network operator, the emphasis being on managerial independence and a compliance programme. These provisions included limitations on the ability to participate in the management of both the network company and other parts of the group, the separation of professional or career interests (reward schemes, salaries, etc.), control and decision-making independence as far as possible, and so on. A compliance programme also had to be set up to prevent discriminatory conduct.

The idea behind the 2003 provisions is that, while it may be argued that if the management and account unbundling, as required by the first regime, is truly operational and implemented in good faith, it is in fact sufficient and the separation of companies to different subsidiaries adds little to the pre-existing situation, the legal unbundling adds to the independence of the network company. It was believed that by creating a separate legal entity, the employees, including the management, would increasingly be able to act independently of the parent company and aim at maximizing the return of the network company.[38]

The idea was therefore to change the corporate identity, from the employee's perspective, through conduct-related rules. It seems, however, that this did not

[35] The Competition Commissioner has made similar remarks concerning the legal unbundling regime. See the speech by Competition Commissioner Neelie Kroes 'A new energy policy for a new era', in a conference: 'European Energy Strategy—the Geopolitical Challenges', Lisbon, 30.10.2006 (SPEECH/06/648), speech by Competition Commissioner Neelie Kroes, 'Improving Europe's energy markets through more competition', Tischgespräch—Industrie-Club e.V. Düsseldorf, 23.3.2007, (SPEECH/07/175), speech of Competition Commissioner Neelie Kroes, 'Improving competition in European energy markets through effective unbundling', Fordham Corporate Law Institute's annual seminar 27.9.2007, (SPEECH/07/574), and Neelie Kroes 'A new European Energy Policy; reaping the benefits of open and competitive markets' in the E-world energy and water conference, Essen, 5.2.2007 (SPEECH/07/63).

[36] For an example of the effects of this new regulatory regime in Member States, see B. Malmendier and J. Schendel, 'Unbundling Germany's Energy Networks', 24(3) *Journal of Energy and Natural Resources Law* (2006) and the country reports in P. Cameron (ed.), *Legal Aspects of Energy Regulation: Implementing the New Directives of Electricity and Gas Across Europe* (Oxford: OUP 2005).

[37] Articles 9 and 13 of the second gas market directive and Articles 10 and 15 of the second electricity market directive.

[38] C. Jones, *EU Energy Law—The Internal Energy Market* (Leuven: Claeys & Casteels 2004), p. 73.

take place. Despite the new rules, significant opportunities for misuse remained. The regime did not appear to achieve the results hoped for. The Commission's Sector Inquiry[39] indicated that severe structural problems were still blocking the path towards an efficiently-functioning internal market for energy. The high degree of vertical integration was specifically identified as a problem, and was also seen as a background factor for many other issues identified by the Commission.[40]

The problem of the existing conduct-related rules—compared to a more drastic corporate restructuring—is that rules, which are not aligned with normal personal and organizational incentives are always a less effective way forward than designing organizational structures which produce the right incentives per se. Despite this, the overall effect of the 2003 directives (once they were properly implemented[41]) was to make discrimination somewhat more difficult for management and to accelerate a probably unavoidable trend towards more complete divestment of ownership and ultimately economic control (ownership or control unbundling), much as is typically required in situations where approval of a merger is accompanied by divestment conditions and more frequently also under Regulation 1/2003.[42]

The 2007 Sector Inquiry threw up numerous examples where the current unbundling regime seemed to fail to achieve its purpose. The various issues uncovered included the top management of a supply company having access to privileged information directly or through board positions, rebates being offered to the supply branch, the favouring of group companies in procurement for network services and balancing, discriminatory behaviour in investment decisions, joint training sessions, shared trading names, the necessity of obtaining approval for major investment decisions, and interpersonal relations.[43] Although it is clear that many of these problems have been rectified since the Sector Inquiry, it is fair to assume that some persist.[44] There is evidence of the existence of persistent problems closely

[39] Preliminary report of the Sector Inquiry under Article 17 Regulation 1/2003 on the gas and electricity markets (16 February 2006) and Communication from the Commission, Inquiry pursuant to Article 17 of Regulation (EC) No. 1/2003 into the European gas and electricity sectors (Final Report) COM(2006) 851 final.

[40] A partial reason for the inefficiency of the past regime can also be a weak regulatory action by the Member State authorities.

[41] See '3rd Legislative Package Input Paper 1: Unbundling' a European Regulators' Group for Electricity and Gas (ERGEG) public document. Ref: C07-SER-13-06-1-PD, 5 June 2007, p. 7, where ERGEG notes that market integration is achieved within countries. This is a further sign of national resistance to market opening. See also Case C-196/07, *Commission of the European Communities v Kingdom of Spain* and Case C-358/05, *Commission v. Spain*, Judgment of 21 June 2007 and K. Talus, 'Role of the European Court of Justice in the Opening of Energy Markets', 8(3) *ERA FORUM* (2007), pp. 435–48.

[42] Commission press releases 'Antitrust: Commission welcomes E.ON proposals for structural remedies to increase competition in German electricity market', (MEMO/08/132), 28.2.2008, 'Antitrust: Commission market tests commitments proposed by E.ON concerning German electricity markets', (MEMO/08/396), 12.6.2008 and 'Antitrust: Commission welcomes RWE proposals for structural remedies to increase competition in German gas market' (MEMO/08/355), 31.5.2008. These cases will be discussed in more detail below in Chapter 4.

[43] DG Competition report on energy Sector Inquiry of 10 January 2007 (SEC(2006) 1724) 10.1.2007, pp. 55–60.

[44] Similarly, see DG Competition report on energy Sector Inquiry of 10 January 2007 (SEC(2006) 1724) 10.1.2007, p. 161.

linked with the vertical integration of energy companies. Recent competition law cases, starting with the 2004 *ENI/Trans Tunisian Pipeline* case[45] and continuing with the *ENI,*[46] *E.ON,*[47] *RWE,*[48] *GDF Suez,*[49] *E.ON,*[50] and *CEZ*[51] cases, all suggest that structural problems related to vertical integration might require radical measures. A similar conclusion can also be drawn from the Commission's energy market progress reports.[52]

Due to these persistent problems, which seemed to stem at least partially from the weak unbundling regime, the Commission proposed the next step: full ownership unbundling.[53] This was to be a clear change to the second energy market directives 2003/54/EC (electricity) and 2003/55/EC (gas), which explicitly excluded the obligation of ownership unbundling.[54] Under the eye-catching heading 'Energising Europe: A *real* market with secure supply',[55] ownership unbundling of the electricity and gas networks was favoured so that 'no supply or production company active anywhere in the EU can own or operate a transmission system in any Member State of the EU'.[56] As a second-best solution, the Commission also proposed the independent system operator model, according to which 'vertically integrated companies [...] retain the ownership of their network assets, but [which] requires that the transmission network itself is managed by an independent system operator—an undertaking or entity entirely separate from the vertically integrated company— that performs all the functions of a network operator'.[57]

However, due to resistance from France and Germany, backed by a number of smaller Member States,[58] and the claims over incompatibility with the right to property and proportionality,[59] the full ownership unbundling option was watered down. Under the new regime, Member States are in effect given a three-way choice. In practice, they may thus decide to opt either for full ownership unbundling,[60]

---

[45] Case A 358, decision by the Italian Autorità Garante della Concorrenza e del Mercato of 15 February 2004.

[46] Case COMP/39.315—ENI.

[47] Case COMP/39.388—German Electricity Wholesale Market and Case COMP/39.389— German Electricity Balancing Market.

[48] Case COMP/39.402—RWE gas foreclosure.

[49] Case COMP/B-1/39.316—Gaz de France (gas market foreclosure).

[50] Case COMP/39.317—E.ON gas foreclosure.

[51] Case COMP/39.727, CEZ. See also Antitrust: Commission opens formal proceedings against Czech electricity incumbent CEZ (IP/11/891) 15.7.2011.

[52] 'Progress in creating the internal gas and electricity market' (COM/2008/0192 final), Report on progress in creating the internal gas and electricity market (COM/2009/0115 final) and Report on progress in creating the internal gas and electricity market (COM(2010)84 final).

[53] See, in particular, 'Questions and answers', (MEMO/07/362), 10 September 2007.

[54] See Article 15(1), 2nd sentence, Electricity Directive 2003/54/EC and Article 13(2), 1st sentence, Gas Directive 2003/55/EC.

[55] See press release, (IP/07/1361), 19.9.2007; emphasis added.

[56] Explanatory Memorandum of the new proposals, p. 7.

[57] Explanatory Memorandum of the new proposals, p. 5.

[58] See for example: Brussels power proposals opposed, *Financial Times*, 6.6.2007 or France warns on energy 'unbundling' plan, *Financial Times*, 7.2.2007.

[59] See, for example, J.-C. Pielow, G. Brunekreeft, and E. Ehlers, 'Legal and Economic Aspects of Ownership Unbundling in the EU', 2 *Journal of World Energy Law and Business* (2009).

[60] Articles 9 (et seq.) of Directives 2009/73/EC (gas) and 2009/72/EC (electricity).

an independent system operator model (ISO),[61] or an independent transmission operator (ITO) model[62] put forward by the Council.[63] This last model, which did not appear in the Commission's original proposals, allows the ownership of the network to be maintained with the supply companies, but attempts to ensure the neutrality and independence of the transmission operator through a set of detailed conditions, including independent management, a supervisory board, a compliance officer, and the possibility of substantial fines in cases of mismanagement. A pessimist might describe this as the 'business as usual' option.

Although both ownership unbundling and the ISO/ITO alternatives require that one company cannot be involved both in transmission and supply/generation, one apparent downside of the new directives is that they yet again contribute to the long list of exemptions and derogations from generally applicable rules.[64] While some vertically integrated companies are forced to sell their network assets, others are not. The Member States where energy companies have close relationships with the political powers are presumably those that will use the opportunity to derogate from full ownership unbundling (provided, of course, that this is what the national energy company wants).[65]

However, despite this defeat at the level of sector specific-regulation, the Commission's strategy to force private companies (so far E.ON[66] for electricity, and RWE[67] and ENI[68] for gas) to sell their network assets and achieve ownership unbundling through the use of general EU competition law is one recent development in the

---

[61] Article 13 (et seq.) of Directive 2009/72/EC (electricity) and Articles 14 (et seq.) of Directive 2009/73/EC (gas).

[62] Articles 17 (et seq.) Directives 2009/73/EC (gas) and 2009/72/EC (electricity).

[63] For an overview of the Third Legislative Package and the unbundling provisions, see J. G. Westerhof, 'The Third Internal Market Package', in M. Roggenkamp and U. Hammer, *European Energy Law Report VI* (Antwerp: Intersentia 2009), pp. 19–35.

[64] On the logic behind exemptions and derogations in the energy sector see K. Talus, 'First Interpretation of Energy Market Directives by European Court of Justice—Case C-17/03, Vereniging voor Energie', 24 *Journal of Energy & Natural Resources Law* (2006), p. 39.

[65] Also the different cultures, traditions, and approaches to energy as a good will undoubtedly have an effect. In France, for example, supply of energy for the population is a central public service function. For France, the national energy company is an element of national independence. Thus energy companies in France have a more central role than, for example, in the Nordic countries. For this see A. Guimaraes-Purokoski, 'Vertikaalinen toimivallanjako EU-oikeudessa. Tutkimus Yhteisön Toimivallan Kehittymisestä Energia-alalla Sekä Julkisen Palvelun Velvoitteen ja Yleispalvelun Sääntelystä Sähkön Sisämarkkinoilla', *Suomalainen Lakimiesyhdistys* (2009), pp. 319–29.

[66] Case COMP/39.388—German Electricity Wholesale Market and Case COMP/39.389—German Electricity Balancing Market. Press release, 'Antitrust: Commission welcomes E.ON proposals for structural remedies to increase competition in German electricity market' (MEMO/08/132), 28.2.2008. See also Summary of Commission Decision of 26 November 2008 relating to a proceeding under Article 82 of the EC Treaty and Article 54 of the EEA Agreement, 8.

[67] Case COMP/39.402—RWE gas foreclosure. Press release, 'Antitrust: Commission welcomes RWE proposals for structural remedies to increase competition in German gas market', (MEMO/08/355), 31.5.2008. For another divestiture (Vattenfall), see Commission press release, 'Energy Commissioner, Andris Piebalgs, welcomes Vattenfall's decision to sell their transmission grids' (MEMO/08/527), 25.7.2008. The Vattenfall case does not seem to be related to a threat of competition law enforcement.

[68] Case COMP/39.315—ENI. 'Antitrust: Commission welcomes ENI's structural remedies proposal to increase competition in the Italian gas market' (MEMO/10/29), 4.2.2010.

enforcement of competition law obligations in the energy sector. By means of this strategy, the Commission seeks to curb the impact of sector-specific regulation regardless of the choice left to the Member States. The Commission's press release indicates that all three companies involved in the above-mentioned cases were behind the proposed structural remedies[69] (ownership unbundling) to settle the ongoing antitrust investigations against them. On the basis of this development, one might say that, while the Commission may have lost the battle on the regulatory front, it is winning the war through the use of general competition law.

3.3.2 The Third Country Clause or '*Lex* Gazprom'

The third country clause, popularly known as the 'Gazprom clause' or '*Lex* Gazprom', is a related issue.[70] This provision will subject operations and investments in the EU market by vertically integrated companies from third countries to the requirement of prior EU consent. The objective of the provision is to ensure that EU interests are secured. In practice, this means avoidance of situations where an external non-EU undertaking has control over EU networks. The decision-making power in this respect will be divided between the Commission and the Member States. Article 11 of Directive 2009/73/EC provides that each Member State retains the competence to decide whether or not to allow a vertically integrated third country company to invest, or whether such investment would be detrimental to its energy security. Here, in addition to the unbundling regime, the general effect on energy security will have to be taken into consideration. The role of the Commission is consultative. Each Member State retains the ultimate power of veto where its energy security is at stake.

Although Article 11 makes a reference to international law and notes that the Commission must take into account the possible agreements 'concluded with one or more third countries to which the Community is a party and which addresses the issues of security of supply', it has been suggested that this provision is at odds

---

[69] While the Commission press release suggests that the initiative came from the companies involved in the investigations, the timing and the Commission activities suggest that the initiative could have come from the Commission. Why would a company that has fiercely opposed ownership unbundling (e.g., see *Financial Times*, E.ON defiant on break-up plan, 4.10.2007) suddenly make a complete change in its opinion, unless it was pressured to do so? The developments under the general competition law regime could also have wider implications, given that Article 52 of third gas market directive provides for a review procedure and requires the Commission to propose further measures in the event that the unbundling regime of the third package proves to be insufficient. If this were to prove the case, would Germany, with two of its main energy companies already being forced to unbundle ownership, still have an incentive to oppose ownership unbundling? While this is, to some extent, a criticism of the Commission approach, it is only partially so. The current situation is also a result of the institutional arrangements chosen by the Member States and the Commission's dual role in the EU. It has an obligation to initiate legislative action where this is necessary and an obligation to enforce EU competition rules. In this case, the Commission is addressing the same issue on both fronts.

[70] A first analysis of this provision is offered in S.S. Haghighi, 'Establishing an External Policy to Guarantee Energy Security in Europe? A Legal Analysis', in M. Roggenkamp and U. Hammer (eds), *European Energy Law Report VI* (Antwerp: Intersentia 2009), pp. 155–88. Haghighi raises certain concerns over some economic and legal effects of this clause.

with the ECT[71] and other instruments of public international law.[72] One practical problem with this provision is the supervision of unbundling in third countries.

Clearly, the 'Gazprom clause' is an extremely political provision. However, given the significance of this clause, the political issues should be separated from more tangible commercial and security-related factors. For example, given that a strong presence in the EU markets means strong commercial interest in maintaining supplies (that generate revenue) and that the penetration of a new company into downstream markets would create new competition, the effects of this clause are somewhat obscure. In this area, company-level linkages can also be seen as strengthening security of supply.

The 'Gazprom clause' may also affect future cooperation between the EU and Russia.[73] The EU emphasizes its need for greater reciprocity in terms of investment and access to the Russian market. However, it is very unlikely that this move will help to achieve the goal of opening up the Russian energy sector to EU companies, or facilitating negotiations relating to a 'new ECT'.

The final issue raised in the context of ownership unbundling is the compatibility of ownership unbundling with general EU law. Even if the ownership unbundling discussion in the context of the third energy law package is now over, it is very likely that the same discussion will re-emerge at some point.[74]

3.3.3 Ownership Unbundling and EU Law

Various authors have suggested that there are considerable concerns regarding the legal enforceability of the introduction of ownership unbundling.[75] Issues raised in this context usually relate to: (i) Article 345 TFEU; (ii) the EU's competences, and the limits of Article 114 TFEU in particular; and (iii) the right to property under the ECHR and the EU legal order.

In essence, the claim is that certain EU and ECHR legal provisions are obstacles to the EU-level adoption of mandated ownership unbundling and that the European

---

[71] A. Willems, J. Sul, and Y. Benizri, 'Unbundling As a Defence Mechanism Against Russia: Is the EU Missing the Point?' 2 *OGEL* (2009).

[72] V. Van Hoorn, '"Unbundling", "Reciprocity" and the European Internal Energy Markets: WTO Consistency and Broader Implications for Europe,' 18 *European Energy and Environmental Law Review* (2009), pp. 51–76.

[73] This concern was also raised, among others, by V. Van Hoorn, '"Unbundling", "Reciprocity" and the European Internal Energy Markets: WTO Consistency and Broader Implications for Europe,' 18 *European Energy and Environmental Law Review* (2009), pp. 51–76. The author notes that the 'EU is building a fence around its garden'. The same concern is noted in S.S. Haghighi, 'Establishing an External Policy to Guarantee Energy Security in Europe? A Legal Analysis', in M. Roggenkamp and U. Hammer (eds), *European Energy Law Report VI* (Antwerp: Intersentia 2009), pp. 155–88.

[74] It is also worth repeating that the same discussion took place in the context of the introduction of TPA.

[75] A. Willems, J. Sul, and Y. Benizri, 'Unbundling As a Defence Mechanism Against Russia: Is the EU Missing the Point?' 2 *OGEL* (2009), M. Hunt, 'Ownership Unbundling: the Main Legal Issues in a Controversial Debate', in B. Delvaux, M. Hunt, and K. Talus (eds), *EU Energy Law and Policy Issues* (Brussels: Euroconfidentiel 2008), and J.-C. Pielow, G. Brunekreeft, and E. Ehlers, 'Legal and Economic Aspects of Ownership Unbundling in the EU', 2(2) *Journal of World Energy Law and Business* (2009).

courts would annul the provisions transposing this idea into law. First, there is Article 345 TFEU. The objective of this provision is to regulate the division of competence between the EU and the Member States, without conferring absolute immunity on property rights from the application of EU law. A certain degree of unification of property law is unavoidable in view of the process of economic integration.[76] Moreover, the purpose of Article 345 TFEU is not to evade the enforceability of the fundamental rules of the Treaty with regard to national systems of property ownership.[77] This means that to some extent the EU has competence to deal with issues involving property rights, and also that national legislators must take into account the EU's general principles and interest in regulating the means of acquisition and enjoyment of property. Article 345 TFEU is not an obstacle to ownership unbundling if we take the view that it will lead to more efficient competition, considered as a matter of public interest. Neither does ownership unbundling exclude Member States' freedom to choose the property ownership regime under which they wish to place the transmission system (e.g. domestic implementation of EU-mandated ownership unbundling could stipulate that the transmission network must remain in public ownership).

Secondly, the focus moves to the legal basis for EU action: Article 114 TFEU. Again, if we agree with the view that ownership unbundling is the best way to achieve a level playing field and agree with the assessment of both national and EU-level regulators that, despite the legislative action taken thus far, a level playing field has not yet been established, then it is clear that further action is necessary. Clearly, ownership unbundling alone is not the 'silver bullet' for securing perfectly-functioning EU energy markets. It is, however, one element of a legislative set up that can deliver efficiently-functioning markets.[78] Therefore, ownership unbundling would eliminate obstacles to the functioning of the internal market.

Thirdly, there is the question of proportionality: in essence, this general principle of EU law requires that there must be a reasonable (proportional) relationship between the means used and the objective desired.[79] While certain tests of proportionality have been developed through the case law of the ECJ,[80] the proportionality test is not always applied in an identical way in every case. In particular, the degree of judicial scrutiny varies according to the background and aims of the provision in question. For example, the Court has ruled that, in matters concerning the common agricultural policy, the EU legislature has a discretionary power, which corresponds to the

---

[76] F. Campbell-White, 'Property Rights: A Forgotten Issue under the Union', in N.A. Neuwhal and A. Rosas (eds), *The European Union and Human Rights* (The Hague: M. Nijhoff 1995), p. 249.

[77] Case C-302/97, *Konle* [1999] ECR I-3099, para. 38; Case C-300/01, *Salzmann* [2003] ECR I-4899, para. 39; Case C-452/01, *Ospelt* [2003] ECR I-9743, para. 24.

[78] While it may be argued that in this case the applicability of Article 95 is rather clear, it may also be noted that the harmonizing effect that is required is not always clear: see, e.g., Case C-217/04, *UK v Parliament and the Council* [2006] ECR I-3771.

[79] See Case 66/82, *Fromançais* [1983] ECR 395, para. 8; Case 181/84, *Man (Sugar)* [1985] ECR 2889, para. 20; Case C-118/89, *Lingenfelser* [1990] ECR 2637, para. 12.

[80] T. Tridimas, 'Proportionality in Community Law: Searching for the Appropriate Standard of Scrutiny', in E. Ellis (ed.), *The Principle of Proportionality in the Laws of Europe* (Oxford: Hart Publishing 1999), p. 68.

political responsibilities imposed on it by the Treaty. Consequently, the legality of a measure adopted in that sphere can be affected only if the measure is manifestly inappropriate having regard to the objective which the competent institution intends to pursue.[81] The Court takes the same approach in cases concerning measures adopted in the sphere of the common commercial policy.[82] Finally, and for present purposes, most significantly, the Court has repeatedly stated that the European legislator has broad discretionary power in situations which require the evaluation of a complex economic situation.[83] Again, the key question comes back to whether ownership unbundling is the appropriate way to bring about competitive energy markets (an objective considered to be in the general interest of the EU). To quote the late Thomas Wälde: 'Save recourse to God, there is no definite method of precisely predicting the future result of economic policies in the interplay with market, institutional, political and other economic and social forces. Accordingly, one cannot require more than a reasonable and plausible relation of the method chosen to the accepted objective within the overall framework of the Treaty.'[84]

The fourth main question raised is whether ownership unbundling is contrary to the case law of the European Court of Human Rights (ECtHR) or the principles developed by the ECJ to protect the right to property and the freedom to pursue an economic activity. These two rights are regularly referred to in tandem, largely following the reasoning and approach taken in the *Nold* case.[85] In *Nold*, the Court expressly denied that these rights were absolute, affirming that they 'must be viewed in the light of the social function of the property and activities protected thereunder'.[86] In others words, prima facie restrictions on property rights and the freedom to pursue an economic activity can justifiably be set aside in the public interest. What counts as being in 'the public interest' must be interpreted in the light of the values and aims of the EU's legal order.[87] Similarly, the Court noted in *Hauer*[88] that the European legislator can establish the basis for restrictive regulation of the use of property within the terms of the pursuit of the general EU interest.

---

[81] Case 265/87, *Schräder* [1989] ECR 2237; Joined Cases C-296 and 307/93, *French Republic and Ireland v Commission of the European Communities* [1996] ECR 795; Case C-120/99, *Italian Republic v EU Council* [2001] ECR 7997; Case T-125/01, *José Martí Peix* [2003] ECR II-865.

[82] Case T-162/94, *NMB and others* [1996] ECR II-427; Case C-150/94, *United Kingdom of Great Britain and Northern Ireland v Council of the European Union* [1998] ECR I-7235; Case T-340/99, *Arne Mathisen* [2002] ECR II-2905.

[83] Case 138/79, *Roquette* [1980] ECR 3333; Case C-4/96, *Northern Ireland Fish Producers' Organisation Ltd* [1998] ECR I-681; Case C-179/95, *Kingdom of Spain v EU Council* [1999] ECR I-6475.

[84] T. Wälde, 'Comment on Einar Hope's Chapter with a Critical Review of Legal and Policy Arguments Driving the Discussion on Third Party Access', in E. Mestmäcker (ed.), *Natural Gas in the Internal Market—A Review of Energy Policy* (London-Dordrecht-Boston: Graham & Trotman 1993), p. 240. Thomas Wälde's opinion relates to the introduction of TPA but given that the arguments of those opposing TPA are the same as those today opposing ownership unbundling, we can extend the argument to cover ownership unbundling.

[85] Case C-4/73, *Nold* [1974] ECR 491. This is the first case in which the applicant maintained an infringement of a right 'akin to proprietary right' and the 'right to the free pursuit of business activity' (para. 12).

[86] *Nold*, para. 14.

[87] *Nold*.

[88] Case C-44/79, *Hauer* [1979] ECR, I-3727.

As for the freedom to pursue trade or professional activities, the Court has ruled that if the applicant can continue to pursue its previous economic activity, the substance of that right is protected.[89] Thus, measures, which interfere with the way in which the companies operate are permitted unless they are manifestly inappropriate in relation to the objective pursued. Furthermore, according to the Court's case law, the substance of the right to property is protected if the compensation provided takes the value of the investments made into consideration.[90]

To date, the Court has settled disputes concerning measures that regulate the use of property (how and how much to produce), whereas in the present case it is a matter of regulating access to property and excluding the energy producers from ownership of network assets. Because of this difference and because of the duality of the human rights regimes in Europe, it is necessary to examine the case law of the ECtHR.[91] Here, one particularly interesting case is *James v UK*,[92] where the ECtHR characterized a compulsory transfer of property as deprivation of property.[93]

Given that the ECtHR has established that there is interference with the right to property, the principle of proportionality is again the key issue in the reasoning of the Strasbourg Court. The ECtHR uses the proportionality principle as a counter weight to the margin of appreciation doctrine.[94] In cases dealing with deprivation of property, the provision and amount of any compensation given is one of the elements of proportionality.[95] As regards the amount of compensation in the *James* case, the ECtHR ruled that 'legitimate objectives of "public interest", such as pursued in measures of economic reform or measures designed to achieve greater social justice, may call for less than reimbursement of the full market value'.[96]

As regards the freedom to pursue an economic activity, ownership unbundling affects the possibility of energy producers pursuing network activities. However, companies active in both production and transmission are not forced to give up all their previous economic activities. If one considers the production of energy to be a company's main commercial activity, interference with the freedom to pursue an economic activity can be considered as proportionate to the objective sought by the interference, since affected companies will be able to continue with their

---

[89] Joined Cases C-184 and 223/02, *Kingdom of Spain and Republic of Finland v European Parliament and Council of the European Union* [2004] ECR I-7789; T-216/05, *Mebrom NV* [2007] ECR 0000, para. 88.

[90] Case C-5/88, *Wachauf* [1989] ECR 2609, para. 19.

[91] The ECJ recognises that the ECtHR plays the role of a guide in the development of the fundamental rights protection: see G. R. Iglesias, 'The Court of Justice, Principles of EC Law, Court Reform and Constitutional Adjudication', 15 *European Business Law Review* (2004), p. 1120.

[92] *James v United Kingdom* [1986] 8 EHRR 123 (ECtHR).

[93] *James v United Kingdom*, para. 40.

[94] See, Y. Arai-Takahashi, *The Margin of Appreciation Doctrine and the Principle of Proportionality in the jurisprudence of the ECHR* (Antwerp: Intersentia 2002).

[95] See, e.g., the discussion in A. Johnston, 'Take-or-Pay Contracts for Renewables: An Analysis of European Legal Issues', in B. Delvaux, M. Hunt, and K. Talus (eds), *EU Energy Law and Policy Issues—ELRF Collection* (1st edition) (Rixensaert: Euroconfidentiel 2008), p. 269, at pp. 277–84; and see also S. Praduroux and K. Talus, 'The Third Legislative Package and Ownership Unbundling in the Light of the European Fundamental Rights Discourse', 9(3) *CNRI* (2009).

[96] *James v United Kingdom*, para. 54.

primary activity. The same argument can of course be used where the main activity of an undertaking is transmission. This conclusion is in line with the case law of the ECtHR.[97] In the *Van Marle* case, where the applicants complained about new legislation which precluded them from continuing to exercise the profession of 'accountants', the Strasbourg Court found no breach of Article 1 of the First Protocol to the ECHR.[98]

In essence, it may be argued that there are no insurmountable legal obstacles if the EU legislature were to decide to adopt ownership unbundling as the only model. This option would guarantee a level playing field without the regulatory intervention coupled with oversight that the current regime requires. However, although this policy choice does not face serious legal obstacles, it must clear daunting political hurdles. These hurdles seem to have posed enough of a difficulty to block full ownership unbundling as far as the third legislative package is concerned. Instead, more exemptions and derogations were added to the EU energy *acquis*, some of which are examined in detail in section 3.4.

3.4 Exemptions and Derogations

As hinted at in sections 3.1–3.3, the number of exemptions and derogations provided from otherwise applicable rules are a notable feature of EU energy law. These exemptions have been seen as a necessary component in the process of transformation from national and monopolistic markets into a competitive and EU-wide market. The pros and cons of the exemptions have been discussed in various commentaries, and they have been seen as either positive[99] or negative factors in EU energy law.[100] While it is clear that such exemptions are a necessary component of the transitional legal regime which will modify the nature of EU

---

[97] The European Convention on Human Rights does not provide for the protection of the freedom to pursue an economic activity, but the Strasbourg court protects the economic enterprise by means of Article 1 of the First Protocol to the ECHR.

[98] *Van Marle v The Netherlands* [1986] 8 EHRR 483.

[99] C. Jones, *EU Energy Law—The Internal Energy Market* (Leuven: Claeys & Casteels 2004), p. 155 and C. Jones, *EU Energy Law—The Internal Energy Market: The Third Liberalisation Package* (Leuven: Claeys & Casteels 2010), p. 443. In the opinion of Jones (et al.), it is not surprising that such exemptions exist but that they are both limited in numbers and strictly controlled. While not disputing the first point, it could also be claimed that the number of different options to derogate is not, in fact, limited. Ultimately this is a question of how one wants to see the issue. Clearly, some exemptions are necessary, but not all.

[100] T. Van Der Vijver, 'Exemptions to Third Party Access for New Infrastructures in European Community Gas Sector—The Exception that Defies the Rule?', 29 *European Competition Law Review* (2008), pp. 229–37. The author notes that while this approach has certain positive elements, the relaxed application of Article 22 might 'harm TPA's status as a legal principle when it comes to new infrastructures' (at p. 137). Similar, but more positive, views are presented by the same author in T. Van Der Vijver, 'Commission Policy on Third-Party Access Exemption Requests for New Gas Infrastructure', in M. Roggenkamp and U. Hammer (eds), *European Energy Law Report VI* (Antwerp: Intersentia 2009), pp. 115–30. Also, based on my own understanding that derives from various presentations of the Commission officials in various conferences and seminars and some subsequent discussions, the Commission seems to be internally divided on this question.

energy markets in a very profound way, it may also be noted that, over the shorter term, each new exemption or derogation is an obstacle on the path towards a level playing field. Therefore, their number should be kept to a minimum.

This section examines some of the most significant exemptions and derogations: the exemption allowing the imposition of a public services obligation; unbundling of small companies; the derogation for emergent or isolated markets; and finally the exemption for major new infrastructure.

3.4.1 Public Service Obligations (PSOs)

Clearly, it is not always possible to offer public services based on pure market mechanisms alone.[101] This is particularly the case where remote and sparsely populated areas are concerned. Full geographical coverage is often difficult to achieve through market-based mechanisms. To remedy this, and other shortcomings (universal service and security of supply, among others), the internal energy market directives offer the possibility to grant exclusive rights.

Article 3(2) of both the third electricity and gas market directives provide that Member States may impose on undertakings operating in either of these two sectors 'public service obligations which may relate to security, including security of supply, regularity, quality and price of supplies [...]. Such obligations must be well defined, transparent and cannot discriminate between companies. It is furthermore added that in relation to security of supply [...] Member States may introduce the implementation of long-term planning, taking into account the possibility of third parties seeking access to the system'.[102] In addition, the Member States should implement appropriate measures to achieve the objectives of social and economic cohesion, environmental protection—which may include means to combat climate change—and to ensure security of supply.

In the name of the PSO, Member States may decide not to apply a number of provisions of the directives where their application would obstruct the performance, in law or in fact, of the obligations imposed on undertakings in the general economic interest.[103] According to the ECJ, the public-service requirements are to be interpreted on a national basis.[104] Where a Member State decides to have recourse to these provisions, it is required that the measure taken does not restrict competition and trade between the Member States more than necessary in order

---

[101] D. Helm, J. Kay, and D. Thompson, 'Energy Policy and the Role of the State in the Market for Energy', in Paul Stevens, *The Economics of Energy Vol. II* (Cheltenham: Edward Elgar Publishing House 2000), p. 415. See also L. Hancher and S. Janssen, 'Shared Competences and Multi-Faceted Concepts—European Legal Framework for Security of Supply', in B. Barton, C. Redgwell, A. Ronne, and D. N. Zillman, *Energy Security—Managing Risk in a Dynamic Legal and Regulatory Environment* (Oxford: OUP 2004), pp. 87–8.

[102] For an overview and an in-depth assessment of various provisions relating to public service objectives in electricity and gas market directives, see C. Jones, *EU Energy Law Vol. 1—The Internal Energy Market* (Leuven: Claeys & Casteels 2004), pp. 113–48.

[103] Article 3(5) of the Gas Market Directive.

[104] Case C-439/06, *Citiworks AG Flughafen Leipzig v Halle GmbH, Bundesnetzagentur* [2008] ECR I-3913, para. 59.

to fulfil the legitimate general interest objectives.[105] The payment of compensation relating to the accomplishment of a public service obligation is not, in principle, considered state aid.[106] However, when examining the question of compensation, the Commission applies the state aid test laid down by the Court[107] in the *Altmark* case.[108]

In discussing the early PSO regime, Hancher and Janssen have noted how the wording of that directive left much scope for subsidiarity.[109] The same can be noted here. The measures adopted by various Member States therefore vary considerably, but must, however, be reported to the Commission.[110] Based on these measures, the Commission will prepare a report and may issue recommendations on appropriate measures to be taken at national level to achieve high public service standards, or measures intended to prevent market foreclosure.[111] The degree of development from the first energy market directives is noticeable. Where the first directives only imposed an obligation to inform the Commission of PSOs that necessitated derogation from these directives, the wording used in the second and third directives requires Member States to inform the Commission of all PSOs, regardless of whether they call for derogations from the directives. This development allows the Commission to acquire information about measures that might distort competition even if they do not require derogation from the directives.[112] It also provides the Commission with information on the overall picture, thus giving it

---

[105] Case C-439/06, *Citiworks AG Flughafen Leipzig v Halle GmbH, Bundesnetzagentur* [2008] ECR I-3913, para. 60. 'However, in order to do so, the Member States must, on the one hand, ascertain whether an unrestricted right of access to the systems would obstruct the performance by the system operators of their public-service obligations and, on the other, determine whether that performance cannot be achieved by other means which do not impact adversely on the right of access to the systems, which is one of the rights enshrined in [the EC energy *acquis*].'

[106] Implementing Note by the Commission concerning the public service obligation. Available at: <http://ec.europa.eu./comm/energy/electricity/legislation/doc/notes_for_implementation_2004/public_service_obligations_En.pdf>. The Commission has been very careful to highlight that these guidelines do not bind the Commission. The issue however is not as simple as it might seem. These guidelines are part of a wider category of 'soft law' comprising a number of non-binding Community instruments such as declarations, resolutions, recommendations, notes of implementation, notices, and codes of conduct. These guidelines are issued by the Commission and further to the principle of legal certainty and the principle of *patere legem quam ipse fecisti*, the Commission should generally be bound by its guidelines. (See, among others, Case T-105/95, *WWF UK v Commission* [1997] ECR II-313.) Therefore it could be suggested that these guidelines should have some effect on the future decision-making of the Commission. On the other hand, the Commission can of course always claim that the guidelines did affect its decision-making but that the particularities of a given case nevertheless dictated a certain outcome.

[107] Note of DG Energy and Transport on Directives 2003/54/EC and 2003/55/EC on the internal market in electricity and natural gas—public service obligations—16.1.2004. Available at:<http://ec.europa.eu/energy/electricity/legislation/doc/notes_for_implementation_2004/public_service_obligations_en.pdf>.

[108] Case C-280/00, *Altmark* [2003] ECR I-7747. This case is discussed in Chapter 4, Section 4.7 on State aids.

[109] L. Hancher and S. Janssen, 'Shared Competences and Multi-Faceted Concepts—European Legal Framework for Security of Supply', in B. Barton, C. Redgwell, A. Ronne, and D. N. Zillman (eds), *Energy Security—Managing Risk in a Dynamic Legal and Regulatory Environment* (Oxford: OUP 2004), p. 97.

[110] Article 3(11) gas directive and Article 3(15) electricity directive.

[111] Article 52(2) gas directive and Article 47(2) electricity directive.

[112] C. Jones, *EU Energy Law—The Internal Energy Market* (Leuven: Claeys & Casteels 2004), p. 130.

the ability to examine the potential effect of a web of PSOs. It may be that granting a single special or exclusive right or other kind of PSO has no significant harmful effect, but that a web of similar grants of rights does have such an effect. This translates into a need to consider the overall effects of various measures and choices at the EU level.

At a more individual level, Article 3(3) of the Electricity Market Directive obliges Member States to take appropriate measures to protect final customers and ensure that there are adequate safeguards to protect vulnerable customers, including measures to help them avoid disconnection. In this regard, the European Parliament pushed the introduction of a new provision in the third electricity market directive (Article 3(7)) which prohibits the disconnection of electricity from 'vulnerable customers' at critical times—i.e. it is intended to prevent pensioners and disabled people being cut off during the winter[113] (although on the basis of subsidiarity the meaning of 'vulnerable customer' is left for Member States to define). The appointment of a supplier of last resort is another new and related concept, which emerged largely because of liberalization and relates to security of supply from a final-customer perspective. Further to Article 3(3) of both electricity and gas market directives, Member States may appoint a supplier of last resort for customers connected to the energy networks. Prior to liberalization of the market, the state monopoly guaranteed the energy supply. This has changed with market liberalization. Market players are now exposed to a number of risks which are inherent in the market-based mechanism. In the worst-case scenario, this may result in a supplier becoming bankrupt as has in fact happened in a large number of cases in, for instance, the UK, the Netherlands, and California. Because of this, Member States may appoint a supplier of last resort which must step in and provide the affected customers with energy until a new supplier has been identified.[114]

The issues of PSOs and security of supply were also debated before the ECJ in 2010. In response to a request for a preliminary ruling from Italy, the Court had the opportunity to pronounce on price security as part of the PSO under Article 3 of the second gas market directive.[115] The case concerned an Italian decree that allowed the national energy market authority (Autorità per l'energia elettrica e il gas (AEEG)) to set 'reference prices' permitting the determination of price levels for supply of natural gas. The decree in question stipulated as follows:

'To comply with the Community law provisions on universal service, [the AEEG] shall set standard terms for the supply of the service and establish, on a transitory basis and based on the actual costs of the service, reference prices ... for supplies of natural gas to domestic customers, which distributors or suppliers shall, within the scope of their public service obligations, incorporate into their commercial offerings (providing also the possibility of a choice between differentiated tariff packages and time tariffs). Article 1, paragraph 375,

---

[113] See EP proceedings of 18 June 2008, amendment 155. (Ref. P6_TA(2008)0294).
[114] U. Hammer, 'Introduction' in M. Roggenkamp and U. Hammer (eds), *European Energy Law Report I* (Cambridge: Intersentia 2004), p. 178. See also T. Vermeir, 'Electricity Market Liberalisation and Supplier of Last Resort in Belgium', in M. Roggenkamp and U. Hammer (eds), *European Energy Law Report I* (Cambridge: Intersentia 2004), pp. 221–33.
[115] Case C-265/08, *Federutility and others* [2010] ECR, p. I-03377.

of Law No 266 of 23 December 2005 ... authorises, within sixty days of the date of entry into force of the law converting this decree, of measures for the protection of consumers in particular circumstances of health or economic disadvantage. The powers of supervision and intervention of the Authority to protect the rights of consumers are also maintained, including in cases of established and unjustified price increases and variations in the terms of service to customers who have not yet exercised their right of choice.'

The applicants in the main proceedings had argued that, as from the date of the full liberalization of the EU natural gas markets, 1 July 2007, the prices should be defined only through the supply/demand mechanism and, as such, the setting of references prices after that date was contrary to EU law.

After noting that in principle price security can arguably be part of the PSO the Member States may decide to impose on private undertakings, the Court's examination of the matter focused essentially on the proportionality test as applied to the PSO and the use of reference prices. The Court concluded that the second gas market directive did not preclude national regulation permitting determination of the price level for the supply of natural gas by the definition of 'reference prices', such as those at issue in the main proceedings, after 1 July 2007, *provided* that such intervention:

- pursues a general economic interest consisting in maintaining the price of the supply of natural gas to final consumers at a reasonable level having regard to the reconciliation which Member States must make, taking account of the situation in the natural gas sector, between the objective of liberalization and that of the necessary protection of final consumers pursued by Directive 2003/55;

- compromises the free determination of prices for the supply of natural gas after 1 July 2007 only insofar as is necessary to achieve such an objective in the general economic interest and, consequently, for a period that is necessarily limited in time; and

- is clearly defined, transparent, non-discriminatory and verifiable, and guarantees equal access for EU gas companies to consumers.

By leaving the proportionality test to the national court, the ECJ in effect also left the price security issue to the national court. The question raised by this judgment is that of whether the national court was adequately equipped to carry out such a balancing exercise. This is particularly the case since it requires taking into consideration the various stages of progress in the national natural gas markets and the balancing of market liberalization and competition with the need to provide for security of supply. Conducting this balancing exercise, which is also required by the Security of Supply Regulation,[116] calls for advanced understanding of the EU and national energy markets and their regulation.

---

[116] The security of supply regulation requires that the measures taken to safeguard the security of gas supply do not unduly distort competition and/or the effective functioning of the internal gas market (Articles 3(6), 10(4), and 10(7)).

3.4.2 Unbundling of Small Companies

Both of the current energy market directives provide an exemption for small distribution companies. Further to Article 26 of both the electricity and gas directives, Member States may decide not to apply the unbundling requirements contained in the energy market directive to an integrated electricity or natural gas undertaking serving fewer than 100,000 connected customers. On this point, it should be noted that even in these cases the exemption does not cover the obligation for account unbundling. The underlying reason for this derogation is the need to consider the particular situation of smaller distribution companies. In these cases, it may be assumed that the added value of the implementation of the unbundling regime is not significant enough to outweigh the cost of restructuring the company.

While the Commission has explained that the 100,000 customers threshold was considered an appropriate figure for the EU as a whole,[117] it seems rather arbitrary. The logic behind the exemption is clear and certainly not disputed, but the specific threshold decided upon is nevertheless questionable. However, this potential problem is mitigated by the fact that Member States are not obliged to adopt this approach and are free to apply lower thresholds or require unbundling from all distribution companies. However, the choice should reflect national circumstances[118] rather than constituting a method of protectionism. The Commission's suggestion was to take a gradual approach in which the larger DSOs, which are still eligible for the exemption from legal unbundling, would be required to adopt functional unbundling, or at least some elements of functional unbundling; and only the smaller DSOs—in terms of the national context—would be exempted from all unbundling requirements.[119]

However, where a company controls several separate network companies, it is the aggregate number of customers that counts. Otherwise it would be easy to circumvent the rule and take advantage of the exemption regime (through the creation of several small and separate distribution companies owned and controlled by a single entity).[120]

Finland is a good example of the use of this exemption. Finland has adopted a two-stage threshold: 50,000 and 100,000 customers for certain unbundling requirements in electricity markets. As distinct from the situation with respect to electricity markets, this exemption does not apply in gas markets, because in this area Finland has the benefit of another exemption: that of isolated markets.

---

[117] Note of DG Energy & Transport on Directives 2003/54/EC and 2003/55/EC on the internal market in electricity and natural gas, 16 January 2004, 'The unbundling regime', p. 17.
[118] Note of DG Energy & Transport on Directives 2003/54/EC and 2003/55/EC on the internal market in electricity and natural gas, 16 January 2004, 'The unbundling regime'.
[119] Note of DG Energy & Transport on Directives 2003/54/EC and 2003/55/EC on the internal market in electricity and natural gas, 16 January 2004, 'The unbundling regime'.
[120] Note of DG Energy & Transport on Directives 2003/54/EC and 2003/55/EC on the internal market in electricity and natural gas, 16 January 2004, 'The unbundling regime', p. 16.

3.4.3 Emergent and Isolated Gas Markets

Article 49 of the gas market directive offers another possibility to derogate from the unbundling requirements and certain other provisions. Where a Member State is not directly connected to the interconnected system of any other Member State and has only one main external supplier (meaning that one supplier has more than 75 per cent of the market), it may derogate from certain requirements of the gas market directive, including the unbundling requirements, the market opening requirement, and the authorization procedure for new gas facilities. The conditions for the derogation for an isolated market cease to exist if one of the above conditions is eliminated. Finland is an example of such an area. The Finnish natural gas markets are not connected to any other Member State markets. The only pipeline into or out of the country is the supply pipeline from Russia.

Article 49 also contains an interesting section which states: 'Articles 4, 9, 37 and/or 38 shall not apply to Estonia, Latvia and/or Finland until any of those Member States is directly connected to the interconnected system of any Member State other than Estonia, Latvia, Lithuania and Finland.' This section became crucial (and political) when the Lithuanian government announced that 'Lithuania is not able to use an exemption provided by the EU Energy Directive, therefore the Baltic country must separate its gas supply from gas transmission through its gas pipelines'.[121] To understand why this would be controversial, it is sufficient to explain that Gazprom holds a 37.1 per cent shareholding in the Lithuanian gas company.

Under a strict interpretation, Lithuania's approach seems correct. The wording of Article 49 does not directly state that it applies to Lithuania, but only to Estonia, Latvia, and Finland. However, if instead one looks at the rationale of the provision and the fact that the same provision goes on to say that the 'subparagraph [referring to Estonia, Latvia, and Finland] is without prejudice to derogations under the first subparagraph of this paragraph' the issue becomes much more complicated. It is most likely (though this is not clear) that the correct interpretation is that as this is an exemption from the rule, it must be interpreted strictly. This approach would be in line with the Court's case law in the third party access cases.[122] However, one could arguably also look at the question in terms of the rationale of the provision.

The provision states:

'Member States not directly connected to the interconnected system of any other Member State and having only one main external supplier may derogate from Articles 4, 9, 37 and/or 38. A supply undertaking having a market share of more than 75% shall be considered to be a main supplier.'

In other words, two criteria must be fulfilled: no connection and only one supplier. Lithuania clearly meets the second one: Gazprom has over 75 per cent market share in supplies. The no-connection criterion is less clear. However, the rationale

---

[121] 'Lithuania must implement 3rd EU Energy Directive despite Russian protests' (29 November 2010) <http://www.lithuaniatribune.com/2010/11/29/ec-lithuania-must-implement-3-rd-energy-directive-despite-russian-protests/>.
[122] Case C-17/03, *VEMW and others* [2005] ECR I-4983 and Case C-439/06, *Citiworks AG Flughafen Leipzig v Halle GmbH, Bundesnetzagentur* [2008] ECR I-3913.

of the exemption for Finland and the Baltic States would suggest that this area is considered to be an 'isolated market' as a whole. Following this interpretation, Lithuania would be able to apply the first paragraph of Article 49 by simply notifying the European Commission that it will do so. Accordingly, internal Baltic connections would not be taken into account.

Similarly, an emergent market may benefit from a similar, but wider, derogation if it would, because of the implementation of the Gas Market Directive, experience substantial problems.[123] An 'emergent market' is defined in Article 2 of the Gas Market Directive as a Member State where the first commercial supply of its first long-term natural gas supply contract was made fewer than ten years earlier. This derogation can also be applied to a certain region within a Member State. A Member State may apply to the Commission for a derogation for an emergent region from the same provisions. When examining the application for an emergent region, the Commission has to take into account the following criteria: the need for infrastructure investment, which might not be economic to operate in a competitive market environment; the level of pay-back prospects for such investment; the size and maturity of the gas system in the area concerned; the prospects for the gas market concerned; the geographical size and characteristics of the area; and socio-economic and demographic factors. The Commission may not grant an exemption unless no gas transmission system has been established in the area or it has been in operation for less than ten years (or 20 years in the case of a distribution system). The temporary exemption may not exceed ten years from the date of the first gas supply in the area (or 20 years in the case of a distribution system). The 20-year exemption for a distribution network is based on the practice of Member States. Greece, at least, has granted 20-year concessions for regional distribution networks.[124] However, the conditions for derogation are examined on a case-by-case basis and the duration of the exemption cannot exceed the period objectively necessary in each case.[125]

The idea behind the derogation is that where the preconditions for free competition do not exist—either because the Member State markets have not been connected to other markets or because the emergence of a market per se is still a very recent phenomenon—the effects of certain provisions of the Directive are likely to be ineffective or even harmful.[126] It is, for example, important to understand that

---

[123] Thomas Wälde discussed the concerns of the Mediterranean countries (Spain, Portugal, Greece, and Italy) that liberalization of energy markets may impede the emergence of their national gas industries. See T. Wälde, 'Comment on Einar Hope's Chapter with a Critical Review of Legal and Policy Arguments Driving the Discussion on Third Party Access', in E. Mestmäcker (ed.), *Natural Gas in the Internal Market—A Review of Energy Policy* (London: Graham & Trotman 1993), p. 231. These concerns seem to have been covered by the exemption regimes included in the directives.

[124] C. Jones, *EU Energy Law—The Internal Energy Market* (Leuven: Claeys & Casteels 2004), p. 166.

[125] C. Jones, *EU Energy Law—The Internal Energy Market* (Leuven: Claeys & Casteels 2004), p. 167. Jones also suggests that the difference in the exemption period for the distribution and other gas infrastructure investments is due to the fact that, for example, when the initial investments in the transmission pipelines are made, they are backed by already concluded gas purchase agreements with large industrial users.

[126] Similarly, C. Jones, *EU Energy Law—The Internal Energy Market* (Leuven: Claeys & Casteels 2004), p. 159.

where capital-intensive infrastructure investment is concerned—which is required in particular in the early stages of the market—there is a need for predictable cash-flow to secure the amortization. That usually involves long-term contractual commitment, with take-or-pay elements or at least some assured quasi-monopoly involving at least temporary preferences for the sponsors to make it economically viable. The significance of the investment costs is in proportion to the risks involved and, mirroring this, the extent of the required special arrangements. Here, this pre-dictability requirement has been translated into an exemption for new emergent markets. However, if it may be concluded that the investment would be made even in the absence of an exemption, such exemption should not be granted.[127]

Article 49(3) provides that the derogation can be partially extended beyond the 10-year period, thus facilitating gradual market opening (with a negotiated access regime for ancillary services and temporary storage).

Article 49 was the key to the Court of First Instance (CFI) judgment in the Portuguese EDP merger judgement, Case T-87/2005.[128] Since Portugal qualified as an emergent market and benefited from a derogation until 2007, the market opening calendar for the Portuguese energy markets became operative only at the end of 2007. There was no real competition on the Portuguese gas markets prior to that date, as the national gas undertaking, Gas de Portugal, dominated all levels of the gas supply chain. In this scenario, the CFI concluded that the absence of competition under the derogation precluded the application of Article 2(3) of the Merger Regulation[129] because 'the creation or strengthening of a dominant posi-tion' requirement[130] could not apply in circumstances where GDP already had a monopoly on the gas supply market. As a monopoly by definition represents the ultimate dominant position, it cannot be strengthened. As to the second cri-terion of Article 2(3)—significant impediment to competition—the CFI noted that, in the absence of any competition, there was no competition that could be impeded.[131]

3.4.4 New Infrastructure

As discussed in detail above, the EU energy *acquis* provides for TPA to all transmission and distribution grids and for LNG facilities. The operator must grant third parties non-discriminatory access to their facilities and in return they earn a regulated return on their investment. However, under Article 17 of the Electricity Regulation

---

[127] C. Jones, *EU Energy Law—The Internal Energy Market* (Leuven: Claeys & Casteels 2004), p. 166.
[128] Case T-87/2005, *EDP v Commission* [2005] ECR II-03745. See also G. Conte, G. Loriot, F. Rouxel, W. Tretton, 'EDP/ENI/GDP: The Commission Prohibits a Merger Between Gas and Electricity National Incumbents', 1 *Competition Policy Newsletter* (2005), pp. 84–7.
[129] Case T-87/2005, *EDP v Commission*, para. 126.
[130] While the previous version of the EC Merger Regulation (4064/89) prohibited 'the creation or strengthening of a dominant position which would have the consequence of significantly imped-ing effective competition' the current version prohibits 'a concentration which would significantly impede effective competition, in particular as a result of the creation or strengthening of a dominant position.'
[131] Case T-87/2005, paras. 117–8.

(EC) 714/2009 and Article 36 of the third Gas Market Directive 09/73/EC, a major new piece of gas infrastructure such as interconnectors and LNG storage facilities can be exempted for a defined period of time from the mandatory TPA, tariff systems, and unbundling obligations provided that certain conditions are fulfilled.

This exemption represents a compromise between two interrelated aims: the promotion of the internal energy market and network investments, and the need to ensure free competition and TPA to the necessary infrastructure. The logic behind such an exemption is to favour long-term efficiency gains over short-term advantage. If capacity reservations and priority rights are necessary for the construction of electricity or gas infrastructure, then they must be accepted, but only for a limited period. To date, the majority of the projects exempted under this scheme have been LNG regasification terminals, but a number of pipelines and electricity interconnectors have also been exempted.[132] Given that this exemption has been discussed in much detail in many previous studies, both by myself (for gas and electricity[133]) and de Hauteclocque (for electricity[134]), this section does not go into detail about the conditions for the exemption. A short comment on the security of supply aspect of the exemption will suffice.

The security of supply aspects largely explain why both the national regulatory authorities and the Commission have been ready to apply the Article 36 exemption to a number of LNG regasification terminals.[135] In addition to enhancing internal energy security by promoting cross-border connections between Member States, this instrument has also become very significant for external energy security. Largely because LNG provides an alternative source of natural gas, with origins such as Qatar, Nigeria, or Trinidad, the EU has so far taken a very favourable attitude towards applications concerning exemption regimes for new LNG terminals. The only situation in which such an exemption would perhaps not be granted is where the owner of the facility is an incumbent and the new facility would further increase its market dominance and/or where this investment would have a negative impact on the investment conditions for other new LNG regasification plants.[136] The logic here is that the anti-competitive effects might outweigh the positive security benefits. Without disputing this logic, it may be noted that a temporary right to supra-normal profits and extended monopoly in exchange for new facilities is not necessarily a scenario that should easily be dismissed. The same logic also lies

---

[132] See the Commission website at <http://ec.europa.eu>.
[133] For gas: K. Talus, *Vertical Natural Gas Transportation Capacity, Upstream Commodity Contracts and EU Competition Law* (Alphen aan den Rijn: Kluwer Law International 2011). For electricity: K. Talus, 'First Experience under the Exemption Regime of EC Regulation 1228/2003 on Conditions for Access to the Network of Cross-Border Exchanges in Electricity', 23 *Journal of Energy and Natural Resources Law* (2005).
[134] A. de Hauteclocque, *Market Building Through Antitrust: Long-term Contract Regulation in EU Electricity Markets* (Cheltenham: Edward Elgar 2012).
[135] For the reasons behind this, see Commission staff working document on Article 22 of Directive 2003/55/EC concerning common rules for the internal market in natural gas and Article 7 of Regulation (EC) No. 1228/2003 on conditions for access to the network for cross-border exchanges in electricity (SEC(2009)642 final), 6 May 2009, p. 9.
[136] See, for example: <http://ec.europa.eu/energy/electricity/legislation/doc/notes_ for_ implementation _2004/security_of_gas_supply_en.pdf>.

behind *Estlink*[137] and *BritNed*,[138] the two decisions on electricity interconnections in which all or some of the investors were transmission system operators with a *de facto* natural monopoly status.[139]

The security of supply discussion in the *Poseidon*[140] pipeline decision is also of interest, though from a different perspective. On this matter, the Commission first noted that the new supply route would increase security of supply. It then noted that the precise effect of the project would also depend on whether it would provide access for new producer countries which had not previously supplied Italy. If this were the case, the positive effect of security of supply, both at national and EU level, would be substantially stronger.[141] The Commission thus appeared to consider the different elements and threats to security of supply.[142] In this regard, the source-related discussion also took into consideration another condition for the exemption, related to the level of risk that the investor must demonstrate. In the *Poseidon* pipeline decision, the Commission first noted that the risks involved in the case of traditional and non-traditional sources of gas supply were different. It then required that this difference in the risks involved be reflected in the final decision and that the national authorities should explicitly determine whether and to what extent different derogation periods should be granted depending on the actual origin of the gas eventually contracted for with respect to the pipeline, and amend the decision based on these factors.[143]

While security and internal market conditions speak in favour of granting these merchant exemptions, the EU competition objective of the liberalization process and the need to balance long-term (dynamic) and short-term (allocative) efficiencies, mean that proportionality constraints are increasingly rigid.

3.5 Security of Supply

The organization of the European energy markets in the pre-liberalization era provided for security of supply. The old government-centred system with monopolies guaranteed security of supply, usually successfully, although often through over-investment with costs passed on to the end-user. This way of organizing the

---

[137] <http://ec.europa.eu/energy/infrastructure/exemptions/doc/doc/electricity/ 2005_ estlink_ decision_ en.pdf>.

[138] <http://ec.europa.eu/energy/infrastructure/exemptions/doc/doc/electricity/ 2007_britned_decision_ en.pdf>.

[139] See the two OGEL special issues on electricity interconnectors edited by K. Talus and C. Zimmermann, 'Electricity Interconnectors' 2 *OGEL* (2006) and 'Electricity Interconnections' 1 *OGEL* (2007) <http://www.ogel.org>.

[140] <http://ec.europa.eu/energy/gas/infrastructure/doc/2007_05_22_poseidon_en.pdf>.

[141] <http://ec.europa.eu/energy/gas/infrastructure/doc/2007_05_22_poseidon_en.pdf>.

[142] For security of supply and its different notions, see K. Talus, 'Security of Supply—An Increasingly Political Notion', in B. Delvaux, M. Hunt, and K. Talus (eds), *EU Energy Law and Policy Issues* (Brussels: Euroconfidentiel 2008).

[143] <http://ec.europa.eu/energy/gas/infrastructure/doc/2007_05_22_poseidon_en.pdf>.

energy market was deemed inefficient from an economic point of view[144] and models drawn from the US and UK suggested that the market could achieve similar levels of security of supply at a lower cost to society. In a somewhat similar fashion, the idea (together with the general internal market impetus) was that a geographically larger market would provide a safety net for national problems. The EU has now moved away from a state-driven system towards a market-based system. It is slowly moving away from national energy markets towards an EU market and even beyond. The number of Member States of the EU has doubled. Energy markets have become more international, which means increased international energy trade and interconnections in energy networks.[145] This is particularly so in gas markets[146] but also in electricity markets (and of course oil markets, which are global). The initial ideology and plan was that the introduction of competition would contribute to security of supply. Energy would respond to the economic rules of the market, going where the prices are highest: its use, substitution and investments responding to prices. However, it is increasingly clear that this did not happen in the real world. Instead, security of supply is a more topical question nowadays than ever before (notwithstanding brief periods of oil shocks in 1973 and 1979, for example).

EU regulation of security of supply covers areas like oil, natural gas, and electricity. In addition, infrastructure security is another area in which the EU takes an increasingly interventionist approach. The EU approach has been to address security of supply issues in both the general energy market directives and in a number of specific instruments focusing on security of supply.

3.5.1 Security of Oil Supply

Oil is traded globally, its availability and price being determined by global markets. Despite efforts to reduce global dependence on oil products through increasing use of renewable energy sources and energy efficiency measures, a report published by the International Energy Agency (IEA) in 2010 confirmed the obvious: oil is likely to remain the dominant fuel in the primary energy mix until at least 2035. Rising oil prices, now often exceeding the magic figure of $100 per barrel, combined with various governmental measures aimed at boosting the use of alternative energy sources, will certainly have a dampening effect on the use of oil and other fossil fuels. But despite this, the demand for oil is set to grow steadily, mainly due to growth in demand in non-OECD countries. China alone may soon account for 50 per cent of the increased demand. In the words of the IEA, during the period from 2010 to 2035:

'Global oil production reaches 96 mb/c1, the balance of 3 mb/d coming from processing gains. Crude oil output reaches an undulating plateau of around 68–69 mb/c1 by 2020,

---

[144] C. von Hirschhausen, T. Beckers, and A. Brenck, 'Regulation and Long-Term Investment in Infrastructure Provision—Theory and Policy', 12(4) *Utilities Policy* (2004), 206–7.
[145] B. Barton et al., 'Introduction', in B. Barton, C. Redgwell, A. Rønne. and D. Zillman (eds), *Energy Security: Managing Risk in a Dynamic Legal and Regulatory Environment* (Oxford: OUP 2004), p. 7.
[146] EIA, World Energy Outlook 2011—special report: 'Are We Entering a Golden Age of Gas?' Same was noted already in IEA, '*Natural Gas Information*' (2007), I.3.

but never regains its all time peak of 70 mb/d reached in 2006, while production of natural gas liquids (NGLs) and unconventional oil grows strongly. Total OPEC production rises continually through to 2035 in this scenario, its share of global output increasing from 41% to 52%. Iraq accounts for a large share of the increase in OPEC output. By contrast, total non-OPEC oil production is broadly constant to around 2025, as rising production of NGLs and unconventional production offsets a fall in that of crude oil; thereafter, production starts to drop.'[147]

Clearly, the global oil supply situation is not going to improve much in the short to medium term. Global oil prices have steadily risen since 2003. Unlike the situation during the oil embargoes in 1973 and 1979, although prices are still affected by political events or embargoes, there has been a fundamental shift, with the primary determining factor now being the delicate balance between supply and demand for oil in the global economy, and the growing concern that the producing countries (Saudi Arabia in particular) will shortly be unable to meet the increased level of demand.[148]

A disruption of supply from a particular source or to a particular state does not affect the supply to or from other states and regions as much as is the case with gas, except for countries with logistical limitations. Supplies shipped in large tankers may be redirected to where they are most needed and where the best price can be obtained. Oil has traditionally been perceived as a highly political commodity. The 1973 oil crisis and other related incidents affecting security of oil supply, the role of OPEC and the creation of IEA, the location of oilfields and other similar factors have made the oil trade very politically sensitive. The past is littered with numerous examples of oil supply disruptions related to political events. The Iranian boycott of 1951–1953, the Suez Crisis of 1956, the Six-Day War in 1967, the Yom Kippur War in 1973, the Iranian Revolution in 1979, the Iran–Iraq War in 1980–1988, and the Gulf Crisis of 1990–1991 are just a few such examples.[149]

Unlike many other energy products and markets, the EU has not been legislating actively in respect of its oil markets. This is due to the very different character of oil markets: their global nature and lesser infrastructure dependency. However, this does not mean that there are no EU level rules relevant to the importation of crude oil into the EU area. The existing rules are mainly focused on security and information-gathering.[150]

---

[147] IEA, World Energy Outlook 2010. Available at: <http://www.worldenergyoutlook.org/>
[148] The lecture of Anas F. Alhajji for the UCL School of Energy and Resources, Australia in September 2010.
[149] P. Stevens, 'Oil Wars: Resource Nationalism and the Middle East', in P. Andrews-Speed (ed.), *International Competition for Resources: The Role of Law, the State and of Markets* (Dundee: Dundee University Press 2008), pp.11–44 and S.S. Haghighi, *Energy Security: The External Legal Relations of the European Union with Major Oil and Gas Supplying Countries* (Oxford: Hart Publishing 2007), p.13.
[150] The main legislative instrument affecting upstream oil markets is the Hydrocarbon Licensing Directive, but this Directive relates to conditions for exploration and production of hydrocarbons rather than importation. (Directive 94/22/EC of the European Parliament and of the Council of 30 May 1994 on the conditions for granting and using authorizations for the prospection, exploration and production of hydrocarbons.) Also, given the potential risk to health, safety, and the environment of oil terminals and storage, EU level regulation of chemical safety is also applicable to oil operators in the oil distribution chain. For this see Council Directive 96/82/EC of 9 December 1996 on the control of major-accident hazards involving dangerous substances, OJ L 010, 14.1.1997, pp. 13–33.

Legislative instruments on the subject of security which relate to the importation of crude oil include the emergency Oil Stocks Directive and the Regulation of Registration for Crude Oil Imports and Deliveries in the European Union. The first-mentioned directive has been modified further to harmonize EU rules with IEA regulation of emergency oil stocks.[151] The objective of the Oil Stocks Directive is to ensure a high level of security of oil supply in the EU through reliable and transparent mechanisms based on solidarity among Member States, through maintaining minimum stocks of crude oil and/or petroleum products and putting in place the necessary procedural means to deal with a serious shortage.[152] Article 3(1) of the directive required Member States to adopt, by 31 December 2012, the necessary laws, regulations, or administrative provisions to ensure that the total oil stocks maintained at all times within the EU for their benefit correspond, at the very least, to 90 days of average daily net imports or 61 days of average daily inland consumption, whichever is greater. This obligation may be imposed on 'economic operators', which presumably includes importers of crude oil.

As to other instrument mentioned, the Regulation on Registration for Crude Oil[153] obliges importers of crude oil from third countries to provide information about the characteristics of the imports to the Member State[154] where the importer is established.[155]

3.5.2 Security of Natural Gas Supply

Compared with oil, the gas trade is much more rigid and more regional. It has traditionally been bound to pipelines, the global LNG trade in more significant quantities being a more recent phenomenon.[156] Because of its network-bound character and because of the costs related to pipeline construction, gas cannot easily be redirected to new locations in the short term. LNG has changed this to some extent. Much like oil, LNG tankers can easily be re-routed to where LNG is most valued and can be sold for the best price.

As with oil, the EU is dependent on an external gas supply. However, unlike oil, gas has not traditionally been a very politically sensitive issue.[157] This, however,

---

[151] The current regime is based on Council Directive 2009/119/EC of 14 September 2009 imposing an obligation on Member States to maintain minimum stocks of crude oil and/or petroleum products, OJ L 265, 9.10.2009, pp. 9–23 (hereafter 'Oil Stock Directive') The previous regime was based on the Council Directive 2006/67/EC of 24 July 2006 imposing an obligation on Member States to maintain minimum stocks of crude oil and/or petroleum products, OJ L 217, 8.8.2006.

[152] Article 1 of the Oil Stocks Directive.

[153] Council Regulation (EC) No 2964/95 of 20 December 1995 introducing registration for crude oil imports and deliveries in the Community (OJ L 310, 22.12.1995, pp. 5–6).

[154] This information includes (i) the designation of the crude oil, including the API gravity, (ii) the quantity in barrels, (iii) the CIF price paid per barrel and (iv) the percentage sulphur content (Article 5 of Regulation (EC) No 2964/95).

[155] Article 1 of Regulation (EC) No 2964/95. The same applies to deliveries from other Member States.

[156] Today, some Member States rely quite heavily on LNG. Spain imports a large percentage of its natural gas as LNG.

[157] This is not to say that no political aspects have been involved in the gas trade. Due to the much smaller significance (and use) of natural gas in the past, these political aspects have not been as visible as for oil.

seems to be changing—one example being the discussion following the incidents between Russia and the transit states of Belarus and Ukraine.[158] Whether these difficulties were politically motivated or whether they can be explained by commercial objectives remains unclear and controversial. Be that as it may, these incidents have highlighted the political aspects of the gas trade.[159]

In brief, risks for the security of the natural gas supply in the EU can be divided into a number of separate but interrelated risks, including reserve depletion, contractual regimes, investment in gas fields and necessary infrastructure, insecurity of transit routes, and insecurity of other energy infrastructure.[160]

In addition to the provisions concerned with security of supply set out in the general internal Gas Market Directive (examined in Section 3.5.5), gas security has also been subject to two consecutive security-specific instruments. While the first Security of Gas Supply Directive, much like the Security of Electricity Supply Directive, mainly increased reporting obligations and clarified the roles of different market players (see the section on electricity below for further details), the main innovation of that first regime was the creation of a gas coordination group. The positive effect of this new institution was exemplified during the 2009 Russia–Ukraine crises. The report written by Kovacevic conveys the impression that the meeting of the EU Gas Coordination Group on 9 January of that year was a necessary component enabling Serbia to arrange emergency imports of 4.7Mcm per day from MOL and EoN.[161] Based on further insights from the 2009 gas crises, during which the gas supply was actually cut in the cold months of the winter, a new EU security of supply instrument was agreed in 2010. Regulation (EU) No 994/2010 concerning measures to safeguard security of gas supply entered into force on 2 December 2010.

The new instrument was now adopted as a regulation, instead of a directive. The content is marked by shifting more responsibility and power to EU level. This is clear, in particular, when looking at the role of the Commission, the level of detail

---

[158] For 2006, see J. Stern, 'The Russia-Ukrainian Gas Crisis of January 2006', 4(1) *OGEL* (2006); A. Belyi, 'Institutional Weaknesses of Intra-FSU Gas Trade', 4(4) *OGEL* (2006); for 2009, see S. Pirani, J. Stern, and K. Yafimava, *The Russo-Ukrainian Gas Dispute of January 2009: A Comprehensive Assessment*, NG 27 (Oxford: Institute for Energy Studies February 2009) and A. Kovacevic, *The Impact of the Russia-Ukraine Gas Crisis in South Eastern Europe*, NG 29 (Oxford: Institute for Energy Studies March 2009).

[159] It has been argued that Russian energy policy is not only guided by economic considerations but also by geopolitical, foreign policy, and security considerations. Weisser is concerned over the growing reliance on Russian gas noting that even the US is known to exert economic pressure on its NATO partners in case of significant political differences. The US/NATO reference is to the Reagan administration when it made attempts to halt further growth in Russian gas trade with Europe after the invasion of Afghanistan. H. Weisser, 'The Security of Gas Supply—A Critical Issue for Europe?' 35(2) *Energy Policy* (2007). This author is of the opinion that there are two components to the energy trade: an economic/commercial and a political one.

[160] S.S. Haghighi, *Energy Security: The External Legal Relations of the European Union with Major Oil and Gas Supplying Countries* (Oxford: Hart Publishing, 2007); J. Stern, *Security of European Natural Gas Supplies: The Impact of Import Dependence and Liberalization* (London: RIIA 2002).

[161] A. Kovacevic, 'The Impact of the Russia–Ukraine Gas Crisis in South Eastern Europe' (NG 29, Oxford Institute for Energy Studies March 2009), p. 13.

(especially when compared to the previous Security of Supply Directive) and the coordination of various issues at regional and EU level.

The detailed rules in the Regulation now cover issues such as: risk assessment; national and regional action plans; the ensuring of 30 days' supply for protected customers (including households); and the creation of a system involving different security of supply responses with different players depending on the seriousness of the disruption (industry—Member State—region—EU level), thus shifting the ultimate responsibility away from the markets to the public sector, where it arguably has always been. It also sets an N-1 standard for infrastructure. This ensures that, in the event of disruption to the single largest gas infrastructure, the capacity of the remaining infrastructure—determined by reference to the N-1 formula—is able to satisfy the total gas demand of the calculated area during a day of exceptionally high gas demand occurring with a statistical probability of once in 20 years. It is noteworthy that the provision does not require preparedness for the supply of gas, but rather the availability of the physical infrastructure capable of supplying the gas. Essentially, the Regulation creates a 'European approach' to gas security and shifts the central role of national authorities to the Commission.

3.5.3 Security of Electricity Supply

Finally we come to the issue of the security of electricity supply. Unlike oil and gas, electricity is not a primary fuel. It is generated from primary fuels such as oil, gas, and uranium, or renewable resources such as hydro, wind, or solar energy. The security of the electricity supply is much less a political or geopolitical question than the security of the oil or gas supply. Security failures are domestic and technical, not external and political. The international trade in electricity is also much smaller than that for natural gas or oil, for understandable reasons.[162] The main concerns for electricity relate to more tangible issues, such as the availability of infrastructure, sufficient investment for generation and transmission,[163] sufficient interconnector capacity to respond to an asymmetric shock in a Member State, and so on.[164] Network security, in particular, has been debated in recent years, largely because a number of alarming events have taken place both in the EU and around the world, such as the large scale blackout in continental Europe in 2006,[165] but also because

---

[162] Electricity is a secondary form of energy and can be generated in various locations using various primary sources of energy such as natural gas, oil, or coal.

[163] K. Talus and T. Wälde, 'Electricity Interconnectors in EU Law: Energy Security, Long-Term Infrastructure Contracts and Competition Law', 32 *European Law Review* (2007), pp. 125–37. See also Eurelectric statement, *Security of Supply—A Key Issue for the European Electricity Industry*, December 2003: available at: <http://www.eurelectric.org>.

[164] K. Talus and T. Wälde, 'Electricity Interconnectors in EU Law: Energy Security, Long-Term Infrastructure Contracts and Competition Law', 32 *European Law Review* (2007), pp. 125–37; and C. Zimmermann, 'Do Electric Interconnectors Improve Long-Term Security of Electricity Supply?' 5(1) *OGEL* (2007).

[165] Other large scale events include, for example, the California power crisis. See World Bank report from April 2001: Energy and Mining Sector Board, *The California Power Crisis: Lessons for the Developing Countries*, 31–7; B. Mclean and P. Elkind, *The Smartest Guys In The Room: The Amazing Rise And Scandalous Fall Of Enron* (New York: Penguin 2003); and the large scale blackout in Italy, see,

of the increasing gap between EU plans for the power sector and the market and investment reality.[166] The impossibility of storing electricity is also a key issue differentiating it from oil and gas. Consequently, ensuring electricity supply is a crucial issue, as is the system's capacity to cope with peak demand periods.[167] Nuclear power is the obvious answer, but remains politically difficult for many countries.

As a response to public concerns over security of supply (or so it seems) the EU adopted a directive concerning measures to safeguard security of electricity supply and infrastructure investment.[168] Its objectives are to: establish ways to safeguard an adequate level of security for the supply of electricity; achieve an adequate balance between supply and demand; and ensure an appropriate level of interconnection between Member States. However, it has significant shortcomings.[169] Its wording is very general, it lacks clear obligations, and the very few obligations which it does contain—such as the clarification of the roles of various market players—are not directly linked to security of supply considerations (although it may be presumed that such clarification will have a positive effect on security of supply). The fact that it was implemented in Finland mostly through pre-existing legislation is illustrative of this relatively 'thin' content, and reflects the dearth of actual legal obligations involved.

The directive aims to increase transparency. The provision of additional and timely information on markets, on supplies, on demand, and on market participants with clearly defined roles and functions, is crucial for energy security. First, this allows the expectations of all parties to be based on clear and accurate data. Secondly, it facilitates the supervision of the various actors and activities. This is important as no central body or single company is responsible for ensuring security of supply.

What is interesting about the directive is that it addresses an aspect of energy security not previously dealt with in an adequate manner: the systemic aspect of energy security. The entire system must be considered when a policy design is drafted.[170] From this perspective, enhanced cooperation in the form of reporting and monitoring (Article 3) will positively contribute to security of supply in EU. The reporting and monitoring obligations will provide the Commission with the information necessary to establish the overall security of supply situation at any

---

K. Talus, 'First Experience under the Exemption Regime of EC Regulation 1228/2003 on Conditions for Access to the Network of Cross-Border Exchanges in Electricity', 23 *Journal of Energy and Natural Resources Law* (2005), pp. 266–81.

[166] This issue is further discussed in Chapter 7, concerning the changing approach and ideology to energy markets and energy market regulation.

[167] See, for example, ETSO, *Winter Outlook Report 2007–2008*. Available at: <https://www.entsoe.eu/publications/former-associations/ucte/other-reports/>.

[168] Directive 2005/89/EC of the European Parliament and of the Council of 18 January 2006 concerning measures to safeguard security of electricity supply and infrastructure investment, OJ L 33/22, 4.2.2006.

[169] K. Talus and T. Wälde, 'Electricity Interconnectors in EU law: Energy security, long-term infrastructure contracts and competition law', 32 *European Law Review* (2007), pp. 125–37.

[170] B. Barton, C. Redgwell, A. Ronne, and D. N. Zillman, 'Introduction', in B. Barton, C. Redgwell, A. Ronne, and D. N. Zillman (eds), *Energy Security—Managing Risk in a Dynamic Legal and Regulatory Environment* (Oxford: OUP 2004), p. 7.

given time. As the EU cannot greatly influence national energy mixes or control national energy policies, it should (and to a certain extent has already) focus on facilitating investment and coordinating national efforts to obtain security of supply.[171]

Taking the above into account, the Directive on the European Critical Infrastructure[172] (energy being one of its central applications[173]) should also be seen as a move in the right direction. The central idea of this directive is to identify and protect infrastructure with an EU dimension.[174] The role of the EU is to assess interdependencies and develop common minimum protection measures.[175]

3.5.4 Infrastructure for Security

To be of any use, the general emergence of the 'solidarity between Member States' approach to energy security and the provisions of the gas security regulation rely on the existence of certain critical elements of EU natural gas infrastructure. While it was thought that these would materialize, the development has been disappointing, though not surprising. In this regard, another set of key security of supply instruments comes into play: the TEN-E framework. These promote trans-European energy networks.

Through the TEN-E framework, particular infrastructure projects are identified as 'projects of common interest' and as 'priority projects' for EU financial aid.[176] On the strength of this status, these projects are more likely to get EU aid and obtain other advantages, on the regulatory front, for example. With the growing investment gap in the EU,[177] there have been calls to revisit and modify the TEN-E framework better to reflect the investment needs of the EU energy markets.[178] To no particular surprise,[179] the main shortcoming of the programme was identified as a lack of

---

[171] In this respect, there is one fundamental question relating to the conceptualization of security of supply that is likely to have tangible effects on EU energy policy: namely, whether the concept 'security of supply' as a legal concept has a different meaning in the EU context from the national context? If there is a difference, security of supply being something else at EU level than at national level, this difference should also be reflected in the measures that are based on security of supply.

[172] Council Directive 2008/114/EC of 8 December 2008 on the identification and designation of European critical infrastructures and the assessment of the need to improve their protection, OJ L 345, 23.12.2008, pp. 75–82.

[173] Annex I of the Directive 2008/114/EC.

[174] Infrastructure located in the EU Member States the disruption or destruction of which would have a significant impact on at least two Member States of the EU (Article 2 (b)).

[175] Commission memorandum, 'The European Programme for Critical Infrastructure Protection (EPCIP)' (MEMO/06/477) 12 December 2006 and Commission Press Release, 'Critical Infrastructure Protection' (IP/08/899), 6 June 2008.

[176] Decision No. 1364/2006/EC of the European Parliament and of the Council of 6 September 2006 laying down guidelines for trans-European energy networks and repealing Decision 96/391/EC and Decision No. 1229/2003/EC. OJ L 262, 22.9.2006, 1–23. See also Communication from the Commission to the Council and the European Parliament, Priority Interconnection Plan (COM(2007)0846 final).

[177] 'Energy 2020: A strategy for competitive, sustainable and secure energy' (COM/2010/0639 final).

[178] European Council Presidency Conclusions of 19–20.3.2009, 7880/09.

[179] The shortcomings now identified by the Commission were highlighted already in a study published in 2007. See K. Talus and T. Wälde, 'Electricity Interconnectors in EU Law: Energy Security, Long-Term Infrastructure Contracts and Competition Law', 32 *European Law Review* (2007).

sufficient financial resources, and a new instrument has been proposed. In 2011, the Commission tabled a Proposal on guidelines for trans-European energy infrastructure, which would repeal Decision No 1364/2006/EC.[180] This proposal is part of the EU infrastructure package from October 2011, and is the latest attempt to provide the missing links in the EU energy markets. The main change to the *status quo ex ante* is the significant increase in direct financing of these projects (up to 70 per cent) in the EU context. The regulation would in many ways follow the TEN-E guidelines and attempt to lay down guidelines for the timely development and interoperability of priority corridors and areas of trans-European energy infrastructure. Many projects had already been identified in the context of the TEN-E guidelines.[181]

In addition to these instruments, the EU, following the example of the US, has granted very significant amounts of funding through the European Energy Programme for Recovery[182] with a view to completing 31 gas infrastructure projects at a cost of EUR 1.39 billion, which includes EUR 1.3 billion support for gas interconnectors. If these measures did not significantly boost the European economy, at least they assisted in getting new energy projects off the ground.

3.5.5 Security of Supply in the General Internal Energy Market Directives

Provisions related to security of supply have been included in virtually all legislative instruments in the field of energy. In addition to the directives on energy savings[183] or those on the promotion of green energy sources or more efficient energy production,[184] the general internal market directives also include several provisions

---

[180] 'Proposal for a Regulation of the European Parliament and of the Council on guidelines for trans-European energy infrastructure and repealing Decision No 1364/2006/EC' (COM(2011)658).
[181] These were also identified earlier in connection to the energy infrastructure priorities for 2020 and beyond—'A Blueprint for an integrated European energy network' (COM(2010)677 final).
[182] Regulation (EU) No 1233/2010 of the European Parliament and of the Council of 15 December 2010 amending Regulation (EC) No 663/2009 establishing a programme to aid economic recovery by granting Community financial assistance to projects in the field of energy and Regulation (EC) No 663/2009 of the European Parliament and of the Council of 13 July 2009 establishing a programme to aid economic recovery by granting Community financial assistance to projects in the field of energy.
[183] For example, Directive 2002/91/EC of the European Parliament and of the Council of 16 December 2002 on the energy performance of buildings, OJ L 1, 4.1.2003, pp. 65–71; Directive 2006/32/EC of the European Parliament and of the Council of 5 April 2006 on energy end-use efficiency and energy services and repealing Council Directive 93/76/EEC, OJ L 114, 27.4.2006, pp. 64–85; Directive 2005/32/EC of the European Parliament and of the Council of 6 July 2005 establishing a framework for the setting of eco-design requirements for energy-using products and amending Council Directive 92/42/EEC and Directives 96/57/EC and 2000/55/EC of the European Parliament and of the Council, OJ L 191, 22.7.2005, pp. 29–58 and Commission Directive 2003/66/EC of 3 July 2003 amending Directive 94/2/EC implementing Council Directive 92/75/EEC with regard to energy labelling of household electric refrigerators, freezers and their combinations, OJ 9.7.2003, L 170, pp. 10–14. For the re-cast plans, see Energy Efficiency Plan 2011 (COM/2011/0109 final).
[184] Directive 2009/28/EC of the European Parliament and of the Council of 23 April 2009 on the promotion of the use of energy from renewable sources and amending and subsequently repealing Directives 2001/77/EC and 2003/30/EC, OJ L 140, 5.6.2009, pp. 16–62; and Directive 2004/8/EC of the European Parliament and of the Council of 11 February 2004 on the promotion of cogeneration based on a useful heat demand in the internal energy market and amending Directive 92/42/EEC, OJ L52/50, 21.2.2004.

which are linked to security. Many of these have been examined in this chapter, including PSOs, merchant exemption for new infrastructure, and others. Furthermore, the energy market directives set up a monitoring mechanism which obliges the Commission to examine and report annually to the European Parliament and Council. This report contains information on: the development of the internal energy markets and the obstacles encountered (including dominance, anticompetitive behaviour and concentration levels); various derogations granted; issues relating to system capacity levels and security of supply in the EU, including current and projected supply and demand balance; and a general overview of the bilateral relations between the EU and its natural-gas-supplying countries as well as transit countries.

In addition to the above-mentioned measures, Articles 42 (electricity) and 46 (gas) also include a provision to deal with a 'sudden crisis in the energy market and where the physical safety or security of persons, apparatus or installations or system integrity is threatened'. In such cases, a Member State has the right temporarily to take the necessary safeguard measures. In practice, it might be expected that this possibility would mainly be used in cases involving system integrity, the functioning of certain energy-related installations, or apparatus being endangered. Based on past experience, it could be claimed that the physical safety of persons is rarely at stake in energy market crisis situations.

These measures are subject to strict proportionality requirements and can only be used in very exceptional and short-term emergency situations.[185] They must be communicated to other Member States and the Commission. The latter has the power to request the Member State to 'amend or abolish such measures, insofar as they distort competition and adversely affect trade in a manner which is at variance with the common interest'.

3.6 Concluding Thoughts: From State to Market and from Monopoly to Competition—How Sector Regulation Created Competitive Markets

The first internal energy market directives were the first constructive and significant steps towards restructuring the EU's energy industries and creating an internal energy market since the Treaty of Rome established the rules on the internal markets and free trade law of the EU. The directives were far from being comprehensive in scope, and it could not have been expected that they would create an internal EU-wide energy market but rather, together with market forces and contemporary attitudes at that time, national energy markets. However, even these markets did not materialize, at least to the extent envisaged. This should not necessarily be considered as a failure of the system. Neither Rome nor the internal European energy market can be created in a day. Energy is a far too 'strategic' and politicized commodity to be amenable to an easy legislative fix. The fact that EU energy

---

[185] C. Jones, *EU Energy Law, Volume 1—The Internal Energy Market* (Leuven: Claeys & Casteels 2004), p. 125.

liberalization has proceeded much more slowly—particularly at the level of cross-border, intra-EU trade, by comparison with the UK after privatization or US states, for example—is due to the fact that, as distinct from the UK, the EU is not a unitary state (or a 'European super-state') but a new type of confederation of states, all of which have very different conditions and types of energy industry. It also has much to do with the different market structures in place, and import dependency. It is difficult to create competitive downstream markets when the upstream supply market is marked by monopoly and state ownership. The Anglo-Saxon model, with its rapid creation of competitive markets, contrasts with the French state-run model (including powerful political constituencies and cultural expectations for the state to deliver energy on egalitarian terms) and the Germanic corporativist model of private, but state-supported cartels and monopolies. The criticism that the EU proceeds too slowly, too ponderously, and in an overly complex way, is therefore based on incorrect assumptions as to how a continent-wide, state-like entity should proceed, which do not take account the federated reality of the EU.

But changes have occurred. As a result of both market forces and the facilitative force and signal effect of new energy regulation, the national markets are moving towards competition in both electricity (more rapidly) and gas (more slowly), and the self-propelling dynamic now created is likely to further that movement, meaning that an internal EU energy market is on the horizon. But this is not likely to happen over night and not with the model that the first engineers of the plan for an internal energy market had in mind.

Energy regulation, with its tension between a free market of autonomous actors and the political expectations for proper energy supply still directed at government, is a complicated matter where regulatory engineering is fraught with uncertainties—as the California energy crisis, where both regulation and policy went awry—illustrates. Avoiding a California scenario will therefore be—and has to be—at the forefront of the minds of the architects of the next phases of national and EU-wide energy reforms. In this context, investment needs over the coming years are significant, both within the EU and outside it. Markets alone are not going to provide for this investment and, after a long period of denial, the EU has come to accept this fact. Significant investment requires regulatory certainty and the ability to predict market conditions with some degree of confidence, together with contractual or other arrangements which match the depreciation periods for energy investment and state support.

In the first years of the new millennium, there was excessive optimism over the ability of an internal energy market to resolve all current energy problems: security of supply, the environment, and competitiveness. The creation of an EU-wide market may mean that localized supply crises can be managed through cross-border supplies from countries with excess capacity. But, on the other hand, a larger system also means that hitherto localized shortages can lead to greater volatility throughout the system. If US refinery shortages can drive up the price of petrol in Europe way beyond the oil price relationship, and if open trade in animals and other agricultural products can easily internationalize otherwise localized risk factors, then a larger market also means larger and more widespread risks and volatilities.

This is the more so as the EU Commission is a monitor, initiator, and to some extent enforcer of EU-wide policies, but does not have the power, trust, or legitimacy to be more than one actor in a field populated by a multitude of actors with limited and narrowed political responsibility and attention. A sudden supply crisis in a Member State, multiplied through free trade can, therefore, irrespective of its true origin and probably diluted responsibility, easily discredit EU-wide energy liberalization policies and the Commission, which can be made a most suitable scapegoat for such crises anyway. It is therefore justifiable to move carefully along the inevitable path towards the creation of an internal European energy market, expanding both eastwards, southwards, and westwards towards a truly global energy market, and developing experience in replacing the reasonably functioning national instruments of regulation, thereby providing this strategic and politicized service to people using a not yet well-known and tested international equivalent.

For the time being, the directives still leave a margin of discretion to Member States in shaping their energy industry, a fact that inevitably causes problems for the internal energy market target: interconnection, interoperability, a level playing field for competition, much higher costs for cross-border trade than at greater distance and—technical—cost within a country. The Commission has not turned into or spawned a European energy regulator. ACER has limited powers, and even the regulatory powers of the Commission are modest, and mainly focused on monitoring proper compliance with directives full of political compromises and leaving much room for national variation, with more significant powers related to all that is an exception from the general regime: derogations, transitional arrangements, the public services, stranded investment, and take-or-pay contract situations. It is logical that the EU machinery seeks larger powers, but to increase their acceptability such powers are constrained by committees, which is not a recipe for rapid insight and action, but rather a way to hide responsibility. The Anglo-Saxon model of an 'independent regulator'—independent from the industry, but also the government—at EU level has also been dropped from the directives and even the 2009 amendments with the creation of ACER. The reason for this is that most EU Member States are not yet ready to cede a large degree of political control to an independent EU-level regulator, which is likely to be less (and certainly not totally) sensitive to ad hoc political pressures.

The directives do not impose the break-up of existing energy monopolies, although that is in the logic of liberalization and seems to be occuring anyway through the strategic use of EU competition law. Currently, at most legal unbundling is required, although the Commission has been pushing towards mandatory ownership unbundling, which would be the logical next step. The issue of energy tax has not been confronted comprehensively as yet, even though different taxation regimes create significant competitive distortions for energy markets. Similarly, while the Commission has discovered the political value of PSOs and environmental references with the European Parliament, unions, and NGOs, there is as yet no EU-wide concept of public service obligations and full harmonization of environmental, energy-related rules is still to emerge. As such, national variations exist and are accepted, even though these may also offer camouflage for protectionism.

4

Treaty Law and the Energy Sector

In keeping with the approach taken in this book, this chapter does not purport to be a general guide to the application of rules on free movement, state aid, or EU competition law as it applies to the energy sector. Several excellent textbook-style works are already available on the market and it is not the intention here to write another book of such general scope.[1] Nor is the intention to describe basic competition law concepts or write an overview of the case law on state aid or free movement. This has been done often enough in both general economic EU law literature and in books focusing on the EU energy markets and their regulation. Instead, this chapter focuses on some central and current issues relating to the enforcement of competition law in energy: access to facilities, long-term energy agreements, destination clauses, external application and the effect of external energy dependency on the application of competition law, and so on. Similarly, the treatment of state aid cases is limited to the most important cases and to areas that are most crucial from an energy perspective. Finally, the chapter also discusses specific issues relating to free movement: the effect of the environmental factors and security of supply.

4.1 EU Competition Law and the Energy Markets

The core of EU competition law is found in Articles 101 TFEU (dealing with anticompetitive agreements and collusion) and 102 TFEU (abuse of a dominant position). EU competition law is closely linked to the evolution of US antitrust law,[2] for reasons of origin, of a similar (though not identical) philosophy, of natural

---

[1] For competition law, for example see C. Jones, *EU Energy Law—Volume II—EU Competition Law and Energy Markets* (Leuven: Claeys & Casteels 2005–2011 editions), P. Cameron, *Competition in Energy Markets: Law and Regulation in the European Union* (Oxford: OUP 2007). Among the older studies, see F. Kriegelstein, *The Application of EC Competition Rules to Liberalised Electricity Markets* (Baden Baden: Nomos 2000).

[2] With an American focus: R. Bolze, S. Peirce, and J. Walsh, 'Antitrust Regulation: A New Focus for a Competitive Energy Industry', *Energy Law Journal* (2000), pp. 79–112, R. Cudahy, 'PURPA: The Intersection of Competition and Regulatory Policy', *Energy Law Journal* (1995), pp. 419–39, R. Pierce Jr 'Antitrust Policy in the new electricity industry', *Energy Law Journal* (1996), pp. 29–58, M. Maedicke, 'Competitive-based Contracts for the New Power Business', *Energy Law Journal* (1996), pp. 103–35.

benchmarking of competition authorities against each other and the competition between the US and the EU in economic terms—although such borrowing from US antitrust law is rarely acknowledged in Europe.[3] The competition provisions are broadly drafted and employ elusive language, and for a long time the Commission had to guide undertakings using various defining regulations, guidelines, and communications. Pursuant to Article 103(2)(c) TFEU, the EU has the power to adopt special competition rules to regulate specific branches of the economy. This competence, however, was never used for energy. Instead, the industry has remained subject to the general rules, including the procedural framework laid down in Regulation 1/2003 and the EU merger control regulation, both of which have become increasingly powerful tools for the Commission in its fight against the ex-incumbents.

Despite the existence of defining regulations, case law retains its key role in clarifying the restrictions and liabilities in the energy sector under the EU competition regime. For a long time, this case law did not emerge and the industry was shielded from the application of general competition law (in some ways it still is—just consider the E.ON/Ruhrgas merger[4]). Initially, monopolistic and corporate 'club' structures meant that the participants in the energy game had little or no interest in airing open disputes. Yet after a period of mutual assessment during and after the introduction of the gas and electricity directives this has been changing as companies are slowly growing more conscious of their role as competitors. This is particularly so in electricity, a bit less so in gas, although times seem to be changing even in the gas sector.[5] The interpretation of primary competition law does not end at the EU level. Decisions made by national competition authorities and in the national courts of Member States lend greater credibility and understanding than would otherwise be the case, as do court decisions from non-EU states which employ similar antitrust and competition regimes. EU competition law is directly applicable and can be directly invoked in national courts (and with private enforcement and decentralization, this occurs more frequently than before), and obligations or allowances under national competition law must stay within the EU framework of Articles 101 and 102 TFEU, and thus, reflect it. For the latter reason, it should be assumed that definitive decisions and clarifications made by national authorities are compatible with EU law. These should therefore be taken more consciously into consideration when interpreting the competition provisions.[6]

---

[3] For some discussion see M. Motta, *Competition Policy, Theory and Practise* (Cambridge: CUP 2004). See also, H. Ullrich, *The Evolution of European Competition Law—Whose Regulation, Which Competition?* (Cheltenham: Edward Elgar 2006).

[4] See OFGEM Letter to the Commission Vice President Loyola de Palacio (Ref: cm73–03cfl), 18.2.2003 and I. Zenke, 'The Merger of E.ON and Ruhrgas: A Never-Ending Story?' (2003) 1 *OGEL*.

[5] K. Talus, 'Winds of Change: Long-term Gas Contracts and Changing Energy Paradigms in the European Union', in C. Kuzemko, A. Belyi, A. Goldthau, and M. F. Keating (eds), *Dynamics of Energy Governance in Europe and Russia* (Houndmills: Palgrave MacMillan 2012).

[6] Just consider national cases on long-term contracts, see for example, <http://www.bundeskartellamt.de/wEnglisch/download/pdf/07_Kurz_TB_e.pdf>. More cases can be found in K. Talus, 'Long-term Natural Gas Contracts and Antitrust Law in the European Union and the United States', 4(3) *Journal of World Energy Law and Business* (2011), pp. 260–315.

Some, albeit cautious, arguments should also be rooted in the application of competition law elsewhere. Both Europe and the US have been net exporters of their largely similar competition law, and many foreign regimes restate European provisions or effectively transpose them with minimal amendment. Care should be taken when provisions remain drafted in a broad and elusive manner, because they may, by stealth, harbour different competition policies and doctrinal exceptions. However, there is no reason why factual arguments and logical considerations, as well as arguments derived from economic theory[7]—on which consideration of the positive and negative effects of EU competition law often relies—should not be transferred into a European context. By way of example, even taking into account the institutional differences, the *Trinko* case from the US Supreme Court is worth reading to gain a better appreciation of the relationship between general competition law and the sector-specific energy regulation (and energy security investment on one hand, and the objective of competitive, integrated EU energy markets on the other).[8] That said, there are differences in the treatment of energy matters between US and European competition law—for instance, concerning the positive effects of joint purchase and sale of energy commodities,[9] long-term gas commodity agreements,[10] and the application of the essential facilities doctrine.[11] Some of these differences are logical and necessary, others are not.

We are not limited to looking at experiences in other countries and regions for guidance on the application of EU competition law in the energy sector. Although the energy industries have their own special features which limit the extent to which competition policies used in other sectors can be applied to them, it is not enough to consider only cases focusing on the conduct of specific energy industries. Various cases from other fields have set precedents for the regulation of similar issues in the field of energy. While this chapter seeks to offer a basic toolkit for the application of EU competition law in the energy sector, one should be aware that a deeper study of EU competition law will reveal many further arguments.[12]

---

[7] See for example D. Hildebrandt, *The Role of Economic Analysis in the EC Competition Rules* (Alphen aan den Rijn: Kluwer Law International 2009).

[8] For example see N. Petit, 'Circumscribing the Scope of EC Competition Law in Network Industries? A Comparative Approach to the US Supreme Court Ruling in the *Trinko* Case', 13 *ULR* (2004) 6. See also K. Talus and P. Kuoppamäki, 'Relationship between General Competition Laws and Sector Specific Energy Regulation', 1 *OGEL* (2010), <http://www.ogel.org>.

[9] See the Commission press release IP/01/830. The GFU case concerns joint sales of natural gas through a single seller, the GFU, from Norway to the EU, since at least 1989. The GFU negotiates natural gas sales contracts with buyers on behalf of all the other natural gas producers in Norway and thus fixes the selling price, volumes and all other trading conditions. The Commission held that, regarding the joint sales of Norwegian gas through the GFU, the members of the GFU infringed what was then Article 81(1) of the EC Treaty and Article 53(1) of the European Economic Area (EEA) Agreement.

[10] K. Talus, 'Long-term Natural Gas Contracts and Antitrust Law in the European Union and the United States', 4(3) *Journal of World Energy Law and Business* (2011), pp. 260–315.

[11] K. Talus, 'Just What is the Scope of the Essential Facilities Doctrine in the Energy Sector: Third Party Access-Friendly Interpretation in the EU v. Contractual Freedom in the US', 48(5) *Common Market Law Review* (2011).

[12] For more detailed examination of the application of EU competition law to energy, see P. Cameron, *Competition in Energy Markets: Law and Regulation in the European Union* (Oxford: OUP 2007).

4.1.1 Fundamental Competition Concepts for the Energy Sector

The application of Articles 101 and 102 TFEU to the energy markets is subject to a number of overarching general issues concerning the application of competition law in the energy sectors, and these should be dealt with together in context.

4.1.1.1 The Relevant Markets

Assessing anticompetitive conduct arising from concentration depends on a market definition, and the more broad the lines are drawn, the less likely one is to find dominance—as required in Article 102 TFEU or the EU Merger Regulation—or any appreciable distortion.[13] Or, to put in another way: when considering the conduct of a supply monopoly in a Member State, it is important to establish whether the relevant market in which its behaviour is benchmarked consists of the whole EU internal energy market, or an internal electricity or gas market, or the territory of a Member State or its sub-regions. Clearly, if the market is defined too narrowly, concentrations that have pro-competitive effects in a wider market might be prohibited; whereas if the market is defined too broadly, the true extent of market power might not become evident. The difficulties involved in defining the relevant markets and the impact that this can have in a particular case are well-illustrated by the Finnish *E.ON—Fortum* merger case.[14] In this case, the Finnish competition authority had concluded that Fortum, the largest energy company in Finland, had a dominant position on the markets and the merger with E.ON's Finnish operations would strengthen that position further. Contrary to this view, the Finnish Market Court took the view that the increased cross-border capacity had reduced the congestion on the border with Sweden to the extent that the markets should be seen as encompassing both Finland and Sweden (at least).[15] Defined in this way, Fortum did not hold a dominant position on the relevant market. In broad terms, identification of the relevant market must take into account both a production and (an ever changing) geographical dimension. The Commission has provided guidance in the form of a notice as to how it applies these concepts.[16] The underlying principle it applies is that undertakings are subject to three main sources of competitive restraints (demand substitutability, supply substitutability, and potential competition) and that demand side substitutability is the principal analytical tool for establishing the relevant market.[17]

---

[13] For the importance of the right market definition see Case C-62/86, *AKZO v Commission* [1991] ECR I-3359 and Case 322/81, *Michelin v Commission* [1993] ECR 3461.

[14] Markkinaoikeus 14 Mar. 2008 nro 123/2008 (Dnro 209/06/KR). This decision by the Market Court has subsequently been confirmed by the Supreme Administrative Court of Finland.

[15] Situation has changed after the case and the price differences are again more prevalent today.

[16] Commission notice on the definition of the relevant market for the purposes of Community competition law (OJ C372, 9 December 1997, pp. 5–13) ('Relevant Market Notice').

[17] See *XXVIIth Report on Competition Policy* [1997], point 44. Supply side substitutability is in practice less important given the time often required for suppliers to switch production and potential competition is taken into account only after the relevant market has been defined to analyse market power in the light of competitive restraints.

In the energy sector, the Commission's assessment of substitutability leads to a rather diverse range of product markets following the common classifications of upstream, midstream, and downstream energy sectors.[18] As far as petroleum is concerned, the exploration of oil and gas is a different product market from the development, production, and marketing of crude oil and gas—which is different again from the distribution (direct sales and service stations) of oil, or the processing, transport, and trading of gas. With regard to electricity, the Commission has identified several different product markets, from transmission, to supply to various customer groups, to balancing power.[19] Definition of the geographical market depends on the product sector involved. Oil and gas exploration and the production market are seen to be global and single, as is the market for the sale of crude oil. In the case of natural gas, the market definition depends on the reach of the pipeline system and the possible use of interconnection. LNG is different from this. However, the geographical reach of direct LNG trade in the EU limits the impact of this type of gas trade. Network-bound transmission and distribution of gas and electricity is usually seen as having a national scope. But, of course, there are exceptions. For example, the power systems of Estonia, Latvia, and Lithuania are part of the power system of north-west Russia. There are no capacity restrictions in the interconnectors between the Baltic States, meaning that unrestricted transmission of electrical energy is therefore possible.[20] For example, Estonia's entire electricity consumption could actually be imported from Latvia using the current connections between the two grids.[21] The supply markets for gas and electricity are essentially national, although this is slowly changing.

As with the geographical scope of the markets, the product markets are subject to periodical changes. Green power is currently emerging as a separate product market. While the power is the same regardless of whether it has been produced through coal or renewables, there are strong customer preferences in favour of green energy, at least in some EU Member States. In many cases, customers are prepared to pay the extra cost involved in using renewable energy.[22]

---

[18] For analysis, see C. Jones, *EU Energy Law—Volume II—EU Competition Law and Energy Markets* (Leuven: Claeys & Casteels 2005), P. Cameron, *Competition in Energy Markets: Law and Regulation in the European Union* (Oxford: OUP 2007) and K. Talus, *Vertical Natural Gas Transportation Capacity, Upstream Commodity Contracts and EU Competition Law* (*The Role of Economic Analysis in the EC Competition Rules* (Alphen aan den Rijn: Kluwer Law International 2011).

[19] For analysis, see C. Jones, *EU Energy Law—Volume II—EU Competition Law and Energy Markets* (Leuven: Claeys & Casteels 2005), P. Cameron, *Competition in Energy Markets: Law and Regulation in the European Union* (Oxford: OUP 2007) and K. Talus, *Vertical Natural Gas Transportation Capacity, Upstream Commodity Contracts and EU Competition Law* (*The Role of Economic Analysis in the EC Competition Rules* (Alphen aan den Rijn: Kluwer Law International 2011)

[20] Decree No 52, 9.2.2005, Exemption decision concerning Estlink project, Estonian Ministry of Economic Affairs and Communications.

[21] Estonian Energy Market Inspectorate, Annual Report 2002, p. 12.

[22] This is the case in Finland where energy companies have 'sold-out' their green power capacities.

4.1.2 Interpretation and Enforcement between EU and National Competition Authorities: The Effect on Trade between Member States

In one of its early judgments, the Court was asked to rule on whether EU competition law and national competition rules could simultaneously be applied to the same cartel.[23] After this initial insight into the question, the matter was then clarified in a notice on cooperation between the Commission and national judges[24] and in a further notice on cooperation between national competition authorities and the Commission, which related to the handling of cases falling within the ambit of Articles 101 and 102 TFEU.[25] The clarification given was later enshrined in various provisions of Regulation 1/2003.[26] In fact, since Articles 101 and 102 are directly applicable, national authorities and national judges are primarily responsible for the application of EU competition law. If national competition authorities or courts apply national competition laws to agreements that may affect trade between Member States, they must also apply EU competition law. The application of national competition law may not prohibit an agreement that is acceptable under Article 101(1) or 101(3) TFEU.

Of course, this decentralization has the effect of reducing the number of cases brought annually before the Commission and gives the Commission the possibility to concentrate on more interesting and important cases. This was one of the underlying ideas when Regulation 1/2003 was enacted: it was no longer necessary for the Commission to handle every single case. The resources of the Commission are limited and it needs to identify those areas where it can add value to the actions of other domestic authorities by applying primary competition law (just consider the impact that this has had on the energy sector). In order to achieve this aim, the Commission may apply Articles 101 and 102, and can adopt decisions addressed to undertakings.

The notion of an internal energy market will make it increasingly difficult to establish exclusive jurisdiction for a Member State in any given case.[27] In fact, even in earlier situations, the Commission and Court have been keen to establish jurisdiction and to avoid the scenario in which national authorities might potentially take a more lenient approach towards their national energy companies. In *Almelo,*[28] the Court followed the *Brasserie de Haecht*[29] and *Delimitis*[30] judgments in holding that the cumulative effect of exclusivity agreements needed to be considered if there was

---

[23] Case 14/68, *Wilhelm v Bundeskartellamt* [1969] ECR 1, [1969] CMLR 100.

[24] [1993] OJ C-39/6. See also Case C-91/95P, *Tremblay* [1996] ECR I-5547. Now replaced by a new notice that was published with the modernization package. See M. Dabbah, *EC and UK Competition Law—Commentary, Cases and Materials* (Cambridge: CUP 2004).

[25] [1997] OJ C 313/3.

[26] For a more detailed picture see for example M. Dabbah, *EC and UK Competition Law—Commentary, Cases and Materials* (Cambridge: CUP 2004), pp. 661–77.

[27] Which exists where effects are confined to one Member State, see Case 8/72, *Vereniging van Cementhandelaren VCH v Commission* [1972] ECR 997, except where its effects constitute a threshold for the commercial actions by companies from other Member States.

[28] Case C-393/92, *Almelo v NV Energiebedrijf Ijsselmij* [1994] ECR I-1477.

[29] Case 23/67, *Brasserie de Haecht* [1967] ECR 525.

[30] Case C-234/89, *Delimitis* [1991] ECR I-935.

an appreciable effect on trade between Member States, and in the *Electricidade de Portugal/Pego*[31] decision the Commission noted that the exclusive supply obligation had the effect of preventing delivery of electricity to consumers in other Member States. In the German *Jahrhundertvertrag* decision,[32] the Commission found that a rather small volume of trade in the area in question did not prevent it from claiming jurisdiction; nor were mere prospects of increases in transmission capacities and the proposed development of cross-border interconnection sufficient in the case of *Scottish Nuclear*.[33] On one occasion, however, the Commission reflected on jurisdiction, when it investigated a notified oral agreement between companies participating in the development of the Britannia gas field in the UK. The agreement concerned a decision between the participating companies to appoint a single sales negotiator on behalf of them all,[34] but it concluded that there was no jurisdiction for it to investigate further because there was no interconnection between the UK and mainland Europe at that time. However, with the growing number of interconnections under the TEN-E projects, and with the linking-up of the last isolated Member States (such as the Baltic States, where one interconnector project has been completed and several more are in the planning stages) the Commission will have EU-level jurisdiction—provided of course that the interconnection capacity is important enough to have an effect.

However, in politically sensitive markets such as energy, the question of jurisdiction is not always just about the law. Just consider the *E.ON/Ruhrgas* merger, a case that shows the political limits of the enforcement of competition law in the energy sector. In this case, the German Federal Cartel Office had prohibited the merger as it would have created a strong, vertically integrated electricity and gas utility by bringing together two dominant companies (in their respective sectors). It also emphasized that the merger would be particularly harmful considering the electricity and gas activities involved and would seriously undermine the transformation of the energy markets towards efficient competition and TPA.[35] In a similar manner to the German Federal Cartel Office, the UK energy market authority, OFGEM, expressed serious concerns over the effects of the merger in a letter addressed to Loyola de Palacio, then the Commissioner for energy and transport. Among other issues, OFGEM's concern was that the merger would impede the emergence of effective competition, would create a vertically integrated utility with activities and interests in all areas of the supply chain in both electricity and gas, and would be counterproductive vis-à-vis the EU's efforts to open up the markets.[36] Both authorities also expressed the opinion that the merger would fall within the competence of the Commission. Despite the opinion of the national energy and competition

---

[31] Case No IV/34.598, *Electricidade de Portugal/Pego Project.*

[32] Commission Decision of 22.12.1992 (Jahrhundertvertrag), OJ [1993] L 50, p. 14.

[33] Commission Decision of 30.4.1991 (Scottish Nuclear) OJ [1993] L 178, p. 34.

[34] See Commission information concerning the Britannia gas condensate field in (1997) 5 *CMLR Antitrust Reports*, p. 192.

[35] I. Zenke, 'The Merger of E.ON and Ruhrgas: A Never-Ending Story?' 1 *OGEL* (2003).

[36] OFGEM Letter to the Commission Vice President Loyola de Palacio (Ref: cm73–03cfl) 18.2.2003.

law authorities, the German government used a special procedure allowing it to disregard the decision of the Federal Cartel Office if 'the restraint of competition is outweighed by advantages to the economy as a whole following from the concentration, or if the concentration is justified by an overriding public interest'.[37] The government thus authorized the merger despite its clear anticompetitive effects. Taking into account the arguments of the German and UK authorities on the jurisdiction of the European Commission in this case, the Commission's passivity can only be explained by reference to political considerations—i.e. the desire to avoid a clash with the German government.

Generally speaking, however, the Commission is keen to encourage decentralized enforcement of EU competition rules under Regulation 1/2003. It has also started to give guidance as to the application of competition rules by Member State authorities—e.g. the specific notice concerning the telecommunications sector.[38] Initially, energy sector players were expected to read these telecoms notices and apply them, *mutatis mutandis*, to their own sector:[39] not a simple task, considering the differences between the two sectors. Today, the energy sector can largely rely on various energy-sector-specific cases and explanations coming from the Commission[40] or the national competition law authorities.[41] The 2007 Sector Inquiry clearly provided the ammunition and resulted in the increasingly intrusive application of EU competition law in the energy sector. Some of these cases are now examined under two headings: Article 101 and Article 102 TFEU.

4.2 Article 101: Cartels and Other Forms of Collusion

Article 101 TFEU can be applied to a number of situations. If long-term contracts are part of a strategy that qualifies as abuse of market power, then invalidity can result from both Article 101 and 102, depending on the details of the case. If an

---

[37] I. Zenke, 'The Merger of E.ON and Ruhrgas: A Never-Ending Story?' (2003) 1 *OGEL*, 1.

[38] Notice on the application of the competition rules to access agreements in the telecommunication sector, OJ C 265, 22.8.1998, p. 15. This notice can be applied *mutatis mutandis* to the energy sector for guidance. While doing this, the significance of interconnectors for EC energy markets must however be kept in mind. See also Use of EC Competition Rules in the Liberalisation of the European Union's Telecommunications Sector—Assessment of Past Experience and Conclusions for Use in other Utilities Sectors (COMP/C/2/HU/rdu, Brussels, 6 May 2001).

[39] See the discussion by M. Albers 'Competition Law Issues Arising from the Liberalisation Process' in D. Geradin (ed.) *The Liberalisation of Electricity and Natural Gas in the European Union* (The Hague: Kluwer 2001), pp. 15 et seq.

[40] The best example here in undoubtedly the COMP/B-1/37966—*Distrigaz* case. This case can be considered as the 'guidance in an appropriate form on the compliance of downstream bilateral long-term supply agreements with EU competition law' that was promised by the Commission in the Proposal for a Directive of the European Parliament and of the Council amending Directive 2003/55/EC concerning common rules for the internal market in natural gas, SEC(2007)1179–1180, (COM(2007)529), 19.9.2007, s. 5.5: 'to reduce uncertainty on the market, the Commission will, in the coming months, provide guidance in an appropriate form on the compliance of downstream bilateral long-term supply agreements with EC competition law.'

[41] Here, one example would be the *E.ON-Ruhrgas* contracts case (Bundeskartellamt, 'Bundeskartellamt pushes ahead with competition in the gas market' (28.1.2005)).

energy monopoly breaches one of these rules, in the absence of a specific derogation under, say, Article 106(2) TFEU, then agreements concluded as a corollary of an anticompetitive and monopolistic corporate strategy will be invalid. As (or perhaps *if*) monopolies gradually disappear, the significance of Article 101 TFEU is likely to increase, since it is through agreements and concerted action that competition can be obstructed in the now slowly emerging oligopolistic markets.

4.2.1 Horizontal Restraints in the Energy Sector: Joint Selling, Price Fixing, and Others

The energy sector, upstream oil and gas in particular, has a long history of inter-company cooperation.[42] The upstream energy sector has traditionally been active in both joint ventures and looser strategic alliances[43] to cope with risk and high capital expenditure. This is less the case with the EU utilities sector, but even here national players have occasionally engaged in joint projects and joint ventures. EU competition law draws a distinction between cooperative and concentrative joint ventures—the latter fall within the ambit of the EU Merger Regulation and are not discussed here.[44] Cooperative and non-full-function joint ventures[45] are governed exclusively by Article 101 together with other horizontal restraints. Horizontal restraints involve agreements or collusion between and among competing entities. It is note-worthy that even this concept is subject to change over time and, for example, it would under certain circumstances be possible to consider electricity and gas companies as competing entities.[46]

Most of the concern regarding antitrust enforcement under Article 101 is related to price fixing and market-sharing. Price is the clearest and most transparent medium of competition, and price fixing elements are present in both horizontal and vertical agreements. As such, there is an abundance of case law concerning price fixing under Article 101, and in relation to the utilities sector.[47] In the energy sector, the pricing question, for natural gas in particular, is somewhat more complicated than in many other sectors. Market-sharing agreements, on the other hand, are not

---

[42] The leading study on the history of petroleum industry is the notorious monograph D. Yergin, *The Prize* (New York: Free Press 1991).

[43] See J. Bellis, 'Liberalisation and the Creation of Strategic Alliances', in D. Geradin (ed.), *The Liberalisation of State Monopolies in the European Union and Beyond* (The Hague: Kluwer Law International 2000), pp. 233–60.

[44] For mergers and acquisitions in energy markets see in particular C. Jones, *EU Energy Law— Volume II—EU Competition Law and Energy Markets* (Leuven: Clayes Claeys & Casteel 2005).

[45] Commission notice on the concept of full-function joint ventures under Council Regulation (EEC) No 4064/89 on the control of concentrations between undertakings. OJ C 66, 2.3.1998.

[46] For instance, the mergers between TRACTEBEL/DISTRIGAZ (Commission Decision of 1 December 1994) and NESTE/IVO (Commission Decision of 2 June 1998) were opposed until the parties had undertaken to divest themselves of their bulk gas sale business to a third party. See the discussion by M. Albers, 'Competition Law Issues Arising from the Liberalisation Process' in D. Geradin (ed.), *The Liberalisation of Electricity and Natural Gas in the European Union* (Deventer: Kluwer 2001), pp. 13 et seq. See also Case T-87/05, *EDP v Commission* [2005] ECR, II-03745.

[47] Most recently, Case C-52/09, *Konkurrensverket v TeliaSonera Sverige AB* (judgment of 17.2.2011), not yet reported.

very complicated, although widely used, in the energy sector. Destination clauses and usage restrictions have traditionally been used in many natural gas contracts, and although there is now ample case law[48] on the topic, these clauses continue to be used.[49]

In addition to agreements between competitors to fix prices and allocate territories or allocate customers, examples of other types of horizontal agreement include those relating to the exchange of certain information or to product standardization.[50] Some of these practices do not in themselves amount to violation of antitrust law, but they may make it easier for competitors to reach a tacit or explicit agreement on pricing or output. Clearly, the coordination of prices may also be achieved by means of agreements for the exchange of information about prices or similar matters. In this regard, the Commission objected to the original form of a joint venture between Shell and Exxon[51] on the ground that it could have encouraged the exchange of market information between them. But opposition seems to depend on the number on participants in the market. Where the market is not oligopolistic, the Commission seems prepared to accept exchanges of individual and confidential information concerning sales volumes and market shares.[52] The exchange of price and other sensitive information is also one of the main concerns in the cooperative type of energy companies present in the Finnish markets. Here the problematic aspects are highlighted when a large number of shareholders are other, normally competing, energy companies that use the cooperative as a power procurement channel.[53] The International Energy Agency (IEA) oil supplies agreements fall into the same category. The Commission's opinion was that, in an emergency, an agreement allocating supplies of essential products may give rise to a breach of Article 101(1). The facts of this matter were that an agreement relating to oil supplies was made between OECD members under the auspices of the IEA, in relation to which the Commission took the view that the exchanges of information associated with the agreement might restrict competition and give rise to market-sharing between the oil companies. Despite this, it granted an exemption under Article 101(3).[54]

Another form of collusion generally not tolerated by the Commission's competition policy is joint selling, the most common form of which in the energy sector

---

[48] Including COMP/38.085, COMP/37.811, and COMP/38.662.

[49] Case 39816—Upstream gas supplies in Central and Eastern Europe. See also 'Antitrust: Commission confirms unannounced inspections in the natural gas sector' (MEMO/11/641), 27.9.2011. For discussion and cases in this area, see K. Talus, 'Long-term Natural Gas Contracts and Antitrust Law in the European Union and the United States,' 4(3) *Journal of World Energy Law and Business* (2011), pp. 260–315.

[50] For a comparison between two cases illustrating Commission's approach to assessment of horizontal agreements and how restrictions by which similar environmental objective is attained may be the determining factor see M. Martinez-Lopez, 'Horizontal Agreements on Energy Efficiency of Appliances: A Comparison between CECED and CEMEP' [2000] *EC C.P.N.*, pp. 24–25.

[51] Notified joint venture EXXON/SHELL, OJ 1994 L144/20.

[52] Eudin, OJ 1996 C 111/8.

[53] For details, see K. Talus et al., *Energy Law of Finland* (Alphen aan den Rijn: Kluwer Law International 2010).

[54] International Energy Agency, 12 December 1983, OJ 1983 L 376/30.

is for the sale of gas from joint production.[55] Although the Commission has stated that an exemption is available if there are compelling reasons to justify it, all lines of argumentation put forward in favour of joint selling of energy have usually been unsuccessful.[56] In the *Corrib Gas Field* case, the production joint venture of Statoil, Enterprise Energy Ireland, and Marathon applied for an exemption for the joint marketing of gas produced at the field for the first five years of production. They argued that this measure was necessary to balance the countervailing purchasing power of the incumbent, state-owned Irish energy companies, Bord Gais Eirean and the Electricity Supply Board. After the Commission raised concerns and started an examination, the Corrib partners refrained from implementing the joint marketing arrangement and withdrew their application for an exemption. Here, two factors appeared to have given rise to doubts about the economic benefits required under European competition law. The first of these was the fact that the field would be Ireland's only domestic gas field following the exhaustion of the existing gas field at Kinsale. The second was that the ongoing process of liberalization would increase the number of eligible customers and that the Irish customer base for its power market was particularly likely to continue its rapid growth, thus offering potential sales outlets for gas suppliers. Arguably, the relative market strength of the partners, especially Statoil, influenced the decision.

On another occasion, the Commission warned Norwegian gas producers that the joint sale of Norwegian gas through the Gas Negotiation Committee (GFU) infringed Article 81(1) of the EC Treaty (now 101(1) TFEU) and, respectively, Article 53(1) of the EEA Agreement.[57] The GFU comprised Statoil and Norsk Hydro and negotiated gas sale contracts with buyers on behalf of all other natural gas producers in Norway. The Commission believed this negotiation to amount to the fixing of sale prices, volumes, and all other trading conditions. The GFU had entered into a large number of long-term supply agreements with European gas operators which had prolonged the adverse effects of joint selling schemes for several years and led to significant rigidity and lack of liquidity in the European gas market.

In this type of case the Commission commonly uses a statement of objection, which is a legal step in proceedings under Article 101 TFEU. It does not prejudice the outcome of the investigation, since the companies involved have the right to reply to the Commission's objections, have access to the file, and to request a formal hearing. Nevertheless, where a Member State supports restrictive measures taken by its national energy companies, this often leads to an immediate discontinuation of

[55] 'Investigation into joint selling concerning the Corrib Gas Field', Commission press release IP (01) 578 (20 April 2001); and Commission statement after the withdrawal of the application for an exemption [2001] 4 CMLR.

[56] Although in Case No COMP/M.6477—BP/Chevron/Eni/Sonangol/Total/JV, the Commission did accept the joint selling arrangement because of the joint venture's moderate anticipated market share, the presence of a number of credible competitors in the market concerned, and competitors' unchanged ability to access re-gasification terminals.

[57] Commission Information on gas joint selling and price fixing by the Norwegian Gas Negotiation Committee, (2001) 5 CMLR Antitrust Reports, 27–28; Commission press release IP (01) 830 (13.6.2001).

such support, as in the case of Norway's GFU[58]—a case which ultimately resulted in Statoil and Norsk Hydro giving commitments to market their gas individually.[59]

Another, more recent, example of behaviour falling under Article 101 TFEU is the *GDF Suez—E.ON Ruhrgas* case.[60] This case concerned a market-sharing arrangement in which the companies involved agreed not to sell gas using the Megal pipeline, which the companies jointly constructed in 1975, to each other's home markets. This arrangement was maintained even after the abolition of the companies' legal or contractual monopolies and the liberalization of the EU natural gas markets. While the parties to the contract declared that they regarded the agreement as void, obviously confirming that both companies understood that the arrangement violated EU competition rules, they continued to abide by this arrangement until September 2005. The Commission took the view that this market-sharing arrangement contributed to the strong market positions maintained by the companies even after liberalization had taken place. Much like destination clauses, these types of arrangements violate both competition and the internal market objectives of EU competition law. As such, and also considering the size of undertakings concerned, it was no surprise that the fines imposed in this case were among the highest cartel-related fines ever imposed by the Commission.[61]

4.3 Article 102: Abuse of a Dominant Position

Abuse falling under Article 102 TFEU can, for example, include discrimination between customers and excessive prices. Others may be more characteristic of state-sponsored monopolies, such as using cross-subsidization from monopoly rent to extend the monopoly to cognate areas, preventing a competitor from offering supply and services using both market power and political or regulatory power, combining state-delegated regulatory authority over a market with commercial operations in the market, and refusing to deal on reasonable terms with a competitor dependent on an 'essential facility' held by the monopoly.

4.3.1 Access to Essential Energy Facilities and Services

The extent to which an undertaking holding a dominant position can refuse to deal with or supply a competitor is one of the most relevant issues for the energy

---

[58] Information on an issued statement of objection concerning the Norwegian Gas Negotiation Committee, [2001] 5 CMLR Antitrust Reports, p. 28.

[59] 'Commission successfully settles GFU case with Norwegian gas producers', IP/02/1084, 17.7.2002.

[60] Case COMP/39.401—E.ON/GDF, see also Commission press release, 'Antitrust: Commission fines E.ON and GDF Suez €553 million each for market-sharing in French and German gas markets', (IP/09/1099), 8.7.2009 and Commission press release, 'Antitrust: Commission action against cartels—Questions and answers', (MEMO/09/323), 8.7.2009.

[61] The fines have subsequently been lowered from over €500 to €320 million for each company by the EU general court (Case T-360/09, *E.ON Ruhrgas v Commission*, judgment of 29 June 2012). The fine can be up to 10 per cent of company's total turnover in the preceding business year.

industries to arise under Article 102. The US-based doctrine of mandatory access to an essential facility is of particular significance in this regard.[62] In essence, it obliges a competitor that controls a service, facility, or intellectual property right to provide access to other competitors on non-discriminatory terms. This obligation requires that the use of the facility is essential for doing business and that replication of it is legally or commercially impractical, and is further subject to objective justification for denial of access.

The essential facilities doctrine has been regularly applied by the European Commission in cases relating to seaports, railways, and other physical infrastructures.[63] The Commission has periodically adopted a rather expansive interpretation of this doctrine.[64] Here, *GVG/FS*[65] provides but one somewhat extreme example. The case concerned a German railway company which intended to provide an inter-national passenger service between Germany and Italy. Here, Petit has noted how 'the Commission only referred to the existence of an "essential facility" concerning the railway infrastructure. Yet, the Commission applied, in substance, a similar test to the other assets at stake (e.g. trains, staff, drivers etc.). A striking feature of the decision thus lies in the fact that the Commission stretches the "essential facilities" concept beyond the purely non-duplicable infrastructure'.[66] To counter the ever-widening scope of the essential facilities doctrine, the Court interfered with this trend, and in *Bronner*[67] the Court made an attempt to limit what may be considered an essential or indispensable service, product, or facility.[68] However, this has had very little impact, as the subsequent case law shows.[69] Recent admin-istrative case law from the European Commission has examined various situations where an allegedly anticompetitive refusal to deal has taken place. These cases

---

[62] Examined in detail in K. Talus, 'Just What is the Scope of the Essential Facilities Doctrine in the Energy Sector: Third Party Access-friendly Interpretation in the EU v. Contractual Freedom in the US', 48(5) *Common Market Law Review* (2011).

[63] Commission Decision of 21 December 1993, Port of Rødby, OJ L 55, 26.2.1994, p.52; Commission Decision of 21 December 1993, Sea Containers/Stena Sealink, OJ L 15, 18.1.1994, p.8; Commission Decision of 11 June 1992, Sealink/B&I-Holyhead, interim measures, not published; among many others.

[64] R. O'Donoghue and A. J. Padilla, *The Law and Economics of Article 82 EC* (Oxford: Hart Publishing 2007), pp. 423–33.

[65] Commission Decision of 27 August 2003, GVG/FS, OJ L 11, 16.1.2004.

[66] N. Petit, 'Circumscribing the Scope of EC Competition Law in Network Industries? A Comparative Approach to the US Supreme Court Ruling in the Trinko Case', 13(6) *Utilities Law Review* (2004).

[67] Case C-7/97, *Oscar Bronner v Mediaprint*, [1998] ECR I-7791.

[68] S. Evrard, 'Essential Facilities in the EU: *Bronner* and Beyond', 10(491) *Columbia Journal of European Law* (2004), pp. 2–15. The author illustrates how under the pre-*Bronner* case law a company was, under certain circumstances, required to provide access just because it held a dominant position and how *Bronner* provided the opportunity for the Luxembourg Court to interfere with this approach. See also, R. O'Donoghue and A. J. Padilla, *The Law and Economics of Article 82 EC* (Oxford: Hart Publishing 2007), pp. 423–33.

[69] See, for example, A. de Hauteclocque, F. Marty, and J. Pillot, 'The Essential Facilities Doctrine in European Competition Policy: The Case of the Energy Markets', in J.M. Glachant, D. Finon, and A. de Hauteclocque (eds), *Competition, Contracts and Electricity Markets: A New Perspective* (Cheltenham: Edward Elgar 2011).

relate variously to nuclear power, to balancing power, to electricity contracts, and to pipeline access requests.[70]

One might have thought that the question of whether and in what cases access has to be granted to energy networks would have lost much of its relevance with the introduction of third party access in both the electricity and gas markets, but this is certainly not the case. In fact, use of Article 102 TFEU has become a significant tool, for the European Commission in particular, to force improvements to access conditions in terms of access, transparency, and even capacity extensions.[71] While *GDF Suez*[72] and *E.ON*[73] are among the competition law cases driven by the Commission under the essential facilities doctrine to open up transportation capacity and alleviate capacity-related foreclosure through significant capacity releases, the *ENI,*[74] *E.ON,*[75] and *RWE*[76] inquiries ended with complete divestiture of certain network assets.

In *GDF Suez* and *E.ON*, the end result was a 50 per cent capacity release. This proportion of 50 per cent of the total capacity represents, according to the Commission, a workable balance between the rights of companies and the need to create competitive conditions:[77] i.e. capacity to compete.[78] Here, it is of particular importance that, in the *E.ON* case, the Commission explicitly noted that 'long-term capacity bookings can be regarded as refusal to supply under Article 102 TFEU' and how the 'mere fact that the current capacities may have been actually used by the essential facility holder for its supply business is not sufficient to exclude an abuse under Article 102 TFEU'.[79] In this situation, according to the Commission, a dominant essential facility holder is under the obligation to take all possible measures to remove the constraints imposed by lack of capacity

---

[70] For an overview, see A. de Hauteclocque, F. Marty, and J. Pillot, 'The Essential Facilities Doctrine in European Competition Policy: The Case of the Energy Markets', in J.M. Glachant, D. Finon, and A. Hauteclocque (eds), *Competition, Contracts and Electricity Markets: A New Perspective* (Cheltenham: Edward Elgar 2011). For electricity, the French nuclear in particular, see C. Defeuilley and A. de Hauteclocque, 'La Production d'Electricité est-elle une Facilité Essentielle?', LARSEN Working Paper 2010.

[71] K. Talus, 'Just What is the Scope of the Essential Facilities Doctrine in the Energy Sector: Third Party Access-friendly Interpretation in the EU v. Contractual Freedom in the US', 48(5) *Common Market Law Review* (2011).

[72] Case COMP/B-1/39.316—Gaz de France (gas market foreclosure).

[73] COMP/39.317—E.ON gas foreclosure.

[74] COMP/39.315—ENI.

[75] COMP/39.388—German Electricity Wholesale Market and COMP/39.389—German Electricity Balancing Market.

[76] COMP/39.402—RWE gas foreclosure.

[77] Commission press release, 'Antitrust: Commission accepts commitments by GDF Suez to boost competition in French gas market', IP/09/1872, 3.12.2009.

[78] The outcome in these two cases follows the same rationale that was adopted on the regulatory front in relation to the Nabucco pipeline. Here, the exemption decision under Article 22 of the Directive 55/2003/EC imposes a capacity cap on the share of annual capacity which the shareholders, all dominant undertakings in their home-markets, can book at the total of all exit points. As such, the exemption from TPA only covers half of the pipeline capacity. The intention is undoubtedly that the decision complies with the requirement that an exemption must enhance competition and that it cannot be detrimental to competition. Commission exemption Decision in Nabucco (CAB D/2008/142), 8 February 2008.

[79] Decision of 4 May 2010 in COMP/39.317—E.ON gas foreclosure, para. 40.

(e.g. by limiting the duration and volume of its own bookings or by expanding its capacities).[80]

Both *GDF Suez* and *E.ON*, as well as other energy-related cases,[81] show the Commission's clear tendency to stretch a refusal to deal or an essential facility-type of approach beyond its original scope. Instead of limiting the application to access refusals, the traditional scope of the doctrine, the Commission has gone much further by demanding capacity expansions or the construction of new capacity on the back of Article 102 TFEU.[82] The mere fact that a dominant company contracts for transportation capacity in its own network has now been deemed to fall within the scope of the doctrine, regardless of whether the capacity is fully in use or not. The earlier destination clause cases,[83] where the Commission pushed for non-contractual remedies, such as capacity expansion,[84] and the more recent *E.ON, RWE, GDF Suez,* and *ENI* cases ending with divestiture of network assets or capacity releases, reinforce this finding. These cases illustrate both the central role played by sufficient transportation capacity in a functional natural gas market and the willingness of the Commission to create the necessary pre-conditions for such a competitive market structure to emerge. While the traditional application of the essential facility doctrine has been limited to requiring access, the Commission's practice in the energy sector includes investment in critical sections of the supply chain.[85] In this respect, the essential facilities doctrine is employed to engineer new and—potentially—more efficient market structures which could not be achieved through sector-specific regulation. However, the creation of administratively-designed markets effectively means that the regulator is making certain assumptions as to the most effective design for natural gas markets. Regardless of this more speculative suggestion, it seems that following the Court's judgment in *Alrosa*[86] it is increasingly difficult to test the limits of the Commission's powers in accepting (or demanding, at least *de facto*) commitments that go far beyond what is strictly speaking necessary or which would correspond to the regulatory choices contained in the sector-specific regulation. The use of seemingly voluntary commitments is not subject to the same kind of proportionality scrutiny that more unilateral Commission measures would be.[87]

---

[80] Decision of 4 May 2010 in COMP/39.317—E.ON gas foreclosure, para. 40.

[81] Cases COMP/39.388—German Electricity Wholesale Market and COMP/39.389—German Electricity Balancing Market, COMP/39.402—RWE gas foreclosure and COMP/39.315—ENI.

[82] Adrien de Hauteclocque notes the same for electricity sector: see A. de Hauteclocque, *Long-term Supply Contracts in European Decentralized Electricity Markets: An Antitrust Perspective*, (PhD Thesis, University of Manchester School of Law, 2009).

[83] Destination clauses and other territorial sales restriction clauses prohibit the buyer from reselling the gas into other countries or other areas than those for which it is intended. By limiting the freedom of the buyer to resell the gas outside a certain area, these clauses enable a supplier to maintain different price areas for the same product. In a series of cases ranging from 2002 to 2007 the Commission negotiated the exclusion of these contracts from long-term gas contracts between the external producers and the EU purchasers. For this case law, see K. Talus, 'Long-term Gas Agreements and Security of Supply—Between Law and Politics', 32(4) *European Law Review* (2007), pp. 535–48.

[84] Commission press release, 'Commission Reaches breakthrough with Gazprom and ENI on territorial restriction clauses', IP/03/1345, 6.10.2003.

[85] This was the case in the Gazprom/ENI case (see Commission press release 'Commission Reaches breakthrough with Gazprom and ENI on territorial restriction clauses' IP/03/1345, 6.10.2003).

[86] Case C-441/07 P, *Commission v Alrosa* [2010] I-05949.

[87] Case C-441/07 P, *Commission v Alrosa* [2010] I-05949, para. 38.

The use of judicial review is restricted to ensuring that the Commission's assessment was not manifestly incorrect.[88]

4.4 Vertical Restraints in the Energy Sector: Long-Term Supply Agreements, Problem Clauses, and Others

Early Commission practice on long-term supply contracts offered a poor model on which to base future practice: the case law which it generated lacked transparency and was neither easy to understand nor of general applicability. On the contrary, there was considerable uncertainty as to why and how a particular solution was reached. For example, in many cases relating to the duration of supply contracts, there was little or no explanation of why the Commission had decided that a particular period of time was the acceptable contract term in a specific case. Only minor distinctions were drawn between upstream and downstream contracts. Similarly, little or no distinction was drawn between electricity- and gas-related cases.

4.4.1 General Developments

Even with the lack of detailed explanation for particular solutions, it was possible to gather that the Commission would permit long-term contracts of less than 15 years' duration.[89] This period was adopted in a number of cases. This seemingly long duration was accepted in the *Electricidade de Portugal/Pego* case, where the Commission suggested reducing the term of the contracts to what it then considered a legitimate period for both financing and investment—i.e. 15 years instead of 28 years.[90] In another long-term power supply agreement, the Commission accepted a period of 15 years, while also insisting on the removal of the right of first refusal by the Portuguese transmission operator (REN) and inclusion of third party access as conditions for supporting this length of period.[91] Similarly, the Commission accepted a period of 14 years for a supply contract for Electrabel, a Belgian monopoly in place at the time. This was reduced from the original 20–30 year period and with a gradual fade-out for the volume of power supplied.[92]

The Commission's decision relating to the reorganization and privatization of the UK energy markets is another case in point. In this case, the Commission required that the duration of certain exclusive take-or-pay agreements relating to nuclear energy be reduced from 30 to 15 years.[93] The UK government had presented

---

[88] Case C-441/07 P, *Commission v Alrosa* [2010] I-05949, para. 42.

[89] See also J. Faull and A. Nikpay, *The EC Law of Competition* (Oxford: OUP 1999), p. 710.

[90] XXIInd Competition Report [1993], 222.

[91] Commission Decision REN/Turbogas, OJ C 118/7, 1996.

[92] XVIIth *Competition Report* [1997], 127. See also R. Tudway (ed.), *Energy Law and Regulation in the EU* (London: Sweet & Maxwell 1999).

[93] Commission Decision of 30 April 1991 relating to a proceeding under Article 85 of the European Economic Community (EEC) Treaty (IV/33.473—Scottish Nuclear, Nuclear Energy Agreement).

detailed argument as to how these agreements and the proposed period was directly linked with the anticipated lifetime of the power stations concerned, and as to how these agreements would replace the previous loose and non-commercial agreements between various public bodies.

In ruling in favour of a 15-year term, instead of the 30 years envisaged by the UK government, the Commission stated:

'This period of validity provides the stability and guarantee necessary for long-term planning and allows the necessary adjustments to be made to the new situation after a reasonable start-up period. However, this period seems necessary to allow Scottish Nuclear to attain full profitability and become competitive.'

It offered no explanation as to how this figure was reached, in the absence of which the 50 per cent reduction from the initial terms seems arbitrary.

There were also exceptions to this rule. For example, the Commission has approved a 25-year take-or-pay agreement for an Algerian company to supply gas to a Spanish power station,[94] the much longer duration being balanced by an increase in security of supply through the development of new Algerian supplies.

This uncertainty in the reasoning applied and approach taken to long-term agreements was also reflected in the more general Commission practice relating to the exemption periods formerly granted under Article 101(3) TFEU. Even the Commission has openly admitted that the early case law, particularly the practice under Article 101(3), TFEU was not always transparent or in line with the underlying economics of the situation at hand.[95] The Commission has indicated that it followed a policy that exemptions would be granted for ten years[96] or for the duration of the agreement if it was less than ten years.[97] Exceptionally, the exemptions under Article 101(3) TFEU could also be for more than ten years.[98] This 'exception' seems to have been quite general in the energy sector, but this is understandable because of the high upfront investment costs involved.

However, this initial confusion and uncertainty has been significantly reduced in more recent case law. For downstream contracts, which are politically much easier to address than upstream contracts, guidance has come though cases starting with *Gas Natural*[99] and then continuing with *Distrigaz*[100] and *E.ON Ruhrgas*.[101] Cases

---

[94] Transgas/Turbogas case, XXVIth Competition Report [1996]. In this case the Commission did require the deletion of restrictions on onwards-sale of power and a reduction in the duration of a provision limiting gas use for power generation only.

[95] European Commission Review of the Council Regulation (EEC) 4056/86 of 22 December 1986. Technical Paper: Burden of Proof (3.12.2003). Available at: <http://ec.europa.eu/competition/consultations/2003_reg_4056_86/elaa_burdenofproof.pdf>. Even if the subject matter of the paper refers to Maritime Transport, the discussion on the practice under Article 101(3) TFEU is general.

[96] With references, among others, to Exxon/Shell [1994] OJ L 144/20, para. 84.

[97] With references, among others, to Jahrhundertvertrag [1993] OJ L 50/14, para. 1 II.C.

[98] With references, among others, to Scottish Nuclear, Nuceast energy Agreement [1991] OJ L 178/31, para. 143. para. 1 II.C. With references, among others, to Scottish Nuclear, Nuceast energy Agreement

[99] COMP/37.542—Gas Natural + Endesa.

[100] COMP/B-1/37966—Distrigaz.

[101] Bundeskartellamt, Bundeskartellamt pushes ahead with competition in the gas market (28.1.2005).

like *Repsol*[102] and *Synergen*[103] are also of particular significance here.[104] Without going into the detail of these cases, which have been discussed in detail in many EU energy law publications, it suffices for the purposes of this discussion to note that the issues which they highlight in relation to the assessment of downstream contracts in terms of competition law are: (i) the volumes tied under the individual exclusivity contract; (ii) duration; (iii) the cumulative effect of a web of contracts; and (iv) efficiencies suggested by the contracting parties.

Clearly, European energy markets, both gas and electricity, have certain features that make the use of long-term contracts somewhat problematic: for example, limited inter-brand competition, very limited intra-brand competition, monopolistic or oligopolistic market structures, and continued division into national markets. However, for gas markets, the structure of EU gas supply must also be considered here.

After a long period of repeating the mantras about market-based methods, an increasing number of researchers have started to question the elimination of long-term contracts and the push for a very much market-based system. In the context of investment, it has been suggested that 'competitive markets can in theory deliver the necessary investments. However, this does not mean that it will happen in the real-world European markets. In addition to the market failures, the reasons for the shortcomings are that the payoff for the security of supply infrastructure is quite speculative, very poorly understood and non-quantifiable'.[105] In essence, the authors argue that to rely on the markets to provide for security of supply in the EU context means that one relies on markets that are not there. They also suggest that it is very questionable whether such markets will ever be there.[106] Similarly, I have argued elsewhere that in the context of gas markets, instead of pushing for competition, maximizing the number of competitors in the markets and notionally seeking the total elimination of long-term arrangements, it is necessary to look at the realities of the EU energy markets and the structure of the supply (from upstream markets in particular) and accept that a state of perfect competition, or even something close to it, is perhaps not the right objective:

'In a sector where the security of supply is of paramount significance for the entire society and where the up-front investments are among the largest of any economic activity, the objective should not necessarily be the maximum amount of competition, at least not with any cost. It may well be that these features of EU energy markets, including significance for the overall economy, the significant investment costs as well as geological and geopolitical

---

[102] COMP/B-1/38348—REPSOL C.C.P.

[103] Commission press release, 'Commission clears Irish Synergen venture between ESB and Statoil following strict commitments', IP/02/792, 31 May 2002. See also Commission Competition Report 2002, 192–3.

[104] Similarly, A. de Hauteclocque, 'EC Antitrust Enforcement in the Aftermath of the Energy Sector Inquiry: A Focus on Long-Term Supply Contracts in Electricity and Gas', in B. Delvaux, M. Hunt, and K. Talus (eds), *EU Energy Law and Policy Issues* (Rixensart: Euroconfidentiel 2008).

[105] J.M.Glachant, D. Finon, and A. de Hauteclocque (eds), *Competition, Contracts and Electricity Markets: A New Perspective* (Cheltenham: Edward Elgar 2011), p. 34.

[106] J.M.Glachant, D. Finon, and A. de Hauteclocque (eds), *Competition, Contracts and Electricity Markets: A New Perspective* (Cheltenham: Edward Elgar 2011), p. 34.

factors, call for a certain minimum company size. In such a situation, the EU should not aim at perfect competition with a large number of market players. Instead, the objective should be the competition between a more restricted numbers of larger natural gas companies. Sometimes "less is more".[107]

4.4.2 Destination Clauses

Destination clauses, or territorial sales restriction clauses, continue to exist despite ample case law prohibiting them. These clauses prohibit the buyer from reselling the gas into other countries (or other areas) than those for which it is intended. As these clauses restrict the freedom of the buyer to re-sell the purchased gas volumes and create artificial barriers to markets, they serve to compartmentalize the market. For these reasons, they are seen as among the most damaging and anticompetitive provisions used in energy contracts, and have the effect of undermining the creation of a pan-European energy market. In the first years of the new millennium, the Commission initiated a dialogue with the parties to upstream contracts, demanding the elimination of destination clauses, use restrictions, and profit-sharing clauses traditionally used in long-term gas supply contracts. In a line of cases from *Gazprom/ENI*,[108] *Gazprom/OMV*,[109] and *Gazprom/E.ON Ruhrgas*[110] to *Nigerian NLNG*[111] and *Statoil and Norsk Hydro*[112] to *Sonatrach*,[113] the Commission negotiated the exclusion of these clauses, although it seems that while such clauses may have been eliminated from these contracts, the same practice continues to take place.[114]

The roots of these territorial restriction clauses lie in the historical segmentation, both horizontal and vertical, of the EU energy markets. Large producers sold gas to national incumbents (not directly to end-customers), which limited their sale to the area where they controlled the pipelines (typically the immediate home state). By limiting the buyer's freedom to resell the gas outside a certain area these clauses enable the supplier to charge different customers different prices at the same delivery point.[115]

---

[107] K. Talus, *Vertical Natural Gas Transportation Capacity, Upstream Commodity Contracts and EU Competition Law* (Alphen aan den Rijn: Kluwer Law International 2011), 278.

[108] COMP/37.811—Territorial Restrictions 1) Algerian gas export contracts 2) Expansion of TAG pipeline. See also Commission press release, 'Commission reaches breakthrough with Gazprom and ENI on territorial restriction clauses', IP/03/1345, 6.10.2003.

[109] COMP/38.085—PO/Territorial restrictions—Austria. See also Commission press release, 'Competition: Commission secures improvements to gas supply contracts between OMV and Gazprom', IP/05/195, 17.2.2005.

[110] Commission press release, 'Commission secures changes to gas supply contracts between E.ON Ruhrgas and Gazprom', IP/05/710, 10.6.2005.

[111] Commission press release, 'Commission settles investigation into territorial sales restrictions with Nigerian gas company NLNG', IP/02/1869, 12.12.2002.

[112] COMP/36.072—GFU—Norwegian Gas Negotiation Committee. See also Commission press release, 'Commission successfully settles GFU case with Norwegian gas producers', IP/02/1084, 17.7.2002.

[113] Commission press release, 'Commission and Algeria reach agreement on territorial restrictions and alternative clauses in gas supply contracts', IP/07/1074, 11.7.2007.

[114] See Antitrust: 'Commission confirms unannounced inspections in the natural gas sector' (MEMO/11/641), 27.9.2011.

[115] 'Delivery point' is the location where the title and risks relating to the gas is transferred from the seller to the buyer or a third party.

While it is hardly surprising that partitioning of the market is prohibited in the energy sector as in other sectors, other aspects of these cases make them interesting for present purposes: the non-contractual commitments in *Gazprom/ENI* and the impact of geopolitical considerations in *Sonatrach*.

We will look first at the 2003 *Gazprom/ENI* case.[116] This settlement closed the first investigation into a number of gas supply agreements between large external suppliers and EU purchasers. It relates not only to destination clauses, which were deleted, but also to other issues. The contractual commitments made by the parties were as follows:[117]

1. territorial restrictions were deleted from all existing agreements and ENI had the right to resell and transport the purchased gas where it wanted;

2. the parties undertook not to introduce similar agreements to any future agreements between each other or any other parties; and

3. the parties deleted the consent clauses (according to which Gazprom was to obtain consent from ENI in order to sell gas to any other customers in Italy) from all existing agreements.[118]

In addition to these contractual commitments, the following non-contractual commitments were made:

1. ENI committed to make significant volumes of gas available for non-Italian customers during the period of five years;

2. ENI committed to promote a capacity increase in the TAG pipeline from Baumgarten to Italy transporting Russian gas to Italy; and

3. finally, ENI undertook to enhance the TPA regime to the TAG pipeline. The commitments made in this respect included the introduction of one-month transportation contracts, a congestion management system, and the creation of a secondary capacity market etc.[119]

The rationale of these commitments was to prevent compartmentalization of the market (contractual commitments) and enable new competition in Italy (the commitment relating to the TAG pipeline) and in other Member States (the commitment relating to the volumes that ENI were to make available to third party buyers). Curiously, the non-contractual commitments seem to have little to do with the destination clauses and seemed to be geared to improving competitive conditions on the Italian gas supply markets more generally.

---

[116] Commission press release 'Commission Reaches breakthrough with Gazprom and ENI on territorial restriction clauses', IP/03/1345, 6.10.2003.

[117] H. Nyssens, C. Cultera, and D. Schnichels, 'The territorial restrictions in the gas sector: a state of play', Competition Policy Newsletter, No. 1, Spring 2004, pp. 49–51.

[118] H. Nyssens, C. Cultera, and D. Schnichels, 'The territorial restrictions in the gas sector: a state of play', Competition Policy Newsletter, No. 1, Spring 2004, p. 50.

[119] H. Nyssens, C. Cultera, and D. Schnichels, 'The territorial restrictions in the gas sector: a state of play', Competition Policy Newsletter, No. 1, Spring 2004, p. 50.

Whereas Where as the Gazprom-related cases were dealt with relatively quickly and without much controversy (greatly helped by the EU-Russia Energy Dialogue[120]), this was not the case in the negotiations with Sonatrach, the Algerian gas company. Destination clauses were also used in Sonatrach's agreements, and as early as 2003 the Commission stated that negotiations were taking place to exclude these clauses from the existing agreements.[121] These negotiations came to an end only in 2007. Despite the fact that the negotiations lasted over three years, the Commission did not embark upon a formal procedure for the exclusion of these clauses. The suggestion here is that this had much to do with geopolitical considerations, and in particular import dependency, for Italy and Spain in this case.

This suggestion can also be further supported by the fact that all the cases featuring an external supplier as a party were closed after extended negotiations (seven years in the case of *Sonatrach*) without a formal decision. The first to end with a formal decision were the *GDF/ENEL*[122] and *GDF/ENI*[123] cases. It seems that the Commission's previous practice—of closing all cases (where large and important non-EU importers were involved) without a formal decision declaring a violation of EU competition law and the willingness to engage in very long negotiations with Sonatrach—is incompatible with the approach adopted in the *GDF/ENEL* and *GDF/ENI* cases. The factual situation in the last-mentioned cases did not call for a formal decision: in both cases the destination clauses had already been abandoned by the parties almost a year before the decision. The Commission has provided two main explanations to why these particular cases were chosen as cases to end with a formal decision. Neither seems convincing. Its main explanation was that, although the parties had stopped the infringement, there was a need to clarify the law.[124] In this context, the Commission also indicated that, although it did not issue any fines in this case, it would do so in any subsequent cases. These statements gave rise to the belief that the Commission would impose substantial fines on companies participating in agreements containing territorial restriction clauses.[125] Considering the very long negotiations on the exclusion of destination clauses from the agreements employed by Sonatrach (and perhaps even others), this explanation is insufficient. First, legal issues concerning straightforward destination clauses are not very complicated. Secondly, the Commission had already indicated that these clauses were anticompetitive in connection with the Gazprom cases. Thirdly, the extended negotiations concerning the same clauses in, at least, Sonatrach's agreements suggest that the Commission should have explained in

---

[120] EU-Russia Energy Dialogue, The Second Progress Report, May 2008. Available at: <http://ec.europa. eu/energy/international/bilateral_cooperation/russia/doc/reports/progress2_En.pdf>.

[121] Commission press release, 'Commission Reaches breakthrough with Gazprom and ENI on territorial restriction clauses', IP/03/1345, 6.10.2003.

[122] COMP/38.662—GDF—décision GDF/ENEL, 26 October 2004.

[123] COMP/38.662—GDF—décision GDF/ENI, 26 October 2004.

[124] COMP/38.662—GDF/ENI, para. 162. See also Commission press release, 'Commission confirms that territorial restriction clauses in the gas sector restrict competition', IP/04/1310, 26.10.2004.

[125] For example, see J. Rodriguez, 'The Growing Impact on EC Competition Law on Gas Sale and Transportation Agreements' *LNG Journal* (2005), p. 33.

more detail why it felt that this particular case, among many other ongoing cases, should be treated differently.

The second reason for the decision appears to be an exercise of the right to a defence. The Commission refers to this as a second reason for a formal decision. It states that the parties disputed the Commission's interpretation of the nature of the relevant clauses.[126] While this explanation would be in line with the Commission's repeated statements to the effect that Gazprom and other significant importers would be treated the same as other companies,[127] it does not seem likely that the reason for a formal decision may be found in the lack of cooperation from a company under investigation. A situation where an undertaking risks facing a stricter application of the law and more severe punishment where it legitimately defends its interests seems to contradict the right to defend oneself, which is a fairly central right in any society based on the rule of law.

Since the Commission's suggestions are not very convincing, the question arises as to the reason behind this enigma. It is submitted that the Commission was influenced by consideration of the political risks involved in 'full-scale' enforcement of EC competition law as far as the Gazprom-EU relationship was concerned—in particular, security of supply issues for the EU—and consequently refrained from taking action in these sensitive cases. This is a classic example of how law can only function within politically acceptable boundaries. However, a change seems to have taken place in this respect.[128] In September 2011, the European Commission initiated the first ever competition inquiry in the energy markets of the Central and Eastern EU Member States.[129] According to the Commission, the unannounced inspections were undertaken as there were concerns that certain anticompetitive practices in the supply of natural gas in Central and Eastern European Member States were taking place. The investigation focuses on the upstream supply level. The Commission suspected exclusionary behaviour, including market partitioning, obstacles to network access, barriers to supply diversification, as well as possible exploitative behaviour, such as excessive pricing. While initial inspection of the premises of various Central and Eastern European companies included both Gazprom and incumbents, the focus has thereafter shifted to Gazprom.[130] The Commission suspects that: (i) Gazprom may have divided gas markets by hindering the free flow of gas across Member

---

[126] C. Cultrera, 'Les Décisions GDF, La Commission est Formelle: Les Clauses de Restriction Territoriale dans les Contrats de Gaz Violent l'Article 81', *Competition policy newsletter*, No. 1, Spring 2005, pp. 47–8.

[127] For example, see Commission Press Release, Commissioner Piebalgs and Minister Bartenstein clarify key points of the EU-Russia gas trade relationship in a letter to the Russian Government, IP/06/556, 2.5.2006.

[128] The suggestion here is that the change has to do with two main factors: success in earlier natural gas and electricity market cases by the Director General of Competition has provided a confidence boost to engage in more complicated cases and the changes in the international gas markets (new volumes of available LNG, reduced demand, and the shale gas revolution) have created a setting where the position of Gazprom is weaker than it was before these events unfolded.

[129] 'Antitrust: Commission confirms unannounced inspections in the natural gas sector' (MEMO/11/641), 27 September 2011.

[130] Case 39816—Upstream gas supplies in Central and Eastern Europe.

States; (ii) Gazprom may have prevented the diversification of supply of gas; and (iii) Gazprom may have imposed unfair prices on its customers by linking the price of gas to oil prices.[131]

The first area of concern, market partitioning, seems to refer to destination clauses or territorial sales restriction clauses. As was seen above, the Commission dealt with these clauses in a line of inquiries in 2002–2007 and negotiated the exclusion of these anticompetitive clauses from the agreements used by Gazprom and other external producers. This investigation suggests that the Commission suspects that destination clauses may still be employed, despite their exclusion from the actual contracts. This was the situation in Megal pipeline case,[132] where GDF Suez and E.ON had declared that they regarded the market sharing agreement to be null and void but in reality continued to abide by this arrangement.[133] The second area of concern seems to relate to capacity hoarding, much like the *GDF* case. The last area that the Commission is looking at is the oil price indexation. Here, it seems that the Commission action is premature. Unlike the US, where gas to gas competition determines the natural gas prices, long-term EU natural gas contract prices have traditionally been based on the market value principle, which means the cost of alternative non-gas fuels. In practice this translates into indexation to heavy fuel oil and light fuel oil or crude oil or a combination of these. Sometimes coal appears in the formula.

This linkage is based on the idea of switching capability of the customer where the price of natural gas would determine whether the customer burns oil or gas.[134] However, today this switching capability is more of a theoretical argument. Even in the longer term, meaning that the linkage could be defended through the argument that the customer will choose to construct an oil burning facility instead of gas or an installation with a switching capability, the argument is largely flawed. No new oil fired generation facilities are being constructed in the EU.[135] The environmental concerns, modernisation of natural gas based power production, limitations on emissions, etc. have all resulted in a situation where the argument based on the switching capability is outdated.[136] Based on these findings, the linkage between the two commodities could be questioned.

This has also been noted in the sector specific regulation where the preamble to the new Third Natural Gas Directive makes a note that 'Natural gas is mainly, and

---

[131] Case 39816—Upstream gas supplies in Central and Eastern Europe. See also Antitrust: Commission opens proceedings against Gazprom, IP/12/937, 4.9.2011.

[132] Case COMP/39.401—E.ON/GDF.

[133] For the other elements including oil price indexation, see K. Talus, 'Long-term Natural Gas Contracts and Antitrust Law in the European Union and the United States', 4(3) *Journal of World Energy Law and Business* (2011), pp. 260–315.

[134] ECT Secreteriat, *Putting a Price on Energy: International Pricing Mechanisms for Oil and Gas* (ECT 2007).

[135] J. Stern, *Is There a Rationale for the Continuing Link to Oil Product Prices in Continental European Long Term Contracts?* (NG 19, OIES 2007), p. 6.

[136] This is widely discussed in J. Stern and H. Rogers, *The Transition to Hub-Based Gas Pricing in Continental Europe* (NG 49, OIES 2011), J. Stern, *Future Gas Production in Russia: is the concern about lack of investment justified?* (NG 34, OIES 2009) and J. Stern, *Is There a Rationale for the Continuing Link to Oil Product Prices in Continental European Long Term Contracts?* (NG 19, OIES 2007).

increasingly, imported into the Community from third countries. Community law should take account of the characteristics of natural gas, such as certain structural rigidities arising from the concentration of suppliers, the long-term contracts or the lack of downstream liquidity. Therefore, more transparency is needed, including in regard to the formation of prices'.[137]

This could be interpreted to mean that while long-term commodity contracts are *per se* seen as a necessary component of the EU natural gas trade, the question of price formation must be addressed at some point. The 2007 Sector Inquiry also addressed the question of the oil price linkage. In essence, the traditional EU importers, the incumbents and the external producers argued in favour of the link. Many of the national regulators, the new entrants and traders considered the link as a symptom of the lack of competition due to contractual structures that continue to affect the markets rather than a technical pricing problem that should be addressed in isolation. In addition, some of these new entities and public bodies argued against the continuation of this linkage.[138]

The situation has radically changed since 2007. A major milestone in the discussions on the correct pricing mechanism took place in August 2010 when the new Chairman of the Board of Management of E.ON Ruhrgas AG indicated that E.ON has moved against the continuing oil price linkage and that the current long-term contracts with this linkage need to be adjusted. This, to quote Professor Jonathan Stern, is nothing short of proposing a "revolution in the industry".[139]

There are several factors that have led to changing behaviour in the EU natural gas industry. These include the rapid and fundamental changes in world LNG markets that have resulted from a decrease in demand and the closure of US markets, linked to the emergence of unconventional gas, both of which have acted as catalysts for change through providing for increasing liquidity in the EU natural gas hubs. However, there is also an important regulatory dimension to this change. This paradigm shift in energy governance—from state to market, from plan to contract, and from monopoly to competition—has significantly changed the way in which EU natural gas markets are regulated and this has had a profound impact on the risk position of the contractual parties. Because of these changes, it is very likely that these changes will lead into a progressive introduction of spot indices in price indexation formulas.[140]

The use of oil indexation in long-term contracts has been further complicated by the above examined downstream markets related decisions from the German Federal Court of Justice in which the Court concluded that it amounted to a

---

[137] Third Gas Market Directive, preamble 37.

[138] Sector Inquiry, p. 219.

[139] J. Stern, *Future Gas Production in Russia: Is the Concern about Lack of Investment Justified?* (NG 34, OIES 2009).

[140] This has been suggested by Jonathan Stern in 2007 and repeated in 2009 and 2011. J. Stern and H. Rogers, *The Transition to Hub-Based Gas Pricing in Continental Europe* (NG 49, OIES 2011), J. Stern, *Future Gas Production in Russia: Is the Concern about Lack of Investment Justified?* (NG 34, OIES 2009) and J. Stern, *Is There a Rationale for the Continuing Link to Oil Product Prices in Continental European Long Term Contracts?* (NG 19, OIES 2007).

disproportionate disadvantage for customers if the strict linkage of the gas price to the oil price allowed the provider not only to compensate price increases but to also generate additional profit out of it.[141] This scenario would become relevant in a situation where, for example, the oil products that are used in the contracts as the basis for gas prices are different in the upstream contract used to import the gas and in the downstream contract that the EU supplier uses with its end-customers. If the price of gas to the final customer goes up more than it does for the EU supplier due to different price developments in different oil products, this would seem to fall under the undue advantage area that the German court was referring to.

As noted above, it would seem that the Commission action in this area is premature. If the EU is still applying a market based approach to energy, should the markets not decide the pricing and should the administrative interference not be limited to clear situations of market failures. There is little need for an antitrust intervention where the market forces are working out the correct pricing mechanism. This is the currently the case and much like the US in the 1980s, the market is working out a new way to trade gas (in US the question related to long-term contracts, in the EU the focus is on pricing). It is both premature and dangerous for the European Commission to intervene and dictate the outcome of this on-going process.

The Commission has been careful to emphasize that the Gazprom case is a 'normal' case and will be decided based on economics. The Commission also tries to draw a line between Gazprom and the Russian State: 'To clarify, this is an investigation which concerns Gazprom, which is a company active in the EU single market, which sells gas to the EU, and so we are looking at the behaviour of this company. This does not concern Russia.'[142]

The interpretation of Gazprom has been somewhat different. According to the Gazprom press release: 'It's no secret that a number of the EU's relatively weak economies continue demanding that Gazprom unilaterally cut down prices, and such statements can be interpreted as nothing else but the European Commission's support to the practice of subsidizing Eastern Europe with cheap gas at the expense of Gazprom. This is an attempt to meet the economic challenges of the EU, particularly of its new member countries, Eastern Europe, at the expense of Russia.'[143] Other responses include those of Gazprom spokesman Sergei Kupriyanov: 'Right now a series of relatively weak EU economies are continuing to demand from Gazprom unilateral concessions on gas prices. You can't view this [the EU probe] as anything other than EC [European Community] support for Gazprom subsidies to eastern Europe. This is an attempt to solve the economic problems of the EC at Russia's cost'; and that of Russia's EU ambassador Vladimir Chizhov: 'EU lawyers can investigate "life on Mars"', or Gazprom deputy chief Alexander Medvedev, who called the EU a 'thief.' Finally, Putin noted that 'someone in the European

---

[141] Bundesgerichtshof, VIII ZR 178/08 and VIII ZR 304/08. This is not a competition but civil code case.

[142] 'First signs of tension after EU move on Gazprom', 5 September 2012. Available at <http://euobserver. com/economic/117441>.

[143] <http://gazprom.com/press/news/2012/september/article143723/>.

Commission decided that we must assume part of the burden of this subsidising [of EU countries]. United Europe wants to retain some political influence and wants us to pay for it'.[144]

In addition to these political responses, there was a legislative response from the Russian side. The Decree No. 1285 of 11 September 2012 (On Measures to Protect the Interests of the Russian Federation when a Foreign Economic Activity is Carried out by Russian Juridical Persons) requires that companies included in the list of strategic enterprises and strategic joint stock companies and their subsidiaries engage in a range of the following specified activities/operations with foreign governments, organizations, and institutions (including foreign regulatory authorities) only after obtaining a prior consent of a federal executive body appointed by the Russian government. These activities cover: (1) submission of information regarding economic activities; (2) making amendments to contracts with foreign entities (as well as documents concerning commercial and pricing policies in foreign States); and (3) selling or transferring shares in foreign entities as well as rights to commercial activity and immovable property located abroad. Importantly, the above-mentioned body will have the authority to refuse to give its consent to the above activities/operations if they have a potential to cause injury to the economic interests of the Russian Federation.[145] In simple terms, the decree refers to the activities of the 'strategic companies', which include Gazprom, and deals with three main aspects: disclosure of information; alteration of contracts; and sale of assets. Translated into EU energy market realities, these became: cooperation with the EU Commission in the competition law case, including providing information under Regulation 1/2003; any changes to long-term gas contracts and oil price indexation in particular; and, finally, sales of network assets under the Lex Gazprom clause.

While the outcome of the case remains to be seen, one thing is clear: this case is not 'just another case'; it is a case loaded with geopolitical considerations.

4.5 Current and Future Standards for the Application of Competition Law in the Energy Industries

As regulated markets replace monopolies, new combinations arise which can undermine the functioning of competition. First, the transitional situation includes the mutation of monopolists into oligopolists, with the possibility of concentration arising through jointly-operated facilities and through influence on the coordination mechanisms now emerging to assure electricity markets. Secondly, similar concentrations can occur (and already have occurred) through alliances between dominant EU traders/transporters and dominant outside suppliers—particularly in Algeria and Russia.[146] Thirdly, the establishment of national regulatory agencies does not

---

[144] 'Putin says "Niet" to EU anti-trust lawyers', 12 September 2012. Available at: <http://euobserver. com/foreign/117515>.
[145] This is a translation of the Russian Decree by Vitaliy Pogoretskyy.
[146] Consider the formation of a Gas-OPEC. See H. Hallouche, 'The GECF: Is it Really a Gas-OPEC in the Making?' (Oxford: Oxford Institute for Energy Studies 2006)

mean that these will automatically guarantee a competitive EU-wide or even global energy market. As long as there is no EU energy regulator, national regulators are likely to be institutionally, politically, and culturally responsive to the interests of national companies as against foreign newcomers. Here, the mandate of ACER falls short of effectiveness. A myriad of opportunities exists for national regulators to include disguised protectionism in the regulation of tariffs, rules on recovery of stranded cost, definition of public service obligations, incentives for production of non-conventional energy, and environmental protection.[147] Illustrations of these can be seen in various examples offered throughout this book. The Commission has tackled this transformation of anticompetitive potential from state-sponsored monopolies to independent regulators by developing first a systematic and then an institutional dialogue with European regulators, but while such dialogue may reduce disguised protectionism and anticompetitive conduct by national energy companies and 'captured' national regulators, it cannot completely exclude it.

4.6 External Dependence, Extraterritorial Application, and Competition Enforcement in an International Energy Context

The issue of the application and enforcement of extraterritorial competition law in relation to foreign energy producers, shippers, etc., is of clear relevance when: import dependency makes it necessary to conclude purchase contracts with non-European corporate entities (e.g. Gazprom); supply networks are administered by non-European system operators (e.g. Sonatrach); or non-European entities decide on the level of production of energy commodities (e.g. OPEC). Internationally, extraterritorial application has been practised in energy matters: just consider the case of the United States NOPEC legislation[148] and other earlier antitrust decisions, which characterized OPEC as an unlawful cartel.[149] The ambit of European antitrust law is wide since its language strikes at any agreement which has an actual or potential effect on trade between Member States and which causes the actual distortion of competition or has the potential to do so as its object or its effect. Clearly, an anticompetitive agreement will be considered invalid when it involves one European energy undertaking, and the same can be said for a non-EU undertaking on the basis of territorial jurisdiction.[150] There are many examples of this in the energy field—just consider

---

[147] On 'regulatory risk' for infrastructure investment, see T. Wälde and A. Kolo 'Environmental Regulation, Investment Protection and "Regulatory Taking" in International Law', *ICLQ* (2001), pp. 811–48.

[148] S. Looper; 'Nopec Goes Bananas: How the Supreme Court Will Thwart Congress's Attempt to Extend U.S. Antitrust Law's Extraterritorial Reach', 1 *OGEL* (2010), <http://www.ogel.org>.

[149] A. Caillard 'EU: US extraterritorial jurisdiction—EU/US agreement' 4(4) *International Trade Law & Regulation* (1998), pp. 54–5 and A. Udin 'Slaying Goliath; The Extraterritorial Application of US Antitrust Law to OPEC', *American University Law Review* (2001), p. 1321.

[150] See generally P. Roth (ed.), *Bellamy and Child, Community Law of Competition* (Sweet and Maxwell 2001), pp. 136 et seq. The concept of extraterritorial application of competition law is in practice most relevant to mergers and acquisitions activities: Case T-102/96, *Gencor Ltd v Commission* [1999] ECR, p. II-00753. See also A. Ezrachi. 'Limitations on the Extraterritorial Reach of the European

the destination clause cases examined in section 4.4.2. Taken a step further, the focus on an appreciable effect on the internal energy market for antitrust considerations could also mean that EU energy undertakings and even non-EU energy undertakings engaging in anticompetitive conduct outside the EU can be subject to the Commission's competition law enforcement efforts under the effects doctrine. This, however, remains somewhat unclear.[151]

It is only where anticompetitive conduct genuinely arises outside European territorial or personal jurisdiction that Commission enforcement is likely to trigger strong reactions on the part of third countries. However, such application is often not as ignorant as perceived. In the US, in response to foreign concerns about the application of their antitrust laws, courts and scholars have developed the concept that the exercise of an extraterritorial jurisdiction may be limited to take account of the important policy interests of another state where the activities in question take place.[152] The case law of the European Commission reflects this approach.[153] But any such attempt needs a functioning system of comity and mutual recognition, which is increasingly practised, but internationally still in its infancy. Viewed against the difficult third party access rights under international agreements such as the Energy Charter Treaty, a quasi-international application of US/EU style antitrust law has the advantage that effective access to dispute resolution mechanisms already exists under national competition enforcement (including injunctions).

However, the EU's dependence on energy imports complicates the extra-territorial application of EU competition laws, particularly in relation to external suppliers. This is clear from the destination clause cases and the responses to the ongoing Gazprom case. It also explains why the Commission has really never attacked upstream contracts or carried out an economic analysis of upstream conditions. One might also look at the negotiations on TPA for the transit pipelines in relation to this issue. In the absence of any other explanation, it seems that (at least in some cases) political decision-making and the role played by security of supply considerations provide the ultimate explanation for this enigma. Law is only applied where it is politically possible to apply it.

4.7 State Aid in the Energy Industries

A free market requires a level playing field where companies compete on the strength of their commercial abilities, not on the strength of their political relations, ability to influence or even capture the regulatory process, and not as a result

---

Merger Regulation', *E.C.L.R.* (2001), pp. 137–46 and M. Broberg 'The European Commission's Extraterritorial Powers in Merger Control: The Court of First Instance's Judgment in *Gencor v. Commission'*, *I.C.L.Q.* (2000), pp. 172–82.

[151] The main case here would be Case 114/85, *Ahlström Oy and others v Commission* [1988] ECR 5193.
[152] See in particular: *Timberlane Lumber Co. v Bank of America*, 549 F. 2d 597, also Restatement (third) of the Foreign Relations Law of the United States, § 403.
[153] See Aluminium Imports form Eastern Europe, OJ 1985 L 92/81, [1987] 3 CMLR 813.

of direct or indirect financial support from their government. In the mercantilist vision of the global economy, it is just the opposite: the state—using private or public companies as tools of national policy—supports its companies by fair means and foul, uses its political leverage to secure overseas contracts and places obstacles in the way of foreign competitors. The state machinery identifies with 'its' companies—and they with the state. The insights gleaned from 'public choice theory' on the relationship between state and society give us an appreciation of the fact that whatever the professed goal and treaty adherence of a government, it is inevitably caught up in attempts made by special interests to capture its regulatory and fiscal machinery. Domestic special interests—trade unions, companies with a competitive advantage—are often able to influence the government and win special privileges through the close linkages between business and politics in the domestic political process, including corruption in the narrow and wider sense.[154] As long as the sphere of the state is not separated from the sphere of business, which in the real world can arguably never be completely distinct, it is natural for companies to seek governmental support. Such support for individual companies obstructs competition based on competence and performance. It also tends to trigger reciprocal races for support, so that companies ultimately compete on their ability to influence their respective governments, consumers, and taxpayers. Furthermore, the prosperity gained through international comparative advantage is undermined. If we have made a decision to adopt a market-based approach to energy, then a properly-functioning international economy (global or European) needs 'constitutional rules' limiting the ability of individual national (and sub-national) governments to distort competition through the use of direct and indirect subsidies. Such rules are not only in the interest of creating a legal framework for the international economy to harness the contribution of competition to global prosperity, but even in the interests of governments themselves: they provide an external constraint which helps governments—as an external, immovable cause (and political scapegoat)—to fend off domestic pressures to provide support to ailing businesses. They also reduce the potential for corruption as governments which are unable to offer subsidies are less susceptible to bribery. These are the reasons in support of international rules to limit subsidies, both at international level, under GATT/WTO law, and at EU level, under Article 107 TFEU. EU rules on state aid had relatively little significance for the energy sector as long as the energy markets were nationally segregated and energy was beyond the reach of EU law. With the opening-up of national energy borders and the development of European (and global) energy trade, the energy companies become vulnerable to international competition, and this tends to make the provision of state aid to energy companies themselves seem quite tempting to governments. On the other hand, the

---

[154] Corruption in the wider (i.e. usually not yet criminalized sense) includes: contributions and other support to political parties; a mutually supportive relationship between senior executives in government, politics, and business—with attractive employment, consultancy, or other commercial contracts waiting for the state's elites upon retirement; and mutual support for senior appointments among small groups of national elites, often related to their class or now mainly common educational background.

pressure for fiscal austerity under the standard rules relating to the Euro currency, in particular in the current debt crisis, together with the waning political and moral legitimacy of state intervention in corporate affairs which have a less pronounced 'national' character, tends to reduce the temptation to intervene surreptitiously, with an inherent opening for corruption, in order to enhance national energy companies' competitive edge.

Article 107 TFEU is based on the objective to reduce state aid, and in particular to distinguish between 'good' state aid justified by environmental, disaster, social, and economic disparity reasons, and 'bad' state aid, which distorts competition and EU trade without having any redeeming virtues. Over the past few decades, the Commission and the Court have—again as part of the internal market programme—spearheaded a significant expansion of the concept of state aid and achieved enforcement successes. The Parliament and Council are less sympathetic, as they tend to be much more vulnerable to domestic pressures than the other European institutions. But enforcement of the prohibition against state aid under Article 107 TFEU is not enough. It is equally important to enhance the transparency of state aid. The process of provision of state aid, as with any activity involving an often dubious relationship between state machinery and commercial interests, inherently prefers shadow to light. Taxpayers and consumers (most of them recipients of minor amounts of state subsidy in one form or other and therefore inclined to see their share and the overall subsidy culture in a positive light) would react very differently if they realized that a significant percentage of overall public expenditure is spent on public subsidy programmes—i.e. that taxes could be significantly lessened if subsidies were eliminated or at least benchmarked against the developed market economies with the lowest state aid figures.[155]

4.7.1 The Structure of Article 107 TFEU

Article 107 TFEU prohibits the granting of state aid by Member States where this distorts competition affecting intra-EU trade. Certain types of aid are excluded under Article 107(2), and others may be excluded at the Commission's discretion under Article 107(3). As far as energy is concerned, Article 107(3) is the more significant of the two provisions. The grant of new state aid must be notified in advance to the Commission, failing which it will be invalid. The procedural provisions are laid down in Article 108 TFEU and complemented by Regulation 659/1999.[156] Article 107 is directed at Member States and involves considerable discretion on the part of the Commission (under Article 107(3), but not 107(2) which is a list of automatic exemptions). There are now policy guidelines on what the Commission views as unjustified state aid.[157] Third parties (i.e. beneficiaries and competitors) are entitled

---

[155] See M. Cini and L. McGowan, *EC Competition Policy* (London: Macmillan 1998), pp. 144–7.
[156] Council Regulation No 659/1999 of 22 March 1999 laying down detailed rules for the application of Article 93 (now Article 108) of the EC Treaty, OJ L 83/1, 27.3.1999, pp. 1–9
[157] Commission notice on the determination of the applicable rules for the assessment of unlawful State aid, OJ C 119, 22.5.2002, p. 22.

to have their voices heard after the Commission has published a communication on state aid procedure (although this is arguably quite a complex procedure). Justifications for state aid cannot only be found in Article 107(2) and (3), but also in the overall derogation in favour of public service functions in Article 106(2), as was affirmed in the earlier *Corbeau*[158] judgment and then in *Altmark*.[159] The Article 106(2) undertakings relating to public service functions are covered by Article 107. This means that such undertakings have to notify new grants of state aid, which are invalid unless justified under Article 107(2) and (3) or, with the strict necessity test, under Article 106(2).[160]

A number of criteria must be fulfilled for a measure to fall under Article 107(1) TFEU. First, there must be intervention by the state or through state resources. Secondly, the intervention must be liable to affect trade between Member States. Thirdly, it must confer a selective advantage on the recipient, which it would not have had under normal market conditions. Fourthly, it must distort or threaten to distort competition.[161] The effect of the arrangement is, or should be, the decisive factor, not its form. However, as discussed in the next paragraph. the notion of state resources as treated in *PreussenElektra* and subsequent cases seems to undermine this effects-based approach. This chapter does not examine all of the criteria set out so far in this section, but instead focuses on the first one, which has continued to pose questions over the years. The other three criteria will only be addressed in passing.

In examining the first of the criteria, it must be underlined that the notion of state aid covers more than just 'subsidies' and has widened over the years. An advantage provided to the recipient can consist of direct subsidies, but also other benefits such as: purchase guarantees like power-purchase contracts;[162] tax benefits; capital increases of loss-making companies; writing-off of debt, preferential interest rates, take-off guarantees;[163] sale beneath market value; or purchase above market values. The concept of 'negative state aid' also falls within the category of state aid.[164] Clearly, the governmental designers of state aid (and the industry recipients) possess great ingenuity: as soon as simple and easily identified types of state aid are detected, new and better disguised ones are invented. If government-controlled companies are involved, typically through the use of tariffs or other contract terms,

---

[158] Case C-320/91, *Corbeau* [1993] ECR I-2533.

[159] Case C-280/00, *Altmark* [2003] ECR I-7747.

[160] Case C-387/92, *Banco de Credit* [1994] ECR I-877.

[161] For example, see Case C-451/03, *Servizi Ausiliari Dottori Commercialisti* [2006] ECR I-2941, para. 56, Case C-206/06, *Essent Netwerk Noord and Others* [2008] ECR I-05497, para 64.

[162] Commission Decision of 4 June 2008 on the State aid C 41/05 awarded by Hungary through Power Purchase Agreements (notified under document C(2008) 2223).

[163] Commission Decision of 4 June 2008 on the State aid C 41/05 awarded by Hungary through Power Purchase Agreements (notified under document C(2008) 2223).

[164] 'Negative state aid' means non-imposition of certain charges on companies in comparable situations therefore mitigating the financial burdens of undertakings. See Joined Cases C-128/03 and C-129/03, *AEM SpA and AEM Torino SpA v Autorita per l'energia elettrica e per il gas and others*, judgment 14 April 2005 (unreported). For an analysis, see: M. Maier and P. Werner, 'ECJ, Judgement of 14 April 2005, Joined cases C-128/03 and C-129/03—AEM v. Autorità per l'energia elettrica e per il gas', 4 *European State Aid Law Quarterly* (2005), pp. 49–52.

the Commission uses the 'market investor principle'[165] to distinguish camouflaged state aid from a legitimate commercial reaction to market conditions. Differentiating between the state as a public actor and the state as a commercial actor is the key here, and the two roles cannot be played simultaneously.[166]

An important standard in practice is that state aid must involve some transfer of a 'resource' from the government to the beneficiary. However, this seemingly clear standard is far from being so in practice, as the case law demonstrates. The issue has been raised in a line of cases from *PreussenElektra*[167] to *Essent*,[168] and we shall go on to examine these cases briefly.

As is well known, *PreussenElektra* essentially concerned a feed-in-tariff scheme in which electricity supply companies were obliged to purchase electricity generated from renewable sources in their areas at a fixed price that was considerably higher than that of electricity produced from non-renewable sources. This scheme had been notified to the Commission under Article 108(3) TFEU and was duly approved. However, it was subsequently modified in the course of the legislative process. The final act included new provisions, such as a hardship clause under which the supplier had the right to receive compensation from the network operator for its additional costs where the proportion of the renewable energy purchased under this scheme exceeded 5 per cent of the energy supplied to end-customers by the supplier. This right was triggered in 1998 and the local energy supplier duly invoiced PreussenElektra. The dispute that followed was heard in the Landgericht Kiel which requested a preliminary ruling from the Court.

There was no dispute among the parties about the economic advantage that followed the mandatory purchase obligation and minimum price, which guaranteed green energy suppliers a higher profit than they would have received in the absence of this type of scheme. Similarly, the distortion of competition and effects on trade criteria seem to have been fulfilled, although this was not made explicit in the judgment.[169] Instead, the main question was whether the requirement had been met that aid must be granted by a Member State or through state resources in any form whatsoever and whether Article 107(1) TFEU had been triggered.

In this context, the Court noted first that the notion of 'by Member States or through state resources' covered advantages granted directly by the state as well as

---

[165] Case C-305/89, *Italy v Commission* [1991] ECR I-01603. C.D. Ehlermann, 'Les Entreprises Publiques et le Controle des Aides d'Etat', *Revue du Marche Commun et de L'Union Europeenne* (1992), p. 613; the comparator used is here a 'holding' company which analyses the strategies of its subsidiaries (including cross-subsidization and loss-leader strategies) from an overall strategic view.

[166] The application of the market investor principle is not always obvious. Just examine and compare the decisions in State aid C 41/05 awarded by Hungary through Power Purchase Agreements (notified under document C(2008) 2223) and Case T-156/04, *EDF v Commission* [2009] ECR II-04503 (appeal pending case C-124/10 P).

[167] Case C-379/98, *PreussenElektra* [2001] ECR I-2099.

[168] Case C-206/06, *Essent Netwerk Noord and Others* [2008] ECR, p. I-05497.

[169] H. Bjornebye, *Investing in EU Energy Security: Exploring the Regulatory Approach to Tomorrow's Electricity Production* (Alphen aan den Rijn: Kluwer Law International 2010), p. 353 and R. Van der Vlies, 'The European Court's *PreussenElektra* Judgment: Tensions between EU Principles and National Renewable Energy Initiatives', 22(10) *European Competition Law Review* (2001), p. 461.

those granted by a public or private body designated or established by the state.[170] Therefore, the allocation of the financial burden arising from a purchase obligation for private electricity supply undertakings as between them and other private undertakings cannot constitute a direct or indirect transfer of state resources.[171] As such, in *PreussenElektra*,[172] the obligation imposed on private electricity supply undertakings to purchase electricity produced from renewable energy sources at a fixed minimum prices did not involve any direct or indirect transfer of state resources to undertakings producing that type of electricity.[173] The Court therefore rejected the view that support measures established by the state (through legislative measures) but financed by private companies[174] are caught by Article 107(1) TFEU.[175]

The Court clearly adopted a very narrow interpretation of the concept of 'state resources' in *PreussenElektra*, and excluded the situation in which aid is not provided using state resources but can nevertheless be attributed to state conduct. The Court therefore essentially followed the approach taken by AG Jacobs.[176] This narrow interpretation was undoubtedly beneficial from a renewable energy and environmental point of view. However, from a wider EU law perspective it is rather problematic as the economic effects of the scheme were essentially the same as in a state aid scheme.[177]

This approach also seems somewhat formalistic as it essentially creates effects that are very similar to state aid, even if the funds never were and never will be at the disposal of German authorities, as emphasized by the AG in his Opinion.[178] It has also been suggested that the link between the public measure and private funding was strong enough for the scheme to be regarded as state aid.[179] This suggestion seems correct. The formalistic approach of the Court in this case seems unwarranted, in particular if one looks at the effects of the measure, instead of its form. This difficulty was manifest in the more recent case of *Essent*.[180] This case

---

[170] Case C-379/98, *PreussenElektra* [2001] ECR I-2099. para. 58.

[171] Case C-379/98, *PreussenElektra* [2001] ECR I-2099, para. 60.

[172] The company on which the state imposed the purchase obligation was privately owned in the *PreussenElektra* case. Had this company been state owned, could the situation been very different. The resources used would have been resources belonging to and controlled by a fully state-owned company. Given the legislative framework in question, the behaviour of the company could have been imputable to the state. This was the situation in Commission Decision of 4 June 2008 on the State aid C 41/05 awarded by Hungary through Power Purchase Agreements (notified under document C(2008) 2223), C-482/99, *Stardust* [2002] ECR I-4397.

[173] Case C-379/98, *PreussenElektra* [2001] ECR I-2099, para. 59.

[174] The Court also emphasized that PreussenElektra was a private company owned by other private companies.

[175] Case C-379/98, *PreussenElektra* [2001] ECR I-2099, para. 63.

[176] Opinion of AG Jacobs in Case C-379/98, *PreussenElektra*, delivered on 26 October 2000. Both the AG and the ECJ made references to the established case law in the area. However, it has been noted that this case law covered quite different situations: J. Baquero Cruz and F. Castillo de la Torre, 'A Note on PreussenElektra', 26 *ELRev* (2001), p. 492.

[177] Similarly, R. Van der Vlies, 'The European Court's *PreussenElektra* Judgment: Tensions between EU Principles and Nationan Renewable Energy Initiatives', 22(10) *European Competition Law Review* (2001), p. 462.

[178] Opinion of AG Jacobs in Case C-379/98 *PreussenElektra*, delivered on 26 October 2000, para. 166.

[179] J. Baquero Cruz and F. Castillo de la Torre, 'A Note on PreussenElektra', 26 *ELRev* (2001), p. 494.

[180] Case C-206/06, *Essent Netwerk Noord and Others* [2008] ECR, p. I-5497.

concerned a national legislation permitting the levy of a surcharge on the price for electricity transmission in favour of a statutorily-designated company which was required to pay stranded costs. These costs that were compensated under the Dutch scheme could not be recovered in the new context of liberalized energy markets. These related to pre-liberalization long-term power purchase contracts, agreements for urban heating projects and a project to produce gas from coal. The scheme was based on what was called a 'protocol agreement' between four regional electricity producers, 23 distribution companies, and SEP, which was owned and created by the regional electricity producers to administer all the produced and imported electricity. The protocol agreement was subsequently incorporated into the Dutch Electricity Act.

In examining the scheme, the Court essentially found that certain amounts under the scheme had their origin in a state resource. This appeared to be so because the charge was imposed by law[181] and the proceeds were administered in accordance with the law.[182] But this was also largely the case in *PreussenElektra*.

No doubt because of these similarities, the Court explicitly distinguished *PreussenElektra*.[183] In that case, the Court reasoned, it was held that the obligation imposed on private electricity supply undertakings to purchase electricity produced from renewable energy sources at fixed minimum prices did not involve any direct or indirect transfer of state resources to undertakings which produced that type of electricity. Unlike in *Essent*, the undertakings in *PreussenElektra* had not been appointed by the state to manage a state resource, but were bound by an obligation to purchase by means of their own financial resources.[184] The difference is subtle.

The result of these two cases seems to be that 'an obligation for suppliers to buy a certain proportion of the electricity supplies from a pre-defined group of producers at fixed terms and prices is not likely to constitute state aid, while a charge levied by TSOs on suppliers and redistributed to producers may constitute state aid'.[185] It has been suggested that this case sheds light on the interpretation in *PreussenElektra*,[186] though others (in my view rightly) maintain that the distinction drawn between *PreussenElektra* and *Essent* is not entirely convincing.[187]

This same distinction was underlined in the later case of *Iride*,[188] where the Court again noted that in *PreussenElektra*, apart from the creation of the legal obligation to purchase at a minimum price, the state had not played any role in the collection and/or redistribution of the funds in question: the sums corresponding

---

[181] Case C-206/06, *Essent*, para 66.
[182] Case C-206/06, *Essent*, para. 67 69.
[183] Case C-379/98, *PreussenElektra* [2001] ECR I-2099.
[184] Case C-206/06, *Essent*, para. 74.
[185] H. Bjornebye, *Investing in EU Energy Security: Exploring the Regulatory Approach to Tomorrow's Electricity Production* (Alphen aan den Rijn: Kluwer Law International 2010), p. 356.
[186] B. Mortensen, 'The European Court of Justice Decision in Case C-206/06', 17(6) *Essent Netwerk Noord BV* (2008) EEELR, p. 392.
[187] H. Bjornebye, *Investing in EU Energy Security: Exploring the Regulatory Approach to Tomorrow's Electricity Production* (Alphen aan den Rijn: Kluwer Law International 2010), p. 356.
[188] Case T-25/07, *Iride and Iride Energia v Commission* [2009] ECR, p. II-0245 (appeal pending: Case C-150/09 P)

to the purchase price were transferred directly between the private sector economic actors, which were the electricity distributor undertakings on the one hand, and the producers of electricity from renewable sources on the other. In the *Iride* case, the revenue from the application of component A.6 of the electricity tariff was collected and managed in a special account by the Equalisation Fund—which is a public body—before being redistributed to the recipient, namely AEM Torino.[189] The Court held that the sums in question must be categorized as state resources, not only because they were under constant state control, but also because they were state property.[190] Even if the funds were not held permanently by the public authorities, the fact that they remained constantly under public control and were therefore available to the competent national authorities sufficed for them to be categorized as state resources.[191] As noted above, the distinction drawn by the Court seems somewhat formalistic. In the context of state-owned entities, it must also be noted that a line of cases on imputability to the state make it clear that is necessary to show that the deployment of the aid to the companies is taking place because of a government decision, the burden of proof being on the Commission.[192] This is relevant in relation to many tariff issues and even certain types of asset sales.

These cases illustrate the difficulty of dealing with state-influenced situations and companies not fully subject to purely commercial strategies. It is also exceedingly difficult to decipher the cost and income calculations of large companies to identify when a tariff covers 'marginal' costs, plus some sort of overhead and rate of return of 'full cost'. Even private companies will often—despite what business school models might indicate—not know very well what cost a particular product line causes, in particular since the allocation of overhead costs is an uncertain art rather than a science. Private companies frequently, by accident, intention, or conscious strategy, run losses in building a business and it will only become clear later whether or not such a strategy has been successful or not. Private companies may well breach all the standards identified as indications of protectionist state aids by a government monopoly. Scrutiny of individual transactions—be it in the context of tax, anti-dumping rules, or state aid—is difficult and often misleading. It also usually overtaxes the time, competence, and resources available in adjudication, illustrating the difficulties involved in regulating the conduct—or the existence—of a state-controlled monopoly. The only argument for continuing such scrutiny is that if the state chooses to keep a tight rein on energy utilities, then it should be viewed with mistrust and kept subject to rigorous, sometimes even excessive, monitoring standards: i.e. more rigorous and onerous than those applied to the

---

[189] Case T-25/07, *Iride and Iride Energia v Commission*, para. 27.
[190] Case T-25/07, *Iride and Iride Energia v Commission*, para. 28.
[191] See, to that effect, Case C-83/98, *P France v Ladbroke Racing and Commission* [2000] ECR I-3271, para. 50, Case C-482/99, *France v Commission* [2002] ECR I-4397, para. 37 and Case T-25/07, *Iride and Iride Energia v Commission* [2009] ECR, p. II-0245, para 25.
[192] Case C-482/99, *France v Commission (Stardust Marine)* [2002] ECR I-4397 and Case T-68/03, *Olympic Airways* [2007] ECR II-2911. For more, see L. Hancher and F. Salerno, 'State Aid in the Energy Sector', in *Research Handbook on European State Aid Law* (Cheltenham: Edward Elgar 2011), pp. 252 and 254.

conduct of private companies operating in reasonably competitive markets. The 'market investor' test cannot do justice to pricing strategies, which will vary from company to company. Perhaps their only justification is that they cause more difficulty and transaction cost to enterprises which, due to their market power and exposure to political pressure provoke legitimate suspicion.

The 2009 *EDF* case,[193] involving France, offers an illustrative example of strong governmental control over its energy companies and the difficulties in applying the 'market investor' test. In that case, the French state essentially cancelled EDF's debt by using various fiscal concessions. During the relevant timeframe, EDF was fully owned and controlled by the French state. Given its undercapitalization and the need to restructure EDF, the Court of First Instance held that the state had acted as any private owner would have done (albeit the means used were slightly different). The Commission had made several mistakes in considering that a private investor could not have invested a similar amount to that involved in the case in the company to facilitate restructuring.

4.7.2 Prominent State Aid Proceedings Relating to Energy

The case law on the provision of state aid in the energy sector has grown substantially since the early 1990s for the reasons outlined in section 4.7.1. It is neither sensible nor feasible to examine all of these cases or even superficially discuss them. Instead, this section provides an overview of various categories of state aid and state aid proceedings particularly relevant to energy. It examines the phasing-out of coal subsidies, preferential tariffs, compensation for stranded costs, aid given for environmental purposes and services of general economic interest. This overview does not cover state aid for regional purposes as such, although this is the single largest aid group in practice.

4.7.2.1 Phasing Out State Aid for Coal

The EU has traditionally accepted aid, even operating aid, given to the coal industry. State aid has been used quite widely to maintain coal-producing capability where such capability existed. In addition to a number of cases on the topic, there was also a specific regulation addressing this question: the Regulation on state aid to the coal industry.[194] According to Article 1 of the Regulation, it was based, *inter alia*, on the need to maintain, as a precautionary measure, a minimum quantity of indigenous coal production to guarantee access to reserves. As such, the instrument was based on security of supply.

One illustrative case on the subsidies provided for domestic coal production is the Commission's *Jahrhundertvertrag*[195] decision. Prompted by state pressure and a

---

[193] Case T-156/04, *EDF v Commission* [2009] II-04503 (appeal pending: case C-124/10 P).
[194] Council Regulation (EC) No 1407/2002 of 23 July 2002 on State aid to the coal industry, OJ L 205, 2.8.2002, pp. 1–8.
[195] *Jahrhundertvertrag* [1993] OJ L 50/14.

state subsidy, German electricity companies committed themselves to use German coal—subsidized at several times the world market price—for a certain percentage of their energy needs. This was accepted for security of supply reasons.

However, with the growth of other energy sources, reliance on coal for security of supply considerations is fading away. Although even today, hard coal support is still the largest single subsidy paid by the German federal government.[196] As a logical continuation of this trend, state aid for the coal industry today mainly focuses on the closure of coal mines,[197] with some exceptions.[198]

4.7.2.2 *Preferential tariffs as State Aid*

Cases involving tariffs provided to national energy producers are of particular interest. In energy-intensive industries (Dutch horticulturists, Belgian fertilizer producers, Italian aluminium producers or iron ore smelters), such tariffs can make or break the competitive strength of an industry. Complaints prompting Commission action and against Commission inaction or acceptance of such practices have therefore often come from commercial competitors. The strength of government influence through the accumulation of both substantial co-ownership (indicated by shareholding and voting strength) complemented by tariff regulation has been a characteristic feature of these cases. The key question is whether or not 'normal' commercial companies would behave in the same way.

The Netherlands is quite often the origin of many energy-related cases which come before the European Courts or the Commission, and tariffs for supply of energy by Gasunie have also been the subject of more than one state aid case. In the *Van der Kooy* case involving Dutch horticulturists,[199] the issue was a lower, preferential tariff for gas supplied by Gasunie. The European Commission and Court regarded Gasunie as a state-controlled enterprise due to the impact of the state's 50 per cent shareholding,[200] intensified by its powers to approve tariffs. Both accepted that a lower tariff was necessary to keep the horticulturalists from switching to—cheaper— coal, but they also found that the tariff reduction was lower than necessary to prevent such a switch. The Court held that the horticultural tariff could not be explained by a commercial justification alone. In another key series of Commission decisions with an intermediate Court decision (*Cofaz I and II*),[201] the issue was again preferential tariffs provided by Gasunie to Dutch fertilizer companies. The fertilizer industry is very energy-intensive. Energy prices have a significant impact

---

[196] <http://ec.europa.eu/competition/consultations/2009_coal/ecorys_study_annex.pdf>.

[197] State aid: Commission proposes Council Regulation on State aid to close uncompetitive coal mines (IP/10/984, 20.7.2010) and State aid: Commission approves Slovenian aid towards the closure of the Trbovlje Hrastnik coal mine (IP/11/804, 29.6.2011).

[198] For example, 'European Commission authorises State Aid for Spanish Coal' (IP/09/1125, 14.7.2009).

[199] Case C-67/85, *Van der Kooy v Commission* [1988] ECR 0129.

[200] At the time of writing, Gasunie is fully owned by the Dutch state.

[201] Case 169/84, *Compagnie française de l'azote (Cofaz) SA and others v Commission (Cofaz I)* [1986] ECR 0391 and Case C-169/84, *Cofaz v Commission (Cofaz II)* [1990] ECR I-3083.

on location. A French competitor—Cofaz—complained about what it alleged to be state aid given by Gasunie to Cofaz's Dutch competitors. At issue again was the question of whether the tariff was commercially reasonable—i.e. one a 'normal' commercial company would, or might, have negotiated in order to keep its Dutch gas consumers from either closing down or migrating to locations with a cheaper gas supply—or whether it was a covert subsidy given by a Dutch state-controlled enterprise to provide Dutch companies with a competitive advantage. Both the Commission and the Court—with varying assessments as to the tariff advantages required to fulfil the commercial aim of holding on to a market—accepted the principle of preferential tariffs for reasons of commercial strategy.

In *Allied Signal* and other cases involving a preferential electricity tariff granted by nuclear power stations to industrial consumers by French EDF,[202] the Commission accepted the use of preferential tariffs in EDF's long-term contracts. First, these were considered to cover at least marginal costs—meaning that dumping was not involved. Secondly, it would have been a reasonable strategy for a private company to seek to develop a new market by offering a long-term cheap supply of electricity to encourage relocation. Leigh Hancher has suggested that the following standards emerged out of these cases: price differentials based on integral tariff systems and for which an objective basis exists and price reduction under commercial pressures are justified, provided there is no ultimate loss of revenue to the state.[203]

It is in practice very difficult to distinguish between state aid and tariffs which are low for some other reason. This difficulty was illustrated in the *Alumix*[204] case from Italy. In the early 1990s, as part of a larger reorganization and privatization process which took place in Italy, aluminium producer Alumix was also restructured, privatized, and sold. The acquisition of Alumix by Alcoa was made conditional upon the provision by ENEL, the state-owned electricity supplier, of a preferential tariff for the supply of electricity to the two smelters. In order to assess the advantage received, the value of the preferential tariff had to be calculated. The problem in this particular case was that there was no market price in Italy. As such, the Commission devised a method to identify the lowest theoretical market price at which a rational market economy supplier would be prepared to sell to its 'best customer' (i.e. the largest consumer with a flat consumption profile) in the specific circumstances of the relevant markets. Using this approach, the Commission assumed that a rational supplier would seek to cover at least its marginal production costs, plus a proportion of its fixed costs.

The relevant market (Sardinia and Veneto) was marked by significant over-capacity in electricity generation which was unlikely to disappear in the next ten years. It was also impossible for generators to export electricity from these regions because of insufficient interconnection with mainland Italy and lack of demand

---

[202] This case was described in L. Hancher, T. Ottervanger, and P.J. Slot, *EC State Aids* (London: Chancery Law 1999), paras. 14.38–14.41.

[203] L. Hancher, T. Ottervanger, and P.J. Slot, *EC State Aids* (London: Chancery Law 1999), para. 14.34.

[204] Case 38/92, *Alumix*, OJ C 288, 1.10.1996, p. 4. See also XXVIth Report on Competition Policy, 1996.

in the nearby regions. Taking these conditions into account, the Commission held that a large industrial client like Alcoa had substantial bargaining power with respect to ENEL, since the closure of the two smelters, which were among ENEL's best customers in Italy, would entail even greater overcapacity and a worsening cost structure for ENEL. Therefore, it was in ENEL's economic interest to supply the smelters with electricity at a particularly low price. As such there was no state aid as ENEL was acting like a rational economic market operator.

With the rise in prices for primary energy, world oil prices in particular, energy-intensive industries have, unsurprisingly, been a frequent recipient of state aid in the form of lower tariffs. One of the high-profile cases in this area was the *Alcoa*[205] case which concerned an electricity price subsidy provided by the state (Italy) in respect of aluminium production. Unlike the earlier *Alumix*[206] case, the Commission was no longer interested in the level of the tariffs and seemed to consider that any state intervention that reduced the tariffs paid by energy-intensive industries (or any customer) will be regarded as state aid regardless of the price and level of support.[207]

Aluminum production is an activity with very high energy intensity. As with the earlier Dutch cases on preferential tariffs for the fertilizer industry, energy costs are a major price component in aluminium production. Under these conditions the carbon leakage type of argumentation[208] on the threat of companies relocating to other countries is logical. Much as was the case in the earlier *Terni*[209] decision, the Commission did not accept this argument and decided that there had been a violation of state aid rules. The industrial relocation argument was considered in more detail in the *Terni* case. In that case, the Italian government argued that 'energy intensive companies in other Member States can also benefit from reduced energy prices and the tariff is required as a transitional measure to avoid delocalization outside the EU pending the full liberalization of the energy market and the improvement of infrastructure'.[210] The Commission refused to accept that argument, noting that 'the fact that a Member State seeks to approximate, by unilateral measures, conditions of competition in a particular sector of the economy to those prevailing in other Member States cannot deprive the measures in question of their character as state aid'. Furthermore, the Italian argument that such state aid could be justified by the existence of other (equally distortive) types of state aid in the EU can be dismissed out of hand. Such an approach would lead to subsidy races and would run counter to the very objective of EU state aid control. With regards

[205] Cases C 38/a/2004 and 36/b/2006, *Alcoa*, OJ L 227, 28.8.2010, pp. 62–94.

[206] This case relates to the earlier *Alumix* case. The decision to open up an inquiry to the state aid because of changes in the scheme was challenged before the CFI. See Case T-332/06, *Trasformazioni v Commission* [2009] ECR II-00029 (appeal C-194/09 P).

[207] L. Hancher and F. Salerno, 'State Aid in the Energy Sector', in *Research Handbook on European State Aid Law* (Cheltenham: Edward Elgar 2011), p. 246.

[208] Carbon leakage refers to industry relocation due to higher costs following the introduction of a price for emissions. This issue is also discussed in the context of Emission Trading at Section 5.5.4.

[209] Commission Decision of 20 November 2007 on the State aid C 36/A/06 implemented by Italy in favour of ThyssenKrupp, Cementir and Nuova Terni Industrie Chimiche, paras. 144 and 145.

[210] Commission Decision of 20 November 2007 on the State aid C 36/A/06 implemented by Italy in favour of ThyssenKrupp, Cementir and Nuova Terni Industrie Chimiche, para. 144.

to the alleged risk of delocalization outside the EU, the Commission noted that there was no precedent in its decisional practice or in the jurisprudence of the EU courts where such an argument has been accepted as a justification for the grant of state aids.[211] This is well in line with the research undertaken by Tscherning, who examined the German markets and concluded that the risk of carbon leakage is exaggerated.[212]

4.7.2.3 Stranded Costs

Another line of cases of significance both for the energy industry and for this book are those involving stranded costs, which address some of the difficult issues involved in making a transition from one system and one ideology to another—from a state-driven to a market-driven system.

In the closed market regime that existed before the liberalization process began, it was normal for the authorities to fix prices in order to guarantee the profitability of all investments made by their national, usually state-owned, electricity companies. Due to this, companies often invested in electricity generation or relatively expensive long-term purchase or supply contracts.[213]

The liberalization of the sector resulted in falling consumer prices for electricity. This could have jeopardized the economic viability of these investments or contracts by generating 'stranded costs'.[214] These often large-scale investments in power generation or large volume purchase agreements, originally made to secure supply for a captive group of customers, albeit at a higher price, became stranded in a system which allows competition and 'releases' those customers to seek less expensive options. In this situation, these companies had few choices. They could pass these costs on in full to their captive customers or find their viability under threat if they continued to provide essential services for individuals or the economy as a whole.[215]

Clearly, transitional solutions were necessary. One solution engineered by the EU was Article 24 of Directive 96/92/EC, which provided for transitional measures to address the question of stranded costs.[216] Another was the so-called 'stranded costs methodology', which allowed for financial compensation for costs resulting from 'well identified and quantified historical commitments that can no longer be honoured in the context of liberalisation'.[217] Here, these arrangements were analysed under Article 107 TFEU.

---

[211] Commission Decision of 20 November 2007 on the State aid C 36/A/06 implemented by Italy in favour of ThyssenKrupp, Cementir and Nuova Terni Industrie Chimiche, para. 145.

[212] R. Tscherning, 'The EU ETS Rules on Carbon Leakage and Energy Intensive Industry in the Federal Republic of Germany' 20 *European Energy and Environmental Law Review* (2011), pp. 2–17.

[213] Such long-term power purchase contracts have been the object of several proceedings at EU level, both in terms of the power contract itself and the related transmission capacity contract. See K. Talus and T. Wälde, 'Electricity Interconnectors—a Serious Challenge for EC Competition Law', 1(3) *Competition and Regulation in Network Industries* (2006).

[214] Stranded costs are costs that were incurred by companies before the liberalization of the electricity sector, and that the effects of the liberalization make it impossible or very difficult to recover.

[215] Commission press release, IP/01/1077, 25.7.2001.

[216] This provision was also examined in Case C-17/03, *VEMW and others* [2005] ECR I-4983.

[217] See P. Cameron, *Competition in Energy Markets* (Oxford: OUP 2007), p. 433.

Due to these special and sector-specific difficulties, the Commission adopted a special assessment method defining the criteria to be used to analyse state aid offsetting these stranded costs, first in the form of a draft memorandum and then in the form of a Communication on the methodology.[218] These criteria include: (i) that the costs are genuinely incurred and directly linked to the liberalization of the sector; (ii) that provision of the aid is time-limited; (iii) that the aid takes account of developments on the electricity market; and (iv) that the aid facilitates the transition to a competitive market.[219]

In practice, these types of stranded costs can take various forms: long-term purchase contracts, investments undertaken with an implicit or explicit guarantee of sale, investments undertaken outside the scope of normal activity, etc.[220] Given the prevalence of these arrangements in the EU,[221] it is hardly a surprise that over a period of time the Commission has applied these assessment criteria to different arrangements in various Member States, including Austria, Belgium Greece, the Netherlands, Luxembourg, Portugal, Spain, UK, Hungary, and Italy.[222] The Hungarian case offers an interesting example. It involved the long-term power purchase agreements under which the national monopoly company was obliged to buy a fixed quantity of electricity at a fixed price from certain generators, covering around 80 per cent of the Hungarian market in electricity generation (during 2001–2004) or 60–70 per cent (in 2005, after which that share slowly decreased).[223] A somewhat similar though not identical situation existed in Poland, and the Commission's case against Poland was very similar to that of Hungary. As noted by Hancher, the similarity of Commission cases seems to have been based on a lot of 'copy-and-pasting'.[224] Given the appeals from the Hungarian case, this chapter will focus on that case.

This case relates to certain power purchase agreements (PPA) entered into in connection with the modernization of the Hungarian electricity markets. The market was first, from 1991 to 2002, arranged under a single buyer model where the state-owned company would act as the single buyer and all power generators would supply energy

---

[218] Commission Communication relating to the methodology for analysing State aid linked to stranded costs—Adopted by the Commission on 26.7.2001.

[219] A more detailed overview of the criteria is presented in See P. Cameron, *Competition in Energy Markets* (Oxford: OUP 2007), pp. 435–8.

[220] Commission Communication relating to the methodology for analysing state aid linked to stranded costs. Available on the website of the Directorate General for Competition: <http://ec.europa.eu/dgs/competition/index_en.htm>.

[221] References to further state aid examinations of long-term purchase power agreements was also made in the context of the energy sector inquiry.

[222] See, for just some examples, Commission press releases: Commission gives partial go-ahead to compensation for Belgian electricity sector, IP/02/605, 24.4.2002; State aids: Commission declares compatible the aid linked to stranded costs in the energy sector in Italy, IP/04/1429, 1.12.2004; and State aid: Commission opens investigation into Italy's plans to grant aid to AEM Torino for stranded costs, IP/06/451, 5.4.2006. An overview of various cases is provided in P. Cameron, *Competition in Energy Markets* (Oxford: OUP 2007), pp. 433–48.

[223] Commission press release, IP/05/1407, 10.11.2005, and Commission Decision of 4 June 2008 on the state aid C 41/05 awarded by Hungary through Power Purchase Agreements (2009/609/EC).

[224] L. Hancher, 'Long-term Contracts and State Aid: A New Application of the EU State Aid Regime or a Special Case?' in J.-M. Glachant, D. Finon, and A. de Hautecloque (eds), *Competition, Contracts and Electricity Markets: A New Perspective* (Cheltenham: Edward Elgar 2011), p. 240.

directly to the single buyer. The single buyer was also required to ensure security of energy supply in Hungary at the lowest possible cost.

The scheme was seen as necessary due to the need to restructure the power industry inherited by the new government from the Soviet era, and at the same time ensure the electricity supply at the lowest possible cost and modernize the infrastructure (with particular regard to the prevailing standards of environmental protection). To achieve these general objectives, the government offered long-term power purchase agreements to foreign investors. These would invest in the construction and modernization of power plants in Hungary in exchange for long-term PPAs with a single buyer.

The PPAs covered the future requirements of the single buyer and went beyond that. They covered both the base-load demand (with lignite-fired and nuclear power stations) and the peak-load demand (with gas-fired power plants). Under the scheme, the generators were obliged to maintain and operate their generation facilities. They reserved all or the bulk of the power plants' generation capacities for the single buyer. This capacity allocation was independent of the actual use of the power plant. Beyond the reserved capacities, each PPA contained a minimum purchase obligation under which a specific minimum quantity of electricity had to be purchased from each power plant. The prices under the PPAs were set by government decrees. These allowed for substantiated operating costs, wholesale and retail prices, and 8–9.8 per cent profit.

Hungary had notified its intention to compensate the single buyer for stranded costs incurred in connection with the PPAs and due to the liberalization. In this case, however, the Commission looked at the situation from a different angle and suggested that the PPAs themselves amounted to state aid for the generators. The Commission suggested that the guaranteed return on investment and the high purchase price secured by the PPAs put power generators operating under a PPA in a more advantageous economic situation than other power generators not party to a PPA. As such, it seemed to confer a selective advantage on those power generators. The Commission also opined that this advantage stemmed from the use of state resources, because the decision to sign the PPAs was a consequence of state policy implemented via the state-owned public utility wholesaler. The Commission assessed the situation using the stranded costs methodology.

The first peculiarity of the case relates to the 'advantage' conferred on the generators. The second peculiarity is the assessment of the value of the advantage. In the context of the presence of PPAs on the markets, this assessment is difficult to make.[225] This section focuses on the first-mentioned element, in respect of which the generators argued that they did not derive any advantage from the PPAs because their behaviour reflected the normal market behaviour of any market economy operator in both the single buyer's and the generators' position. They argued that any private actor in the same position (under the legal obligation of security of supply as a single buyer) would have chosen to enter into the PPAs, and that the economic advantage derived from the PPAs did not go beyond what, in the circumstances of

[225] L. Hancher, 'Long-term Contracts and State Aid: A New Application of the EU State Aid Regime or a Special Case?' in J.-M. Glachant, D. Finon, and A. de Hauteclocque (eds), *Competition, Contracts and Electricity Markets: A New Perspective* (Cheltenham: Edward Elgar 2011), p. 240.

the immature Hungarian energy market of the 1990s, was a normal commercial advantage for the parties. This view tends to dictate that the decision should have taken into account the legal requirements and economic reality current at the time of conclusion of the PPAs. Interestingly, the Commission suggested that it did not question the fact that it was necessary to enter into PPAs in the circumstances prevailing at the time those agreements were concluded, but that this did not in any way mean that the PPAs did not confer an advantage on the generators.

The Commission agreed that, when examining the existence of state aid, it was obliged to assess the situation prevailing at the time the measure entered into force, but it maintained that such assessment is not always limited to that *moment* in time. There are exceptional circumstances that merit a different approach. The Commission's approach in the case was that the fundamental change in the legal and economic circumstances that took place on Hungary's accession to the EU meant that the existence of state aid should be assessed under the new economic and legal circumstances. It went on to say that any other approach would lead to a situation where the economic conditions of the pre-accession and pre-liberalization period could be perpetuated long after the country's accession. This was especially the case given that no exceptions were provided for the energy markets in the Hungarian Accession Act. The Commission accordingly took the view that, in joining the liberalized internal energy market, Hungary agreed to apply the principles of that market's economy to all the players on its existing market, including all existing commercial relations. Therefore, the Commission examined the measure against the state aid criteria as of the day Hungary joined the EU.

As such, the Commission concluded that the PPAs in question provided certainty both as regards the reimbursement of fixed and capital costs and the level of use of the generation capacities. This is not the case under normal commercial arrangements like spot markets or forward contracts. The main terms and conditions of the purchase obligation enshrined in the PPAs—i.e. the capacity reservations and guaranteed off-take by Hungarian Magyar *Villamos* Művek (MVM) under such conditions as to ensure the return on investment of the power plants by shielding them from the commercial risks of the operation of their plant—constituted state aid within the meaning of Article 107(1) TFEU. This state aid was the result of the combination of the capacity reservations, the minimum guaranteed off-take, the pricing mechanism based on a capacity fee and an energy fee to cover fixed, variable and capital costs, over a long duration beyond normal commercial practice.

The Commission noted that several elements of the main principles constituting the PPAs in this case did not meet the requirements identified in the stranded costs methodology. First they failed to fulfil the requirement that the arrangements for paying the aid must take account of future developments in competition. The price-setting mechanisms of these PPAs were designed in such a way as to take into consideration only the specific parameters of the power plant concerned in order to establish the price. Prices offered by competing generators and their generation capacities were not considered. Secondly, the PPAs also contradicted the principles under which the financing arrangements could not conflict with the EU interest, notably competition. The salient principle in this regard is that financing arrangements cannot have the effect of deterring outside undertakings or new players from entering certain national or regional markets. However, the system of capacity reservation and capacity fee present in this case had the effect of deterring MVM—which is by far the largest buyer on the wholesale market—from shifting to producers other than those under PPAs. Furthermore, the opening of the market and the conditions under the PPAs compelled MVM to purchase more electricity than it needed, leading it to resell that electricity on the free market through release mechanisms. This in itself hampered new entries on the wholesale market. Finally, the Commission considered that the PPAs caused distortions of competition on the Hungarian wholesale electricity market over a period considerably in excess of that necessary for a reasonable transition to a competitive market.

Not only is this case illustrative of stranded-cost-related questions, but it also potentially has much wider implications. This case and the Polish case decided in parallel with it suggest that a change might have occurred in certain methods used by the Commission in examining aid given to companies in the energy sector. These two cases essentially placed the emphasis on 'where it was most efficient to allocate risk in energy markets and to some extent attempted to analyse how different forms of vertical arrangement would deliver this allocation of risk'.[226] However, no actual market analysis was carried out in the decision. Instead, the decision seems to be based on the idea that had the long-term contracts not been in place, a liquid wholesale market would have developed (more) rapidly. This, as has been seen in relation to other EU countries, is a dangerous assumption. But, as Hancher notes,[227] 'perhaps the Commission always knows best' …

4.7.2.4 Services of General Economic Interest

The Court takes the view that public service requirements are to be interpreted on a national basis.[228] Where a Member State decides to have recourse to these provisions, the measure must not restrict competition and trade between the Member States more than is necessary in order to fulfil the legitimate general interest objectives.[229] The payment of compensation relating to the accomplishment of a public service obligation is not, in principle, considered to amount to state aid. However, when examining the question of compensation, the Commission applies the state aid test formulated by the Court in the *Altmark* case.[230] This comprises four cumulative conditions which schemes must meet in order not to be ruled illegal:

1. the company must be responsible for the implementation of clearly defined public service obligations;

---

[226] L. Hancher, 'Long-term Contracts and State Aid: A New Application of the EU State Aid Regime or a Special Case?' in J.-M. Glachant, D. Finon, and A. de Hauteclocque (eds), *Competition, Contracts and Electricity Markets: A New Perspective* (Cheltenham: Edward Elgar 2011), p. 233.

[227] L. Hancher, 'Long-term Contracts and State Aid: A New Application of the EU State Aid Regime or a Special Case?' in J.-M. Glachant, D. Finon, and A. de Hauteclocque (eds), *Competition, Contracts and Electricity Markets: A New Perspective* (Cheltenham: Edward Elgar 2011), p. 248.

[228] Case C-439/06, *citiworks*, para. 59.

[229] Case C-439/06, *citiworks*, para. 60.

[230] Case C-280/00, *Altmark* [2003] ECR I-7747. See the guidance of the Commission on SGEI: Communication from the Commission on the application of the European Union State aid rules to

2. the parameters for the cost calculations must be pre-established in an objective and transparent manner;

3. the compensation must not exceed what is strictly necessary (yet allowing for a reasonable return); and

4. the selection of the company that is subject to the PSO must be made through a public tendering procedure or the compensation level must be calculated by comparing the cost to that which a well-managed and adequately resourced company would incur (again allowing for a reasonable return).

When these criteria are met, the measure is not considered to be state aid and do not need to be notified as such to the Commission. These criteria have been applied in a large number of cases in the energy sector over the last few years, some of which are briefly examined in this section.[231]

The question of services of general economic interest (SGEI) was raised in the Hungarian PPA case discussed in section 4.7.2.3, in which some of the generators argued that the scheme was in fact a SGEI scheme. The Commission responded to the various elements of these arguments but found that the PPAs could not be considered to be services of general economic interest. Not only did the PPAs not fulfil all the criteria laid down in the *Altmark* judgment, but the Commission also viewed the objective of security of supply as being of a very general nature. To some extent, the view could be taken that any generator in the electricity sector contributes towards achieving this objective.[232] It also noted that, while security of supply could clearly be a SGEI, it should have complied with the requirements of Article 11(4) of Directive 2003/54/EC, which states that '[a] Member State may, for reasons of security of supply, direct that priority be given to the dispatch of generating installations using indigenous primary energy fuel sources, to an extent not exceeding in any calendar year 15% of the overall primary energy necessary to produce the electricity consumed in the Member State concerned'. This criterion was not fulfilled in this case.

An example of a situation falling within the scope of the *Altmark* criteria was the Irish generation capacity scheme.[233] In this case, the Irish TSO had indicated the emergence of a generation capacity gap from 2005 onwards. By 2007, this

---

compensation granted for the provision of services of general economic interest, OJ C8, 11.1.2012, pp. 4–14, Commission Decision of 20 December on the application of Article 106(2) of the Treaty on the Functioning of the European Union to State aid in the form of public service compensation granted to certain undertakings entrusted with the operation of services of general economic interest, OJ L7, 11.1.2012, pp. 3–10; and Communication from the Commission, European Union framework for State aid in the form of public service compensation (2011) OJ C8, 11.1.2012, pp. 15–22.

[231] See, also, Commission Decisions in cases N 34/99, Austria—compensation for stranded costs, OJ C 5, 8.1.2002, p. 2; NN 49/99 Spain—Scheme for competition transition costs, OJ C 268, 22.9.2001, p. 7; N 6/A/2001 Ireland—Public service obligations imposed on the electricity supply board with respect to the generation of electricity out of peat, OJ C 77, 28.3.2002, p. 25.

[232] Commission Decision of 4 June 2008 on the State aid C 41/05 awarded by Hungary through Power Purchase Agreements (notified under document C(2008) 2223).

[233] State aid N 475/2003—Ireland—Public Service Obligation in respect of new electricity generation capacity for security of supply (OJ 2004 C 34/8).

gap would grow to around 10 per cent of the total generation capacity in 2003. To address this potential problem, the Irish Commission for Energy Regulation decided to launch a process aimed at facilitating the entry of significant amounts of new capacity on to the national market. This meant that, under a specific scheme of up to ten years' duration, Capacity and Differences Agreements (CADA) would be granted to generators that would undertake the construction of this new generation capacity. As the CADAs served a security of supply purpose, the Commission examined the scheme under the *Altmark* criteria.[234] It noted that:

'Electricity is a product that is vital for the economy and even for the everyday life of European citizens. Electricity breakdowns have huge, sometimes life threatening, impact. Ensuring that no such breakdown occurs even in peak demand periods and under all weather conditions is therefore clearly necessary for the public interest.'

The Commission then went on to take the view that, in line with earlier case law, ensuring security of supply can be considered as a legitimate objective of general economic interest. The assessment then turned to the proportionality question. The Commission considered that, while cross-border interconnectors would in many ways be the preferable option—as they provide for more market-based schemes, allow for the sharing of reserve capacity, etc.—this is not an option in Ireland's case. It also underlined the distinction between 'reserve capacity' and 'normal capacity'. After considering these and many other factors, the Commission accepted the scheme as falling within the *Altmark* criteria.

Another similar case dealing with the relationship between security of supply and state aid comes from Latvia, where a generation deficit loomed following the decommissioning of the Ignalina nuclear power plant in Lithuania at the end of 2009 and the renovation of the Narva oil-shale power plant in Estonia at some point in the near future. The Commission had authorized aid that Latvia intended to grant by way of tender for the construction and operation of a 400 MW thermal power plant between 2015 and 2025. The aim of the measure is to ensure security of supply (that future electricity demands are met by available supplies and to reduce the dependency on gas as the dominant fuel source). In order to diversify Latvia's energy mix, the plant is due to use either LNG regasified in Latvia or solid fuel, such as coal, lignite or peat, mixed with at least 10 per cent biomass.[235]

4.7.2.5 Environmental State Aid

Given the EU's '20–20–20 by 2020' target and the shortcomings of the market-based schemes, it is natural that state aid is used to create the necessary preconditions for an 'environmentally sound' energy infrastructure. The amounts

---

[234] The examination differentiated between possible state aid to the generators, which are examined here, and the public electricity supply branch of the Irish Electricity Supply Board, which is not covered here.

[235] State aid 675/2009—Tender for Aid for New Electricity Generation Capacity (decision of 14.6.2010).

involved are very significant: for example, for 2008 environmental protection aid amounted to around EUR 12.7 billion.[236] In addition, aid for green energy production and research and development in this area is provided under other schemes, such as regional aid. State support for green energy production is also enshrined in Article 8 of Directive 2009/72/EC, which provides the possibility to launch a tendering procedure for new generation capacity in the event that the authorization scheme under Article 7 has failed to deliver the investment necessary to ensure security of supply. Both the authorization scheme and the tendering scheme allow for discrimination in favour of environmentally sound production (and/or energy savings).[237] Additionally, state aid is allowed for this purpose. The EU has adopted a number of instruments facilitating state aid which has an environmental objective. The guidelines on state aid for environmental protection[238] and the General Block Exemption Regulation[239] are among these instruments.[240]

The starting-point for the guidelines in this area is that market-based instruments are preferable and state aid that incentivizes companies to invest in environmentally sound technologies is only a second-best option. The idea is that if companies can avoid making sufficient environmental investment because they receive state aid, this will not only distort competition but will also frustrate the very objective of meeting the EU's ambitious targets for the environment. As such, state aid should—so the theory goes—only be used in situations where the 'polluter pays' principle does not deliver the required outcome in a particular Member State. In reality, some form of state aid is very often a precondition for green investment. State aid corrects the market failure linked with environmental negative externalities and can, if carefully designed, also induce behavioural change and lead to the adoption of more environmentally-friendly processes or investment in greener technologies. It may also allow Member States to adopt measures that go beyond the support scheme employed by the EU.[241]

In essence, the guidelines are based on certain core principles: the polluter-pays principle; aid should incentivize a behavioural change in the concerned companies; proportionality; the concept of eligible costs; the split between standard and detailed assessment, the distinction between investment aid and operating aid and larger amounts of aid for SMEs.[242] The guidelines allow state aid for various

---

[236] L. Hancher and F. Salerno, 'State Aid in the Energy Sector', in *Research Handbook on European State Aid Law* (Cheltenham: Edward Elgar 2011), p. 246.

[237] These schemes have been examined in detail in H. Bjornebye, *Investing in EU Energy Security: Exploring the Regulatory Approach to Tomorrow's Electricity Production* (Alphen aan den Rijn: Kluwer Law International 2010).

[238] Community guidelines on state aid for environmental protection, OJ C 82, 1.4.2008, p. 1.

[239] Commission Regulation (EC) No 800/2008 of 6 August 2008 declaring certain categories of aid compatible with the common market in application of Articles 87 and 88 of the Treaty.

[240] Others would include the Temporary Community framework for state aid measures to support access to finance in the current financial and economic crisis (OJ 2009, C 16/1). The temporary Framework also emphasizes environmental aids.

[241] 'Frequently asked questions'—MEMO/08/31, 23.1.2008.

[242] These are discussed in detail in L. Hancher and F. Salerno, 'State Aid in the Energy Sector', in *Research Handbook on European State Aid Law* (Cheltenham: Edward Elgar 2011), pp. 259–70.

projects on renewable energy, CHP, CCS, energy savings, waste management, environmental studies, aid involved in tradable permit schemes, energy efficient district heating, etc., up to 100 per cent of the extra costs.[243] The division between investment aid and operating aid is of course relevant in this regard.

In addition to these guidelines, the General Block Exemption Regulation, which also covers environmental aid, was adopted in 2008. This greatly simplifies and codifies the pre-existing scheme and allows for measures like investment in energy savings and renewable energy sources and aid in the form of environmental tax reductions. From an energy perspective, the Block Exemption Regulation and the guidelines cover very similar ground. However, there is a significant difference in practices, which is that the Regulation is subject to a maximum amount. Due to this cap, it does not apply to the large-scale energy projects which are often the norm in the energy industry, although it does apply to many smaller-scale projects.[244] It also includes a number of conditions, largely inspired by the guidelines, to ensure that the aid has a positive environmental effect. By way of summary, without going into further detail, it can be said that, following adoption of the General Block Exemption Regulation, state aid in this area can be assessed using a three-step approach:

1. below a certain threshold, straightforward investment aid measures fall under the General Block Exemption Regulation, while less straightforward aid, operating aid measures are subject to standard assessment under the Guidelines;

2. above the thresholds, the investment or operating aid measure will fall under detailed assessment; and

3. exemptions/reductions from environmental taxes will either fall under the General Block Exemption Regulation or be subject to a stand-alone set of provisions outside the usual standard/detailed assessment matrix.

There are some Finnish examples of state aid assessed using this approach. In 2011, Finland introduced a system of guaranteed prices for new wind and biogas installations up to a certain total capacity.[245] The price covers the difference between production costs and the market price for electricity. The installations able to benefit from the 2011 support scheme are made subject to certain conditions. First, they must be located in Finland or its territorial waters. Secondly, they must also be connected to the electricity network and be participants in the Nordic electricity markets. This operating aid for energy production from wind and biogas constitutes state aid within the meaning of Article 107(1) TFEU and has been approved by the Commission.[246] Similarly, Finland has another support scheme

---

[243] The eligible cost methodology is also provided in the Guidelines (paras. 80–84.)
[244] For some discussion on this, see H. Bjørnebye, *Investing in EU Energy Security: Exploring the Regulatory Approach to Tomorrow's Electricity Production* (Alphen aan den Rijn: Kluwer Law International 2010), pp. 369–85.
[245] Act on operating aid for electricity produced from renewable energy sources (1396/2010).
[246] State aid SA. 31107 2011/N—FI. Decision of 15 March 2011 (C (2011) 1750).

for power plants using renewable energy sources.[247] The conditions are again quite similar: the installations able to benefit from this support scheme based on this direct grant, which is calculated per MWh of produced electricity, must be located in Finland or its territorial waters. These wind power, hydropower, biogas, and forest chips installations must also be connected to the electricity network. This fixed operating aid for power plants using renewable energy sources again constitutes state aid and has been approved by the Commission.[248] Another example of state aid assessed under the environmental state aid guidelines was the *Austrian Feed-In Tariffs* case (N 446/2008). In 2009, the Commission authorized a subsidized feed-in tariffs scheme in Austria for producers of green electricity. The rationale of the aid was to accelerate and increase the development production of renewable electricity while avoiding over-compensation for extra costs. Environmental aid can also be granted to advance certain technologies—for instance, the authorization of aid totalling EUR 10 million to a Dutch company for a CO_2 capture demonstration project.[249] Finally, it must also be noted that environmentally-flavoured aid can also be granted under other state aid schemes. An example of this would be the EUR 17 million granted in 2010 as regional investment aid for a German company for the production of solar modules in Germany.[250]

Looking at the success rates for environmental aid, reflecting the general concern over the environment, climate change and other related issues, environmental reasons are the most suitable cover for state aid. Similarly, as new forms of clean energy are not yet economically feasible, state support is often given in the form of state aid. These can exceed what is legitimately required. They can also intentionally or accidentally be so structured as to favour domestic industry over foreign competitors. A simple minimum obligation to purchase energy from renewable energy sources (RES-purchase obligation) may lead to favouritism, and not contain enough assurances of transparency and non-discrimination. Accepting a measure that has a legitimate environmental motivation may bring short-term public approval, but may compromise a longer-term environmental policy aimed at optimal results.

4.8 Free Movement of Energy and the Exceptions

The main difference between an EU internal energy market and 27 liberalized national energy markets is their integration through unhindered cross-border trade in energy. Such a system embraces competition where new market entry is difficult to achieve in domestic upstream production or generation, whether for practical or encrusted legal reasons. This is the starting-point for devising an ideal set

---

[247] Act on operating aid for electricity produced from renewable energy sources (1396/2010).
[248] State aid SA. 32470 2011/N—FI. Decision of 22 March 2011 (C (2011) 1951). In addition to these, Finland also grants operating aid for small wood fired CHP-plants and forest chips fired power plants (State aid SA. 31204 2011/N—FI).
[249] N 190/2009—CO2 Catch-up pilot project at Nuon Buggenum plant (decision of 25.5.2010).
[250] N 641/2009—LIP—Solibro GmbH (decision of 20.7.2010).

of rules: it must give priority to cross-border trade, work to overcome practical obstacles, and give guidance on restricted exceptions where the EU's peremptory aims are concerned (social cost, environment, security), without forgetting the need to facilitate the establishment of energy undertakings from other Member States. However, as distinct from internal energy market interests, the Treaty does not contain a clear and coherent legal regime dealing with the enhancement of, and restrictions on, trade—thus posing an obstacle to economic integration—by former state-sponsored monopolies engaged in energy production, trade, or services.

The rules on free movement of goods and the exceptions to these rules are the starting-point here. However, the difficulty in applying these Treaty provisions in practice lies in the fact that they are short, general, and inevitably in need of further interpretation, especially in relation to their exceptions—an area that is constantly evolving.[251] Article 34 TFEU prohibits total or partial restraints on imports. Measures of equivalent effect comprise all trading rules enacted by Member States which are capable of hindering, directly or indirectly, actually or potentially, intra-EU trade. Such measures need not be binding upon undertakings, and may even include measures adopted by independent professional bodies on which powers have been conferred by the state to govern the conduct of their members.[252] This means that the provision is likely to apply to measures (access and grid codes, etc.) taken by independent regulatory authorities or associations of energy industry groups. It is not even necessary to demonstrate an *appreciable* effect on trade between Member States (although the idea of a *de minimis* rule for Article 34 has been suggested by AG Jacobs),[253] unlike for the competition provisions of Articles 101 and 102 TFEU. Only where measures applicable without discrimination are too uncertain and indirect may a measure fall outside Article 34. The same caveat applies to exports under Article 35 TFEU.[254]

The jurisprudence of the Court has not yet developed a consistent system for the application of these rules to the energy sector. There is a line of decisions, both on trade and on monopolies, which seems to have gone from extensive justifiability of extensive monopolies to a more rigorous scrutiny of even more limited monopolies, but there is no full consistency even between the more recent decisions. It would therefore be wrong to try to construct a doctrinally rigid system of presumed consistency with an ability to reasonably predict future Court decisions as is sometimes attempted. The Court, with its varying composition and majority thinking, is influenced by considerations of dominant paradigm and political

---

[251] For example, Cases C-112/00, *Eugen Schmidberger, Internationale Transporte und Planzüge v Austria* [2003] ECR I-5659, C-36/02, *Omega Spielhallen* [2004] ECR I-9609 and C-470/03, *AGM-COS. MET v Tarmo Lehtinen and Finland* [2007] ECR I-02749. See, for example, P. Oliver, *Free Movement of Goods in European Union* (Oxford: Hart Publishing 2010).

[252] Cases 266 and 267/87 *R v Royal Pharmaceutical Society of Great Britain, ex p. Association of Pharmaceutical Importers* [1998] ECR 1295.

[253] Opinion in Case C-112/00, *Eugen Schmidberger, Internationale Transporte und Planzüge v Austria*, delivered on 11 July 2002, paras 65–84.

[254] Note the interesting Case 174/84, *Bulk Oil v Sun International* [1986] ECR 559 where a restriction on the delivery of oil to Israel amounted to a measure under Article 29 EC but was not contrary to it, because it involved exports to a third country.

acceptability, technical feasibility, and judicial restraint, all of which prevent it from embarking upon more comprehensive policy-making than is suitable for a court which deals with individual cases often emerging at random. It also tends to recognize the retention of large areas of policy discretion by both governments and the Commission, and is given to accepting the policy compromises hammered out between the Commission, Member States, and other influential forces, instead of trying to interfere with them. The decisions of the Court and their impact upon legal doctrine nevertheless serve to structure the form of argument used, although this does not necessarily mean that any particular decision can be predicted, as the Dutch case, C-17/03, *VEMW and others*,[255] showed. This judgment, whether a result of lack of proper understanding of the energy market mechanism or of well-informed and thorough deliberation—opinions tend to diverge—came as a surprise to the industry. Because Articles 34 and 35 TFEU are now applied extensively to restrict quantitative restrictions on cross-border trade and measures having equivalent effect (the *Dassonville* formula: directly or indirectly, actually or potentially), the focus of the analysis here is not on these rules but rather on the apparent exceptions to them.

4.8.1 Exceptions in the Name of Security and the Environment

The need to include exceptions to the free movement provisions at Treaty level was conceived as necessary from the beginning. In the most basic terms, other values exist in addition to seeking to maximize competition and realise an internal market, and consequently exceptions need to be made. As far as energy is concerned, one needs only to consider the objectives of EU energy policy to see factors that compete with a pure competition/internal market objective: notably, security of supply and sustainability. These are the two areas on which that this section focuses.

Article 36 TFEU contains the key explicit exception to Articles 34 and 35 TFEU and in an energy context it has been applied to justify national restrictions on energy to maintain public security. During the 1970s oil crisis, a limitation of Article 34 regarding free and competitive trade through EU secondary legislation was tolerated in the light of security of supply fears.[256] In the mid-1980s, in the *Campus Oil* case,[257] the Court ruled on the meaning of the term 'public security'

---

[255] Case C-17/03, *VEMW and others* [2005] ECR I-4983.
[256] C. Bickler and M. Renger, 'European Union', in R. Tudway, *Energy Law and the Regulation in Europe* (London: Sweet and Maxwell 1999), p. 1015 with references to Council Directive 77/186/ EEC [1977] OJ L 61/23 amended by Council Decision 79/879/EEC [1979] OJ L 270/58; these provisions have since been abolished.
[257] Case 72/83, *Campus Oil Ltd v Minister of Industry and Energy* [1984] ECR 2727, for the measure: the Petroleum Oils (Regulation or Control of Acquisition, Supply, Distribution or Marketing) Order 1983 and the continuing Petroleum Oils (Regulation or Control of Acquisition, Supply, Distribution or Marketing) (Continuance) Order 1997; for further discussion see E.D. Cross, L. Hancher, and P.J. Slot, 'EC Energy Law', in M. Roggenkamp et al. (eds) *Energy Law in Europe* (Oxford: OUP 2001) pp. 225–8, with further references to P. Oliver, *Free Movement of Goods in the European Community* (London: Sweet and Maxwell 1996), pp. 200–1; L. Gomley, *Prohibiting Restrictions on Trade within the EEC* (1985), p. 138l; and C. Ehlermann, 'Die rechtlichen Instrumentarien zur Verwirlichung des gemeinsamen Markted nach dem EWG Vertrag', in R. Lukes (eds), *Ein EWG Binnenmarkt für Elektrizita: Realitat oder Utopie* (1988), pp. 39–41.

contained in Article 36 TFEU, and found it to justify an obligation relating to the purchase of supplies at pre-determined prices from the Irish state-owned refinery to keep it running in the interest of public security, even if the state pursued further economic interests normally contrary to Article 34. Yet, in another case concerning an oil refinery monopoly in Greece, the Court dismissed the claim that security of supply necessitated exclusive rights[258] but reaffirmed the requirement that an exception could only be granted if there was proof that the refinery would not be able to sell at competitive prices without the discriminatory measure.[259]

In *Cassis de Dijon*,[260] the Court recognized so-called 'mandatory require-ments', such as consumer protection, could be exempted from the application of Article 34 TFEU, but required a restrictive measure to be proportionate. There is no exhaustive list of these overriding interests and the Court has accepted and will create new ones. To reduce the uncertainty regarding mandatory requirements, the Court introduced a methodology to benchmark impediments of trade against other EU interests by reference to their discriminatory (distinctly applicable) or non-discriminatory (indistinctly applicable) nature.[261] Where discriminatory meas-ures were concerned, the Court would apply the exceptions contained in Article 36 to the case at hand. By way of a second step, it also would also consider whether the measure in question was nevertheless disproportionate (arbitrary discrimination, disguised restriction). Where non-discriminatory measures were concerned, the Court would first determine whether the measure was a selling arrangement or arguably a comparable measure with the same effect, for these measures fall outside of Article 34 TFEU. If it was not a selling arrangement, the Court would then decide whether a mandatory requirement in the EU interest would justify keeping the measure in place regardless of its negative effect. However, this methodology was abandoned when its application proved too rigid to include changes in political priorities.[262] Sustainability and environmental protection provide prime examples in this context. The Court now looks for mandatory requirements even in discrimi-natory cases, which in effect renders the exhaustive catalogue contained in Article 36 useless, but leaves it with some persuasive character.[263]

---

[258] Case C-347/88, *Commission v Greece* [1990] ECR-I 4747.
[259] P. Oliver, *Free Movement of Goods in the European Community* (London: Sweet and Maxwell 1996), p. 202 and D. Cross, L. Hancher, and P. J. Slot, 'EC Energy Law', in M. Roggenkamp et al. (eds), *Energy Law in Europe* (Oxford: OUP 2001), p. 227, with further references to guidelines on national measures seeking to ensure security of supply in SEC (90) 1248, Brussels, 14 September 1990.
[260] Case C-120/78, *Rewe v Bundesmonopolverwaltung für Branntwein* [1979] ECR 649.
[261] Case C-268/91, *Keck and Mithouard* [1993] ECR 6097. There are also cases on Sunday trading, pharmaceutical advertising, and retail sale of tobacco in Italy (Banchero) and so on.
[262] Joined Cases C-34/95, C-35/95, and C-36/95, *De Agostini* [1995].
[263] Case C-379/98, *PreussenElektra* [2001] ECR I-2099. H. Bjornebye, *Investing in EU Energy Security: Exploring the Regulatory Approach to Tomorrow's Electricity Production* (Alphen aan den Rijn: Kluwer Law International 2010), p. 105, J. Baquero Cruz and F. Castillo de la Torre, 'A Note on PreussenElektra', 26 *European Law Review* (2001), pp. 497 et seq. and A. Johnston et al., 'The Proposed New EU Renewables Directive: Interpretation, Problems and Prospects', 1(3) *European Energy and Environmental Law Review* (2008), p.132. However, the original approach marked by a strong demarcation between discriminatory and non-discriminatory measures have started to fade also more generally. P. Pecho, 'Good-Bye-Keck? A Comment on the Remarkable Judgment in Commission v Italy, C-110/05', 36(3) *Legal Issues in Economic Integration* (2009), p. 269.

4.8.1.1 Exceptions for Security of Supply

Security of supply was the central issue raised in the infamous *Campus Oil*[264] case, which was examined by the Court under the public security exemption contained in Article 36 TFEU. The case concerned a 1982 Irish Order for the maintenance and provision of supplies of fuel. This required all importers of any petroleum product within its scope to purchase a proportion—around 30–40 per cent—of the amount of petroleum products they required from the national refinery, Irish National Petroleum Corporation (INPC), at a predetermined cost-based price.

INPC's share capital was owned by the Irish state, its basic function being to improve the security of the Irish oil supply. The company owned the only refinery in Ireland. The purchase obligation was disputed before a national court, which decided to request a preliminary ruling. The questions involved related to the free movement of goods, Article 34 TFEU, and the exceptions contained in Article 36 TFEU.

In the proceedings, the Irish government maintained that 'Ireland's *heavy dependence* for its oil supplies on imports from other countries and the *importance of oil for the life of the country* make it indispensable to maintain refining capacity on the national territory, thereby enabling the national authorities to enter into long-term delivery contracts with the countries producing crude oil'.

The Irish government also argued that the purchase obligation in place at the time was the only way to guarantee the existence and continued operation of the national refinery. As this was indispensable for security of supply—the argument went on—the public security exemption was applicable to the case.

The Court accepted this argument, which was essentially based on security of supply, on that occasion. Relying on the 'exceptional importance' of petroleum products as energy sources in the modern economy and their 'fundamental importance for a country's existence (since not only its economy but above all its institutions, its essential public services and even the survival of its inhabitants' depend thereon), the Court found that Article 36 TFEU allows Member States to protect public security using means that restrict the free movement of goods within the meaning of Article 34 TFEU.

It is significant that the Court maintained that, despite the fact that the European Community and the IEA had enacted legislation with the object of securing the supply of energy among its Member States, a Member State still has the competence to enact further legislation going beyond the measures agreed upon at EU and IEA level. As noted by AG Jacobs, the special economic role of petroleum products was a decisive factor in the Court's rather exceptional judgment in *Campus Oil*.[265] That degree of emphasis on security of supply was thus already unusual at the time of the *Campus Oil* judgment and the Court's subsequent case law, discussed in the

---

[264] Case 72/83, *Campus Oil* [1984] ECR 2727.
[265] Opinion in Case C-379/98, *PreussenElektra AG v Schleswag AG*, delivered on 26.10.2000, para. 209.

rest of this Section, suggests that such a decision would be unlikely nowadays, even where petroleum products were concerned.[266]

An interesting epilogue to this case was that, despite this reliance on security of supply and claims of indispensability, Ireland decided in 1995, only ten years after the Court's decision, to close its refinery because it apparently now considered that security of supply in Ireland could be sufficiently guaranteed through other means (in particular through its commercial partners).[267] This example shows how security of supply is a relative and flexible notion. It may well be asked how the national refinery suddenly became less than indispensable for national security in the ten years following the judgment. At any rate, the dependence on imports and the importance of oil to the country did not disappear. What did happen, however, was that the underlying ideology changed from a state-driven system, in which security of supply was to be guaranteed by the state, to market-driven essentially by market forces, where security of supply could be entrusted to the market players.[268] It may be that the difference in approach can be traced to this change in the conception of the role of the state in energy security. It may also be that other objective factors are behind the change, the case having occurred at a point where oil prices were historically high, with the anticipation that prices were going to increase further. Perhaps in these circumstances the Irish government took a narrow view of security of supply and wanted physical possession of the infrastructure. Later, prices fell significantly, stayed low for a few years, and government fears regarding oil shortages disappeared. Possession of the refinery no longer mattered—oil and oil products were freely available; and since refining has not been a very lucrative business in financial terms since 1973, the Irish government woke up to the risk that it was going to have to subsidize a refinery instead of simply buying 'cheap' products. Alternatively, there may also have been a less objective reason for the change. It may be that the security of supply argument has less to do with objective factors and more to do with the appeal this line of argumentation has to a non-energy expert combined with the state's keenness to win the case before the Court.

A somewhat similar matter came before the Court only a few years later.[269] In 1988, the Commission initiated proceedings against Greece. This case concerned the exclusive right of the Greek state to import and market a quantity of petroleum products corresponding to 65 per cent of the requirements of the domestic market. All distribution companies were required to obtain their supplies

---

[266] Cameron also notes that a lot has changed since *Campus Oil*: the interconnections between Member States are growing, etc. P. Cameron, *Competition in Energy Markets: Law and Regulation in the European Union* (Oxford: OUP 2007), pp. 549–50.

[267] M. Ayral, *Droit Communautaire de l'Energie* (Paris: Joly Editions, 1997), p. 6. Since then the refinery has been sold several times, the most recent owner being ConocoPhillips. The refinery was for sale in 2007 (*The Irish Times*, Deutsche Bank to handle Whitegate sale, Saturday, 12 May 2007).

[268] For an interesting comparison, see Commission press release, 'Competition: Malta Opens Petroleum Products Market to Competition; Infringement Procedure Closed', IP/07/1952, 18.12.2007.

[269] Case C-347/88, *Commission v Greece* [1990] ECR I-4747. An interesting detail in the *Campus Oil* proceedings is that the government of Greece also participated in the proceedings and supported Ireland, perhaps in anticipation of finding itself before the ECJ in a similar matter.

from Greek public-sector refineries to the extent of a percentage of the requirements of the domestic market corresponding to the unadjusted part of the marketing monopoly. The rationale behind this obligation was to secure an outlet for the products of its public sector refineries.

In this case, the Greek government sought to justify certain exclusive rights enjoyed by public sector refineries on public security grounds, following the argument successfully used in *Campus Oil*. Greece argued that its 'special geopolitical situation makes it essential to adopt measures designed to ensure that the country has a regular supply of crude oil and petroleum products. That aim can be achieved only by maintaining public-sector refineries in operation. Accordingly, it is necessary to require distribution companies to obtain a proportion of their supplies from those refineries until such time as it is possible for them to market their products at competitive prices.'

In this case, the Court recalled that it had held in *Campus Oil* that:

'[a] Member State which is totally or almost totally dependent on imports for its supplies of petroleum products may rely on grounds of public security within the meaning of Article 36 TFEU for the purpose of requiring importers to cover a certain proportion of their needs by purchases from a refinery situated in its territory at prices fixed by the competent ministry on the basis of the costs incurred in the operation of that refinery, if the production of the refinery cannot be freely disposed of at competitive prices on the market concerned.'

Nonetheless, it concluded that Greece had failed to demonstrate that, if the state's rights with regard to the importation and marketing of petroleum products were not maintained in force, the public sector refineries would be unable to dispose of their products on the market at competitive prices and thereby ensure their continued operation. The proportionality test was thus unfavourable for Greece.

Greece lost a very similar case only ten years later.[270] The matter before the Court was a Greek law obliging undertakings engaging in import to hold a minimum stock of petroleum. The law gave companies the right to transfer that obligation, in whole or in part, to refineries located in Greece from which they had acquired products during the previous year. This right to transfer the stock-holding obligation covered a maximum quantity equal to the volume of products which the refineries had supplied to them during a 90-day period in the previous year.

In the Commission's view, this possibility to buy petroleum products from refineries established in Greece in order to be able to transfer the storage obligation constituted an obstacle to the free movement of goods,[271] because if companies wanted to purchase products from other Member States, they lost the opportunity to transfer the storage obligation. Defending its national solution, Greece argued that the free movement of goods had not been restricted and even if it had been,

---

[270] Case C-398/98, *Commission v Greece* [2001] ECR I-7915. A different interpretation is offered in C. Barnard, *The Substantive Law of the EU—The Four Freedoms* (Oxford: OUP 2004), p. 72. In that discussion, the entire system of transposing the obligation to hold a 90-day stock of petroleum products is seen as 'extremely onerous'. This system, however, is not uncommon in the EU. Similar requirements imposed on importers to hold certain percentages of the total annual imports of oil and/ or natural gas are in force in Poland, Italy, and France, among other states.

[271] Case C-398/98, *Commission v Greece*, [2001] ECR I-7915, para. 16.

the solution it applied could be justified under Article 36 TFEU as a system necessary to safeguard the security of supply of petroleum products.[272]

The Court noted, with references to *Campus Oil*, that the Greek government was right in claiming that maintenance on national territory of a stock of petroleum products allowing continuity of supplies to be guaranteed constitutes a public security objective. However, since Greece's arguments were of purely economic nature, they could not serve as justification for a quantitative restriction within the meaning of Article 36 TFEU.[273]

The Court also noted that less restrictive means were available. In particular, with reference to AG Colomer's opinion, it pointed out that there was no inevitable linkage between the transfer of the storage obligation and the purchases from the national refineries and the system could be built on the basis of a competitive and market-based scheme.

It is of interest that the Court also referred explicitly and approvingly to the AG's opinion, in which he noted that products covered by a system contrary to Article 34 TFEU but justified under Article 36 TFEU cannot 'exceed the minimum supply requirements without which the public security of the State concerned would be affected or the level of production necessary to keep the refinery's production capacity available in the event of a crisis and to enable it to continue to refine at all times the crude oil for the supply of which the State had entered into long-term contracts'.[274]

Just as with the previous case, the Greek system was seen to create an obstacle to the free movement of goods that could not be justified under the security of supply argument successfully used in *Campus Oil*. In addition to the economic nature of the arguments put forward by the Greek government, the Greek scheme went too far to be justifiable under Article 36 TFEU.

4.8.1.2 Is the Security of Supply Defence Still Applicable?

Given the substantial changes which have occurred in the EU and international energy markets and their regulation over the years following *Campus Oil*, the question whether the decision in the case remains applicable or whether new market developments have made it moot is interesting and somewhat open. Clearly, the more that national markets are integrated into the EU markets, and the further the harmonization of national energy legislation is pushed, the less scope remains for national security of supply measures.[275] It also seems clear that security of supply is not to be considered an overriding instrument or a wild card that beats the rules on

---

[272] Case C-398/98, *Commission v Greece*, para. 21.

[273] Case C-398/98, *Commission v Greece*, paras. 29 and 30.

[274] Opinion of AG Ruíz-Jarabo Colomer in Case C-398/98, *Commission v. Greece*, delivered on 15.2.2001, para. 47.

[275] Case C-326/07, *Commission v Italy* [2009] ECR I-2291, paras. 67 and 68. This suggestion was also made by AG Jacobs in *PreussenElektra* where he noted how: 'it is doubtful whether recourse to Article 36 is still possible given the fact that the electricity directive provides for types of measures necessary to ensure security of supply.' See Opinion in Case C-379/98, *PreussenElektra AG v Schleswag AG*, delivered on 26.10.2000, para. 209.

free movement of good whenever evoked. On the contrary, while it is possible to invoke security of supply as a defence under Article 36 TFEU as a public security factor, it can only be accepted under very strict proportionality requirements. The security of supply defence can only be accepted under exceptional circumstances[276] and purely economic arguments cannot be used as a part of the security of supply line of defence.

It must also be noted that, in addition to these free movement of goods cases, the Court has looked into the security of supply argument in the so-called 'golden share' cases.[277] In these cases, which related to the free movement of capital, and freedom of establishment in some cases, the question to be decided was essentially whether the state could retain the power to veto decisions made by privatized companies and, if so, under what conditions. One of these conditions could have been the risk to the security of energy supply. The approach taken by the Court was largely the same as in the free movement of goods cases: the scope of national measures to ensure security of supply is narrow and must fulfil the proportionality test. In the early golden share cases, the Court, while admitting that this was a possible justification, refused to accept the attempts to justify restrictions on free movement of capital on the grounds of security of supply as a legitimate public interest factor.[278] The case of *Commission v Belgium* followed, in which the Court finally accepted a formula under which the security of supply defence could be successfully invoked. The Court held that the Belgian legislative scheme could be justified by the objective of guaranteeing energy supplies in the event of a crisis because the government's golden share entitled the state to block a decision made by Distrigaz. This criteria to which this right was subject were that it was: (i) subject to strict time-limits; (ii) limited to certain decisions concerning strategic assets of the companies in question and could only be invoked where there was a risk that national energy policy objectives might be compromised; (iii) required a formal statement of reasons; and (iv) could be subject to an effective review by the courts.[279] In the event that this set of criteria is fulfilled, security of energy supply may therefore be invoked in future cases as an overriding requirement of general interest which is considered as: (a) non-discriminatory; (b) non-discretionary; and (c) satisfying the principle of proportionality.[280]

---

[276] Similarly, see P. Cameron, *Competition in Energy Markets: Law and Regulation in the European Union* (Oxford: OUP 2007).

[277] See cases C-367/98, *Commission v Portugal* [2002] ECR I-4731; C-483/99, *Commission v France* [2002] ECR I-4781; C-503/99, *Commission v Belgium* [2002] ECR I-4809; C-462/00, *Commission v Spain* [2003] ECR I-4581; C-98/01, *Commission v Great Britain* [2003] ECR I-4641; C-174/04, *Commission v Italy* [2005] ECR I-4933; C-274/06, *Commission v Spain* [2008] ECR I-165; C-326/07, *Commission v Italy* [2009] ECR I-2291.

[278] Case C-367/98, *Commission v Portugal* [2002] ECR I-4731; C-483/99, *Commission v France* [2002] ECR I-4781.

[279] Case C-503/99, *Commission v Belgium* [2002] ECR I-4809, paras. 49–51. This case is discussed from a free movement of capital point of view in C. Barnard, *The Substantive Law of the EU—The Four Freedoms* (Oxford: OUP 2004), pp. 479–80.

[280] The Court did not accept the Commission's claim that the same objective could be attained by Belgium through less restrictive means (long-term gas supply agreements, diversification of supply sources, or some form of licensing scheme).

In other words, it seems that the Court interpreted the security of supply defence very restrictively in this case. It has refused to accept this defence in most other cases,[281] holding that the public security defence may be invoked only in cases where there is a 'genuine and sufficiently serious threat to a fundamental interest of society'.[282] For example, a simple acquisition of more than 10 per cent of the share capital of the national energy company cannot be regarded as a real and serious threat to national security of supply.[283]

Throughout its case law, the Court has rigorously applied a proportionality test to avoid decisions where restrictive national legislation has gone further than necessary to satisfy the security of energy supply objective. The proportionality test has, in particular, meant that national provisions providing special rights to the state must be precise and objectively verifiable. From an investor's point of view, these requirements translate into much-needed legal certainty.

As noted, the further that the harmonization of national energy legislation is pushed, the less scope remains for national security of supply measures.[284] However, this option should always remain, as national circumstances vary from country to country. Finland and Spain have very different security of supply risks and this difference must be reflected in measures, legislative and other, aiming to strengthen their security of supply. One size does not fit all.

4.8.1.3 Exceptions for Environmental Reasons

It is nowadays settled case law that national measures capable of obstructing intra-EU trade may be justified by overriding requirements relating to the protection of the environment, provided that the measures in question are proportionate to the aim pursued.[285] The internal energy markets and free movement of energy are no exception to this. The question is principally that of what types of restriction are acceptable. The Court has examined this issue in a number of cases, *PreussenElektra* in particular. Even before *PreussenElektra* the Court had the opportunity to examine discriminatory national treatment in the *Outokumpu* case.[286] This case centred around the issue of environmental taxation and concerned excise duty on electricity imported into Finland from Sweden. Under the Finnish laws on the taxation of energy then in force, excise duty on electricity was levied in Finland on electricity produced there, the level of duty depending on the method of production. Essentially,

---

[281] Among others, C-462/00, *Commission v Spain* [2003] ECR I-4581; C-98/01, *Commission v Great Britain* [2003] ECR I-4641; C-174/04, *Commission v Italy* [2005] ECR I-4933; C-274/06, *Commission v Spain* [2008] ECR I-165; C-326/07, *Commission v Italy* [2009] ECR I-2291.
[282] See Case C-54/99, *Église de Scientologie* [2000] ECR I-1335, para. 17; C-483/99, *Commission v France* [2002] ECR I-4781, para. 48; C-503/99, *Commission v Belgium* [2002] ECR I-4809, para. 47.
[283] Case C-274/06, *Commission v Spain* [2008] ECR I-165, paras. 38 and 51.
[284] A recent security of supply related case is also Case C-265/08, *Federutility and others* [2010] ECR, p. I-03377.
[285] Case C-320/03, *Commission v Republic of Austria* [2005] ECR, I-9871, para. 70; Case C-463/01, *Commission v. Germany* [2004] ECR, I-11705, para. 75; Case C-309/02, *Radberger Getränkegesellschaft and S. Spitz* [2004] ECR, I-11763, para. 75.
[286] Case C-213/96 *Outokumpu* [1998] ECR I-1777.

hydropower and nuclear power were taxed at a lower rate than electricity produced from more polluting sources, such as coal or oil. This scheme was, according to the drafting history of the law, based on environmental grounds. However, the amount of duty chargeable on imported electricity was not determined on the basis of the production method. The excise duty chargeable on imported electricity was lower than the highest excise duty chargeable on electricity produced in Finland. However, it was higher than the excise duty chargeable on electricity produced in Finland through hydropower or nuclear power. The scheme did not allow the importer to provide evidence that the imported electricity was produced through hydropower or other renewable energy sources and therefore benefit from the lower duty.

AG Jacobs examined the case and concluded that the scheme, and the differentiated treatment involved, was justified because of its environmental objective and the lack of effective alternatives. The Court found differently. After noting the central position of environmental protection in both the general EU law and EU energy policy in particular, the Court examined the discriminatory nature of the scheme. It took the view that practical difficulties in determining the origin or production methods of imported electricity could not justify discriminatory taxation. On this point, it was of relevance that the scheme did not allow the importer the opportunity to demonstrate the origin and production method of the imported electricity. As the Finnish taxation system discriminated against electricity produced in other Member States, it was found to violate Treaty provisions on non-discriminatory taxation.

It may well be thought that, had it been possible for the importer to prove the origin of the imported electricity, the outcome might have been different. The Court has been ready to allow schemes which, in the name of environmental protection, have an impact on trade between Member States and are also discriminatory, as long as the potential importers from other Member States have a possibility to participate.[287] As will be seen, the discriminatory nature of the German renewables scheme at issue in *PreussenElektra* did not prevent the Court from accepting it.

As is well known, the *PreussenElektra* judgment concerned a feed-in-tariff scheme in which electricity supply companies were obliged to purchase electricity generated from renewable sources in their areas at a fixed price considerably higher than the price of electricity produced from non-renewable sources. This purchase obligation only covered renewable energy generated in Germany. The scheme raised two separate issues, which were addressed by the Court: (i) that of state aid for environmental purposes and the requirement that aid is granted by a Member State or through state resources; and (ii) the relationship between the Treaty's free movement of goods provisions and environmental protection. While the first issue has been tackled in the section on state aid, this section focuses on the second issue.

In respect of the relationship between the internal market objective and the support of the green energy production, the Court, after repeating the *Dassonville*

---

[287] D. Chalmers, G. Davies, and G. Monti, *European Union Law* (Cambridge: CUP 2010), p. 773.

formula, stated the obvious, with reference to *Campus Oil* and other cases:[288] an obligation placed on traders in a Member State to obtain a certain percentage of their supplies of a given product from a national supplier limits to that extent the possibility of importing the same product by preventing those traders from obtaining supplies in respect of a proportion of their needs from traders situated in other Member States.[289] The Court held that in this case the purchase obligation imposed on electricity supply undertakings applied only to electricity produced from renewable energy sources within the scope of the German statute and within the respective supply area of each undertaking concerned, and was therefore capable, at least potentially, of hindering intra-Community trade.[290] In fact, it was clear at the time that the purchase obligation only applied to renewable energy produced in Germany,[291] and due to this the provision in question could easily be classified as a 'buy-local' requirement and was directly discriminatory.[292]

One of the shortcomings of the judgment is that the Court did not explicitly discuss the discriminatory nature of the scheme. This would have required taking a stand on the promotion of environmental objectives, a mandatory requirement under the case law stemming from *Cassis de Dijon*,[293] and a discriminatory measure that promoted this objective.[294] As explained, discriminatory measures can, in theory, only be accepted under the exhaustive list contained in Article 36 TFEU. As environmental concerns were not considered as crucial at the time of negotiating the EEC Treaty as they are today, this element is not part of that list, nor has it been added to the list, despite several opportunities to do so.[295] In the absence of this addition, the current state of affairs is still marked with uncertainty.[296] It is clear, however, as discussed in Section 4.8.1.4, that the proportionality question has become the major criterion of assessment in these types of environmental cases.[297]

---

[288] Case 72/83, *Campus Oil* [1984] ECR 2727, para. 16 and Case C-21/88, *Du Pont de Nemours Italiana* [1990] ECR I-889, para. 11.

[289] Case C-379/98, *PreussenElektra* [2001] ECR I-2099, para. 70.

[290] Case C-379/98, *PreussenElektra* [2001] ECR I-2099, para. 71.

[291] A. Johnston et al., 'The Proposed New EU Renewables Directive: Interpretation, Problems and Prospects', 1(3) *European Energy and Environmental Law Review* (2008), p. 132.

[292] H. Bjørneby, *Investing in EU Energy Security: Exploring the Regulatory Approach to Tomorrow's Electricity Production* (Alphen aan den Rijn: Kluwer Law International 2010), p. 105.

[293] Case 120/78, *Rewe-Zentral* (Cassis de Dijon) [1979] ECR 649.

[294] H. Bjørneby, *Investing in EU Energy Security: Exploring the Regulatory Approach to Tomorrow's Electricity Production* (Alphen aan den Rijn: Kluwer Law International 2010), p. 105, J. Baquero Cruz and F. Castillo de la Torre, 'A Note on PreussenElektra', 26 *European Law Review* (2001), pp. 497 et seq. However, the judgment in C-2/90, *Commission v Belgium* (Walloon Waste) [1992] ECR I-4431 a discriminatory measure was justified on environmental grounds. For a recent discussion on the application of free movement of goods provision to discriminatory measures, see P. Pecho, 'Good-Bye-Keck? A Comment on the Remarkable Judgment in Commission v Italy, C-110/05', 36(3) *Legal Issues in Economic Integration* (2009).

[295] A. Johnston et al., 'The Proposed New EU Renewables Directive: Interpretation, Problems and Prospects', 1(3) *European Energy and Environmental Law Review* (2008), p.132

[296] However, the original approach marked by a strong demarcation between discriminatory and non-discriminatory measures have started to fade also more generally. P. Pecho, 'Good-Bye-Keck? A Comment on the Remarkable Judgment in Commission v Italy, C-110/05', 36(3) *Legal Issues in Economic Integration* (2009), p. 269.

[297] See, in particular, Case C-320/03, *Commission v Austria* [2005] ECR 1–9871. This case is discussed in section 4.8.1.4.

This question was raised by AG Jacobs, who considered the question of whether directly discriminatory measures can be justified as being of fundamental importance by reference to mandatory requirements. AG Jacobs seems to have favoured a more flexible approach to the mandatory requirement of environmental protection: (i) due to the integration principle in Article 11 TFEU; and (ii) because to hold that environmental measures can be justified only where they are applicable without distinction risks defeating the very purpose of the measures. National measures for the protection of the environment are inherently liable to differentiate on the basis of the nature and origin of the cause of harm, and are liable to be found discriminatory precisely because they are based on such accepted principles as that 'environmental damage should as a priority be rectified at source' (Article 191(2) TFEU). Where such measures necessarily have a discriminatory impact of that kind, the possibility that they may be justified should not be excluded.[298] Despite this invitation on the part of the AG, the Court declined to embark upon a discussion of the merits of discriminatory measures versus environmental protection.

In assessing the case, the Court nevertheless considered it necessary to consider both the aim of the German law and the particular features of the electricity market. It found that the use of renewable energy sources for producing electricity, which was the objective of the German law, is useful for protecting the environment insofar as it contributes to the reduction in emissions of greenhouse gases in line with the commitments of the EU and its Member States. The growth in the production of renewable energy was among the key objectives which the EU and its Member States intended to pursue in implementing the obligations agreed under the United Nations Framework Convention on Climate Change and its Kyoto Protocol.[299]

After noting that these measures are also designed to protect the health and life of humans, animals, and plants, and having made reference to the integration principle in Article 11 TFEU, the Court went on to refer to the preambles of the first electricity directive, recital 28 of which stated that it is for reasons of environmental protection that the directive authorized Member States to give priority to the production of electricity from renewable sources, and recital 39 of which stated that the directive constitutes only a further phase in the liberalization of the electricity market and left some obstacles to trade in electricity between Member States in place.[300]

The Court also noted that, once electricity has been allowed into the transmission or distribution system, it is difficult to determine its origin and, in particular, the source of energy from which it was produced.[301] As such, the system of certificates of origin for electricity produced from renewable sources being planned at the time was essential.[302]

---

[298] Opinion of AG Jacobs in Case C-379/98, *PreussenElektra*, delivered on 26.10.2000, paras. 229–233.
[299] Case C-379/98, *PreussenElektra* [2001] ECR I-2099, paras. 72–74.
[300] Case C-379/98, *PreussenElektra* [2001] ECR I-2099, paras. 75–78.
[301] Case C-379/98, *PreussenElektra* [2001] ECR I-2099, para. 78
[302] An interesting comparison is the earlier Case C-213/96, *Outokumpu* [1998] ECR I-1777, where the Court adopted a very different approach to a similar suggestion regarding the nature of electricity by the government of Finland.

In a somewhat abrupt ending, in particular after laying out what Bjørnebye has called a 'smorgasbord of arguments and considerations',[303] the Court concluded as follows:

'Having regard to all the above considerations, the answer to the third question must be that, in the current State of Community law concerning the electricity market, legislation such as the amended Stromeinspeisungsgesetz is not incompatible with Article 30 of the Treaty [now Article 36 TFEU].'

The reference to the 'current State of Community law concerning the electricity market' obviously poses the question of whether the judgment is applicable now, in 2013, following the appearance of two new energy market packages and a green energy package. Does the rationale of the judgment apply to discriminatory measures that contribute to environmental protection?[304] Does the reference to certificates of origin mean that, with the emergence of these certificates shortly after the judgment, the judgment is now longer relevant? These issues are examined in section 4.8.1.4.

4.8.1.4 *The Continuing Applicability of* PreussenElektra

While the fight against climate change and the corresponding and very ambitious renewable targets in the EU have increased the need to support renewable energy production, a common EU renewable support scheme has yet to emerge. While it falls short of setting forth this type of scheme, the clear intention of the Directive 2009/28/EC is to strike a balance between the right of each Member State to select the most suitable and effective way to reduce its emissions and the need to collaborate in the fight against climate change at EU level.

Renewable energy generation investments are far from being market-based investments, as are many of the other types of energy infrastructure investments in the EU. After a long period of denial, the EU is now coming to grips with this reality.[305] In the absence of EU support schemes, there is a practical need to allow Member State support schemes, which undoubtedly have an effect on trade between Member States.[306] It has also been argued that the choice of legal base, Article 192 TFEU, and the use of flexible mechanisms under Directive 2009/28/

---

[303] H. Bjørnebye, *Investing in EU Energy Security: Exploring the Regulatory Approach to Tomorrow's Electricity Production* (Alphen aan den Rijn: Kluwer Law International 2010), p. 108.

[304] These questions have also been raised already in J. Baquero Cruz and F. Castillo de la Torre, 'A Note on PreussenElektra', 26 *European Law Review* (2001), pp. 489–501.

[305] See for example, 'Energy 2020: A Strategy for Competitive, Sustainable and Secure Energy', (COM/2010/0639 final). The document speaks heavily in favour of public sector involvement in future investments.

[306] An interesting option is provided by A. Johnston et al. who question whether a feed-in-tariff would constitute a trading rule and thus fall under the scope of the free movement provisions in the first place. Under this approach, a feed-in-tariff, instead of being a trade mechanism, would be seen as a national energy policy instrument. A. Johnston et al., 'The Proposed New EU Renewables Directive: Interpretation, Problems and Prospects', 1(3) *European Energy and Environmental Law Review* (2008), pp. 137–8.

EC show that the EU legislator has accepted the existence of 27 different national regimes which may have a discriminatory effect.[307]

One way of looking at whether the *PreussenElektra* judgment remains relevant is to say that, given the rationale of the judgment and the continuing relevance of Article 11 TFEU, now coupled with the increasing urgency for reductions in greenhouse gas emissions, it would seem that measures introduced or specifically allowed through secondary EU law would comply (*de facto* at the very minimum[308]) with Treaty rules on the free movement of goods, even where these have a discriminatory effect.[309]

Given the obligations related to renewables contained in Directive 2009/28/EC and the generally recognized need to cut emissions both very significantly and very rapidly, one could argue that there is a practical need to allow Member States a large degree of flexibility in their choice of mechanisms.[310] This requires that Member States have full liberty 'to develop the most suitable and effective national support mechanisms given the current full range of possibilities, from energy taxation, to [feed-in-tariffs] or other systems providing for a technology-specific premium'.[311] Adopting this type of approach, the main criteria in assessing the national schemes that promote renewable energy would be the necessity and the proportionality of the scheme.

The issue of the proportionality of environmental measures was highlighted in the judgment handed down in *Commission v Austria*.[312] In that case the Court stated that it was settled case law that national measures capable of obstructing intra-EU trade may be justified by overriding requirements relating to protection of the environment, provided that the measures in question are proportionate to the aim. After reiterating the importance of environmental protection[313] and making reference to the integration principle, emphasizing the fundamental nature of that objective and its extension across the range of those policies and activities, the Court looked at the question of the proportionality of the measures aiming at

---

[307] R. Van Der Elst, 'Les Defis de la Nouvelle Directive sur les Energies Renouvelables', in S. Hirsbrunner, D. Buschle, and C. Kaddous (eds), *European Energy Law/Droit Européen de l'Énergie* (Brussels: Bruylant 2011), p. 198.

[308] Compare this to the solution under general EU competition law (Articles 101 and 102 TFEU) where the approach has sometimes been to circumvent the difficult questions of quantifiability or non-economic nature of the benefit by not dealing with these issues. See K. Talus, *Vertical Natural Gas Transportation Capacity, Upstream Commodity Contracts and EU Competition Law* (Alphen aan den Rijn: Kluwer Law International 2011). For the role of environmental gains under the public procurement rules, see Case C-513/99, *Concordia Bus Finland* [2002] ECR I-7213.

[309] However, Johnston et al. suggest that Article 11 TFEU only refers to the EU legislator and would not help where the question relates to compatibility with Treaty provisions. See A. Johnston et al., 'The Proposed New EU Renewables Directive: Interpretation, Problems and Prospects', 1(3) *European Energy and Environmental Law Review* (2008), p. 134.

[310] Similarly, A. Johnston et al., 'The Proposed New EU Renewables Directive: Interpretation, Problems and Prospects', 1(3) *European Energy and Environmental Law Review* (2008), p. 142.

[311] A. Johnston et al., 'The Proposed New EU Renewables Directive: Interpretation, Problems and Prospects', 1(3) *European Energy and Environmental Law Review* (2008), p. 143.

[312] Case C-320/03, *Commission v Austria* [2005] ECR 1–9871.

[313] Para. 72 with further references to Case 240/83, *ADBHU* [1985] ECR 531, para. 13; Case 302/86, *Commission v Denmark* [1988] ECR 4607, para. 8; Case C-213/96, *Outokumpu* [1998] ECR I-1777, para. 32.

environmental protection.[314] It examined whether the restriction was proportionate having regard to the legitimate aim pursued in this case, namely the protection of the environment. As it turned out, the proportionality test proved fatal and the Court found that the Austrian regulation was incompatible with the Treaty.

Looking at cases like *PreussenElektra* and even the earlier case of *Bluhme*[315] and the efforts made at international, EU, and national level to reduce greenhouse gas emissions and curb climate change, it might not be excessively rash to suggest that, where necessary in order to provide an effective response to the looming environmental crises, the Court is prepared to adopt a more relaxed approach to measures taken by Member States than it would in other situations.[316] In essence, the Court is prepared to accept that the application of law must be sensitive to the surrounding realities. As such, it would not lightly strike down effective and proportionate environmental measures taken at national level.

Finally, in some areas the free movement provisions have already been incorporated into the renewable energy schemes at EU level. An example of this is the use of guarantees of origin, a scheme based on mutual recognition. The use of guarantees of origin is regulated at a general level through Directive 2009/28/EC, Article 15(9) and (10) of which requires Member States to recognize guarantees of origin issued by other Member States in accordance with this Directive exclusively as proof that the electricity has been produced from renewable energy sources.

A Member State may refuse to recognize a guarantee of origin only when it has well-founded doubts about its accuracy, reliability, or veracity. If it does have such doubts, it must notify the Commission of the refusal and the reasons for it. If the Commission finds that a refusal to recognize a guarantee of origin is unfounded, it can adopt a decision requiring recognition of the guarantee of origin in question.

The mutual recognition system has, unsurprisingly, not proved entirely unproblematic. In 2009, the Commission issued a reasoned opinion to Italy for failure to recognize certain guarantees of origin from other EU Member States, namely France, Greece, and Slovenia, for renewable energy produced in 2005.[317] This categorical refusal was, according to the Commission, unjustified.[318]

4.9 Concluding Thoughts: From Nothing, to Supporting, to an Increasingly Powerful Tool

The Treaty of Rome gave the Commission extraordinary powers, for that point in time but also for today. Under the Treaty—then the EEC Treaty, now the TFEU—the

---

[314] Case C-320/03, *Commission v Austria* [2005] ECR 1–9871, para. 85.

[315] Case C–67/97, *Bluhme* [1998] ECR I–8033.

[316] D. Chalmers, G. Davies, and G. Monti, *European Union Law* (Cambridge: CUP 2010), p. 896.

[317] The obligation in 2005 was based on Directive 2001/77/EC of the European Parliament and of the Council of 27 September 2001 on the promotion of electricity produced from renewable energy sources in the internal electricity market, OJ L 283/33, 27.10.2001.

[318] 'Renewable electricity: Commission sends reasoned opinion to Italy for not accepting guarantees of origin', IP/09/426, 19.3.2009.

Commission has the legal power to change the way in which the energy business is run, regardless of the approaches taken by Member States. What is more, the Commission's powers extend to central areas of national decision-making. The support Member States give to their energy companies can be prohibited under the EU state aid provisions of the Treaty. Measures taken by a national energy company can be prohibited and circumvented through the creative use of EU competition laws. Preferences for certain types of power generation can be called into question and the national security of supply arrangements can be undermined.

The changes which have taken place over the last few years in EU competition law could hardly have been greater: from almost complete non-application to the energy sector, the approach to enforcement moved to being 'supportive' of sector-specific regulation, and then to increasingly intrusive enforcement. Now companies are required to sell off assets, invest in cross-border infrastructure, and refrain from using their own and legally-acquired transportation capacity. In part, this has required the re-thinking of certain competition law concepts, such as essential facilities.

The liberalization process has triggered a dramatic restructuring of the industry, with winners but also, and inevitably, many losers. National authorities are naturally tempted to use state aid (ideally by way of regulation) to help the losers to survive (and to turn national winners into EU winners). The principle should be that the state should not interfere with such restructuring nor waste its resources on propping up losers—since this will just end up creating bigger losses for society—but rather seek to mitigate the social consequences of the inevitable, and desirable, restructuring.

The stronger weight now given to environmental objectives means both that protectionism will increasingly seek environmental camouflage and that advocacy of environmental purposes will urge that the environmental failure of markets requires correction by means of public subsidies. A choice needs to be made from among competing economic philosophies: does one trust the market as ultimately the best agent of environmental policy; or, on the basis of an environmentalist revival of mercantilism, does one look to the state? The current ideological limbo, in which a market-based philosophy is coupled with a state-centred reality does not provide a workable solution.

5

Environment and Energy

On a Bumpy Road Towards a Clean Energy Future

5.1 EU Environmental Policies for Energy: Contradictions and Dilemmas

Inherent human and societal anxiety needs an object, and with wars within the territory of the EU a thing of the past and peace and relative prosperity in abundance, concern over the global environment is now an essential part of the mindset of the Western middle classes. These concerns have led to a significant improvement in the quality of the environment in the rich countries—the players in the political process have to respond. The EU and its largely faceless actors—the Commission, Parliament, and Council—have to respond even more vigorously as they lack the political legitimacy that was once vested in the nation state.[1] The institutions of the EU are hence compelled to respond to environmental concerns and, even more to the point, to be seen to be doing so. This is a close to impossible task, and the ingenuity, perseverance and strategic skill of the European Commission, in particular, demands admiration. It has accomplished a lot.

Environmental action is often based on uncertain science, a fact which is clearly in evidence where it presently matters most—climate change. In an increasingly global economy and an even more increasingly integrated internal market, environmental action requires policies beyond national borders, because if this is not the case then competition is bound to lead economic actors to relocate. This is not only a theoretical threat, as the companies relocating to China and other countries have shown.[2] But such international action, even in the closer framework of the EU, touches on core sentiments of national sovereignty with respect to tax and the environment versus economic cost trade-offs reflected and formally enshrined in Articles 192 and 194 TFEU, which are essentially based on the principle of subsidiarity. Furthermore, environmental action, if serious, rapidly runs into a serious

---

[1] While it could be argued that the European Parliament is there to fill the democratic deficit and that its powers have been increased to accommodate this, it is still far from comparable to a national parliament.

[2] It is, however, necessary to note that the fears of massive relocations are perhaps over-exaggerated. See R. Tscherning, 'The EU ETS Rules on Carbon Leakage and Energy Intensive Industry in the Federal Republic of Germany', *European Energy and Environmental Law Review* (2011), pp. 2–17.

contradiction: the middle classes now ruling the EU are keen on green policies, but unwilling to see the luxuries of prosperity seriously threatened. The right to travel and to own cars are now regarded as sacrosanct. Idealistic young Europeans are keen to help the disenfranchised people of the Third World, but do not really wish them to enjoy the same material and environmentally damaging comforts. The issue is most acute in the field of energy. Energy is what fuels modern economies—a machine that has created endless prosperity and comfort. At the same time, consumption of the sources of energy, which are key both now and for the foreseeable future, constitutes the gravest environmental threat to the planet. This is a circle that is hard to square. But the contradiction to be faced is even worse: with climate change as a result of hydrocarbon consumption being the clearly identified main danger, nuclear energy, which has been safe for decades in the West, is not affected by security of supply problems, and is among the cleanest energy sources available, should be the obvious answer. But in most EU countries this source of power is burdened with the tradition of anxiety of the last generation engendered by the ever-present prospect of nuclear war in the 1950s and 1960s—and thus not really regarded as an acceptable saviour. While nuclear power in France is responsible for approximately 80 per cent of national power production and the share of nuclear power in electricity generation in Finland is approximately one-third,[3] the situation in many other countries is very different. While not long ago certain EU countries, Sweden and Germany in particular,[4] faced with climate change and security of supply challenges, were revisiting previous decisions to phase-out nuclear power, and other countries were becoming more open to this option, the Japanese nuclear crises that followed the tsunami of March 2011 brought an abrupt halt to most of these plans.[5] European environmental politics in the energy field are therefore riddled with contradictions and there is great pressure on the European institutions to buy legitimacy through high-flying targets which do not ultimately seem to be based on much science.[6]

This chapter surveys the main issues for EU environmental policies and law in the field of energy, but does not deal with EU environmental law as such. The chapter focuses on the development of EU policies in the areas of energy, the environment, and climate change.

---

[3] International Energy Agency, *Energy Policies of IEA Countries, Finland 2007 Review*, pp. 85, 87, 103.

[4] Here, the direct link between the political reactions and the public opinion is particularly visible.

[5] Even if the Energy Roadmap 2050 includes a heading entitled 'Nuclear energy as an important contributor', the text in that section is carefully crafted so as not to take any positions vis-à-vis nuclear. It essentially explains that some states are for, others against, nuclear power and then focuses on safety aspects. See Communication from the Commission to the European Parliament, the Council, the European Economic and Social Committee and the Committee of the Regions, 'Energy Roadmap 2050', (COM(2011) 885/2).

[6] This was highlighted by the former Prime Minister of Finland, Paavo Lipponen, in his 'Foreword', to B. Delvaux, M. Hunt, and K. Talus (eds), *EU Energy Law and Policy issues* (Brussels: Euroconfidentiel 2008). Examples of this approach will be given in this chapter.

5.2 Key Questions, Concepts, Legal Frameworks

Why should the EU take any environmental action, particularly by way of imposing legal obligations on Member States?[7] Would it not be better left to Member
States to lay down national environmental laws which reflect the balancing of the
costs and benefits of environmental regulation in the national political process,
the attitude towards scientific uncertainty and risk and the *quid pro quo* between a
higher environmental quality attained nationally and the relocation of industries?
Could not the market respond to the environmental preferences of its participants
and develop, without interference by the state, instruments that bring about the
desired environmental quality? Environmental policy needs to be considered in the
light of the tension raised by these questions. The standard economic justification
of such regulation is that it 'internalizes' what are known as the 'external' environmental costs not borne directly by the actors which cause such effects. Markets
sometimes 'fail' to internalize such external costs, due to lack of competition or,
more often, due to the high 'transaction costs' which would be incurred if the many
affected by environmental damage had to be organized to pay for the prevention
of environmental damage. State action, in this economic view, is justified to correct
'market failure'. State action taken purely at national level is often insufficient as
environmental damage transcends the limits of national jurisdiction. Furthermore,
tighter national regulation may encourage polluters to relocate, thus undermining the
bargaining power implicit in state regulation, and compete unfairly with national
producers subject to a high level of environmental regulation, but both subject
to the competition of global markets. That is often used to justify EU-wide, or
ideally worldwide, minimum or even high environmental standards, by export of
high national standards, by trade restrictions against goods and services imported
from countries with a lower level of environmental regulation or by other forms of
extraterritorial regulation: e.g. use of financing, trade and tax sanctions, and other
forms of economic and political leverage.[8]

However, none of the above concepts are foolproof. Market failure is a very
ambiguous concept and needs to be contrasted with 'state failure'—which occurs
when the regulatory action taken by state (and intergovernmental) institutions does
not deliver what is expected, but is mired in inefficiency, fails to achieve targets,
and the regulatory machinery is hijacked by vocal minorities who, pursuant to the
'logic of collective action', bring their intensely-held beliefs to bear on the process
to the detriment of the interests of the majority at large.[9] Regulation can create

---

[7] For this, see K. Lenaerts, 'The Principle of Subsidiarity and the Environment in the European
Union: Keeping the Balance of Federalism', 17 *Fordham International Law Journal* (1993),
pp. 846–95.

[8] For a survey of key concepts in environmental law and policy from an energy perspective, from
a mainly US perspective but still useful, see: F. Bosselman, J. Rossi, and J. Weaver, *Energy, Economics
and the Environment, Cases and Materials* (New York: Foundation Press 2010).

[9] J. Rossi, 'Public Choice Theory and the Fragmented Web of the Contemporary Administrative
State', 96 *Michigan Law Review* (1998), pp. 1746–77.

competitive disadvantages for those subject to it (though also competitive advantages for those made subject at a very early stage to high standard regulation likely to spread), but there is also virtue in accepting 'regulatory competition': i.e. letting societies compete through their variety rather than imposing uniformity. A 'race to the bottom', driven by 'environmental dumping', is often alleged to be the consequence of regulatory competition, but it has to be recognized that such competition may under certain conditions also identify the most competitive social systems which combine both environmental quality and efficient ways to attain them—i.e. lead to an efficient race to the top. EU-wide regulation is also, quite apart from the economic language deployed, a way to express 'shared common values' in the EU. They do undoubtedly exist: EU citizens have a common interest in environmental quality. But such values are not shared and developed as they emerge in the national political and cultural discourse. There are wide divergences in national attitudes, for instance with respect to nuclear power (e.g. France or Finland versus the now mainly anti-nuclear societies like Germany or Sweden), or with respect to high environmental standards (e.g. the Nordic societies versus the UK). The logic of the EU discourse is to pretend the existence of shared common values and to formulate them in the many declaratory and even legislative instruments deployed, but the realities of a not-yet common culture, or rather cultural process, often creates complications and regulatory inefficiencies. One size does not always fit all—at any rate not efficiently. The legal foundation and political underpinnings of EU environmental policy in the energy sector are positioned in this framework of debate.

The legal foundation of EU environmental action is principally to be found in Articles 191 and 192 TFEU and the general energy Article 194 TFEU with reference to new and renewable energies, plus the general reference to the environment and sustainable development in Article 11 TFEU. Although the requirement for a 'high level of environmental protection' in respect of EU action under Article 37 TFEU is a goal, it is a difficult one to achieve despite the increasing number of directives and regulations to the same effect. This difficulty stems from the use of the principle of subsidiarity, the recognition of national differences and the exercise of governmental discretion in shaping policies based on often uncertain assumptions. Constitutional powers are significant here: a directive which is aimed, at least to a significant extent, at contributing towards the internal market does not require unanimity, but matters of tax, choice between energy sources (nuclear, renewables, and coal are particularly noteworthy in this context) and the general structure of its energy supply, does (Articles 192(2) or 194(2) TFEU). Member States may maintain a higher level of environmental protection in the light of scientific evidence, even after EU-wide harmonization has occurred, but the obvious potential for protectionist abuse is tightly controlled by the Commission, other Member States, and ultimately the ECJ.[10] Measures taken at national level are to be struck down if

---

[10] The ECJ has in particular placed emphasis on the proportionality scrutiny of national environmental action. See, as just one example, Case C-320/03, *Commission v Austria* [2005] ECR 1–9871 and the case law.

they constitute arbitrary discrimination, a disguised restriction on trade within the EU, or an obstacle to the functioning of the internal market.[11]

The intention here is not to develop an in-depth analysis, but to at least point to situations that would test the above provisions. First, they would be tested if, following the implementation of harmonization measures, a Member State further raised its environmental standards. Such action would both reflect the 'high level of environmental protection' sanctioned by the Treaty, but also constitute protection of its domestic industry in one way or another. For example, Germany, with the leverage available to it by dint of its very large market, might require higher environmental standards for gasoline, impose import restrictions on electricity generated by nuclear plants with lower safety standards[12] or by other power plants able to operate with lower emission standards.[13] From the Member State's perspective, such measures could be justified under Article 193 TFEU as long as they were not discriminatory and could be seen as based on reasonable environmental criteria, plus the need to create a level playing field between domestic companies subject to high standards of environmental regulation and foreign competitors not subject to such standards. But would such measures be legal under EU law—in particular the free movement of goods provisions or Article 114(5) TFEU? The content of Article 114(6) TFEU suggests that, since such import restrictions are a 'restraint on trade between Member States' (and not even disguised) and an obstacle to the functioning of the slowly emerging internal energy market, they infringe Article 114 TFEU and the free movement of goods provisions.

Even if one admits the right of a Member State to impose, without discrimination, higher product standards, the fact remains that Member States with large market leverage can *de facto* impose their policy on industries in other Member States dependent on access to their markets. Regulatory control over large markets therefore inevitably confers a *de facto* extraterritorial regulatory power intervening in other Member States'—and the EU's—regulatory sovereignty.

Another energy-specific issue that can be developed out of Article 192(2) is that, under current law, Member States cannot be compelled by a majority to give up energy sources which are environmentally seen as more questionable— e.g. German coal, French nuclear power, or perhaps in the future UK oil and gas. Article 194(2) explicitly states that 'measures [taken under Article 194 TFEU and majority voting] shall not affect a Member State's right to determine the conditions for exploiting it energy resources, its choice between different energy sources and the general structure of its energy supply, without prejudice to Article 192(2)(c)'.

---

[11] Case C-320/03, *Commission v Austria*; see also R. Van Der Elst, 'Les Defis de la Nouvelle Directive sur les Energies Renouvelables', in S. Hirsbrunner, D. Buschle, and C. Kaddous (eds), *European Energy Law/Droit Européen de L'Energie* (Brussels: Bruylant 2011) and even the discussion in D. Chalmers, G. Davies, and G. Monti, *European Union Law* (Cambridge: CUP 2010), p. 896.

[12] For a discussion in Finland relating to power imports from Russia with connection to nuclear power, see V.A. Lappalainen, 'Proposed Finland-Russia Interconnector Rejected', 1 *OGEL* (2007), <http://www.ogel.org>.

[13] This type of scheme was essentially accepted in the *PreussenElektra* case but instead of clear guidance on the question of discriminatory nature of measures that contribute to the environment, the ECJ provided for a plethora of arguments and accepted the discriminatory scheme.

Article 192(2)(c) TFEU provides that 'measures significantly affecting a Member State's choice between different energy sources and the general structure of its energy supply' are subject to a requirement for unanimity. As such, the new energy title should *a priori* not restrict Member States' choices with respect to energy sources. However, the current practice, which pre-dates the TFEU, suggests that the matter might not be so simple. Law in the books is different from law in action.

In order to reach the EU-wide target of 20 per cent renewable energy production by 2020, Directive 2009/28/EC on the promotion of the use of energy from renewable sources set 'mandatory' national targets and requires Members States to prepare and establish national action plans to reach their respective targets. The national targets that in principle translate into an overall EU target of 20 per cent increase in renewable energy production vary considerably from Member State to Member State. For example, the UK target is 15 per cent (from a 2005 level of 1.3 per cent!) while Latvia has a target of 40 per cent (from a 2005 level of 32.6 per cent) and Sweden has a target of 49 per cent (from a 2005 level of 39.8 per cent). Finland's target is 38 per cent (from a 2005 level of 28.5 per cent) and the French target is 23 per cent (from a 2005 level of 10.3 per cent).

Looking at these figures, it is clear that the environmental requirements under the EU energy *acquis* requires that countries achieve what in some cases like Latvia or Finland are very significant shares of total renewable energy production. In these cases, the renewables targets clearly restrict the right of the Member States to decide on their energy mix. Given that Directive 2009/28/EC was adopted under Article 175(1) EC [now 192(1) TFEU]—except for the biofuels-related requirements which were adopted under the internal market Article 95 EC [now 114 TFEU]—and by a majority vote, it seems that the Directive 2009/28/EC was adopted under the wrong legal basis, and is therefore in conflict with the Treaty, provided of course that a requirement that approximately half the national electricity production be from renewable energy sources instead of nuclear, coal, natural gas, or other options is considered to 'significantly affect' the right of a Member State to choose between different sources of energy supply.

5.3 Specific Environmental Issues of Energy

5.3.1 Extractive Industries

Internationally, most environmental sensitivities are relatively 'normal', localized and manageable at the production stage: i.e. the mining and extraction of oil and gas, coal, and uranium. The sensitivities here are partly traditional: e.g. subsidence and emission of particles in water effluents in the case of mineral extraction. Spillage of oil and flaring of gases in oil and gas extraction without proper environmental safeguards have a sad history, with well-known areas of severe environmental degradation where oil and gas extraction has occurred (e.g. Lake Maracaibo in Venezuela, Baku on the Caspian Sea, parts of Western Siberia, Delta in Nigeria, the OK Tedi and Fly River in Papua New Guinea and Ecuador jungle). Vulnerabilities tend to increase as oil and gas extraction moves, as happens increasingly, into deeper offshore areas, as the Macondo blowout in the Gulf of Mexico showed.[14] But while the damage caused by improper operations can be severe and have a wider geographical scope, modern industry practices relying on both constantly emerging technology in conjunction with governmental regulation, industry self-regulation, and internal corporate regulation (environmental impact statements, management plans, civil liability risk, and proper management of environmental responsibilities) seem to have brought these risks essentially under control. Of course, accidents happen in any areas of economic activity. Any incident in this area will necessarily be followed by an inquiry, an assessment of the adequacy of the existing regulatory framework, and some corrective measures. This type of failure-correct approach was taken on a global scale following the much-publicized oil disaster in Gulf of Mexico. In addition to litigation and changes to laws and policies in the US, it also led to changes in the EU legislative framework for offshore drilling. Comment from the EU Commission crystallizes this:

'Safety is non-negotiable. We have to make sure that a disaster similar to the one in the Gulf of Mexico will never happen in European waters. This is why we propose that best practices already existing in Europe will become the standard throughout the European Union.'[15]

While the Hydrocarbons Directive (1994/22/EC) already included an obligation to consider the technical and financial risks, as well as the obligation for applicants seeking exclusive exploration and production licences to disclose their past record of responsibility, the Macondo incident led to further regulation in this area. The new draft regulation on the safety of offshore oil and gas prospection, exploration, and production activities[16] provides for a more holistic approach and covers the whole lifecycle of all exploration and production activities from design to the final removal of an oil or gas installation. As this might suggest, significant environmental issues are also involved in the phase of decommissioning and abandonment of extraction, production, and transportation facilities. These are not completely new—traditional mining law was replete with obligations to restore old mining works at least to a condition of safety. These obligations were not always well implemented, in particular in countries with institutional weakness: i.e. in developing and transition countries.[17] The current tendency is towards a full clean-up, not just to ensure safety, but also to remedy the environmental damage caused either to the *status ex quo ante* (which is often not feasible) or to an acceptable new status (turning an open cut mine into a lake or similar). The emerging consensus in the EU is that offshore platforms have to be completely removed,[18] mining sites

---

[14] For this, see O. Anderson and J. Lowe (eds), 'Special Issue on Oil Spills', 3 *OGEL* (2010).

[15] 'Offshore oil drilling: European Commission envisages EU safety rules', IP/10/1324, 13.10.2010.

[16] Proposal for a Regulation on safety of offshore oil and gas prospection, exploration and production activities (COM/2011/688).

[17] T. Wälde, 'Environmental Policies Towards Mining in Developing Countries', 10(4) *Journal of Energy and Natural Resources Law* (1992), pp. 327–51.

[18] This is also the approach under the 1989 IMO Guidelines and Standards for the Removal or Offshore Installations and Structures on the Continental Shelf and in the Exclusive Economic Zone, available at <http://www.imo.org>. See also the OSPAR Decision 98/03, available at <http://www.ospar.org>.

(e.g. East German lignite) restored to a safe and attractive natural environment, and disused transport facilities (pipelines, transmission lines) completely dismantled and the natural state of the land restored—or a reasonably attractive equivalent achieved. The same applies to decommissioned nuclear facilities, although here special safety issues need to be taken into account. These issues may of course cause problems relating to modern, environmentally safe investment in sites left behind following the collapse of former Communist countries. Solutions in this regard involve financing clean-up of the site from the asset value still left and, directly or indirectly (though tax incentives), from the public purse.

5.3.2 Transportation

In the transportation phase, risks occur primarily with the onshore and offshore transport of oil. Onshore pipelines are vulnerable to sabotage, and many major environmental accidents have been caused by intentional destruction of pipelines, resulting in serious spillages (e.g. in Colombia). Faulty pipeline systems have also led to spillages of over 10 per cent of the total flow in Siberia. Certain problems are also involved in laying oil and gas pipelines through vulnerable environments—in particular arctic environments (e.g. Alaska—but this will also become an issue if exploration and production in the Arctic region starts[19]).

Offshore oil transport is mainly a matter of maritime safety,[20] although EU law applies to oil spills within EU waters.[21] Public attention has been drawn to such risks as a result of several tanker accidents, such as the Erika tanker accident off Brittany in northwest France in 1999 or the Prestige accident off the coast of Spain in 2002.[22] The fact that only an infinitesimally small amount of all transported oil is spilled is an indication of how well safety systems in fact work. Improvement here may be achieved through extension of safety management systems from in-house corporate organizations to shippers, through the use of safety training, standards (e.g. a double-hull obligation for tankers), liability systems, and better monitoring of flag of convenience ships, plus the expansion of responsibility from the harder to monitor shippers to easier to control oil companies.[23] The point of leverage here is, first, on the oil companies (who have leverage through subcontracting and

---

[19] For this, see the *OGEL* special issue edited by J Lloyd Loftis, 'T. J. Tyler and A. Goins, Arctic Region: Boundaries, Resources and the Promise of Co-operation', 2 *OGEL* (2012).

[20] For an overview of the applicable rules, see E. Smith, J. Dzienkowski, O. Anderson, J. Lowe, B. Kramer, and J. Weaver, *International Petroleum Transactions* (Colorado: Rocky Mountain Mineral Law Foundation 2010), pp. 846–69.

[21] See case C-188/07, *Commune de Mesquer v Total France* [2008] ECR I-4501. The Court concluded that hydrocarbons accidentally spilled at sea following a shipwreck, mixed with water and sediment and drifting along the coast of a Member State until being washed up on that coast, constitute waste within the meaning of the Waste Directive.

[22] For these see, I. Patricia Garcia, '"Nunca Mais!" How Current European Environmental Liability and Compensation Regimes are Addressing the Prestige Oil Spill of 2002', 25 *The University of Pennsylvania Journal of International Law* (2004), p. 1395.

[23] Offshore oil pollution from ships is addressed in O. Anderson and J. Lowe (eds), 'Special Issue on Oil Spills', 3 *OGEL* (2010).

shipping contracts) and, second, through using port control to bypass the innate laxity of flag-of-convenience states.[24]

5.3.3 Environmentally Sustainable Power Production

While the environmental impact of hydrocarbon-based energy is clearly the most significant of all energy sources, renewable energy also has an impact on the environment. Just consider hydropower or wind power. The impact of hydropower on the environment principally occurs in terms of the mostly localized changes caused to natural habitats by the building of dams. This method of generating power was formerly heralded as a sign of progress, and is currently in principle highly commendable for its zero contribution to climate change, but is also now much criticized. Since hydro-dams have been more or less built to potential in most of the EU, the issues here are rather related to the effect of new dams built in developing countries—which may include damage to sensitive natural habitats, population displacement, and sometimes a safety risk. One example from the other side of the world is the Australia/Papua New Guinea project, the Wabo hydropower project. This project envisages the construction of a large hydropower plant in Papua New Guinea, and the transmission of a large proportion of its output via an undersea cable to the northern part of Australia—meaning power for the Australians; development, electrification, and displacement of traditional landowners for the Papua New Guineans.

Wind power, like hydropower, should be hugely popular, since it has the potential to replace the very problematic burning of hydrocarbons, thus avoiding the emission of gases contributing to climate change. On paper and at the level of EU and Member State policies, it is all this. However, in the normal contradiction between generally shared soft environmental sentiments and much less tractable interests closer to home, wind farms up close are greatly disliked, due to noise emissions and unsightliness—leading to the infamous NIMBY ('not in my backyard') effect.[25] There are also claims of adverse health impact, without serious scientific evidence to back them up. Wind power is also problematic in other ways. In Finland, for example, calls to increase wind-based generation are voiced in various fora. However, the peak demand period in Finland is January–February, the cold period, where the temperature frequently drops to between –20° C and –40° C. During this period, wind-based production is often not an option, since power production is not significantly higher during the cold peaks and wind may even be absent during a period of extreme cold, in February in particular. Also, when the temperature drops below –30° C, which is not infrequent in Finland, wind power is not always available because of use restrictions in cold weather.

---

[24] D. Anderson, 'Port States and Environmental Protection', in A. Boyle and D. Freestone, *International Law and Sustainable Development* (Oxford: OUP 1999), pp. 325–45.

[25] NIMBY effect here is meant as a catchphrase, not as scientific concept. In this context, see P. Devine-Wright, 'Beyond NIMBYism: towards an Integrated Framework for Understanding Public Perceptions of Wind Energy', 8 *Wind Energy* (2005), pp. 125–39.

Therefore, wind generation is not always a suitable replacement for fossil fuels when peak-load capacity is required. This problem might partially be overcome through the creation of a pan-European energy network, but as this is unlikely to happen in the foreseeable future, today's market structure does not easily allow for a significant wind-based production capacity in Finland, even though the government is pushing for that. These peak-load-capacity-related problems are further aggravated by the introduction of the Kyoto Protocol and the EU Emission Trading Scheme (ETS). In many cases, the reserve capacity to address demand spikes followed by cold weather in northern Europe or hot spells in southern Europe is based on coal-based generation, as in Finland, or oil-based generation, as in Southern Europe, from older generation plants. Such plants are, needless to say, not as environmentally friendly as new generation plants.

Environmental sensitivities increase as hydrocarbons (coal, oil, gas) move to the consumption phase. The refining of oil into commercial products used to produce large noxious emissions of particles and gases. But, under the impact of technological change, regulation, and the increasing integration of environmental consciousness into all phases of engineering design, these emissions also seem to have been brought under control, at least within the EU.

However, the major environmental challenge in the energy sector is the large-scale emission of 'greenhouse gases' (CO_2, methane, etc.) through the burning of hydrocarbons at the consumption stage. Transport (cars and trucks), households (heating as well as, increasingly, air conditioning), industry—in particular the electricity industry—are the main contributors to this problem. One needs to bear in mind that noxious emissions per unit of energy are by far the highest for coal, followed by oil, and last (but not least) gas. There is now a wide scientific consensus—even within the US government, and possibly even the US oil industry—that the emission of these greenhouse gases through industrial processes is responsible at least for a substantial part of the global warming currently observed, and will potentially have a detrimental effect on nature, the weather, and societies over the next 50 to 100 years.

Given that observable climate change is to a large extent caused by hydrocarbon emissions, a major part of current environmental attention is focused on stabilizing (as in the United Nations Framework Convention on Climate Change from 1992, Article 2) and reducing (as in the Kyoto Protocol) these emissions. Such policies cannot avoid confronting the nuclear dilemma. The nuclear industry developed in the Cold War era. Perception of the industry has historically been inextricably linked to the, perhaps not unreasonable, great fear about nuclear war and the memories of the US dropping nuclear bombs on Hiroshima and Nagasaki in 1945. Political opposition to nuclear weapons in the 1950s and 1960s made no distinction between peaceful and military uses of nuclear energy. The Chernobyl accident in Ukraine in 1986 may have been a consequence of the in-built institutional weaknesses of socialist systems, but it did not allay the prevailing fears concerning nuclear energy, in particular in Germany and Austria. The Green parties in these and other countries emerged largely as an anti-nuclear movement. The post-2000 era, marked by growing energy prices and environmental awareness, created the preconditions for the emergence of a more positive view of nuclear-based power generation. However, the earthquake and the tsunami that followed it in 2011, with its devastating impact on the Fukushima nuclear power plant, put an end to the so-called 'revival of nuclear' in the EU and elsewhere. The dilemma now is that nuclear energy has been proven to produce, on a very large-scale, energy that is free of greenhouse gas emissions, at the production stage. As such it is, in terms of the Kyoto Protocol on Climate Change, hugely superior to hydrocarbons, the current mainstay of EU energy demand. It is also, at least at this time and for the foreseeable future, a much more certain source of large-scale energy supply than the currently fashionable and much-promoted renewable sources of energy (e.g. wind power, solar power, and biomass). The contribution made by these sources of energy to total energy production is currently very small, apart from largely non-expandable hydropower. The potential of nuclear is very different. Just consider France, with nearly 80 per cent of its electricity being produced from nuclear facilities and over 40 per cent of its total energy supply being nuclear-based.[26]

While the unconventional and renewable sources of energy are now much promoted (and indeed should be promoted), their realistic contribution to large-scale energy production is still largely untested. The political dilemmas and ideological contradictions involved here are well reflected by the case of Germany—a country which may be regarded as among the most vigorous proponents of environmental protection, reflecting the values strongly held by its middle class. Nevertheless, the country is also a very large emitter of greenhouse gases and a user of very heavily polluting, economically inefficient, and massively subsidized domestic coal. In 2001, it made a decision to exit gradually from the nuclear industry by 2022. Then in 2010, the phase-out of the remaining nuclear power plants was postponed by 12 years. Then, just one year later, the old timetable was back on. All nuclear power plants in Germany are, according to current plans, to be closed by 2022. Given that gas is the greenest of the fossil fuels, it might be assumed that natural gas will play a key role in making up the difference once nuclear power generation ceases. On the other hand, nuclear-based power might be imported from France or the Czech Republic.

5.4 Process, Objectives, and Instruments of EU Environmental Policy for the Energy Industries

Better environmental quality at a reasonable cost through the integration of environmental concerns into all phases and elements of the energy industries can perhaps be seen as the key objective of EU policy in this respect. A 1998 communication of the Commission listed energy efficiency, and increased share of cleaner energy sources as specific goals, in addition to the self-evident objective of reducing the

---

[26] See International Energy Agency, 'Executive Summary and Key Recommendations for Energy Policies of IEA Countries—France', (2010), p. 1, available at: <http://www.iea.org/Textbase/npsum/France2009sum.pdf>.

environmental impact of the production and use of energy sources.[27] In 2007, the EU Heads of states and governments set a series of climate and energy targets to be met by 2020, known as the '20-20-20' targets. These targets are not so different from the 1998 objectives. They include a 20 per cent reduction in greenhouse gas emissions, a 20 per cent share of renewable energy sources, and 20 per cent energy savings.[28] The key determinant of a list of objectives, though, is not the rarely justifiable declaration of a lofty overall goal, but rather its rank and weight within often conflicting objectives. The reference to a 'high level of protection' in Article 191 TFEU and the need to integrate the environment into all other EU activities under Article 11 TFEU have been relied on to suggest priority[29] over the more mundane aspects of energy supply. But this would be a legalistic view not in conformity with the political and legal processes out of which EU energy policy and law emerges. As with any authoritative legal instrument, the Treaty—and EU practice—includes several often contradictory objectives. The main opponent of the more purist concept of a 'high level of environmental protection' is security of supply, another of the EU's energy policy objectives,[30] which is even recognized as a legitimate key interest by the ECJ.[31] Security of supply is not merely a legal concept, but expresses the essential dependence of all EU activities on the continuous supply of energy, in many cases (and increasingly) from outside the Union.[32] If security of supply

[27] 'Communication on strengthening environmental integration within Community energy policy' (COM (98) 571), p. 8.
[28] 'Renewable Energy Road Map Renewable energies in the 21st century: building a more sustainable future' (COM(2006) 848 final), Brussels, 10.1.2007.
[29] A. Schaub, *Europäische Energiebinnenmarktpolitik und Umweltpolitik* (Baden Baden: Nomos 1996), p. 262.
[30] For example, see Article 3(1) of the Third Gas Market Directive: '[…] with a view to achieving a competitive, secure and environmentally sustainable market in natural gas.' See also Communication from the Commission to the European Parliament, the Council, the European Economic and Social Committee and the Committee of the Regions, 'Second Strategic Energy Review: an EU energy security and solidarity action plan' (COM(2008)0781 final), Green paper, 'A European Strategy for Sustainable, Competitive and Secure Energy' (COM(2006)105 final), 8.3.2006. The security of supply objective is defined as tackling the EU's rising dependence on imported energy through: (i) an integrated approach—reducing demand, diversifying the EU's energy mix with greater use of competitive indigenous and renewable energy, and diversifying sources and routes of supply of imported energy, (ii) creating the framework which will stimulate adequate investments to meet growing energy demand, (iii) better equipping the EU to cope with emergencies, (iv) improving the conditions for European companies seeking access to global resources, and (v) making sure that all citizens and businesses have access to energy. See also the Communication from the Commission to the European Parliament and the Council, 'Energy Infrastructure and Security of Supply' (COM(2003)743 final), 10.12.2003, p. 3 and Council Resolution of 23 November 1995 on the Green Paper for a European Union Energy Policy, OJ C 327/3, 7.12.1995, p. 3.
[31] See the free movement of goods cases: C-72/83, *Campus Oil Ltd v Minister of Industry and Energy* [1984] ECR 2727, C-347/88, *Commission v Greece* [1990] ECR I-4747, Case C-398/98, *Commission v Greece* [2001] ECR I-7915 and the free movement of capital cases: C-367/98, *Commission v Portugal* [2002] ECR I-4731, C-483/99, *Commission v France* [2002] ECR, p. I-4781, C- 503/99, *Commission v Belgium* [2002] ECR I-4809, C- 462/00, *Commission v Spain* [2003] ECR I-4581, C-98/01, *Commission v United Kingdom* [2003] ECR I-4641, C-174/04, *Commission v Italy* [2005] ECR I-4933, C-274/06 *Commission v Spain* [2008] ECR I-26 and C-326/07, *Commission v Italy* [2009] ECR I-02291.
[32] On energy dependency and its impact on EU energy policies, see S.S. Haghighi, *Energy Security: The External Legal Relations of the European Union with Major Oil and Gas Supplying Countries* (Oxford: Hart Publishing 2007) or A. Biava, 'L'action de L'Union Européenne Face au Défi de la Sécurisation de son Approvisionnement Energétique', 22 *Politique Européenne* (2007), pp. 107–23.

were seriously disrupted in the EU or a major part of it, one should have little doubt that political and public pressure would very quickly make energy supply an absolute priority with little or no regard paid to environmental implications. It is only in a situation where energy supply is not a problem that the question of relative rank and priority can reasonably be raised.[33] The order of priority of one of these sometimes conflicting objectives is therefore a question that depends on the particular situation at hand and can change quite easily. This was, to a certain extent, witnessed during the 2006 and 2009 gas supply crises.[34] The challenge for the European institutions is to seek out actions that allow both objectives to be achieved at the same time: i.e. look for pareto-optimal rather than zero-sum solutions. Given that such situations are a good way to gain capital in terms of political legitimacy, it is not surprising that the European Commission currently focuses on energy efficiency and renewable energy sources, as these promise to deliver results both on the environmental and security of supply counts.

The other area of conflict for the objective of high levels of environmental protection is with cost. There is no disagreement if a better environmental solution can be achieved at no cost—with nobody having to pay–but environmental policy choices often involve heavy trade-offs between cost and benefit. If the cost is narrowly distributed and the benefit widely distributed, lobbying against the policy will often be successful. But also if the cost is widely distributed, but visible—e.g. in the case of taxes on energy leading to high gasoline taxes—popular resistance may emerge, which can be hard for governments and environmentalist NGOs to override. Again, successful strategy by the European Commission means seeking out policies where environmental benefits can be efficiently achieved—as happens when they are combined with the efficiency gains of liberalization, or where blame for the cost can be hidden or shifted to national governments.

One also needs to realize that environmental and energy policies at EU level evolve out of a political process in Brussels, where the cards are stacked in favour of the technocrats of the Commission, large (mainly energy) companies with expertise and lobbying resources, and vociferous NGOs with the ability to set up focused public opinion campaigns. The general consumer, the public at large, or elected representatives (whether in national parliaments or the European Parliament) seem to have a lesser, sometimes invisible role in this dialogue of the keenly materially or ideologically interested which seek legitimacy by claiming to be 'civil society'.

---

[33] It has been suggested that under the legislation on EU energy security, the environmental protection objective had been compromised to promote competition and security of supply. Z. Shu Yu, 'The Proposed EU Energy Security Package vis-à-vis EU Law', *European Environmental Law Review* (2004), pp. 170–6. However, given the content of the energy security directives, it is difficult to agree with the author.

[34] For 2006, see J. Stern, 'The Russia-Ukrainian Gas Crisis of January 2006', 4(1) *OGEL* (2006); A. Belyi, 'Institutional Weaknesses of Intra-FSU Gas Trade', 4(4) *OGEL* (2006); for 2009, see S. Pirani, J. Stern, and K. Yafimava, *The Russo-Ukrainian Gas Dispute of January 2009: A Comprehensive Assessment*, NG 27 (Oxford: Institute for Energy Studies February 2009) and A. Kovacevic, *The Impact of the Russia-Ukraine Gas Crisis in South Eastern Europe*, NG 29 (Oxford: Institute for Energy Studies March 2009).

The result of this process—part dialogue, part bargaining, part law, and part invisible manoeuvring—is the formulation and use of the relevant policy and legal instruments. What will be required is 'improvements in the implementation of existing legislation, integrating environmental concerns into other policies, encouraging the market to work for the environment, and empowering citizens and changing behaviour'.[35] As this Commission quote illustrates, the idea is to persuade citizens to do what is expected of them on a voluntary basis, and if this approach does not work—i.e. if empowered citizens do not behave as the elite expects them to—then they must be compelled to act as required by harder instruments of law. In practice, this is what has largely taken place. After testing the waters with less formal instruments of persuasion, which are still used in some areas, the Commission has moved to these harder instruments of law. The EU moved from 'voluntary targets' for renewables and biofuels, used in the first directives in this area, to binding targets under the current Directive 2009/28/EC.

The initial 'soft' instruments included 'voluntary agreements' with industry groups (mainly 'voluntary agreements' between industry sector competitors, often grouped together in an industry association, facilitated by and then formally notified by the Commission[36]), e.g. for introducing more energy- or environment-efficient equipment;[37] best practice initiatives aimed at identifying and then spreading environment-efficient innovations; efforts to build up 'EU energy/environmental labels' into 'environmental brands' able to attract a consumer following; and the setting of 'targets' for energy efficiency intended to focus attention on and galvanize efforts to achieve the target.[38] Some of these instruments relied on the facilitation and agenda-setting power of the Commission, others on the implicit need for environmental 'branding', for an authoritative source for setting and controlling standards. Others evidently relied on the prospect of future legislation if the voluntary agreement approach failed to work. Ultimately, this last threat did materialize.

Section 5.5 examines the legal instruments used to push the (in)famous EU '20-20-20 by 2020' objectives in energy efficiency, renewable energy, and emission reductions.

---

[35] Comission, 'European Climate Change Programme, Report' (June 2001), pp. 45–46. It is not clear if the democratic-participatory goal ('empowering') is fully compatible with the technocratic-paternalistic ('changing behaviour') goal. What happens if empowered citizens do not wish to change their behaviour as the technocratic elites around the Commission services think they should?

[36] 'A unilateral commitment of the industry that the Commission takes note of and covers by a corresponding recommendation addressed to industry.' See for example para. 32 of the Green Paper on greenhouse gas emissions trading within the European Union (COM/2000/0087 final).

[37] E.g. agreement with the lamp manufacturers to increase the sale of CFLs [compact fluorescent lights] by 2005; with the car industry on reduction of CO2 emissions, EUC Climate Change Report of June 2001 at p. 46; with the European Automobile manufacturers association, with Japanese and Korean car manufacturers, see: COM (1999) 4446 final; COM (1996) 561; COM (1998) 495 final; EU Green Paper on greenhouse gas emissions trading, COM (2000) 87 final at pp. 20, 21.

[38] Note in particular the discussion of initiatives in the Comission Report, 'European Climate Change Programme' (June 2001); for an example of Commission initiatives to encourage oil companies to undertake voluntary agreements to refrain in the future from chartering tankers older than 15 years—COM (2000) 603 final of 27 September 2000; P. Cameron, 'Note on Energy', 11(3) *YIEL* (2001), p. 3.

5.5 Areas of Primary EU Action

5.5.1 Energy Efficiency

One of the core areas of EU action is the promotion of energy efficiency and energy savings. As noted, energy savings also promote energy security and, as such, this is a logical primary area of action for the EU. An example of the complementary nature of the two EU energy policy objectives is the Energy Services Directive.[39] This directive was adopted under the environmental provisions of the Treaty, namely what is now Article 192(1). However, the first recital of the directive describes how it contributes to improved security of supply.[40] This is of course based on the idea that greater energy efficiency reduces energy demand, and that this contributes to the fulfilment of environmental objectives by leading to less electricity generation and transmission, which in turn contributes to security of supply by reducing energy dependence through demand side management.

At Treaty level, the issue of energy savings is now explicitly mentioned in Article 194 TFEU giving the EU the competence to promote energy efficiency, which has now firmly established itself in the EU energy *acquis*. The lack of a precise legal basis was not an issue even at an earlier stage, since these measures were often taken under the environmental competences of the EU, as was seen in the case of Energy Services Directive from 2006. Policy action, translating into legislative action, has also been boosted by the 20-20-20 goals, which also includes a specific target of a 20 per cent reduction in primary energy use compared with projected levels, to be achieved by improving energy efficiency.

In 2006, the Commission adopted the Energy Efficiency Action Plan.[41] This action plan had the objective of suggesting various measures to be taken to real-ize the 20 per cent energy savings potential that was seen to be necessary both from an economic viewpoint, by achieving significant monetary savings, and from a sustainability viewpoint, by reducing emissions though less energy consumption. This Energy Efficiency Action Plan, together with EU policy initiatives in this area, led to the adoption of a large number of energy efficiency measures. These included Directive 2010/31/EU on the energy performance of buildings; Directive 2010/30/EU on the indication, by labelling and standard product infor-mation, of the consumption of energy and other resources by energy-related

---

[39] Directive 2006/32/EC of the European Parliament and of the Council of 5 April 2006 on energy end-use efficiency and energy services and repealing Council Directive 93/76/EEC, OJ L 114, 27.4.2006, pp. 64–85.

[40] 'In the Community there is a need for improved energy end-use efficiency, managed demand for energy and promotion of renewable energy production, as there is relatively limited scope for any other influence on energy supply and distribution conditions in the short to medium term, either through the building of new capacity or through the improvement of transmission and distribution. This Directive thus contributes to improved security of supply.'

[41] Communication from the Commission of 19 October 2006, 'Action Plan for Energy Efficiency: Realising the Potential' (COM(2006) 545).

products; Regulation (EC) No 1222/2009 on the labelling of tyres with respect to fuel efficiency and other essential parameters; Regulation (EC) No 106/2008 on a Community energy-efficiency labelling programme for office equipment; Regulation (EU) No 1015/2010 implementing Directive 2009/125/EC with regard to ecodesign requirements for household washing machines; Regulation (EC) No 859/2009 amending Regulation (EC) No 244/2009 as regards the ecodesign requirements in respect of ultraviolet radiation for non-directional household lamps; and so-on.

These measures provide for schemes involving soft, non-mandatory energy savings targets, energy labelling, the energy certification of buildings, the raising of awareness, and the gathering of information. These are EU-wide schemes, but mostly contain soft obligations for the Member States. In itself, this EU-level action is only logical. For example, where labelling schemes are concerned, purely national (or private) schemes would in most cases be unlikely to gain consumers' trust beyond national borders (except where a country's labelling scheme was particularly credible and well-publicized), so there is a strong logic behind EU-inspired labelling.

However, these measures have not been enough, and it is now clear that the EU is still far from reaching the 20 per cent target. As part of a review of the 2006 Energy Efficiency Action Plan, the Commission will attempt further to reinforce the EU's policies in the area of energy efficiency. The new plans will focus particularly on the building, utility, and transport sectors. The plan is that recasts of the Energy End-Use Efficiency Directive and Energy Services Directive will also form part of the revised Energy Efficiency Plans.[42] While this review was to take place in 2009, the revised plans were finally published in March 2011.[43] The revised Energy Efficiency Plans from 2011 confirm the failure of the previous actions, legislative and policy, suggesting that governance and awareness issues were to blame. The measures proposed by the new plans include mandatory refurbishment for public buildings with binding efficiency targets ('leading by example'), new incentives and audits, and so on. Furthermore, legally binding national energy savings targets are to be put in place if sufficient progress is not made by 2013.[44] The movement from 'soft' and 'less formal instruments of persuasion' to harder instruments of law is clear.

5.5.2 Renewable Energy

Modern society has lived off hydrocarbons—coal, oil, and gas—for well over a century. Since the 1950s, nuclear power has been added to the arsenal. Replacing these sources as the essential component of energy supply would spell liberation in many directions—liberation from the overwhelming dependence on external oil and gas (such as the OPEC countries, Russia, and other producing countries); liberation from the anxiety, the safety risk and the decommissioning uncertainty of

---

[42] Directive 2006/32/EC of the European Parliament and of the Council of 5 April 2006 on energy end-use efficiency and energy services and repealing Council Directive 93/76/EEC, OJ L 114/64.
[43] Energy Efficiency Plan 2011 (COM/2011/0109 final).
[44] Energy Efficiency Plan 2011 (COM/2011/0109 final).

nuclear energy; and liberation from the guilt engendered by contributing massively to climate change through greenhouse gas emissions from hydrocarbons, while preaching the virtues of low emission sources of energy to developing countries. As a consequence of the pressure exerted from all these directions, the EU has re-oriented its energy policy, with increasing speed and substance, and with wide support within the Union, towards the development of unconventional or renewable energy sources (RES) of an environmentally innocuous character. There is opposition to this development, first from the external energy suppliers, mainly OPEC, and, on a more latent basis, from the industrial communities in the conventional energy industries (coal, oil, and gas).[45] However, the international energy companies at least have already embarked upon a similar re-orientation process, with established oil companies such as Shell and BP maintaining renewable energy subsidiaries. In this context, one pertinent question is: since we are going to continue to be dependent on fossil fuels, why do we expect major oil and gas companies to promote renewable energy instead of focusing on their role in the global energy markets? Should they not concentrate on finding badly-needed sources of oil and gas and let others deal with renewable energies?

In 2010, renewable energy contributed about 18 per cent to total EU electricity production,[46] but the major component of this 18 per cent was large-scale hydropower, which, it appears, cannot be expanded to any great extent.[47] It is sometimes hard to find the truth behind ideological claims about the economic viability of unconventional energy made by environmental pressure groups. It does appear to be the case that these sources have, in the past, received much less support than established ones; but this may also be due to the much greater importance of conventional energy sources as against the much smaller potential of non-renewable energy. What is clear however, is that the cost—both the capital cost of investment and operating costs—for these new sources of energy is coming down. At the moment, they are still an uneconomic hobby for the rich or only viable with state support—principally by way of subsidy or mandatory purchase requirements. One would expect that, with economies of scale, experience with large-scale production (even offshore) and technologies evolving, both due to expected market demand and governmental incentives, and with the transition of companies involved in such energy production from cottage industries to large industrial players, such energy sources will become more viable. After all, the growth rates for this industry are impressive.[48] The direction in which technology and markets will evolve is,

---

[45] This opposition is by no means restricted to the EU but is present everywhere. An illustrative example is the opposition from BHP Billiton to the 2011 Australian decision to implement a carbon tax as a pathway to an emission trading scheme.

[46] Commission Communication on renewable energy (MEMO/11/54), 31 January 2011.

[47] Around 70 per cent of total EU renewable energy is based on biomass and waste, hydropower having approximately 20 per cent share. However, in electricity production, the share of hydropower is much higher, around 60 per cent. See <http://epp.eurostat.ec.europa.eu/statistics_explained/index.php/Renewable_energy_statistics>.

[48] <http://www.ewea.org/fileadmin/ewea_documents/documents/publications/reports/Green_Growth.pdf> (last accessed 9.8.2012).

however, far from clear. One negative effect of the current public-sector-designed support mechanisms is that governments are effectively making choices about the 'right' technologies for the future. This should, in a market-based system such as the EU claims to have, be left to the markets. If not, we should make an open and transparent departure from a market-based system and recognize the role of the state in the energy markets.

The progress to the status quo in the EU has been a result of progressive steps towards the binding targets that exist under Directive 2009/28/EC. As a first step, Directive 2001/77/EC on the promotion of electricity produced from renewable energy sources in the internal electricity market,[49] which followed the 1997 White Paper,[50] set an indicative target of doubling the share of renewables in EU energy consumption from 6 per cent to 12 per cent in 2010. This meant a share for electricity production of 22 per cent.[51] This overall EU target was then translated into national targets. Both targets were related to the EU's Kyoto commitments. To achieve the targets Member States *could* provide for rules giving renewable energy sources priority access to transmission and distribution channels on a mandatory basis.[52] However, it should be noted that Article 8(3) of the 1996 Electricity Directive already provided that 'a Member State may require the system operator, when dispatching generating installations, to give priority to generating installations using renewable energy sources or waste or producing combined heat and power'. Member States also had to introduce effective certification of origin under Article 5, in order to minimize the obvious and large potential for fraud. Furthermore, they had to remove administrative and other regulatory barriers, including ensuring that connection costs are transparent and non-discriminatory.

In a similar way, Directive 2003/30EC promoted the use of biofuels in road transport. That directive aimed at promoting the use of renewable fuels in transport but, based on its actual content (which was short, indicative, and oriented towards reporting), it was easy to predict its failure.

These first generation renewable energy directives were replaced by Directive 2009/28/EC on the promotion of the use of energy from renewable sources.[53] This directive adopted a more holistic approach to renewable energy and made an attempt to reach the 20-20-20 target in terms of renewable energy. It also set a mandatory share for the use of renewable energy—biofuels—in the transport sector, amounting to at least 10 per cent of final energy consumption in the sector by 2020.

---

[49] Directive 2001/77/EC of the European Parliament and of the Council of 27 September 2001 on the promotion of electricity produced from renewable energy sources in the internal electricity market, OJ L 283, 27.10.2001, pp. 33–40.

[50] Commission draft for a Renewable energy electricity directive, 10 May 2000; COM (2000) 279 final; White Paper: COM (97) 599 final;

[51] Article 3 (4) of Directive 2001/77/EC.

[52] Article 7 (1) of Directive 2001/77/EC.

[53] Directive 2009/28/EC of the European Parliament and of the Council of 23 April 2009 on the promotion of the use of energy from renewable sources and amending and subsequently repealing Directives 2001/77/EC and 2003/30/EC, OJ L 140, 5.6.2009, pp. 16–62.

In order to reach the EU-wide target of 20 per cent, Directive 2009/28/EC sets mandatory national targets and requires Member States to prepare and establish national action plans to reach their respective targets. As discussed in Section 5.2, the national targets that in principle translate into an overall EU target of a 20 per cent increase in renewable energy production vary considerably from Member State to Member State. For example, the target for Finland is 38 per cent (from a 2005 level of 28.5 per cent) and the French target is 23 per cent (from a 2005 level of 10.3 per cent). These targets can be achieved by using various measures within the country but also through joint projects[54] or statistical transfers. They can even be achieved through cooperation with non-EU countries[55] as long as the electricity is consumed within the EU, under certain conditions which eliminate the most obvious problems connected with third country cooperation, such as only new installations and no double support. In a similar manner to its predecessor, the Directive contains rules on guarantees of origin[56] and on the easing of administrative burdens.[57]

The Directive takes several important steps forward in turning indicative targets into mandatory targets. Among many other innovations, it turns 'may' into 'shall' as far as the duty to provide for priority access is concerned, thus ensuring that TSOs provide for priority access or guaranteed access.[58]

The Directive makes several significant improvements to the regulatory framework for biofuels. Among other provisions, it is now required, under Article 4, that each Member State 'shall ensure that the share of energy from renewable sources in all forms of transport in 2020 is at least 10% of the final consumption of energy in transport in that Member State'. This serves to eliminate any question-mark over the mandatory nature of 'indicative targets'. The Directive also introduces a sustainability criterion which excludes, for example, raw materials originating from lands with high biodiversity value to avoid negative impacts on the ecological processes in these areas, protected areas or areas containing rare or endangered ecosystems.[59]

5.5.2.1 Cogeneration of Heat and Power

Another instrument promoting the 20-20-20 by 2020 objective is Directive 2004/8/EC on the promotion of cogeneration based on useful heat demand in the internal energy market.[60] In essence, cogeneration is a technology which allows the simultaneous generation of power and heat, capturing heat as a by-product which can be used for domestic or industrial heating purposes. As such, it has a substantial potential to increase energy efficiency and reduce environmental impact.

---

[54] Articles 7 and 8 of Directive 2009/28/EC.   [55] Article 9 of Directive 2009/28/EC.
[56] Article 15 of Directive 2009/28/EC.   [57] Article 13 of Directive 2009/28/EC.
[58] Article 16(2) of Directive 2009/28/EC.
[59] Article 17 and, for the verification scheme, Article 18 of Directive 2009/28/EC.
[60] Directive 2004/8/EC of the European Parliament and of the Council of 11 February 2004 on the promotion of cogeneration based on a useful heat demand in the internal energy market and amending Directive 92/42/EEC, OJ L 52, 21.2.2004, pp. 50–60.

Compared with the Renewables Directive, this Cogeneration Directive is in many ways much more modest in scope. Even if the objective of the Directive is somewhat similar to the Renewables Directive, the means of promoting cogeneration are clearly less effective.

Article 1 of the Directive states that its objective is to 'increase energy efficiency and improve security of supply by creating a framework for promotion and development of high efficiency cogeneration of heat and power based on useful heat demand and primary energy savings in the internal energy market, taking into account the specific national circumstances especially concerning climatic and economic conditions'. The means to be used to achieve this aim include guarantees of origin,[61] national analysis of the potential for high-efficiency cogeneration,[62] support schemes[63] and facilitated administrative procedures,[64] plus, of course, reporting.[65] Pursuant to Article 8, states *may* also facilitate access to the grid system of electricity produced from high-efficiency cogeneration from small scale and micro cogeneration units. Here the Directive falls short of the approach taken in the Renewables Directive, in which 'may' was changed to 'shall'. The Cogeneration Directive therefore adopts the same approach as the old renewable electricity production directive from 2001. This is logical, as the Cogeneration Directive dates back to 2004. As with the Renewables Directive, the principle of subsidiarity applies to national support schemes, which may include investment aid, tax exemptions or reductions, green certificates, and direct price support schemes.

Section 5.5.3–5.5 examine the instruments relating to climate change and the EU's efforts in respect of emission reduction in greater detail.

5.5.3 Climate Change Mitigation

The world is now undeniably in a phase of global warming. Many of the last 20 years rank among the warmest years since 1850 as far as global surface temperature is concerned, the linear warming trend over the 50 years from 1956 to 2005 (0.13 [0.10 to 0.16] °C per decade) is nearly twice that for the 100 years from 1906 to 2005, and the average temperatures in the Arctic have increased at almost twice the global average rate over the past 100 years. Land regions have warmed faster than the oceans.[66]

While there have been many periods of warming and cooling over the last 1,000 years and before, the opinion now shared by most scientists is that the current phase of warming is related to the emission of greenhouse gases (mainly CO_2 but also N_2O, methane and others) produced by burning of fossil fuel (hydrocarbons). Greenhouse gases form a protective mantle around the Earth, retaining some of the heat reflected back off the Earth. The suggestion is that the production of greenhouse gases now exceeds the natural capacity to absorb them. Most of the man-made CO_2 emissions are attributable to the energy sector—oil, natural gas,

---

[61] Article 5 of Directive 2004/8/EC.   [62] Article 6 of Directive 2004/8/EC.
[63] Article 7 of Directive 2004/8/EC.   [64] Article 9 of Directive 2004/8/EC.
[65] Article 10 of Directive 2004/8/EC.   [66] IPCC, Assessment Report 4 (2007).

and coal in particular (with coal producing most per unit of energy). Somewhat simplistically, one might say that power generation and refineries account for around 30 per cent of total emissions, transport for around 20 per cent, industry for under 20 per cent, and other factors around 30 per cent (this last figure includes households, agriculture, etc.).

The Kyoto Protocol is the main international response to the concerns over global warming. While the EU is not among the major producers of CO_2 (at 15 per cent of world emissions in 2005, compared with the US at 22 per cent and China currently at 19 per cent but projected to grow rapidly to 26–27 per cent by 2030),[67] it made a commitment under the Kyoto Protocol to stabilize its CO_2 emissions at 1990 levels in 2000 and reduce them by 8 per cent from the 1990 level by 2012. These targets are legally binding as the Protocol entered into force on 16 February 2005.[68] Even before agreeing these targets, the EU expressed its intention to adhere to its commitments regardless of what other countries might choose to do, in order to exert political pressure on other countries—in particular the US—and develop an exportable model on how to meet the Kyoto targets. In 2007, the EU made a unilateral commitment to cut its emissions by at least 20 per cent of 1990 levels by 2020, and pledged to raise this figure to 30 per cent if major industrial countries followed through on their respective commitments.[69] This obviously does not mean that a uniform reduction level of 20 per cent or even 8 per cent has been adopted. Under the original burden-sharing agreement within the EU, the overall EU target was allocated to Member States, with the largest cuts to Germany (21 per cent) and the UK (12.5 per cent). France, which was the lowest producer, had to stabilize its emissions.[70] These figures have evolved over the years and, under the new 'Effort Sharing Decision' for the non-EU ETS sectors,[71] Member States have agreed that from 2013 to 2020 they will limit their greenhouse gas emissions quite significantly as compared to 2005 greenhouse gas emissions levels: Germany and France have agreed on a 14 per cent reduction, Denmark on a 20 per cent reduction, and the UK on a 16 per cent reduction. For the poorer Member States, the figures look very different: Bulgaria (20 per cent increase), Poland (14 per cent increase), the Baltic States (ranging from 11 to 17 per cent increase), and Romania (19 per cent increase).

Most EU energy action—in particular the promotion of energy efficiency, of renewable sources of energy, of technology and regulatory measures to reduce

---

[67] Figures from European Environment Agency, <http://www.eea.europa.eu>.

[68] Article 25 of the Kyoto Protocol provides for the mechanism for entry into force. This Protocol shall enter into force on the ninetieth day after the date on which not less than 55 Parties to the Convention, incorporating Parties included in Annex I which accounted in total for at least 55 per cent of the total carbon dioxide emissions for 1990 of the Parties included in Annex I, have deposited their instruments of ratification, acceptance, approval or accession.

[69] There have been opinions voiced by some Member States that the EU should unilaterally adopt the 30 per cent target.

[70] Annex 1 of COM (1999) 230 final.

[71] Decision No 406/2009/EC of the European Parliament and of the Council of 23 April 2009 on the effort of Member States to reduce their greenhouse gas emissions to meet the Community's greenhouse gas emission reduction commitments up to 2020, OJ L 140, 5.6.2009, pp. 136–48.

greenhouse gas emissions—can now be placed within the context of the Kyoto targets and even beyond. To some extent, these are compatible with other EU energy policies, and aim—at least to a certain extent—to reduce its energy dependence and create an internal energy market. However, it is also clear that some of these measures run counter to other EU energy policy objectives and pose practical problems. In the absence of a common EU support scheme or, more likely, schemes, national support mechanisms need to be tolerated even where these might conflict with the internal market objective. The intermittent nature of many renewable energy sources, solar and wind in particular, remains an issue yet to be fully resolved. The failure to internalize the environmental costs of greenhouse emissions properly through the EU ETS, which has had its share of problems (including disputes and litigation before the European Court of Justice,[72] and significant price variations: 2005: EUR 30 per tonne; May 2006: EUR 6.5 per tonne; August 2008: EUR 25 per tonne; 2009: EUR 8–15 per tonne). This scheme is discussed further in section 5.5.4. The climate policies also place the EU at loggerheads with its major oil and gas suppliers, mainly OPEC and Russia, which largely depend on exports of oil and gas, just as the EU depends on imports from them. A successful move away from oil and gas would undermine the economic and thus political viability of such exporting countries. These issues have not been thoroughly explored, nor have serious efforts been made to identify whether there are ways in which the level of conflict may be reduced. If technology were to bring CO_2 emissions from oil and gas use down to a reasonable level, the nascent antagonism between the EU and its major suppliers might be amenable to management. In the same vein, action on climate change should not focus solely on pushing renewable energy, with its possible inbuilt limitations, but also on finding common ground with the EU's oil and gas suppliers. Finally, it should focus not just on preventing global warming, but also on finding ways to manage global warming if it should prove inevitable, whether for man-made or natural reasons.

5.5.4 Emissions Trading

Two principal state policies are used to tackle emission reductions: emissions trading and carbon taxation. It is of course possible to adopt both, as in the EU where it is proposed that a carbon tax be used to complement emissions trading; or to use the carbon tax as a pathway to an emissions trading scheme, as in Australia—although this path in no way represents a logical 'transition' to an emissions trading scheme. In essence, emissions trading is the flipside of carbon tax. While carbon taxation puts a negative value on emissions and thereby creates an incentive to reduce them, emissions trading is more flexible and better mobilizes the efficiency

---

[72] For example, Cases C-127/07, *Arcelor Atlantique and Lorraine and Others* [2008] ECR I-09895 or T-183/07, *Poland v Commission* [2009] ECR II-03395 and the appeal: C-504/09 P, *Commission v Poland (not yet decided)* or C-505/09 P, *Commission v Estonia*, judgment of 29 March 2012 (not yet reported).

of the market: it assigns emission rights, on a historical or current activity basis, by benchmarking against typical operations or on the basis of auctioning, often with some gradual phase-out method, and then opens up trading in such rights. The first economic incentives work like a carbon emission tax: the right-holder has an interest in reducing emissions since this allows it to realize the value implicit in emission rights through sale. But there is a second, possibly more powerful incentive: by using market-based trading, emission rights can move to those operators who most need them—i.e. those for whom achieving emissions reductions is most costly—while those able to reduce emissions at less cost are likely to prefer to sell the emission rights and undertake the necessary investment. The system does not by itself reduce emissions (except through decreasing caps), but provides incentives to find the lowest cost of achieving a given emissions reduction target; the lower the cost, the likelier is it that greater reduction targets become politically and commercially acceptable. This should lead to maximum abatement at a given cost, or to least cost for a given abatement (and probably to a combination of both). Society thus achieves a larger abatement effect than would be achieved by using a pure carbon tax (where no trading takes place), at the level that society is ready to accept, since those with the greatest competence in reducing emissions would do most and would specialize much more in emissions control than in the use of a a rigid carbon tax scheme. Emissions control would then become not only an incentive gradually to reduce one's emissions to save cost, but a competitive business based on freeing-up the value implicit in reducing emissions. That, at least, is the theory. In reality, a wide range of problems with the EU ETS have distorted the mechanism used. Economic models rarely seem to work when it comes to the energy industries.

In principle, an emissions scheme operates as follows: a national (corporate, EU-wide, global) ceiling of CO_2 emissions is determined; normally, on the basis of historical emissions, with a gradual phase-down in the future towards agreed targets (such as the targets in the Kyoto protocol for countries and regions, or in the EU by way of the 'burden-sharing agreement' (*supra*) with sub-targets allocated for each country). Commercially tradable emission rights are then awarded to each significant operator (with the scheme being more suitable for large-scale operators than for small ones) or, within a company, to each significant project (e.g. a refinery). This requires considerable attention to be paid to metering, certification, monitoring, and compliance control. The right-holders/operators can then trade, typically on a formal trading exchange with rules and transparency. Those able to reduce emissions most cheaply will sell in order to free-up the—presumably higher—cash value of the emission right. Those with the highest cost of abatement will purchase—it being presumably cheaper to buy the right than to invest in abatement measures (in this respect, prices such as EUR 6 per tonne of CO_2 will hardly make the necessary difference). Those most efficient in abatement would gain most, and the most inefficient would have to pay most. This in turn would lead to technological progress and abatement investment driven by a competitive market rather than command-and-control government regulation.

Noting the success of the Acid Rain Program[73] in the US, the EU, following Article 17 of the Kyoto Protocol,[74] created its own emissions trading scheme (EU ETS) under Directive 2003/87/EC (EU ETS Directive). The EU ETS Directive entered into force on 1 January 2005.[75] Article 1 of the Directive states the objective of establishing a scheme for greenhouse gas emission allowance trading within the EU in order to promote reductions of greenhouse gas emissions in a cost-effective and economically efficient manner. The EU ETS Directive allows major industrial greenhouse gas emitters to buy and sell emission credits and, following the model discussed, this market-based scheme provides for economically efficient reduction in greenhouse gas emissions.[76] As noted this type of cap-and-trade system should in theory permit the internalization of the negative externalities most efficiently. Under the EU ETS, the covered installations are permitted to emit a predetermined amount of CO_2 into the atmosphere[77] and, if necessary, purchase extra allowances to offset these excessive emissions. The more efficient installations can then sell their extra allowances. As long as the carbon price is high enough, it should provide for incentives to invest in low emissions technologies. However, one of the main problems in the EU ETS has been the volatility of this price. For obvious reasons, this hinders investment in this area.

The EU has just completed its second trading period (the first period ran from 1 January 2005 and ended on 31 December 2007,[78] while the second started on 1 January 2008 and finished at the end of 2012).[79] The third trading period started on 1 January 2013 and will run all the way to the end of 2020.[80] Currently, the scheme covers four sectors: energy, ferrous metals, minerals, and wood pulp.[81] New sectors have joined and will join the scheme in 2012 (the aviation sector)[82] and 2013 (petrochemicals, ammonia, and aluminium).[83] One of the issues raised

---

[73] The so-called US Acid Rain Program, established under Title IV of the Clean Air Act of 1990, 104 Stat. 2468 (1990).

[74] Article 17 of the Kyoto Protocol to the United Nations Framework Convention on Climate Change.

[75] Directive 2003/87/EC of the European Parliament and of the Council of 13 October 2003 Establishing a Scheme for Greenhouse Gas Emission Allowance Trading within the Community and Amending Council Directive 96/61/EC, OJ L 275/32, 25.10.2003.

[76] The difference between the trading under Kyoto Protocol and EU ETS is that Kyoto applies to States and EU ETS applies to installations. The EU ETS is linked to trading under Kyoto through the Linking Directive. Directive 2004/101/EC of 27 October 2004 amending Directive 2003/87/EC establishing a scheme for greenhouse gas emission allowance trading within the Community, in respect of the Kyoto Protocol's project mechanisms, OJ L338/18, 13.11.2004.

[77] Article 9 of Directive 2003/87/EC.

[78] Article 11(1) of Directive 2003/87/EC.

[79] Article 11(2) of Directive 2003/87/EC.

[80] Directive of the European Parliament and of the Council amending Directive 2003/87/EC so as to improve and extend the greenhouse gas emission allowance trading scheme of the Community, OJ L 140/63, 5.6.2009.

[81] Annex I of Directive 2003/87/EC.

[82] Directive 2008/101/EC of the European Parliament and of the Council of 19 November 2008 amending Directive 2003/87/EC so as to include aviation activities in the scheme for greenhouse gas emission allowance trading within the Community (OJ L 8/3, 13.1.2009)

[83] Directive 2003/87/EC.

within these highly energy-intensive industries is 'carbon leakage': i.e. relocation to the Chinas and Indias of this world. There are provisions in place to prevent this, both in terms of flexibility in the system and in terms of trade sanctions.[84] Here, the question of international law, and WTO law in particular, emerges.[85] Similarly, the inclusion of aviation in the EU ETS is not without problems of its own.[86]

The multi-year trading periods are based on national action plans (NAPs) which cap the total quantity of allowances in the Member State in question for the trading period.[87] One problem with these NAPs has been overestimation of emissions and the subsequent over-allocation of emission permits by the Member States. After these problems materialized in the first trading period, the Commission became less willing to approve the NAPs under Article 9 of the EU ETS Directive, which has led to litigation. For very obvious reasons, these types of problems create effects both at EU level and at national level. In addition to the discriminatory nature of the scheme—in that the impact varies for producers in different Member States and facilitates windfall profits for the power industry—these problems undermine the social acceptability of an emissions trading scheme.

The third trading period, which started on 1 January 2013, will see many changes to the scheme, since, pursuant to the 2008 Climate Change Package, the EU ETS was amended in April 2009.[88] The main changes include: the expansion of covered installations to include petrochemicals, ammonia, and aluminium;[89] an EU-wide cap for the third trading phase onwards;[90] a progressive decrease in freely-allocated emission allowances at a rate of 1.74 per cent per year, arriving at a 20 per cent reduction by 2020; and a comparable increase in auctioned allowances.[91] However, this last change does not apply to the power industry, where 100 per cent of the allowances are to be auctioned,[92] except in certain predefined situations—these

---

[84] See R. Tscherning 'The EU ETS Rules on Carbon Leakage and Energy Intensive Industry in the Federal Republic of Germany', *European Energy and Environmental Law Review* (2011), pp. 2–17 and H.H.B. Vedder, 'The Climate Challenge to Competition', in M. Roggenkamp and U. Hammer (eds), *European Energy Law Report VII* (Antwerp: Intersentia 2011), pp. 3–20. This issue has been addressed in Articles 10a to 10c of the Directive 2009/29/EC.

[85] See for example, B. de Bruijne; H.H.B. Vedder, 'The Interface between EU Energy, Environmental and Competition Law in the Netherlands', 4 *OGEL* (2012), <http://www.ogel.org>.

[86] See the Opinion of AG Kokott in Case C-366/10, *Air Transport Association of America, American Airlines, Inc, Continental Airlines, Inc, United Airlines, Inc v The Secretary of State for Energy and Climate Change*, 6.10.2011. See also <http://ictsd.org/downloads/2012/05/the-inclusion-of-aviation-in-the-eu-ets-wto-law-considerations.pdf>.

[87] Article 9 of Directive 2003/87/EC.

[88] 2009/29/EC of the European Parliament and of the Council of 23 April 2009 amending Directive 2003/87/EC so as to improve and extend the greenhouse gas emission allowance trading scheme of the Community, OJ L 140, 5. 6.2009, pp. 63–87.

[89] Annex 1 of the 2009/29/EC of the European Parliament and of the Council of 23 April 2009 amending Directive 2003/87/EC so as to improve and extend the greenhouse gas emission allowance trading scheme of the Community, OJ L 140, 5.6.2009, pp. 63–87.

[90] Article 9 of Directive 2009/29/EC of the European Parliament and of the Council of 23 April 2009 amending Directive 2003/87/EC so as to improve and extend the greenhouse gas emission allowance trading scheme of the Community, OJ L 140, 5.6.2009, pp. 63–87.

[91] Article 9 of Directive 2009/29/EC of the European Parliament and of the Council of 23 April 2009 amending Directive 2003/87/EC so as to improve and extend the greenhouse gas emission allowance trading scheme of the Community, OJ L 140, 5.6.2009, pp. 63–87.

[92] Article 10a(1) of Directive 2009/29/EC.

being related to the windfall profits that the sector was receiving as it passed on the costs of reductions to the end-customers while receiving free allowances.[93] Finally, acknowledging the existence of a world beyond the EU, each Member State has the right to take financial measures in favour of sectors it decides are exposed to significant risk of carbon leakage due to costs relating to greenhouse gas emissions passed on in electricity prices, in order to compensate for those costs.[94]

5.5.5 Energy Taxation

A logical consequence of a modern environmental policy would be to 'internalize' external environmental costs in the financial calculus of the actor with the closest control over the impugned action.[95] The levying of taxes that reflect the calculated, or even roughly estimated, environmental cost, should be one of the easiest, most effective and most transparent ways to internalize environmental externalities. Using this approach and ideology, the power of competitive markets is harnessed to develop and apply the right technologies and select the optimal energy mix to minimize payments of such tax, leading to the minimization of emissions at the least cost to consumers. If the tax is in substance (and not merely for purposes of political salesmanship) an environmental one, and not simply a method of maximizing tax revenue, it would logically work toward its own oblivion.

The choice between the two principal carbon-reduction methods—emissions trading and carbon taxation—depends on policy choice. This choice is not obvious and while emissions trading has its benefits, it also carries risks: system failure can create a financial crisis, and low or fluctuating prices will not provide for investment incentives for the industry, among other issues.

The EU clearly seems to have chosen the emissions trading scheme (EU ETS) as the primary method of reducing carbon emissions. However, this does not mean that carbon taxation plays no role at EU or Member State level.

At Member State level, energy taxation can be seen as one of the instruments that Member States may use to fulfil the objectives and national targets set in the context of the EU '20-20-20 by 2020' policy. As Member States can still use their own systems of taxation to guide the industry towards sustainable options, or to increase state revenue, this may be a powerful tool.

---

[93] D. Behn, 'Methods for Allocating Allowances Under the EU Emissions Trading Scheme: Assessing its Interaction with the EU State Aid Rules', in B. Delvaux, M. Hunt, and K. Talus (eds), *EU Energy Law and Policy Issues* (Cambridge: Intersentia 2011).

[94] Article 10a(9) of Directive 2009/29/EC of the European Parliament and of the Council of 23 April 2009 amending Directive 2003/87/EC so as to improve and extend the greenhouse gas emission allowance trading scheme of the Community, OJ L 140, 5.6.2009, pp. 63–87.

[95] One can call this the 'polluter pays' or causation principle. In reality, causation is quite complex. In the case of a pollution effect, many actors are involved in the causation process. It makes sense to select among the many actors the one which is best capable to control the effects most efficiently: i.e. from the many involved in pollution, the one—usually a commercial company—is selected because it is considered the best placed to influence the environmental impact.

While the EU ETS, based on Directive 2003/87/EC[96] as amended, is clearly the cornerstone of the EU-level emissions reduction scheme, the EU has also taken measures in the areas of energy taxation. A minimum tax harmonizing directive covering energy products and electricity entered into force at the beginning of 2004.[97] However, judging by its contents, the fight against climate change does not appear to be the primary objective of this directive. Instead, it is concerned with issues such as the internal market and economic gains. Recital 4 of the directive is illustrative: 'Appreciable differences in the national levels of energy taxation applied by Member States could prove detrimental to the proper functioning of the internal market.' However, the Directive does include references to the Kyoto Protocol and notes that taxation is one of the instruments that can facilitate achievement of the Kyoto objectives.

However, the EU has recently taken steps to place taxation measures in a more prominent role to fight climate change.[98] The new draft directive could make significant changes to Directive 2003/96/EC.

At an ideological level, the new draft directive now targets emission reductions, in particular in those sectors not subject to EU ETS. For these sources of CO_2, the draft directive attempts to introduce a cost-effective scheme available to Member States in order to achieve their emission reduction targets. As such, it complements the EU ETS in respect of emission reduction efforts. Reflecting this ideological change, it requires Member States to distinguish between CO_2-related taxation and general energy consumption taxation.[99]

The draft directive is also sensitive to the overlaps between the CO_2 taxation and the EU ETS, and attempts to strike a balance between the new scheme and the EU ETS so as to ensure that the first taxation complements the EU ETS rather than distorts it.[100] Overall, it is clear that the EU ETS continues to be the primary method of reducing CO_2 emissions. This scheme is complemented by the proposed energy tax directive.

While the choice of the EU ETS over taxation instruments is undoubtedly based on policy choices, it is worth noting that this is also the easier option under primary EU law. Article 192(2) TFEU, which was used as the legal basis for the EU Emissions Trading Directives [then Article 175(1) EC], provides for decision-making under the 'ordinary legislative procedure' which, under Article 294 TFEU, requires the Council to act under qualified majority voting. Contrary to this, unanimity is required to establish measures primarily of a fiscal nature (Article 194(3) TFEU and Article 113 TFEU). The proposed legal basis for

---

[96] Directive 2003/87/EC of the European Parliament and of the Council of 13 October 2003 establishing a scheme for greenhouse gas emission allowance trading within the Community and amending Council Directive 96/61/EC.

[97] Council Directive 2003/96/EC of 27 October 2003 restructuring the Community framework for the taxation of energy products and electricity.

[98] Proposal for a Council Directive amending Directive 2003/96/EC restructuring the Community framework for the taxation of energy products and electricity (COM(2011)169/3).

[99] Article 1(2) of the draft directive.

[100] See Article 1(1)–(4) for the relationship and balance between the two.

the new draft directive for energy taxation is Article 113 TFEU, which requires unanimous action in accordance with a special legislative procedure. As such, the more prominent role of the EU ETS is also logical from a Treaty perspective.

Finally, a proper carbon tax would make sense if fully aligned with the actual carbon emissions in order to encourage the use of both cleaner fuels and cleaner combustion technologies. The first step, though, should be to remove all state aid for coal; the subsidization of an energy source which, given the environmental damage it causes, should really be heavily taxed is an anachronism. It makes sense for EU energy tax legislation to be harmonized in order to avoid the environmental and economic distortions which currently occur. But there is no compelling need for full energy tax harmonization. Countries should decide for themselves how, where, and at what level to collect taxes if such taxation does not severely distort cross-border trade in electricity or gas. While tax competition is a thorn in the side of high-tax countries and of a Commission ever-bent on creating uniform conditions, it is a good thing from the perspective of individual taxpayers and national economies. The worst that could come out of energy tax harmonization is an external reason to raise taxes: i.e. the ability of politicians to place the blame for taxation on an external institution, while making political capital from spending.

Sections 5.6–5.8 introduce and examine certain other EU environmental measures that have an impact on energy activities.

5.6 Examples of Other Environmental Measures Taken by the EU in the Energy Field

In addition to the policies and legislative actions examined and discussed so far in this chapter, there is a large number of other environmentally-oriented regulatory acts in the EU, which either target the energy sector or have a direct impact on energy activities. The intention here is not to examine all of these measures, but to provide examples of various relevant legislative measures.

Pollution and prevention control for high polluting sectors—Directive 2008/1/EC concerns integrated pollution prevention and control,[101] and aims at achieving the integrated prevention and control of pollution arising from industrial and agricultural activities with high pollution potential. These activities are listed in Annex 1 and the energy industry appears prominently as the first industrial area falling within the scope of the directive. These activities are subject to specific permits that limit pollution and other negative impact from these installations.[102]

If the gas emitted from the installation falls under the EU ETS, the permit does not include an emission limit value for direct emissions of that gas (unless it is necessary to ensure that no significant local pollution is caused). Furthermore, if the

---

[101] Directive 2008/1/EC of the European Parliament and of the Council of 15 January 2008 concerning integrated pollution prevention and control, OJ L 24, 29.1.2008, pp. 8–29.
[102] Articles 4–9 of Directive 2008/1/EC.

activity falls under the EU ETS scheme, Member States may choose not to impose requirements relating to energy efficiency in respect of combustion plants.[103]

Management of waste from extractive industries—Directive 2006/21/EC on the management of waste from extractive industries[104] provides for measures, procedures, and guidance to prevent, or where this is not feasible, reduce as far as possible any negative effects on the environment (including water, air, soil, fauna and flora, and landscape) and any resultant risks to human health, brought about as a result of the management of waste from the extractive industries.[105]

While the directive is a response to events where chemicals, heavy metals, or corrosive material have been discharged into the environment—in accidents like Aznalcóllar (Spain, 1998) where a tailings dam failure released very significant amounts of toxic tailings slurries and liquid into a nearby river, or the similar Baia Mare and Baia Borsa accidents (Romania, 2000)—energy activities are within the scope of the directive. Waste from drilling and extraction of energy fuels are among those commercial activities that require permits and various plans regarding construction, operation, and closure. However, it should also be noted that there are exclusions of certain activities and products from the scope of the Directive that are of significance to the energy industry (under Article 2 of the Directive). An example of this is the injection of water containing substances resulting from the operations for exploration and extraction of hydrocarbons or mining activities, and the injection of water, for technical reasons, into geological formations from which hydrocarbons or other substances have been extracted.

Looking at these two specialized initiatives among many others, it appears that the Commission tends to jump in with initiatives reflecting prevailing public opinion if a conspicuous crisis seems to call for at least the appearance of energetic action. In some areas, there may be a proper EU rationale (i.e. the need for EU-wide action rather than purely Member State action): for example, if there are cross-border effects or if common action will reduce evasive action and strengthen enforcement. On the other hand, it is not that clear that the Commission should intervene if the environmental effect is purely localized and national, and no significant distortion of competition takes place. Would it not be more democratic and more in keeping with the principle of subsidiarity if in such situations the political process in the country involved led to decisions with particular trade-offs, rather than to an EU-wide process involving countries and actors with no immediate interest involved? The Commission makes a short-term political gain by appearing to be responsive to public opinion, but in effect decision-making is removed from a more democratic to a less democratic and more opaque process.

Procedural environmental protection: Environmental Impact Assessment (EIA) Directive—First adopted in 1985, Council Directive 85/337/EEC on the assessment

---

[103] Article 9(3) of Directive 2008/1/EC.
[104] Directive 2006/21/EC of the European Parliament and of the Council of 15 March 2006 on the management of waste from extractive industries and amending Directive 2004/35/EC—Statement by the European Parliament, the Council and the Commission, OJ L 102, 11.4.2006, pp. 15–34.
[105] Article 1 of Directive 2006/21/EC.

of the effects of certain public and private projects on the environment[106] has been amended a number of times to keep it up to date as compared with other subsequent instruments, principally of international law, as follows:

1. Directive 97/11/EC to consider the UN ECE Espoo Convention on EIA in a trans-boundary context;

2. Directive 2003/35/EC to align the Directive with the Aarhus Convention on public participation in environmental matters; and

3. Directive 2009/31/EC to include new areas in the scope of the Directive, such as CCS.

The directive provides for procedural environmental protection, but does not provide for substantive environmental standards. It requires assessment of the environmental projects likely to have significant effects on the environment. Many energy-related projects—such as most nuclear installations, large power plants, certain large-scale oil and gas production, dams, and pipelines—fall within the scope of Article 4(1) as they appear in Annex 1 and are therefore be subject to a mandatory EIA.

However, other energy projects, such as certain types of drilling, mineral extraction through dredging, the surface storage of gas or other fossil fuels or wind farms, fall under Annex II. As far as these types of projects are concerned, Member States can decide whether an individual project is subject to an EIA either on a case-by-case examination or through thresholds or criteria set by the Member State. As one might well imagine, this discretion has been the subject of disputes before the ECJ. Essentially, the Court has noted that, while Member States have this discretion to assess whether an Annex II project is subject to an EIA, their discretion is limited by the obligation set out in Article 2(1) of that Directive. Article 2(1) provides that projects likely to have significant effects on the environment, particularly by virtue of their nature, size or location, shall be subject to an impact assessment.[107] More specifically, the Court has ruled that Article 4(3) obliges Member States to take into account, when establishing the criteria or thresholds mentioned, *all* the relevant selection criteria set out in Annex III. This annex lays out the following criteria to be taken into account: (i) the characteristics of projects which must be considered, having regard, in particular, to their size, the accumulation with other projects, the use of natural resources, the production of waste, pollution and nuisances and the risk of accidents; (ii) the location of projects, so that the environmental sensitivity of geographical areas likely to be affected by projects must be considered, having regard, in particular, to the existing land use and the absorption capacity of the natural environment; and (iii) the characteristics of the potential impact, having regard, *inter alia*, to the geographical area involved and the size of the population

---

[106] Council Directive 85/337/EEC of 27 June 1985 on the assessment of the effects of certain public and private projects on the environment, OJ L 175, 5.7.1985, p. 40 (as amended).

[107] See for example, Cases C-121/03, *Commission v Spain* [2005] ECR, p. I-07569, para. 87; C-72/95, *Kraaijeveld and Others* [1996] ECR I-5403, para. 50; C-392/96, *Commission v Ireland* [1999] ECR I-5901, para. 64.

living there. A Member State cannot, for example, decide to take into account the size of the project only and disregard the other criteria.[108]

5.7–5.8 of this chapter look at two future possible mechanisms to counter climate change. While the first of these, carbon capture and storage (CCS), has been the subject of many studies; the second, geo-engineering, is only now making an appearance in serious academic discussion.

5.7 Carbon Capture and Storage: From a Regulatory Reality to Making a Difference?

In brief, the idea behind CCS is that it is a bridging technology that captures some of the CO_2 from certain industrial installations, which is then transported to be stored permanently in the suitable geological formations under the ground. The intention is obviously not to disincentivize reductions in CO_2 emissions or research and development into renewable energy sources, but to complement them. Essentially, it means admitting that we are still going to need fossil fuels for the years to come and that the world is not going to change instantly.

While the normal pattern is that the legislature and, consequently, the law follow the technological or other developments and breakthroughs in the industry by reacting to change, the opposite is true in the context of CCS. Here, the legislature seems to have taken the lead. While the EU does not have any new serious CCS projects,[109] it has a legislative framework ready for these operations, in the event that they take off. At present, the CCS legislation is primarily a theoretical exercise (or 'enabling legislation') and CCS remains only a 'regulatory reality'. However, it has been estimated that as much as 160 million tonnes of CO_2 could be stored by 2030.[110]

Following indications emanating from the Commission over a period of years to the effect that this option would form a part of the EU '20-20-20 by 2020' strategy, Directive 2009/31/EC[111] was adopted in 2009 for implementation by Member States by June 2011. The Directive deals with the full life-cycle of a CO_2 storage project, from issues like exploration and storage permits,[112] both onshore and offshore, to third-party access regimes to transport pipelines and storage facilities, and to closure and post-closure transfer of responsibilities. In addition to the CCS Directive, CCS projects are obviously subject to a range of other national and

---

[108] Case C-66/06, *Commission v Ireland* [2008] ECR I-158, paras. 62–64.
[109] Although the Norwegian Sleipner and Snovhit projects are worth noting.
[110] Preamble 5 of Directive 2009/31/EC of the European Parliament and the Council of 23 April 2009 on the geological storage of carbon dioxide and amending Council Directive 85/337/EEC, European Parliament and Council Directives 2000/60/EC, 2001/80/EC, 2004/35/EC, 2006/12/EC, 2008/1/EC and Regulation (EC) No 1013/2006, OJ L 140, 5.6.2009, pp. 114–35.
[111] Directive 2009/31/EC of the European Parliament and the Council of 23 April 2009 on the geological storage of carbon dioxide and amending Council Directive 85/337/EEC, European Parliament and Council Directives 2000/60/EC, 2001/80/EC, 2004/35/EC, 2006/12/EC, 2008/1/EC and Regulation (EC) No 1013/2006, OJ L 140, 5.6.2009, pp. 114–35.
[112] Article 5 for exploration permits and Articles 6 et seq. for storage permits.

EU regulations at various stages of the process, such as the Integrated Pollution Prevention and Control (IPPC) Directive[113] in respect of capture, and the EIA Directive for various parts of the CCS chain (capture facilities, pipelines etc).[114]

While CCS is excluded from the scope of water and waste laws in the interests of achieving certainty,[115] it remains subject to EU laws on the protection of groundwater.[116] Here, an interesting comparison may be made with the US, where the hydraulic fracturing that led to domestic success in shale gas was exempted from the 2005 Safe Drinking Water Act by the 2005 Energy Policy Act.[117] This exclusion led to a great deal of discussion once evidence regarding the impact of hydraulic fracturing on drinking water started to emerge.

The main responsibility for granting permits and imposing conditions remains at Member State level, although minimum requirements for permits are provided for. Article 11 of the CCS Directive also specifically notes that storage permits are subject to such future changes as may be necessary to respond to technological changes and certain other issues. These would certainly include new information concerning CO_2 storage, which is currently largely restricted to the reinjection of CO_2 for enhanced oil recovery. Similarly, Article 10 states that the Commission has a consultative role, and provides for a non-binding opinion in the decision-making on storage permits.

The EU measures relating to CCS are not taking place in a vacuum. Similar measures are also being discussed at international level,[118] where legislative measures have been taken to facilitate CCS in geologically suitable areas beneath the seabed. In particular, legal barriers for storage have been removed through the adoption of related risk-management frameworks under the 1996 London Protocol to the 1972 Convention on the Prevention of Marine Pollution by Dumping of Wastes and Other Matter (1996 London Protocol) and under the Convention for the Protection of the Marine Environment of the North-East Atlantic (OSPAR Convention). Amendments dating back to 2006, decisions and guidelines have been put in place to ensure environmentally safe CCS operations. Much like the prohibition of underwater CO_2 storage under the CCS Directive,[119]

---

[113] Directive 2008/1/EC of the European Parliament and of the Council of 15 January 2008 concerning integrated pollution prevention and control, OJ L 24, 29.1.2008, pp. 8–29.

[114] For a comprehensive overview of the decision-making relating to a CCS project, see A. Ming-Zhi Gao, 'The application of the European SEA Directive to carbon capture and storage activities: the issue of screening', 17(6) *European Energy and Environmental Law Review* (2008), pp. 314–71.

[115] It has been noted that the potential for CCS projects is negatively affected by regulatory complexity. See M. White, 'Carbon Capture and Storage: Becoming a Regulatory Reality in Europe', in B. Delvaux, M. Hunt, and K. Talus (eds), *EU Energy Law and Policy Issues* (Brussels: Euroconfidentiel 2008), p. 224.

[116] Such as the Directive 2006/118/EC of the European Parliament and of the Council of 12 December 2006 on the protection of groundwater against pollution and deterioration, OJ L 372, 27.12.2006, pp. 19–31.

[117] For the US shale gas revolution and its backgrounds, see F. Geny, 'Can Unconventional Gas be a Game Changer in European Gas Markets?' NG 46 (Oxford: OIES 2010).

[118] An overview of the international law context is provided in M. White, 'Carbon Capture and Storage: Becoming a Regulatory Reality in Europe', in B. Delvaux, M. Hunt, and K. Talus (eds), *EU Energy Law and Policy Issues* (Brussels: Euroconfidentiel 2008), pp. 242–3.

[119] Article 2.

a decision to prohibit the dumping of CO_2 into the sea or on the seabed has also been taken, due to the obvious potential risks that such activities may present.

One of the main problems with CCS, at least on a large scale, is the cost of the infrastructure and the physical space it (currently) requires. Even more so than with renewable energy, CCS requires significant investment. Therefore, while this regulatory reality may one day reflect actual practice within the EU, it is far less likely that it will be adopted in the poorer countries of the world. Another question, of course, is how much CO_2 can actually be stored before we run into difficulties.

5.8 When All Else Fails: The Geo-engineering of Climate Change?

'Globally, we need to realise that although research and investment in mitigation and adaptation is essential, it may not be enough. Investment in geo-engineering research has begun and, without international governance structures, schemes could soon be implemented unencumbered by the safeguards needed.'[120]

Since the adoption of the United Nations Framework Convention on Climate Change (UNFCCC), international efforts have been made to control greenhouse gas levels. While some progress have been made, it has become increasingly clear that it is difficult to achieve a global regime with the potential to reduce emissions on a sufficient scale. While efforts are still being made to conclude an international treaty on climate change mitigation, companies and countries have started to look at alternative technological options to prepare for the situation. This is also the case for the EU.

According to the head of the climate change unit at the European Commission's Joint Research Centre, the 'EU is also doing earth modelling to test how different geo-engineering approaches would impact upon the entire earth system: not just the atmosphere, but the oceans and the biosphere as well'.[121]

Geo-engineering of climate change can be seen in two ways: it can constitute a cost-reflective method of combating climate change used in combination with other climate change mitigation methods, and it can also be seen as a back-up system in case other measures fail. In this case, geo-engineering is seen as a radical method of intervention in the Earth's climate system. There are various ways to do this, and the methods can be placed in two general groups:

(I) the first group of schemes concerns solar radiation management, where the objective is to reduce the Earth's exposure to sunlight. The methods used to achieve this would include; marine cloud whitening, stratospheric aerosols, and space-based sunshades. The risks associated with these methods include: the necessity to create an artificial balance between global warming and solar radiation that should be

---

[120] <http://www.guardian.co.uk/environment/2011/jun/13/geoengineering-research-guidelines?IN TCMP=SRCH>.
[121] <http://www.euractiv.com/en/climate-change/eu-climate-scientist-casts-doubt-geo-engineering/ article-185287>.

maintained over very long time periods (even centuries); the risk of project failure at a later stage, creating a rapid increase in global temperature; the same risk of rapid increase in temperature relating to termination of the programme; little or no impact on current CO_2 levels; and potential ozone layer depletion;

(II) the second group of schemes involves carbon dioxide removal, where carbon dioxide is moved from the atmosphere and then stored in land- or sea-based sinks. Examples of carbon dioxide removal include: CCS, ocean fertilization, and land-based weathering. The risks associated with these methods include: potentially significant effects on natural ecosystems, high costs, and the long-term nature of the projects.

Because many of the most radical measures with the potential for significant effect on ecosystems are not highly capital-intensive and the technology to realize these measures exists, a single country has the potential to revert to these methods if its national interest so demands. Because of this potential, and because a more radical intervention by a specific state in the future cannot be ruled out, there is an urgent need to create a regulatory framework capable of effectively dealing with this issue. Similarly, given that even the testing phase may have severe negative effects on local or wider ecosystems, it could be argued that the testing phase should be regulated at an international level.

A decision would have to be made on whether an international instrument dealing with testing and/or deploying geo-engineering schemes to stop climate change should be created in the framework of the UNFCCC. This would have the benefit of using an existing institutional framework and providing a common starting-point. However, it could also be argued that the use of UNFCCC would have the downside of channelling the discussions and negotiations to the pre-existing venues and problems. If these fears turn out to be well-founded, it could prove to be counterproductive.

5.9 Concluding Thoughts: From Ideological Change to a Reality Check

The energy industries in the EU are now well advanced in the process of transition towards a liberalized EU-wide market. Liberalization should lead, and perhaps in certain ways is leading, towards technological modernization and greater energy efficiency. Competitive markets complement environmental policies. Among other things, they create transparency—i.e. they facilitate the pinpointing of otherwise hidden subsidies and charges—which in turn allows the markets to operate efficiently. In this way, a much greater environmental benefit is achieved at less cost than in situations where monopolies and state ownership camouflage the protection of vested interests under pious, increasingly environmental, labels. But liberated energy markets *do* require an effective and transparent regulatory and fiscal framework. External costs—e.g. pollution or contribution to climate change—need to be identified, measured, and then added to the cost of operation. Through the use of economic instruments (e.g. trading of emissions rights, green certificates, public service obligations, priority grid access or dispatch priorities, minimum demand guarantees, and environmental premiums for 'clean energy' or levies to internalize external environmental costs), markets can achieve much greater environmental benefits at a cost society is willing to accept for environmental quality than command-and-control rules. However, the problems here include the willingness of the markets to embrace the low carbon future and the opportunities it provides, and the flaws in the exiting market-based schemes, which seem to fail their purpose. Market failure is apparent in the EU ETS. However, at the other extreme, State driven schemes are not necessarily much better. Market failure must be contrasted with state failure. Such command-and-control systems cannot activate technological innovation and rapid diffusion as effectively as competitive markets. They are therefore bound either to require cost and investment for environmental purposes far beyond what society is ready to tolerate, or achieve much less in environmental terms than market-based solutions. One should bear in mind that reborn environmental communism is bound to fail to fulfil its own objectives, either through society baulking at the cost involved, or through conspicuous failure to achieve environmental quality at a cost which society will tolerate. Environmental lawyers, who mostly have no economic training or interest (and may even be hostile to economic analysis of environmental issues) and who are steeped in the prohibit–allow culture of public law and in sympathy with morally attractive—though often practically irrational—NGO campaigning are quite vulnerable to such forces, which pull them away from a realistic assessment of the cost and benefit[122] of environmental action. Consider this example from Finland: voices from within some Member States have opined that the EU should unilaterally adopt a 30 per cent target. According to a high-ranking official in the Finnish ministry responsible for energy, the emissions reductions made in Finland by moving from 20 per cent to 30 per cent reduction by 2020 correspond to the CO_2 emissions China makes in seven hours. This clearly raises the question of effect of measures in the EU versus similar investments in developing countries, or even in the European Energy Community Member States.

The general emphasis on environmental quality in the prosperous West European countries reflected in a large number of initiatives at the EU level is important and commendable. However, they include significant shortcomings and flaws.

First, they rely on the rest of the world to produce the intended results. The EU cannot produce the intended results by itself. The difficulties involved here are well illustrated by the recent rounds of climate change negotiations. Here, the rise of the BRICs [Brazil, Russia, India, and China] and others has already led to, and will continue to drive, fundamental changes in the nature of some aspects of

---

[122] C. Malin, 'Politics, Economics and Environment: Experience of the US Oil and Gas Industries', in N. Steen (ed.), *Sustainable Development and the Energy Industries* (London: RIIA 1994), pp. 157–74 and V. Fogleman, 'Economic Impacts of Environmental Law: The US Experience and its International Relevance', in N. Steen (ed.), *Sustainable Development and the Energy Industries* (London: RIIA 1994), pp. 81–102.

international negotiations and even international law, especially for multilateral instruments such as those relating to climate change. Just consider the setup at the time of Kyoto and compare it to Cancun.

Secondly, looking at the regulatory framework for renewable energy, several issues emerge: the starting-point with the Renewables Directive, and more generally the EU energy *acquis*, is that investment in renewable energy should be market-based. The EU has opted for a scheme where national targets are set through a centralized scheme and the choice of means used to achieve this target is left to the subsidiary level. These investments should be triggered by price signals. However, it has been rightly questioned how much reality there is in the market-driven ideology, given that investments are made mainly pursuant to government subsidy and support schemes.[123]

Thirdly, many of the initiatives could in principle be undertaken at national level, with some consultation and best-practice dialogue at EU level. But the internal market generally, and now particularly as it emerges very late in the energy industries, requires some measure of harmonization at EU level. Otherwise, one cannot realistically expect Member States to give free access to competing products and services from other states if these are not subject to at least a minimum and agreed level of environmental rules—the prospect of otherwise likely trade sanctions against environmental and energy dumping practices makes it necessary to create a common environmental regime. Apart from increasingly tough emissions control, the EU's environmental objectives for energy are largely oriented towards support for market penetration by hitherto uneconomic clean energy sources on the supply side, and energy-saving and efficiency on the demand side. Nuclear power—which is optimal from a climate perspective, but problematic in terms of risk perception and waste management—continues to pose a dilemma, particularly in the post-Fukushima world.

The Commission—like all institutions dependent on public approval—exploits the occasional crisis to increase its low levels of political legitimacy. There is nothing wrong with this in principle, since the Commission is an absolutely essential driver of European integration and European commonalities, and as such needs to be seen to reflect commonly-held values; but in some areas this tendency, which runs counter to the well-founded principle of subsidiarity, may not be sufficiently counter-balanced, in particular if public agitation regarding one of the crises which regularly occur makes sober assessment of the matter at European level impossible.

EU energy policy, as the environment-energy interface, provides an excellent socio-economic laboratory of economic regulation that mirrors the process of globalization by providing extranational solutions to problems that exceed the regulatory power of nation states. To this extent, it constitutes a model of governance in the global economy, where state sovereignty does not disappear but is shared by an international community. But, in the case of the EU, the challenges of developing such innovative forms of intra-EU governance often lead to self-absorbed navel-gazing.

---

[123] H. Bjornebye, *Investing in EU Energy Security: Exploring the Regulatory Approach to Tomorrow's Electricity Production* (Alphen aan den Rijn: Kluwer Law International 2010), pp. 157–8.

The EU is not alone in the world. It is a partner and competitor with other, in some respects stronger, forces. Its energy policy is an outstanding example, with its overwhelming dependence on external supplies from many regions, and with competition for these supplies from other, partly more prosperous and energy-intensive, partly much more populated regions of the world. EU energy policy, therefore, also has an external, international dimension. This is what Chapter 6 is about.

6

The International Dimension of EU Energy Law and Policy

6.1 The Shaping of the EU's International Energy Policies: Players, Policy, and Issues

In the past, the EU's focus has often been markedly inward-looking. That is natural for a community of sovereign states engaged in the difficult process of integration and of developing, and accepting, joint institutions. There is little time to look outside when what happens inside is so absorbing. But the EU is not the sole inhabitant of a lonely planet, and this is nowhere less so than in the field of energy. Without energy the EU societies would not function, and most of the energy they use comes from abroad, and mostly from countries which are difficult, volatile, risky, have problems with human rights, the environment, and good governance—in short, not members in good standing of the community of 'civilised nations'.[1]

In the old world of state ownership and monopoly, energy was a strictly national matter, and companies went out as national champions to find coal, and later oil, sponsored and supported by their home government. This mercantilist approach— with governments trying to ensure security of supply by dealing with other governments—informed the energy policy of most EU countries until fairly recently, is visible in most of the EU's external energy actions of the past and is far from disappearing from the mindset of most agencies and people involved. If the going gets tough and energy supply anxieties arise, the state is expected to secure the supply, using all of its powers—the 1991 Gulf War may have had a legitimate basis in the defence of the integrity of an independent state against a neighbour's aggression, but it is unlikely to have happened if the Gulf had not been of principal importance to the energy security of both the US and the EU. But with the energy markets becoming both regional (e.g. electricity and gas) and increasingly global (e.g. oil, but also LNG and coal), the long-established connection between anxiously observed 'energy dependence' and strategic state, or EU-wide, action, to assure 'security of supply' is no longer automatic. Apart from during the two World Wars, serious supply disruptions have been extremely rare,[2] while

---

[1] As in Article 38 of the Statute of the International Court of Justice.

[2] The 2009 Russia-Ukraine gas crisis being the main example. For the background and consequences of this crisis, see: S. Pirani, J. Stern, and K. Yafimava, 'The Russo-Ukrainian Gas Dispute of January 2009: A Comprehensive Assessment', NG 27 (Oxford Institute for Energy Studies, February 2009)

'energy dependence' has relentlessly increased. Countries with very high degrees of energy self-sufficiency—e.g. the former Soviet Union—on the other hand, have done rather badly.[3]

The EU Green Paper on security of energy supply of November 2000 reflected this transition from a *dirigiste*, intergovernmental, and mercantilistic view of security of supply to a more market-based one. It detailed the energy dependence of the EU and concluded that the future would bring greater dependence on oil and gas imports. It also highlighted the significant contribution that coal (with better environmental technology) and nuclear power (with no effect on climate) could make, and identified the market-oriented steps to be taken to ensure a functioning market, both through market-facilitative institutions and instruments, and through support for investment in significant physical infrastructure (mainly pipelines and interconnectors). But the Green Paper was still mired in the self-absorptive perspective typical of EU institutions. While it identified 'dependence'—i.e. where oil and gas come from and are likely to come from in the future—it failed to make the necessary next step and ask not only what the EU expects, but also what the external parties' interests and constraints are, and how to strike deals based on a reciprocal congruity of interest. This same approach has characterized much of the EU's external energy action throughout the liberalization process. The external dimension of EU energy policy needs to be understood in internal and regional (e.g. eastwards, southwards) terms, as well as in terms of the global state of play of energy production, transport and supply.

Within the EU, the Directorate –General (DG) for Energy represents the technocratic energy focus, with greatest concern over energy flows to the EU, also defending its own international turf against other actors within the European Commission. Together with DG Competition, it is responsible for creating competitive markets, both in the EU and in the wider European territories. There is a special relationship—the application of EU energy law to the EEA countries (mainly Norway) to watch over. EEA countries have to incorporate EU internal market law (e.g. competition, internal trade law and the energy directives) as it evolves, with consultation, but no participation. As the largest oil and gas producer in Europe, but outside the EU, Norway is therefore now subject to EU energy and competition law. This became very clear in the *GFU* case,[4] which forced a significant change in the Norwegian gas trade with EU companies. While previously gas from Norway was traded through the gas negotiation committee, each Norwegian producer must now conclude separate contracts with EU buyers. But Norwegian

---

and A. Kovacevic, 'The Impact of the Russia-Ukraine Gas Crisis in South Eastern Europe', NG 29 (Oxford: Oxford Institute for Energy Studies March 2009). Unlike the 2006 crisis, the 2009 crisis and the consequent supply cut had severe but variable effects in the South Eastern Europe. In some countries, district heating was disrupted during a period of extreme cold. In other countries industrial activities were halted, with significant financial consequences. See A. Kovacevic, 'The Impact of the Russia-Ukraine Gas Crisis in South Eastern Europe', NG 29 (Oxford: Oxford Institute for Energy Studies March 2009).

[3] J. Mitchell (ed.), *The New Economy of Oil* (London: Earthscan 2001), pp. 176–207.

[4] COMP/36.072—GFU—Norwegian Gas Negotiation Committee.

energy policy has always been strongly statist and protectionist,[5] and its participation in the ECT negotiations focused on maximizing Norwegian carve-outs from the ECT liberalization policies. In addition to ensuring a privileged role for the state in oil and gas, the Norwegian policies on ownership of its greatest source of electricity—hydropower—also aims at ensuring public control over these resources.[6]

The EU's wider-ranging foreign policy interests include building economic collaboration with Russia and the Central Asian/Caucasus countries where energy is again a major factor in economic growth, ever-growing supply interest and investment interest for the EU, but also a source of internal and external tensions over control of oil and gas wealth. The EU's direct interest in border security also extends to those Mediterranean countries which have energy resources but are unstable—particularly Algeria, but also Tunisia and Morocco (oil transit), as well as Syria and Egypt (oil supply). Iran is also a key country in this regard, in terms of regional security, oil and gas supply from Iran direct, and in terms of its political and transit leverage over the countries involved in oil and gas production in the Caspian region (Azerbaijan, Turkmenistan, Kazakhstan, and Uzbekistan). Tensions with the West over nuclear power (and other issues) are complicating supply and providing a window of opportunity to Chinese energy companies. Turkey is a pivotal country, for reasons of regional security and transit from the Caspian, both through the Bosporus and through oil and gas pipelines (BTC oil pipeline but also many other oil and gas pipelines). Its relationship with the EU is unstable because of the uncertain fate of its accession requests. There are serious problems of cultural compatibility, both in terms of the EU's relationship with Turkey and in terms of Turkey's internal political make-up. The Middle East's role as a major supplier to the EU is likely to grow in the medium term and beyond, as North Sea oil and gas supplies fade and to the extent that Russian energy production is absorbed domestically as the Russian economy grows. Unconventional oil and gas will not be able to curb this trend, at least in the medium term. The Middle Eastern countries are all troublesome. Not one oil and gas producer in the Middle East (or the Mediterranean or Caspian region) reflects contemporary Western expectations of good governance, democracy, and respect for human rights. Violently divisive and modernized feudal structures predominate, although this might be changing with the events dubbed the 'Arab Spring'. At the time of writing, it is too early to tell. If there is a linkage between these values and political stability, then any of these countries can be thrown into political turmoil and external conflict, as was witnessed in spring 2011 (the 'Arab Spring'). If the EU takes seriously the resurgence, under a different label, of the 'civilised nation' concept, then it should not be doing business with countries like Syria—which are, however, crucial for the EU's energy supply. Whether Islam is a major risk factor for stable energy trade relations with the EU, or a factor which

---

[5] S. Anderson, *The Struggle over North Sea Oil and Gas: Government Strategies in Denmark, Britain and Norway* (Oslo: Scandinavian University Press 1993). This type of approach is of course understandable and well in line with many other resource rich countries. Why would you not extract maximum rent for your resources.

[6] Case E-2/06, *EFTA Surveillance Authority v The Kingdom of Norway*, Judgment of 26 June 2007, EFTA Court Report 2007, p. 164.

can stabilize the relationship based on mutual respect is an interesting question.[7] While the EU increasingly relies, with no realistic alternative in the medium term, on these problematic countries as major oil and gas suppliers, one should not forget that these countries themselves rely at least to an equal extent—and probably more so[8]—on exporting their energy. With growing demands from growing populations and with no realistic industrial alternative (although some developments suggest that this might change in the future), the oil and gas producers—whatever their regime and even during civil war, as in Libya—are in much more desperate straits: they do have to export to the market and if they do not or the price is too low, the thin fabric of their countries' institutions is immediately and seriously in peril. Just consider the recent investment wave in the Middle East and Northern Africa (MENA) region, largely initiated as response to unrest among younger members of the population: Saudi Arabia: $160 billion has been spent on new homes, decreasing education costs, stipends for students, 60,000 new jobs, increasing minimum wages; Kuwait: $5 billion cash handouts and free food; Oman: a 40 per cent increase in minimum wages; Algeria: pay increases for public workers, higher subsidies on food, job creation, new homes; and Bahrain: wage increases, increased food subsidies, increased social welfare allowances. All of this requires a high oil price, and exports.[9]

The EU is also involved in energy relations outside this circle of core interest, both of a political and of an energy-based character. West African countries (notably Nigeria and Angola) have acquired a growing role in energy (oil, LNG) supplies which requires nurturing. In Asia, the EU has encountered a large, growing. and competing supply interest (e.g. for Siberian, Central Asian and Middle East oil and gas), but also a market for investment and export of equipment and services. In Latin America, there is both a traditional cultural (Spain) and economic (UK, Germany) interest for the EU. In both Asia and Latin America, there is a strong, not always clearly visible, counter-interest in balancing the overwhelming US interest by developing relations with the more economically-focused and less power-oriented EU. The US itself is one of the relations to consider in energy matters. Traditionally, US international energy policy has been more assertive (e.g. the Gulf War) and more self-confident—i.e. less interested in consensual, multilateral solutions (e.g. the US forced entry into and then made a surprise exit from the Energy Charter Treaty).[10] Throughout the world, EU and US companies, often

---

[7] N. Oystein, *Oil and Islam: Social and Economic issues* (Research Council of Norway: J. Wiley & Sons 1997); Samuel Huntingdon's clash of culture prediction—S. Huntingdon, *The Clash of Civilisation and the Remaking of World Order* (New York: Simon & Schuster 1997)—is one way of looking at it, but the modern European way would rather tend towards respect and tolerance for Islam; Islam itself is torn between a need to modernize and fundamentalist tendencies which may in due time lead to a modernization of Islam incorporating Islam's traditional respect for property, contract, and trade.

[8] J. Mitchell (ed.), *The New Economy of Oil* (2001), pp. 177 and 203.

[9] P. Stevens, *The Arab Uprisings and the International Oil Markets* (London: Chatham House 2012).

[10] W. Fox, 'The United States and The Energy Charter Treaty: Misgivings and Misperceptions', in T. Wälde (ed.), *The Energy Charter Treaty: An East-West Gateway for Investment and Trade* (London: Kluwer 1998).

with home-state and EU support, compete for access to oil and gas acreage, investment, and sale of equipment and services—with US companies often hindered by the use of domestically-motivated US economic sanctions: e.g. against Iran, Libya, Cuba, or North Korea.[11] The US has also played a key role in the Caspian region and was largely behind the success of the BTC oil pipeline. The US involvement in the Nabucco project seems to be much less central, possibly because of the different geopolitical significance of the two projects. China is the most recent major and global participant in the energy game. With strong government backing and less concern for international sanctions, Chinese oil and gas companies have signed deals in places and for products like US shale gas, Canadian oilsands, Australian coalbed methane, Russian oil and gas, but also in more problematic places, including many African countries and Iran.[12]

It would be wrong to portray the relevant actors only within the traditional model of states and their strategies. EU (and US, perhaps even Chinese[13]) foreign policy is very much influenced by non-state actors. These include: non-governmental organizations (NGOs), which now represent themselves as the truest guardians of Western cultural values; multinational companies, which are now obliged to present themselves not only as profit machines, but as 'forces for good';[14] business organizations, which tend to represent the common denominator of corporate interest; and the press, through which the actions of all actors are filtered and magnified. Not all that is seen by governmental actors as good for business (e.g. the MAI negotiations up to 1998 or the ECT) is viewed in the same way by the companies themselves. Close corporate-government relations—e.g. between the former state company Elf and the French government—tend to give way to greater distance as international capital markets exercise more influence on corporate management than their home governments. International organizations in which the EU Member States or the EU itself participate develop at times a dynamic of their own, driven either by the secretariat or by a caucus of like-minded and similarly-oriented government delegates. Within WTO processes, the emphasis is on free trade; within the OECD, the emphasis is on free movement of capital; within the IEA, the emphasis is on identifying current trends and prospects and recommending governmental action, plus consultation with the producing countries; within the World Bank, the traditional emphasis on good project lending has given way to a much more diffuse effort to leverage lending to influence economic (and energy investment/privatization) policies and now the 'hard' imposition of 'soft' cultural policies (in relation to the environment, human rights, participatory democracy, and the eradication of

---

[11] T. Wälde, 'Managing the Risk of Sanctions in the Global Oil and Gas Industry', 36 *Texas International Law Journal* (2001), pp. 184–230 and K. Talus and M.A. Nunes, 'Regulation of Oil Imports in the United States and the European Union', 2 *OGEL* (2011), <http://www.ogel.org>.

[12] For the activities of Chinese oil and gas companies, and Chinese energy policies more generally, see the articles of Philip Andrew-Speeds on *OGEL* (<http://www.ogel.org>).

[13] For the drivers behind policies of Chinese oil and gas companies, see International Energy Agency, Overseas Investments by Chinese National Oil Companies: Assessing the drivers and impacts (IEA 2011), pp. 25–8.

[14] J. Mitchell (ed.), *Companies in a world of conflict* (London: RIIA 1998), pp. 209 et seq.

poverty).[15] In UN fora (e.g. in particular United Nations Conference on Trade and Development (UNCTAD)), where the EU participates, but is not in a position of strength, the emphasis is rather on defending developing countries against the imposition of economic and now cultural policies mainly representing the Western countries. A critical assessment of liberalization and privatization in markets which may not be ripe for this, and a proposal for *quid pro quo* energy trade deals, is developed here.[16] The financial institutions (the World Bank, mainly under US influence; European Bank for Reconstruction and Development (EBRD)—under European, but not EU influence; European Investment Bank (EIB)—under EU influence) have their own policy contribution to make.[17] In the energy field, their role lies in exercising financing leverage to obtain favourable investment terms and in supporting infrastructure facilities for which private banks are by themselves and without public guarantees not ready. Generally speaking, the Member States prefer to retain their national powers and influence over international institutions like the IMF or the World Bank, and the role of the EU is reduced to that of seeking to reconcile the divergent opinions of its Member States.[18]

With OPEC, the EU has a dialogue (but possibly one of the deaf); both OPEC and EU environmentalist (and tax) interests are in favour of the consumer paying a high oil price, but they differ on who is to collect the rent (OPEC prefers taxes and high prices in favour of the producing country; the EU high consumption taxes in favour of EU Member States). OPEC is, however, politically very useful to the EU. First, it contributes, now perhaps more effectively than in the past, to the maintenance of reasonably high and stable oil prices by better production control. Secondly, because it is outside the jurisdiction of EU law and not vulnerable to internal EU political and public pressure, it serves where necessary as a convenient scapegoat for high energy prices. In a way, it now does the dirty business for consumers and international oil companies, neither of which, for competition law and public opinion reasons, can do it themselves.

Given the multitude of fora and elements in EU international energy policy, and the legal instruments deployed, its approach is not always to achieve a carefully planned outcome of a political process through a unitary actor such as the European Commission. In practice, the policy that emerges is rather the unplanned—and in fact unplannable—result of many players acting both within and outside the EU. The particular measures taken often require consent and involvement by outside actors. In most cases, these measures are generated by coalitions of like-minded actors:[19] e.g. climate change policies by officials from DG Climate Action, DG Energy, and DG Environment, environmental ministries, NGOs and executives from climate-change divisions in major energy companies, international energy

---

[15] H. Bergesen and L. Lunde, *Dinosaurs or Dynamos? The United Nations and the World Bank at the Turn of the Century* (London: Earthscan 1999).
[16] UNCTAD, *Energy Services in International Trade: Development Implications* (10 April 2001).
[17] For criticism, see in particular the work of Joseph Stiglitz.
[18] D. Chalmers, G. Davies, and G. Monti, *European Union Law* (Cambridge: CUP 2010), p. 639.
[19] R. D. Putnam, 'Diplomacy and Domestic Politics: The Logic of Two-level Games', 42 *International Organization* (1988), pp. 427–60.

policy/legal assistance from linked groups in DG Energy, DGs with international focus (from development to trade to foreign policy), aid industry lobbies, NGOs and institutional and individual beneficiaries in the recipient countries. It is not surprising that the EU's international policy in the energy field is sometimes contradictory, with the transnational environmental coalitions transcending organizational borders producing multilateral environmental agreements (MEA) calling for trade restrictions, while the corporate-Commission trade-focused groups produce treaties and WTO panel-based trade law aimed at excluding MEAs.[20] In this process, certain dominant themes are generally present, though these are often dominant only in their particular arenas. These include energy security for DG Energy, integrated competitive markets for DG Competition, climate change for DG Climate Action and DG Environment, and building stability by economic and energy investment in former Soviet countries[21] and the Mediterranean for the internationally focused DGs. Development aid plays a role here, but EU development aid suffers from lack of focus and the tension between 'selfless' aid, on one hand, and more 'selfish' aid tied to the donor's interest, on the other, with no clear understanding as to which approach is in the final analysis better for both donor and recipient. New themes pervading all other activities relate to the current enthusiasm for exporting Western cultural values to, and imposing them on, countries which do not conform to Western governance concepts—i.e. a revived form of nineteenth century concepts of missionary colonialism and the civilizing mission of the West. There are also more technical imperatives for external EU energy action: some issues (e.g. global warming) require global action, though national and EU-wide policies can serve as a laboratory for global policies (and provide a competitive advantage to EU companies thus forewarned of regulations to come). The chief example of this is the EU emissions trading scheme, though this scheme is used as an example both by those in favour of such a scheme and by those opposing it.[22]

As global energy markets emerge (as is already largely the case for oil and to some extent now for gasoline, LNG, coal and—more slowly—pipeline gas), regulatory solutions have to be found,[23] and EU external energy policy will then be about creating a global regulatory framework. The harbingers of such developments are the—as yet unsuccessful—efforts to create a global investment code. The pooling of regulatory powers in the form of EU economic (including energy) law should only be a first step to pooling global regulatory powers in international institutions, although the resistance observable in the EU is likely to be even more

---

[20] T. Wälde, 'Sustainable Development and the 1994 Energy Charter Treaty: Between Pseudo-action and the Management of Environmental Investment Risk', in F. Weiss et al. (eds), *International Economic Law with a Human Face* (London: Kluwer Law 1998), pp. 223–71.

[21] T. Wälde, 'International Good Governance and Civilised Conduct among the Caspian Sea States: Oil and Gas Lever for Prosperity of Conflict', in W. Ascher and N. Mirovitskaya (eds), *The Caspian Sea: A Quest for Environmental Security* (London: Kluwer 2000), pp. 29–51.

[22] This has been the case in, for example, Australia.

[23] For an international regime for cross-border pipelines, see C.I.A. Siddiky, *Cross Border Pipeline Arrangement: What Would a Single Regulatory Framework Look Like?* (London: Kluwer Law International 2011).

intensive on a world scale, and thus progress is likely to be very gradual. In the fullness of time and an ideal world, external EU energy law should be nothing but a regional component of international energy law.

6.2 The Legal Instruments and Legal Authority of the EU's External Energy Policy

To pursue its energy goals, the EU primarily uses treaties and money. Treaties create a network of legal—and thus also political and administrative—obligations and procedures with the partner countries. No systematic analysis of the role of energy in such treaties has so far been conducted.[24] While energy is mentioned in most treaties of the economic cooperation type, it is rarely the focus of such a treaty.[25]

For a long time, the 1994 Energy Charter Treaty was the only treaty dedicated to energy to which the EU had acceded, and only in 2005 was the Energy Community Treaty signed. It should be no surprise that the majority of the language in the more general treaties amounts to friendly expressions of goodwill with respect to trade, investment, and the environment—and in the more recent treaties (e.g. the 2000 Cotonou Agreement, etc.), good governance, civil society, and human rights are also mentioned.[26] Specific legal obligations are thin on the ground in these treaties, and mostly relate to trade. Energy trade has only recently become a more significant topic in EU treaty negotiations. One can perhaps understand EU treaty-making as, first, an effort to develop a significant, and acknowledged, foreign policy role, hamstrung by the absence of the traditional levers used to project political and military power abroad. Secondly, it is based on the explicit or implicit strategy to develop 'reasons to talk' with governments of interest to the EU. Treaties thus involve a process of dialogue, from negotiation to the stage of implementation, which in most cases is rather about discussing with governments the general, hortatory principles contained in such treaties.

Traditionally, international law is regarded as a creation made for states by states as the principal actors in international law and international legal relations. The emergence of the EU as a significant actor in international law and policy results from developments at both internal EU level (legal personality with the Treaty on the EU and growing competence to act within those areas specifically conferred to it by the Member States) and international level (the general recognition of the EU

---

[24] This is particularly so at bilateral level. On the environmental front, this type of study was carried out by Gracia Marin Duran and Elisa Morgera, see G. Marin Duran and E. Morgera, *Environmental Integration in the EU's External Relations: Beyond Multilateral Dimensions* (Oxford: Hart Publishing 2012).

[25] This is the case even with the major energy exporting countries. See, for example, Euro-Mediterranean Agreement establishing an Association between the European Community and its Member States, of the one part, and the People's Democratic Republic of Algeria, of the other part, OJ L 265/2, 10.11.2005.

[26] Article 9 of Cotonou Agreement refers to human rights, democratic principles, and rule of law. (The Cotonou Agreement was revised in 2005 ([2005] OJ L 209/27).)

as an international actor[27]). The EU[28] has legal personality (Article 47 TEU) and by default also has international legal personality. It can therefore act on the international stage as a state-like actor. This means that it can conclude international agreements without the signatures of Member State representatives—although Member State interests are guarded by the Council of Ministers, which takes decisions alone or jointly with the Parliament (Article 218 TFEU, for common commercial policy, Article 207 TFEU). It can also take trade measures, such as imposing anti-dumping regulations. International agreements concluded by the Union are binding both on the institutions of the Union and on its Member States.[29]

Given the innovative nature of EU as an actor in international stage (not really a federal state—yet, at any rate—but not really an international organization either), triggered some debate at first, but the initial difficulty of the EU acceding to international law instruments has been solved by defining the EU as a 'Regional Economic Integration Organisation'. Today, the EU is a full member of numerous international organizations like the WTO. In other organizations, like the OECD it plays a less formal, but in practice often an influential, role.[30]

The EU's external competences are based either on the explicit authority of the Treaty or are the external manifestation of internal powers ('external/internal parallelism'). Article 216(1) TFEU invests the EU with competence to conclude international agreements where this is necessary in order to achieve one of the objectives of the EU or is provided for in a legally binding act of the EU or is likely to affect common rules or alter their scope.[31] In the *Open Skies* judgments of 5 November 2002,[32] the Court did note that an international agreement was not necessary in these cases and that it had not been demonstrated that the internal competence could effectively have been exercised only at the same time as the external competence. However, in those cases the second option applied—i.e. the EU's exclusive competence arising from a legally binding act of the EU. The judgments in these cases clearly meant that, because the EU had exclusive competence with regard to certain aspects of international air services, Member States could no longer enter into international agreements themselves.

---

[27] G. Marin Duran and E. Morgera, *Environmental Integration in the EU's External Relations: Beyond Multilateral Dimensions* (Oxford: Hart Publishing 2012), pp. 6 and 7.

[28] More generally, see D. Chalmers, G. Davies, and G. Monti, *European Union Law* (Cambridge: CUP 2010), pp. 630–73.

[29] Article 216 (2) TFEU. This provision has been interpreted to extend to customary international law and general principles of international law (Cases C-T-115/94, *Opel Austria v Council* [1997] ECR II-39 and C-162/96, *Racke & Co v Hauptzollant Mainz* [1998] ECR I-3655).

[30] Supplementary Protocol to the Convention on the OECD of 14 December 1960, the signatory countries agreed that the European Commission should take part in the work of the OECD. European Commission representatives work alongside Members in the preparation of texts and participate in discussions on the OECD's work programme and strategies, and are involved in the work of the entire Organization and its different bodies (see <http://www.oecd.org>).

[31] Case 22/70, *ERTA* [1971] ECR 263.

[32] Court cases C-466–469/98, C-467/98, C468/98, C-469/98, C-472/98, C-475/98, and C-476/98 of 5 November 2002. See also Communication from the Commission on the consequences of the Court judgments of 5 November 2002 for European air transport policy (COM/2002/0649 final).

Articles 2 to 6 TFEU distinguish explicitly between 'exclusive', 'shared', and 'supportive' EU powers. In this context, energy appears as a 'shared' competence (Article 4(2)(i) TFEU), which is specified under title XXI (Energy) and in Article 194 TFEU. With the emergence of more and more detailed and comprehensive EU energy law through the three packages of energy directives and Article 194 TFEU, there are more and more areas where there are strong arguments for exclusive EU competence to conclude treaties with respect to energy. This is clearly the case in certain other areas of energy: mineral oil, natural gas, and even electricity are goods which are subject to trading and can therefore fall within the scope of the Common Commercial Policy under Articles 206 and 207 TFEU. The Common Commercial Policy is an exclusive competence of the Union in the sense of Article 3(e) TFEU. In this context, the European Parliament's involvement in the formulation of the EU's Common Commercial Policy, insofar as its consent is now required, is a significant change brought about by the Lisbon Treaty.[33]

The second major instrument of EU international energy policy is money, mainly funds allocated to technical assistance projects in the energy field. The EU regularly requires a treaty before committing to the provision of technical assistance (the older term is 'development aid') funds. Treaties and money thus complement each other. Technical assistance provided under the manifold and (regrettably) periodically changing EU-typical acronyms, like TACIS, PHARE, SYNERGIE, ALTENER, SAVE, INOGATE and others serve multiple purposes. They are intended to help the recipients obtain expertise which they do not have and cannot pay for themselves. They represent a means of influencing partner countries' policies in the EU direction. They provide work for the large EU consultancy industry. They help this industry and larger EU companies to penetrate new markets, often in competition with US (USAID) technical assistance pursuing a similar strategy. Their main benefit is probably that they facilitate the emergence of knowledge-based networks (consultants, academics, officials, corporate executives, NGO experts, specialized press), privileging the outreach of EU specialists.

Treaties (and money) never deliver what they promise in their high-sounding preambles and press releases. They are often not taken seriously on both sides: their hortatory language, replete with expressions of goodwill, friendship, and morally welcome purposes, lack direct impact. Nevertheless, it would be wrong to deny the usefulness of these instruments. Deployed *en masse*, they project the EU as a prosperous partner with overwhelmingly cooperative and commercial interests. The web of treaties and the professional networks created by technical assistance are a conduit for channelling EU influence through concepts, methods, models, precedents, and best practices to countries which need such models and are unable to develop effective approaches to governance on their own. The EU's influence on partner countries' energy policies is therefore rarely a matter of power and direct pressure, but of persuasion and intellectual osmosis facilitated by trust and the common quest for peace and prosperity. It is not the way of hard power, but rather that of collaborative dialogue.

---

[33] See Article 218(u) and (v), and Article 207(2) TFEU.

6.3 Technical and Financial Assistance Programmes

With its technical and financial assistance programmes, the EU tries to influence partner countries' energy policies in an EU-friendly direction: liberalization, the opening-up of the energy industries for (preferably EU) investment, increased trade relations (the export of EU equipment and services, import of partner-state oil and gas), better environmental performance—particularly in relation to greenhouse gas emissions and other emissions with a cross-border effect on EU environmental quality (e.g. air pollution, the survival of forests)—and nuclear safety. This sometimes direct, but more often informal, underpinning of EU assistance is not necessarily in conflict with the overall objectives of host states. Most of the countries which have an energy relationship with the EU—i.e. Russia and various countries in Central Asia, the Mediterranean, the Middle East and West Africa—are mired in systems of economic governance which obstruct development: communist organizational structures and attitudes[34] have been inherited and not replaced by a functioning market and a system of institutions and culture which supports the market.[35] The problem with most of these projects is not that they are supposed to preach EU principles and policies, but that their duration and impact is typically short, minimal, and localized. There seems to be no systematic reflection and strategic planning as to what the EU wants to achieve and how it is to be done, given the ever-complex circumstances of post-communist and developing countries where advice (rather than the perquisites of foreign aid) is often not wanted—at least, not by the right people—is not professionally rendered, relies more on the recounting of EU systems than on transposing concepts and experience to the often very different host state context, and is rarely absorbed with lasting effect. This problem affects the grant of all technical assistance in such circumstances (e.g. World Bank, UN, EBRD, bilateral agencies: DFID (Department for International Development) in the UK or GIZ (Deutsche Gesellschaft für Internationale Zusammenarbeit) in Germany), but may be particularly acute in the case of the EU, which lacks systematic in-house expertise on the giving of policy and legislative reform advice. While DG Energy (and other DGs) does have energy expertise,[36] it is elusive and not effectively transferred. It is sometimes hard to avoid the impression of a giant funding system operating without a focused and expert mind watching over such activities and learning from them. Managing administrative challenges seems to prevail over the more relevant challenge of thinking seriously about real, rather than purely formalized, objectives.

---

[34] See T. Wälde and J. Gunderson, 'Legislative Reform in Transition Economies', 43 *International & Comparative Law Quarterly* (1994), pp. 347–79, T. Wälde and C. von Hirschhausen, 'Legislative Reform in the Energy Industry of Post-Soviet Societies', in R. Seidman, A. Seidman, and T. Wälde (eds), *Making Development Work: Legislative Reform for Good Governance* (London: Kluwer 1999).

[35] M. Olson, *Power and Prosperity* (New York: Basic Books 2000).

[36] It is also worth noting that after the Lisbon Treaty the only DG responsible for implementation of instruments of EU external assistance is DG for Development and Cooperation (EuropeAid).

6.3.1 Examples of Earlier Cooperation Programmes

6.3.1.1 SYNERGY, PHARE, and TACIS

SYNERGY was a cooperation programme managed by the DG for Transport and Energy (DG TREN). It financed cooperation activities with non-EU countries relating to the formulation and implementation of energy policy. The scheme was based on earlier energy-related cooperation projects following the oil crises of the 1980s, beginning with the 'EC International Energy Co-operation Programme', which then evolved into the SYNERGY programme. SYNERGY was the international cooperation component of the 'Energy Framework Programme' which ran from 1998 to 2002. SYNERGY's aim was to improve the competitiveness of EU industries, enhance security of supply, promote sustainable development, and improve energy efficiency. Its guidelines[37] stated that the implementation of the programme should refocus on activities related to security of supply and the implementation of the Kyoto Protocol. Unlike other EU programmes, which were of a more general nature and included energy as one of several aims, SYNERGY was a specific energy policy programme covering the external dimension of EU actions in the energy policy sector.

PHARE can be characterized as the main channel for the European Union's financial and technical cooperation with Central and Eastern European countries (CEECs). It focused on preparing the then candidate countries for EU accession. In the energy field, this meant review of the regulatory and institutional situation in the CEEC countries to bring them—by legislative reform, institution-building, and training—into conformity with EU energy law. The EU energy directives, the Energy Charter Treaty and EU competition law were perhaps the most relevant benchmarks for reform of the energy sector in Eastern Europe. Support for a twinning mechanism between partner institutions was also provided.

In the end, these programmes were about creating professional networks, explaining the rationale, methods, and concepts of the energy directives and helping the accession countries gradually to reach a similar stage, first formally, and then, hopefully, also with proper understanding and absorption. The main weakness of most projects was their short-term nature. Developing a relationship of reciprocal understanding between the EU and the CEEC partner takes a year—by which time the project had usually come to an end. The cumbersome nature of the procurement machinery meant that the largest amount of funds and time was not spent on professional communication across often substantial cultural borders, but on dealing with the Commission's departments. The development of long-term partnerships between competent institutions—the only effective way to build a productive professional and intellectual partnership—failed to occur.

---

[37] Council Decision of 9 April 2001 laying down the new guidelines applicable to actions and measures to be taken under the multiannual programme to promote international cooperation in the energy sector (1998 to 2002) under the multiannual framework programme for actions in the energy sector and connected measures, OJ L/125, 5.5.2001, pp. 24–6.

The EU TACIS programme provided technical assistance to Russia and other post-Soviet countries.[38] The stated objective was to facilitate the transition to a market economy and to reinforce democracy and the rule of law. In the former Soviet Union, the situation was again very different from the accession countries. Here, there were sometimes, or even usually (except in the case of Ukraine), ample national reserves and production. The issue was rather that of how to create a regulatory regime that would encourage investment in upstream oil and gas development, fair access to transportation pipelines, and market-based incentives for efficient production, transport, and consumption. At all levels, these clear objectives were confronted by Soviet-style obstruction, involving: extensive resentment against foreign investment in Russia; an opaque, volatile, and corrupt culture interposed between investor and the government's licensing system; the absence of a culture of trust, commitment, and law; and a very close relationship between business and state, which prevented the state from regulating effectively and prevented business from focusing on commercial and competitive performance. The policy requirements here were very different. The energy directives had only limited usefulness as benchmarking models. The Energy Charter Treaty, with its emphasis on the introduction of a market economy, respect for property, non-discrimination, and access to transit and transport facilities, was probably more relevant at this stage.

Russia did not need to manage the importation and distribution of energy (as did the CEEC countries), but rather to produce and distribute more efficiently. Furthermore, it was not—and never will be—a candidate for EU accession, given that it is very large and has a tradition of perceived supremacy. The EU model should therefore have been offered, not on the basis of the obligation to adopt EU law for accession purposes, but through persuasion on the basis that it was the right model for Russia's needs. While the TACIS programme's funds were substantial, they were not sufficient to exercise financial leverage on Russia to adopt foreign-imported policies. There is, or rather was, also acute competition between the US (or Anglo-Saxon) models that underpinned Russia's early shock reform efforts (also driven by the IMF and the World Bank), and the EU model which contained the flexibility to emphasize more liberal (e.g. the UK) and more statist (e.g. France) versions. This programme ran from 2000 to 2006 and was then replaced by the European Neighbourhood and Partnership Instrument (ENPI)[39] for the period from 2007 to 2013.[40]

6.3.1.2 Europe Agreements

Before moving to the agreements which now exist, an 'in between' group of agreements will be examined: the Europe Agreements. These were the instrument used

---

[38] Armenia, Azerbaijan, Belarus, Georgia, Kazakhstan, Kyrgyzstan, Moldova, Mongolia, Russian Federation, Tajikistan, Turkmenistan, Ukraine, and Uzbekistan.

[39] Regulation (EC) No 1638/2006 of the European Parliament and of the Council of 24 October 2006 laying down general provisions establishing a European Neighbourhood and Partnership Instrument, OJ L 310, 9.11.2006, pp. 1–14.

[40] Similarly, the MEDA program in the Mediterranean region was replaced by ENPI from 2007 onwards.

to prepare Eastern European countries for accession to the EU. At the time of writing, only Bulgaria and Romania still have Europe Agreements.

With the EU as the dominant partner, the Europe Agreements established a programme for preparing the partner countries for eventual accession. They provided the means whereby the EU offered the associated countries the trade concessions and other benefits normally associated with full EU membership. The Europe Agreements aimed to establish free trade in industrial products and in services, limited freedom of movement, introduction of competition law (including state aid rules) over a gradual, transitional period, although the EU opened its markets more quickly than the associated country. As a result, industrial products from the associated countries had virtually free access to the EU from the beginning of 1995. The Agreements also contained provisions regarding the free movement of services, payments, and capital in respect of trade and investment, and the free movement of workers. When establishing and operating in the territory of the other party, enterprises were to receive treatment not less favourable than national enterprises. Under the Agreements, the partner countries also committed themselves to approximating their legislation to that of the EU, particularly in areas relevant to the internal market. Energy was mentioned as one of the areas of economic cooperation and nuclear safety was mentioned as a special concern.[41] The form of the obligations was not specific; they referred to a general policy in the sector (e.g. the opening-up of the energy sector), defined a best-efforts obligation, enabled financial and technical assistance, and defined full approximation as the ultimate target, but without a specific timetable. They also formed the basis for several PHARE projects to assist the accession countries to develop regulatory regimes for energy (including competition) in line with EU law and the energy directives.

Sections 6.4 to 6.6 examine some of the current elements of EU external energy policy. In essence, EU action in this area can be, and often is, multilateral. The EU participates in international efforts in a given area like energy security, access to energy markets, or protection of energy investments. In addition to this, energy cooperation may be integrated in bilateral or inter-regional instruments. In this area, the EU negotiates bilateral legal and policy instruments with a range of developing and developed countries and regions. The chapter first focuses on examples of bilateral mechanisms (although the Cotonou Agreement is, arguably, regional in scope) (see section 6.4), and thereafter provides an overview of the multilateral mechanisms for energy cooperation using the ECT and the Energy Community Treaty as examples (see sections 6.5–6.7).

---

[41] Articles 79 and 80 of the EU-Bulgaria Europe Agreement (Europe Agreements are virtually identical); these provisions mention as areas of cooperation energy efficiency, savings, development, transfer of technology, diversification of supply, transit, environmental impact, and opening up of the sector including modernization. This is an antechamber to full accession in the energy area. Article 81 includes, with a similar intention, environmental (including climate change) obligations.

6.4 Bilateral Aspects of EU External Energy Policy: From Associations to Dialogues

6.4.1 Association and Economic Cooperation Agreements

The EU has concluded several types of economic cooperation agreements. They differ in terms of the level of economic integration aimed at: goodwill discussions only; a basis for development aid and trade preferences involving an intention to move to a customs union; or a customs union plus gradual adoption of EU law by the partner state to prepare for accession. They have no specific energy focus, although energy may be mentioned as an object of development aid, included in a customs union and the adoption of EU law. They also tend to formulate goodwill declarations concerning foreign investment, but do not contain hard and specific legal obligations like those we see in the bilateral investment treaties, which now, post-Lisbon, are concluded by the EU and not by the Member States.

6.4.1.1 Association Agreements

Association agreements are a special case, and have been since the early days of the European Community. The Treaty of Rome invested the EU (then the EEC) with the competence to conclude agreements establishing an association with both third countries and international organizations. Without a formal definition of the objectives and scope of these associations, the EU has used this competence over the years to conclude associations with a large number of countries for very different purposes and objectives.[42] Duran and Morgera distinguish between four categories of association: association as a prelude to EU membership (as is currently the case with Turkey and certain South-Eastern European countries); association as a substitute for EU membership (as is currently the case with Norway and the countries in the Euro-Mediterranean Partnership); association as a development tool (as is the Cotonou Agreement); and association as an instrument for inter-regional cooperation (e.g. the association agreements with Chile and South Africa).[43]

These association agreements can also cover energy, as in the Association Agreement with Albania (which was signed on 12 June 2006 and entered into force on 1 April 2009), Article 107 of which states:

'Energy Cooperation shall focus on priority areas related to the Community acquis in the field of energy, including nuclear safety aspects as appropriate. It shall reflect the principles of the market economy and it shall be based on the signed regional Energy Community Treaty with a view to the gradual integration of Albania into Europe's energy markets.'

---

[42] The current legal basis in Article 217 TFEU seems to suggest that association agreements can be concluded to cover all EU policies and activities. Similarly, see G. Marin Duran and E. Morgera, *Environmental Integration in the EU's External Relations: Beyond Multilateral Dimensions* (Oxford: Hart Publishing 2012), p. 60.

[43] G. Marin Duran and E. Morgera, *Environmental Integration in the EU's External Relations: Beyond Multilateral Dimensions* (Oxford: Hart Publishing 2012), pp. 58 and 59.

Certain factors stand out. First, for those associations that are a prelude to EU membership, the financial assistance offered is often tied to progress made in fulfilling the objectives of the association agreement.[44] The EU monitors progress in the association country in terms of approximation of laws. As such, it is ultimately the EU that evaluates the 'merits' of association countries' 'compliance'.[45] A somewhat similar issue can be raised in the context of EU relations with its neighbouring countries. Article 8 TEU states: 'The Union shall develop a special relationship with neighbouring countries, aiming to establish an area of prosperity and good neighbourliness, founded on the values of the Union [...].' Examples of this type of neo-colonialism are readily available.

Association agreements can provide preferential access to EU markets, often with a view to a later customs union. There is institutional machinery for dialogue (a Council or Committee), which is increasingly also competent to deal with governance issues: i.e. a way for the EU (but never, in practice, for the partner country) to raise, with some financial, trade, and political leverage in the background, governance issues. There is an emphasis, pushed in particular by the southern EU countries, towards closer relations with the Mediterranean countries. Association agreements exist with most Mediterranean countries,[46] with Turkey being a special case.[47] These agreements were originally implemented by the MEDA programme, which contained a number of projects relating to energy. There are no specific 'energy' agreements in the EU-Mediterranean relationship; some of the countries have looked at the ECT, but felt that the 'hard law' obligation and direct enforcement (by investment arbitration) was not acceptable. This situation reflects the internal political circumstances of most Mediterranean countries: weak governance; religious problems where fundamentalist Islam is challenging governments which provide no significant popular participation; inter-ethnic strife; and suppression of minorities (e.g. Turkey, Israel, Algeria, and Syria). From an energy perspective, these countries are of great importance, in particular to southern Europe: oil and gas investment supply from Syria, Egypt and Algeria and through Turkey, Tunisia, and Morocco. As in the case with Russia and the Caspian/Caucasus countries, the EU wishes for good commercial relations with all of these countries. Through the use of treaties, dialogue, professional community-building, and assistance, it can help positive governance elements to grow, but in essence it cannot, on its own and

---

[44] Article 112 in the Association Agreement with Albania. Available at <http://ec.europa.eu/enlargement/pdf/albania/st08164.06_en.pdf>.

[45] G. Marin Duran and E. Morgera, *Environmental Integration in the EU's External Relations: Beyond Multilateral Dimensions* (Oxford: Hart Publishing 2012), p. 74.

[46] Just see Decision 2005/690/EC, Decision 2004/635/EC, Decision 2002/357/EC, Decision 2000/384/EC, Decision 2000/204/EC, Decision 98/238/EC, concerning the conclusion of a Euro-Mediterranean Agreement establishing an association between the European Communities and their Member States, of the one part, and, respectively, the People's Democratic Republic of Algeria, the Arab Republic of Egypt, the Hashemite Kingdom of Jordan, the State of Israel, the Kingdom of Morocco, and the Republic of Tunisia.

[47] Council Decision 2008/157/EC of 18 February 2008 on the principles, priorities and conditions contained in the Accession Partnership with the Republic of Turkey and repealing Decision 2006/35/EC, OJ L 051, 26.2.2008, pp. 4–18.

without strong domestic allies, guarantee the creation of stable systems of good and democratic governance.

6.4.1.2 The Cotonou Agreement

The most important partnership agreement between the EU and the developing world is the Cotonou Agreement. Created in 2000, it functions as the framework for the EU's relations with 79 countries from Africa, the Caribbean and the Pacific (ACP). The ACP countries are most of the former colonies of EU Member States (the UK, France, Portugal, Belgium, and Spain), with some important exceptions (e.g. India, and the Latin American countries). It acts to some extent, and in tension with WTO commitments and former colonial preferences, as the legal basis for substantial development aid. Energy, which used to have a section devoted to it in the Lomé Agreement, appears in the Cotonou Agreement only as a series of passing references,[48] mainly to renewable energy. The promotion of investment promotion—relevant to the substantial investment of EU companies, for example, in Nigeria, Trinidad and Angola—is commented on positively, with the prospect of unspecific EU investment guarantees and future specific investment protection treaties. This aspect was also emphasized in the 2005 and 2010 revisions. The Cotonou Agreement is long on hortatory and other general policy declarations in the style of a preamble or UN General Resolutions, but short on specific mechanisms and obligations in the style of a BIT or the ECT. It reflects a neo-missionary revival in Western countries[49] by providing for a consultation procedure for human rights, democratic principles, the rule of law and corruption, but without the specificity of, for example, the OECD Anti-Corruption Convention.[50]

In line with the current trend in international cooperation, the 2010 revisions also highlighted climate change as a new area of cooperation. This is logical, considering that many of the ACP countries are highly vulnerable to the potential negative effects of climate change (including extreme weather or rising water levels). In line with this, renewable-energy-related cooperation now has a more prominent role than before. As the other side of the coin, the new additions also include a specific reference to environmental measures not being used for protectionist purposes.[51]

It is hard to assess the effectiveness of both the very open-ended goodwill obligations and the massive development aid (including finance) for which the agreement

---

[48] In this context, also the ACP-EU Energy Facility is noteworthy. See Communication from the Commission to the Council and the European Parliament of 26 October 2004 on the future development of the EU Energy Initiative and the modalities for the establishment of an Energy Facility for ACP countries (COM(2004) 711 final).

[49] M. Ottaway, 'Reluctant Missionaries', July–August 2001, *Foreign Policy*, available at: <http://www.foreignpolicy.com/articles/2001/07/01/reluctant_missionaries> (last accessed 6.8.2012).

[50] See generally, L. Low, T. Sprange, and M. Barutciski, 'Global Anti-corruption Standard and Enforcement: Implications for Energy Companies', 3(2) *Journal of World Energy Law and Business* (2010), pp. 166–213.

[51] Second revision, 19 March 2010. Text available at: <http://ec.europa.eu/development/icenter/repository/second_revision_cotonou_agreement_20100311.pdf>.

serves as a legal basis (for the period from 2008 to 2013, the amount allocated for this cooperation is EUR 22.7 billion[52]—not an insignificant amount). One approach is to look at most of the language as a public relations exercise meant to placate the European Parliament and NGOs; the other is to view this as a step towards more effective measures to support good governance. Good governance itself can—if applied and imposed on weaker developing countries—be seen as the right move to make the world a better place, or as the continuation, albeit under different labels, of the economic and cultural dominance over what were formerly colonies, and are now underdeveloped and aid- and finance-dependent countries: i.e. the contemporary format of cultural colonialism with a newly revived, strong missionary element.

6.4.2 Partnership and Cooperation Agreements

Partnership and cooperation agreements envisage neither accession nor a customs union. They provide a basis for economic and trade policy dialogue, as well as for technical assistance. This form has been chosen for the EU's relationship with Russia and most post-Soviet states.[53]

The 1994 Partnership and Cooperation Agreement with Russia is of particular interest from an energy perspective, given Russia's role in relation to the EU's energy supply. It entered into force in 1997, and is a general agreement with objectives ranging from democracy and cultural cooperation to free trade and the transition of the Russian economy to a market-based system.[54] Article 65 deals specifically with energy, cooperation in this field being carried out 'within the principles of the market economy and the European Energy Charter, against a background of the progressive integration of the energy markets in Europe'.[55] The parties agreed to initiate negotiations for a new EU/Russia Agreement to replace the current version at the EU-Russia Summit in June 2008.[56] Negotiations started in July 2008 but the 12 rounds of negotiations that were undertaken by the end of 2012 have not brought these discussions very far.[57] In the field of energy, this instrument has been

[52] Details available at: <http://ec.europa.eu/europeaid/where/acp/overview/cotonou-agreement/index_en.htm>.

[53] Council and Commission Decisions 99/602/EC, 99/614/EC, 99/515/EC, 99/490/EC, 99/491/EC, 98/401/EC, 97/800/EC, 98/149/EC, 99/593/EC, 2009/989/EC on the conclusion of the Partnership and Cooperation Agreement between the European Communities and their Member States, of the one part, and the Republic of Armenia, the Republic of Azerbaijan, Georgia, the Republic of Kazakhstan, the Kyrgyz Republic, the Republic of Moldova, the Russian Federation, Ukraine, and the Republic of Uzbekistan, Tajikistan of the other part, respectively.

[54] Agreement on partnership and cooperation establishing a partnership between the European Communities and their Member States, of one part, and the Russian Federation, of the other part—Protocol 1 on the establishment of a coal and steel contact group—Protocol 2 on mutual administrative assistance for the correct application of customs legislation—Final Act—Exchanges of letters—Minutes of signing, OJ L 327, 28.12.1997, pp. 3–69.

[55] Article 65(1) of the Agreement on partnership and cooperation.

[56] See 'The Joint Statement of the EU-Russia Summit on the Launch of Negotiations for a New EU-Russia Agreement'. Available at: <http://www.eu2008.si/en/News_and_Documents/download_docs/June/0627_eu_RUS-izjava.pdf>.

[57] Generally, see <http://eeas.europa.eu/russia/>. See also, R. Leal-Arcas, 'The EU and Russia as Energy Trading Partners: Friends or Foes?' 14(3) *European Foreign Affairs Review* (2009), pp. 337–66.

largely mute. This is only logical when compared to the developments in other energy-related cooperation efforts aiming at pushing the ideal of a market economy into the Russian energy markets—the Energy Charter Treaty in particular.

6.4.3 Energy Dialogues

The EU has a number of institutionalized Dialogues in place. These Dialogues are often dominated by EU approaches and EU policies (even if coined as 'shared values' and 'shared objectives'). The approach is often that of persuasion (i.e. the EU persuading the partner countries) instead of real negotiation. The Dialogues with developing countries—which enable EU supervision of third countries in terms of internal, domestic, implementation of the Dialogues based on EU standards and the EU's understanding of sufficient performance—are a good example of this.[58] As noted by Leino-Sandberg, the problem is partly the special nature of the EU as an international actor. Given that the EU's position is created through negotiations and bargaining between its 27 Member States, the EU's approach is often already cemented prior to commencement of the Dialogue.[59] This is particularly problematic when institutionalized Dialogues are used to discuss negotiation positions for, say, climate change negotiations.[60]

The situation is somewhat different in energy Dialogues with producing and supplying countries. Here, the EU cannot impose its solutions and views as it can in some other situations. Think of OPEC as the partner in the Dialogue,[61] or Russia. An Energy Dialogue between the EU and Russia was initiated in October 2000, and covers issues such as energy security, energy efficiency, infrastructure, investment, and trade. In essence, the aim of this quite innovative institution established by EU and Russia is to improve the mutual understanding of the energy policies of the two partners. In some ways, the Energy Dialogue has been a successful institution, despite significant shortcomings.

This cooperation represents a policy level cooperation and the actual decision-making powers of the states involved are of course not affected in any way. The stated objective of this partnership is to promote energy security on the European continent, though its actual contribution remains thin. The main example of a positive effect in this respect, at least on paper, is the so-called Early Warning Mechanism, which requires mutual information-sharing in case of potential oil and gas supply and demand problems, including transit. Such problems may be technical, commercial, or political in nature.[62]

---

[58] For this, see P. Leino, 'The Journey Towards all that is Good and Beautiful: Human Rights and "Common Values" as Guiding Principles of EU Foreign Relations Law', in M. Cremona and B. De Witte (eds), *EU Foreign Relations Law* (Oxford: Hart Publishing 2008).

[59] P. Leino, 'The Journey Towards all that is Good and Beautiful: Human Rights and "Common Values" as Guiding Principles of EU Foreign Relations Law', in M. Cremona and B. De Witte (eds), *EU Foreign Relations Law* (Oxford: Hart Publishing 2008), p. 679.

[60] G. Marin Duran and E. Morgera, *Environmental Integration in the EU's External Relations: Beyond Multilateral Dimensions* (Oxford: Hart Publishing 2012), p. 231.

[61] For details, see <http://ec.europa.eu/energy/international/organisations/opec_en.htm>.

[62] On this and other developments, see <http://ec.europa.eu/energy/russia/overview/index_en.htm>.

While the Energy Dialogue may cover a wide range of issues, there are clear differences in emphasis between the parties: while the EU is mainly addressing issues of access to Russian markets and security of EU energy supply, Russia appears concerned about investment in export infrastructure. At least in part because of these differences, the success of the Energy Dialogue in the area of natural gas has been limited. The main point that has been resolved through the Dialogue is the resolution of the destination clause issue.[63] In this sense, the Dialogue has produced positive results.

In addition to these differences, there are also less sensitive areas which are therefore treated in more detail. It is important to note that the Dialogue is not only concerned with oil and gas, although it seems that this was the original emphasis of the parties. Electricity markets and electricity trade were included in the agenda at an early stage, and even nuclear issues are addressed as a central part of this cooperation. One area often debated in this context is energy savings.[64] The fact that this is a much less politically sensitive issue than the trade in natural gas, for example, undoubtedly has a bearing. There are many more common concerns and benefits here than in other areas. Similarly, electricity is much less sensitive because, unlike natural resources, it is not considered to be a strategic asset.[65]

While this partnership might be beneficial for both parties, it still faces significant challenges. Some of the current issues affecting the cooperation with Russia include the gradual foreclosure on investment by companies established in one of these areas into another area. Russia has limited foreign investor participation in developing its natural resource base and the EU has, through the Third Country Clause,[66] done virtually the same.[67] It was specifically noted by the Russian representatives at a meeting as a 'potential' issue that could impair further cooperation. Similarly, environmental issues continue to be a difficult area.[68]

In addition to cooperation, the Energy Dialogue is also used as a platform for discussing sensitive issues upon which the opinions of the parties might diverge. However, as mentioned, the tangible results from these discussions are limited. A good example of this is the fate of long-term upstream gas agreements. While discussions on the negative and positive effects of these agreements continue in the EU, the Dialogue has been used to exchange views on this question,[69] without major breakthroughs.

---

[63] EU-Russia Energy Dialogue, 'The Second Progress Report' (May 2008). Available at: <http://ec.europa.eu/energy/international/bilateral_cooperation/russia/doc/reports/progress2_en.pdf>.

[64] For the developments in this respect, see A.V. Belyi and K.V. Petrichenko, 'Energy Efficiency Policy in Russia', 1 *OGEL* (2011), <http://www.ogel.org>.

[65] Electricity is a secondary energy source, not primary like natural gas or oil.

[66] For the Third Country Clause and its relation to international law and EU-Russia relations, see A. Willems, J. Sul, and Y. Benizri, 'Unbundling as a Defence Mechanism Against Russia: Is the EU Missing the Point?', in K. Talus and P. Fratini (eds), *EU-Russia Energy Relations* (Rixensart: Euroconfidential 2010) and S.S. Haghighi, 'Establishing an External Policy to Guarantee Energy Security in Europe? A Legal Analysis', in M. Roggenkamp and U. Hammer (eds), *European Energy Law Report VI* (Antwerp: Intersentia 2009).

[67] <http://ec.europa.eu/energy/russia/joint_progress/doc/progress9_en.pdf>.

[68] <http://ec.europa.eu/energy/russia/joint_progress/doc/progress9_en.pdf>.

[69] Interim Report by the Parties of the EU-Russia Energy Dialogue, para. 3. Available at: <http://ec.europa.eu/energy/russia/joint_progress/doc/2006_05_25_interim_report_en.pdf> and The Ninth

There is also a bilateral EU-Norway Energy Dialogue mechanism in place. This Dialogue aims primarily at the coordination of energy policies (including research and technological development in the sector) and relations with other energy-producing countries. The current cooperation between Norway and the EU focuses, among other things, on the internal energy market, renewable energy (offshore wind in particular), and Carbon Capture and Storage projects.[70]

Norway is a special case in many ways. It is in a very different position from other external energy producers. It is regarded as 'politically stable and secure'. EU-Norway relations are governed by the European Economic Area (EEA) Agreement, which covers areas such as the single market legislation, including competition law, public procurement and state aid and the free movement of goods. In these areas, Norway is in many ways much like an EU Member State, despite two negative referendums in 1972 and 1994. This is particularly so in the energy sector. First, Norway is under an obligation to implement the internal energy market legislation and must follow the competition law articles of the EEA Agreement, which are identical to those of the EU competition law provisions. Energy issues are, in particular, dealt with in Annex IV of the EEA Agreement. Secondly, in electricity Norway is an integral part of the common Nordic wholesale electricity market and the Nordpool power exchange. The Norwegian energy market authorities are also part of the Nordreg cooperative organization.

Section 6.5 focuses on the multilateral side of EU external energy relations.

6.5 Multilateral Aspects of the EU's External Energy Policy: From Energy Charter Treaty to Energy Community Treaty

Even with the emergence of the Energy Community Treaty, the ECT is still the EU's primary international (institutional) instrument in the energy area, athough its importance for EU decreased significantly (but has not disappeared altogether) after Russia indicated that it would not ratify the ECT and would cease its provisional application.[71]

From its inception, the ECT was conceived, initiated, promoted, and supported by the EU. It expresses the EU interest in safe energy supplies, stable political relationships, and trade and investment along its borders (parallel to TACIS, PHARE,

Progress Report, October 2008. Available at:<http://ec.europa.eu/energy/russia/joint_progress/doc/progress9_en.pdf>.

[70] Commission press release, 'EC-Norway Energy Dialogue: Boosting Cooperation in the Internal Energy Market, Offshore Wind and Carbon Capture and Storage Projects', IP/08/817, 29.5.2008. See also Press Release, 'CCS, Market Liberalisation and Energy Security Dominate the Agenda of the EC-Norway Energy Dialogue', IP/09/849, 28.5.2009 and the Press Release from 22.6.2012, available at: <http://ec.europa.eu/energy/international/bilateral_cooperation/doc/norway/120622_press_announcement.pdf>.

[71] For this, see A. Konoplyanik, 'A Common Russia EU Energy Space (The New EU Russia Partnership Agreement, Acquis Communautaire, The Energy Charter and the New Russian Initiative)', in K. Talus and P. Fratini (eds), *EU-Russia Energy Relations* (Rixensart: Euroconfidentiel 2010).

SYNERGY, cooperation agreements and the establishment of EBRD). Its content is influenced by investment treaty practice, but also by the EU energy policy trends of those days (the Licensing Directive and the first internal energy market directives). With the problems relating to the Transit Protocol and the non-ratification of the ECT by Russia, the nature of the ECT is now changing. Here, a potential problem with the close proximity of the ECT to the EU has been flagged:

'One wonders to what extent this Treaty, with an independent Secretariat and Conference, can become a self-sustaining international arrangement able to survive independent of the European Union. There is a public perception that the ECT is a key instrument of EU policy towards the East, and it is perhaps not surprising that the Treaty is still widely, and incorrectly, called the "European" Energy Charter Treaty. One may question whether this proximity will allow the Energy Charter process to evolve outside of the flows of EU energy and Eastern policy.'[72]

This section examines the Energy Charter Treaty as a part of the external elements of EU energy law and policy. In keeping with the approach taken in this book, the focus will be on the development of the ECT over time, rather than on detailed examination of its legal provisions. As it is in many ways a logical extension of the examination of the ECT, the chapter also discusses the Energy Community Treaty.

6.5.1 Energy Charter Treaty: Past, Present, and Future

6.5.1.1 The Evolution of the Energy Markets and the Energy Charter Treaty

Two main factors contributed to the creation of the ECT. The events of the early 1990s—the dissolution of the USSR and the COMECON system, the fall of the Berlin Wall and related events—offered a window of opportunity for East-West cooperation and the possibility to create an international law instrument to facilitate this type of transnational cooperation between former ideological opposites. However, it is quite likely that the ECT would have seen the light of the day without these events. The increasingly international nature of energy markets and energy trade also called, and still calls, for the creation of this type of international institution. The growth of international energy trade is complemented by new international instruments and international institutions supporting this internationalization development.

Energy markets have developed in stages and through a particular logic. The first step involved local markets with one producer and few customers, and within a specific territory or state. At the very first stage, the development of the gas sector usually started with vertically-integrated local companies, which provided limited supplies to the nearby located consumers. The initial investment that had to be made at this stage was smaller than it would be in the later stages. This initial stage was then followed by the process of internationalization, where the geographical

---

[72] C. Bamberger and T. Wälde, 'The Energy Charter Treaty', in M. Roggenkamp et al. (eds), *Energy Law in Europe* (Oxford: OUP 2008).

markets expanded and the trade became international, or regional. Here, markets evolved to include more complex commercial institutions. This process led first to regional markets, which is largely the current situation. The final stage is that of the future internationalization or even globalization of energy trade. The globalization trend then leads to globalization of the markets for energy products, as has been the case for oil and coal to a certain extent. For gas, there is no international market but only regional markets. However, we can see a trend towards that type of development in the case of LNG. This, however, requires future development and investment.

It is against this background that the ECT is examined. As an investment protection and stimulation mechanism, the ECT represents the limits of the political process in the international arena. At the time of its negotiation, and today, it is the leading multilateral framework in this area. It introduced several innovations and pushed international law relating to this area to new levels.

6.5.1.2 Why an International Law Instrument—Why the ECT?

In the first stage, local or national markets, there are two options, the choice depending largely on the maturity of the country's legal and socio-economic situation. In developing or transition economies, stabilization is required in order to attract investment. Given the state of national legislation or political and/or legal institutions, there is a need to create mechanisms which increase stability for large and capital-intensive investment. This type of risk usually requires a project-specific response, which can be included in the investment agreement with the state (by way of production-sharing agreement, concession, host government agreement on pipelines, and so on). At the time of the dissolution of Soviet Union, this situation was characteristic of the Russian legal and political system. The movement from a socialist system towards a market-based economy created transition risks. More generally, this issue affected all the ex-Soviet countries who decided to change their system. However, it must be noted that this type of transition risk is not absent from the more developed market economies. Just consider the progress in the EU energy markets from the first, to the second and to, currently, the third energy market package,[73] or some of the measures adopted to address climate change. These constant legislative changes also create legal uncertainty about future regulation and the impact these changes have on prior investment.[74] The changes in the levels of unbundling are but one example of changes undermining investment stability for long-term energy investment.

---

[73] Also, the case-by-case antitrust treatment of long-term contracts in the EU significantly increases business risks for the market actors. See K. Talus, 'Just What is the Scope of the Essential Facilities Doctrine in the Energy Sector: Third Party Access-friendly Interpretation in the EU v. Contractual Freedom in the US', 48(5) *Common Market Law Review* (2011).

[74] This risk has been emphasized in K. Talus, *Vertical Natural Gas Transportation Capacity, Upstream Commodity Contracts and EU Competition Law* (Alphen aan den Rijn: Kluwer Law International 2011).

The second option is then the creation of a predictable and stable domestic legal framework for energy investment. Here, specific investment laws as well as other related laws, on taxation for example, are designed to provide investment stability, and the protection offered does not cover a specific agreement or project but is wider, covering all types of investment activities. These options are available and typically used when the projects are national in scope and energy markets are local or national.

The second stage in the development of the market, brought about through the internationalization of energy markets, creates a need for an international response to international projects and markets. Here, international law instruments come into play. Again, there are two options at this stage. The first is to enter into bilateral agreements with the main commercial partners: bilateral investment treaties ('BITs') and double taxation treaties. Such instruments have a long history and nowadays number in their thousands. However, one problem with this approach is that the relevant instruments date back to different decades and, as such, are the product of different trends in international law and international relations. This is also reflected in their content, which differs in each case (although strong similarities also exist).

The second option is the use of multilateral instruments and treaties. This is a more recent phenomenon. Unlike BITs, a multilateral framework applies to all those countries which have opted to join the framework in the same manner and its application is therefore more predictable. Well-known multilateral legal instruments (which are international treaties) include the WTO and the ECT, but the EU legal system itself can be regarded as a multilateral legal framework. The focus here is on the ECT.

6.5.1.3 *The Energy Charter Treaty and its Origins*

The ECT is an energy-specific multilateral instrument covering issues such as free trade in energy-related products (based on GATT/WTO rules), freedom of transit (as specified in the Transit Protocol—here, certain parallels to the WTO can be seen, although the ECT takes the transit issues much further), the protection and promotion of foreign investment (national treatment/most favoured nation treatment), and dispute settlement (both between states and between investors and states). The ECT's objective is to 'establish a legal framework in order to promote long-term cooperation in the energy field, based on complementarities and mutual benefits, in accordance with the objectives and principles of the Charter'.[75] These principles include secure energy supply and sustainable economic development.[76]

Given the nature of energy investments—which are highly capital-intensive and have long lead times and payback periods—and the internationalization of the energy trade, it is no surprise that this industry-specific investment protection scheme appeared in the 1990s.

[75] Article 2 of the Energy Charter Treaty.
[76] Energy Charter Secretariat, 'The Energy Charter Treaty and Related Documents—A Legal Framework for International Energy Cooperation', p. 13.

The process leading towards this legally binding document dates back to the early 1990s and was from the beginning geared towards securing EU energy supplies.[77] The ECT was signed in 1994 and entered into force in April 1998 after the 30th signature. The initial focus of the ECT process was East-West energy cooperation within Europe[78] and the major stakeholders in the early 1990s were the EU and its Member States, the Russian Federation, and the Energy Charter Secretariat itself. In essence, the need for this international law framework came from the uncertainty created by the fall of the Soviet Union. This was also reflected in the motivations of the parties to the ECT process in the early days.

For the EU, the major driver behind the ECT was the need to use international law to protect existing East-West and anticipated West-East investment flows. The aim to export the Western model of the rule of law and the EU energy *acquis* to the ex-Soviet states was also a motivating factor. This last issue was obviously based on the first EU energy law package, the content of which is strongly reflected in the ECT legal framework.

For Russia, the main driver was the need to compensate for the lack of an adequate legal framework for energy investment (and more generally any investment), which was a result of the transition from the former socialist system to a capitalist system. This compensation was sought through adopting the most advanced international law solutions for energy trade and energy investment protection and stimulation. The idea was of course to bring in much-needed foreign capital and investment.

Both sides believed that the creation of common rules of the game for energy markets and energy investment would bring about the necessary stability for cooperation between the two partners.

The Energy Charter Secretariat was the third stakeholder in the negotiations, and was to a significant extent to thank for their successful conclusion. This issue, while important for the final outcome of the ECT process in the early days, is not discussed here.

6.5.1.4 *The Energy Charter Treaty and Energy Charter Process*

As mentioned, the Energy Charter Treaty covers various areas of energy cooperation, including investment, trade, energy efficiency, and dispute settlement. It applies to energy materials, energy products, and energy-related equipment. It has a significant group of stakeholders including over 50 Member States, over 20 observer states and over 10 international organizations as observers.[79]

---

[77] S.S. Haghighi, *Energy Security: The External Legal Relations of the European Union with Major Oil and Gas Supplying Countries* (Oxford: Hart Publishing 2007), p. 188. The process was initiated in June 1990 when the European Council gave the Commission the task of finding the best way to implement the cooperation between ex-Soviet countries and the EU. Further to this request, the Commission proposed that a European Energy Charter be created. This has been seen as the first formal step in the ECT process. (C. Bamberger and T. Wälde, 'The Energy Charter Treaty', in M. Roggenkamp et al. (eds), *Energy Law in Europe* (Oxford: OUP 2008), pp. 145–94.)

[78] Illustratively put in the heading of one of the most significant publications on ECT: T. Wälde (ed.), *The Energy Charter Treaty: An East-West Gateway for Investment and Trade* (London: Kluwer Law International 1996).

[79] For the list of members and observers, see <http://www.encharter.org/index.php?id=61>.

The Energy Charter Process is the name given to the process of implementation of the Energy Charter Treaty, which is based on monitoring procedures with regular reviews of the implementation of ECT provisions in Member States. It is, in essence, a highly specialized forum for advanced discussions (in the working groups) on the evolution of energy markets and new risks for energy projects that might arise from such evolution. Once identified, it attempts to address these risks in cooperation with governments and other stakeholders. As such, it is also a platform for further developments and the preparation of new legally binding instruments to reduce those related risks. In this sense, the role of the Energy Charter Process is to deepen (in terms of moving further on the detail: for example, Article 7 on transit has been complemented by the Transit Protocol which goes into much more detail in terms of transit) and broaden (both in terms of geographical coverage and product scope) the ECT. Given recent developments, with Russia withdrawing from the provisional application, but not from the Energy Charter Process itself, the process can be used to improve the Treaty or to discuss its details.

6.5.1.5 *The ECT as the First Multilateral Investment Agreement*

The ECT is based on well-established BIT practice, and is clearly influenced by Chapter XI of the North American Free Trade Agreement (NAFTA) (on investment), the now-abandoned OECD project on Multilateral Agreement for Investment, as well as the EU's first energy law package.[80] It represents the combined effect and legal force of more than 1,200 BITs.

The ECT includes two types of investment protection. It contains binding 'hard law' obligations for the post-establishment phase of energy investment (non-discrimination, etc.), and 'soft law' obligations for the pre-establishment phase (the stage of making the investment). It provides protection against certain key political and regulatory risks, including expropriation or nationalization, breaches of individual investment contracts, or unjustified restrictions on the transfer of funds. It provides for most-favoured-nation (MFN) treatment and national treatment. It also prohibits discrimination, etc.

These, and other, substantive rules on investment protection are reinforced by the provision of access to binding international dispute resolution mechanisms. The ECT also provides for both state-to-state and investor-to-state arbitration. The latter mechanism gives the investor direct access to his or her chosen investment arbitration forum: ICSID, ICC Stockholm or UNCITRAL. The awards rendered under these mechanisms are final and directly enforceable.

In terms of legal innovation, Article 10 on the promotion, protection and treatment of investments contains two interesting principles:

(1) *Standstill* in Article 10(5)(a): 'Each Contracting Party shall, as regards the Making of Investments in its Area, endeavour to limit to the minimum

---

[80] But also the Directives on Transit and Hydrocarbons Licensing Directives, Articles 101 and 102 TFEU and notions of special responsibility incumbent on State and private enterprises with a publicly privileged but dominant market position. See C. Bamberger and T. Wälde, 'The Energy Charter Treaty', in M. Roggenkamp et al. (eds), *Energy Law in Europe* (Oxford: OUP 2008).

the exceptions to the Treatment described in paragraph (3) [national treatment and MFN]';

(2) *Rollback* in Article 10(5)(b): 'Each Contracting Party shall, as regards the Making of Investments in its Area, endeavour to: progressively remove existing restrictions affecting Investors of other Contracting Parties.'

The standstill provision requires the state not to introduce new restrictions on investment. The rollback provision requires reduction of all investment restrictions. These are not legally binding obligations, as the use of the word 'endeavour' suggests. However, they do reflect the general objective of the provisions of the Treaty on investment protection.

6.5.1.6 *The ECT and its Geographical Scope*

The initial focus of the ECT process was East-West energy cooperation within Europe, in the widest sense. This was a natural consequence of the widening geographical scope of the energy markets, the internationalization of European energy markets and the developments in the internal arena more generally. While certain OECD countries like the US and Canada participated in the negotiations, they did not ultimately sign up to the ECT.[81] The geographical focus has now been widened significantly[82] to include the Caspian region and even Japan and Australia. The current expansion of observer countries is quite logical, and includes North African, Eurasian, and Australasian countries. This development was initiated by the 2004 Policy Review[83] which directed attention to these geographical areas. These regions and developments reflect the internationalization of the energy markets and the energy value chain.

However, despite the continuing discussions, none of the main suppliers of gas to the EU—i.e. Russia, Algeria, and Norway—have ratified the ECT.[84] More generally, it is rather obvious from the list of Member States that those countries that are keen to adopt the ECT are the consuming countries, not the producing countries.[85] This is without doubt the major shortcoming of the ECT from the

---

[81] Illustratively put in the heading of one of the most significant publications on ECT, T. Wälde (ed.), *The Energy Charter Treaty: An East-West Gateway for Investment and Trade* (London: Kluwer Law International 1996).

[82] This was specifically noted by the Secretary General of the ECT secretariat: <http://www.enchar-ter.org/fileadmin/user_upload/SG_s_speeches/ECT_10th_anniversary_speech_rev.pdf>.

[83] CC 298 and Summary Record the Fifteenth Meeting of the Energy Charter Conference (CC 294).

[84] Although Russia did apply the ECT provisionally until summer 2009, which meant that Russia applied the ECT 'to the extent that such provisional application is not inconsistent with its consti-tution, law or regulations', according to Article 45 of the ECT. For the provisional application, see K. Hobér, 'The Energy Charter Treaty—Recent Developments', 5 (2007) 2 *OGEL* or C. Bamberger and T. Wälde, 'The Energy Charter Treaty', in M. Roggenkamp et al. (eds), *Energy Law in Europe* (Oxford: OUP 2008).

[85] D. Doeh, A. Popov, and S. Nappert, 'Russia and the Energy Charter Treaty: Common Interests or Irreconcilable Differences?', 5 (2007) 2 *OGEL*; and C. Bamberger and T. Wälde, 'The Energy Charter Treaty', in M. Roggenkamp et al. (eds), *Energy Law in Europe* (Oxford: OUP 2008).

EU perspective. However, from this EU perspective, it must be noted that the list of Member States includes Ukraine, which is a significant transit country for the EU.[86] While it is significant that some of the most of the ambitious 'emerging oil and gas producers' are part of the ECT community, the Caspian region and Kazakhstan in particular, and that this could prove to be very significant in the future from an EU perspective,[87] it is also possible that these countries will withdraw from the ECT when their economic or political situation so demands.

6.5.1.7 *The Development of the Activities of the ECT and the Energy Charter Process in Terms of Focus*

Looking at the activities and priorities of the ECT and the Energy Charter Process, it is also possible to see development and movement along the cross-border energy value chain. The activities and priorities of the ECT in the early 1990s were largely focused on production and upstream supply of energy. Towards the end of the 1990s and the early 2000s, the focus shifted to include the whole value chain, including trade and transit, thus facilitating risk-mitigation along the entire supply chain. Energy security also emerged as a major theme during this period. Current activities seem largely concerned with such issues as energy efficiency and environmental protection, thus moving the focus from production and transit to consumption (demand and equipment). This might signal a more permanent shift in focus. Furthermore, the number of topics and areas covered in the Energy Charter Process has been growing over the years, and an increasing number of investment arbitrations are taking place under the ECT framework.

6.5.1.8 *Attitudes of the Key Parties: The EU and Russia*

6.5.1.8.1 Current Issues from a Russian Perspective

As discussed, Russia has not ratified the ECT. There are various reasons for this. Politically, there has been a quite natural reaction from Russia to the external pressure to ratify the ECT, principally exerted by the EU and the European Commission.

Russia also considers that, from a producer perspective, the balance of the ECT is too consumer-friendly, and does not contain the necessary balance between the consumer and producer countries. In addition to Russia's more valid concerns, there have also been misunderstandings and misinterpretations of the ECT on the Russian side (for instance, that the ECT would force Gazprom to open up gas transportation system to all at the low domestic tariff rates).

The Transit Protocol has been one of the major obstacles to Russian acceptance of the ECT—a more serious obstacle than the other objections against the ECT raised in discussions within Russia. Negotiations on the Transit Protocol were

---

[86] Ukraine has also ratified the Energy Community Treaty. The Ukrainian Parliament ratified this Treaty on the 15 December 2010.

[87] For a more detailed discussion, see also A. Konoplyanik and T. Wälde, 'Energy Charter Treaty and its Role in International Energy', 24(4) *Journal of Energy and Natural Resources Law* (2007), pp. 523–58.

initiated in 1991. Negotiations on the text of the Protocol started in 2000, and were provisionally suspended in 2003 after it became clear that the text could not be unanimously adopted as it stood.[88] The thorniest issues preventing the adoption of the Transit Protocol related to EU-Russia relations. Before Russia gave notification that it would not ratify the ECT and would cease to apply the ECT provisionally,[89] the most significant issues were: (1) the Regional Economic Integration Organisation (REIO) clause;[90] (2) the issues relating to access to pipelines and tariff-setting procedure;[91] and (3) the right-of-first-refusal on renewal of transit terms for existing users.[92] These issues mostly relate to the ever-widening geographical scope of the EU, and are explained below.

Because of the historical Cold War era division of Europe, the delivery points for Russian gas were previously located on the border of Western Europe and Soviet-controlled Eastern Europe. The choice of delivery point was naturally based on the possibility of influencing or controlling the transmission of gas on either side of the 'Iron Curtain'. The situation changed radically in 2004 (changes had, of course, already taken place prior to this in the 1990s) since the delivery points for Russian gas moved from the EU border to a location within the EU.[93]

These evolutions brought about significant changes, in that title and the related risks were now being transferred to the buyer (or a third party) at the EU border. With the 2004 enlargement, the delivery points were suddenly located in the EU area, and Gazprom found itself in a situation in which its gas was flowing in EU pipelines which were now subject to EU regulation. This change was significant and further complicated the situation with Gazprom's long-term agreements.

The Gazprom gas that reaches the EU customer is, structurally speaking, subject to various contractual arrangements. For the purposes of our discussion, it suffices to separate the agreement to purchase gas from the agreement to purchase transfer capacity in a pipeline. Under the current scheme, the customer (for example, the Italian company ENI) buys an agreed amount of gas from Gazprom, which delivers it to one of the delivery points (for example, Baumgarten). Until delivery, transmission of the contractual amount of gas is Gazprom's responsibility. Prior to reaching

---

[88] See generally: <http://www.encharter.org>.

[89] For this, see A. Konoplyanik, 'A Common Russia EU Energy Space (The New EU Russia Partnership Agreement, Acquis Communautaire, The Energy Charter and the New Russian Initiative)', in K. Talus and P. Fratini (eds), *EU-Russia Energy Relations* (Rixensart: Euroconfidentiel 2010).

[90] It seems that while the two other points may be overcome through negotiations, the REIO clause is the most difficult item to resolve. The EU refuses to allow the Transit Protocol to be applicable to transport within the EU area.

[91] Auctions as a method of transit capacity allocation and the requirement of cost-reflectiveness of transit tariffs. The Transit Protocol requires that all transit tariffs be cost reflective. Through negotiations that lead to Article 10bis, the issue was largely solved.

[92] For an explanation of these difficulties see, for example, C. Bamberger and T. Wälde, 'The Energy Charter Treaty', in M. Roggenkamp et al. (eds), *Energy Law in Europe* (Oxford: OUP 2008); D. Doeh, A. Popov, and S. Nappert, 'Russia and the Energy Charter Treaty: Common Interests or Irreconcilable Differences?', 5(2) *OGEL* (2007).

[93] A very detailed discussion is provided in A. Konoplyanik, 'Russian Gas to Europe: From Long-term Contracts, On-border Trade and Destination Clauses to … ?' 23(3) *Journal of Energy and Natural Resources Law* (2005), p. 282.

the Baumgarten delivery point, the gas travels through Slovakia and the Czech Republic, both EU Member States. In order to get the gas to the delivery point, Gazprom must contract with the Slovak and Czech gas pipeline operators to ensure capacity in their pipelines. The problem is obvious: a mismatch in the duration of the two separate agreements and the impossibility of renewing the transportation agreement makes it impossible for Gazprom to fulfil its contractual obligations.[94]

In the past, this mismatch problem did not exist as long-term capacity reservations were concluded for the amount of gas specified in the long-term gas supply agreement (also reflected in the capacity purchase agreement). Today, the situation regarding long-term capacity reservations is more complicated.[95]

The transmission of gas to Europe by Gazprom was not previously affected by competition law concerns. Today, given the efforts to apply competition law in the energy sector and the growing congestion problems, this is an increasing concern for Gazprom.[96] It therefore comes as no surprise that long-term gas supply agreements (the question of the so-called 'right of first refusal') and access to pipelines remain among the principal issues preventing Russia from ratifying the Energy Charter Treaty.[97] And because of these, and other, concerns, Russia notified the Depository of the Treaty in October 2009 that it would not ratify the ECT and would cease to apply the ECT provisionally.[98] It has also suggested the negotiation of a new investment treaty.[99]

These concerns should be taken seriously. It is crucial to recognize that the EU is not alone in the world and must consider the concerns of its partners with an open mind. For Russia eventually to join the ECT, substantiated and valid Russian concerns must be addressed (though at the same time it must be stressed that not all Russian concerns are well-founded or valid—not even close—as discussed).

---

[94] This approach follows the scheme of a more detailed analysis of the problem: see A. Konoplyanik, 'Russian Gas to Europe: From Long-term Contracts, On-border Trade and Destination Clauses to … ?'. 23(3) *Journal of Energy and Natural Resources Law* (2005), p. 282.

[95] K. Talus, *Vertical Natural Gas Transportation Capacity, Upstream Commodity Contracts and EU Competition Law* (Alphen aan den Rijn: Kluwer Law International 2011).

[96] For criticism to the approach of the Commission under general competition law, see K. Talus, 'Just What is the Scope of the Essential Facilities Doctrine in the Energy Sector: Third Party Access-friendly Interpretation in the EU v. Contractual Freedom in the US', 48(5) *Common Market Law Review* (2011).

[97] For an explanation of the current difficulties in the ECT process, see, for example, C. Bamberger and T. Wälde, 'The Energy Charter Treaty', in M. Roggenkamp et al. (eds) *Energy Law in Europe* (Oxford: OUP 2008) and D. Doeh, A. Popov, and S. Nappert, 'Russia and the Energy Charter Treaty: Common Interests or Irreconcilable Differences?', 5(2) *OGEL* (2007). For the provisional application by Russia, see K. Hober, 'The Energy Charter Treaty—Recent Developments', *OGEL* (2007) Vol. 5. For the right of first refusal, see A. Konoplyanik, 'Stiff Competition Ahead—As Russia Moots Ways to Increase Presence on European Gas Market', 2(1) *OGEL* (2004). See also 'Putting a Price on Energy: International Pricing Mechanisms for Oil and Gas' (2007) Energy Charter Treaty Secretariat, p. 174.

[98] For this, see A. Konoplyanik, 'A Common Russia EU Energy Space (The New EU Russia Partnership Agreement, Acquis Communautaire, The Energy Charter and the New Russian Initiative)', in K. Talus and P. Fratini (eds), *EU-Russia Energy Relations* (Rixensart: Euroconfidential 2010).

[99] Before the notification to the contrary, Russia had agreed to apply the ECT provisionally. This meant, according to Article 45 of the ECT, that it applied the ECT 'to the extent that such provisional application is not inconsistent with its constitution, law or regulations'. For an analysis of the proposal and the background see: 'OGEL Special on EU-Russia Relations', 2 *OGEL* (2009), available at <http://www.ogel.org>.

However, Russia should recognize that ratification of the ECT would bring it a number of benefits. It would, first, protect Russian investments abroad. Here, the risk created by the EU's measures to liberalize the energy market is particularly relevant. The fact that it does not seem very likely that Russian efforts to come up with an alternative to the ECT will result in much speaks in favour of Russian ratification of the current ECT. Compared with the early 1990s, when there was a window of political opportunity, the present day political atmosphere is not as favourable to this new Treaty. The Russian side must also distinguish between valid concerns and those which are based on misinterpretation of the ECT, or possibly even voiced without having read the text of the ECT!

6.5.1.8.2 Some Issues from the European Front: It's not all about Russia

Even if it is the Russian Federation that has withdrawn from the provisional application of the ECT, Russia is not the only one causing problems. Arguably, the EU is partially blocking Russian access. Several issues on the EU side have made the negotiations rather problematic, including:

1. long-term monopolization of participation in the Energy Charter Process by DG Energy (formerly DG TREN) at a low level and without adequate coordination with and/or within the EU Member States;

2. absolute priorization of the norms of the *acquis Communautaire* and unwillingness even to discuss the issues relating to the relationship between the EU's energy law and the ECT;

3. unwillingness to resolve the issues relating to intra-EU transit and the REIO clause;

4. attempts to use the ECT as a subordinated instrument of EU external policy; and

5. diminished interest in the Energy Charter Treaty in favour of the Energy Community Treaty.

However, there is also fault on the Russian side. Such difficulties include Russia's negative attitude towards (the political leadership of) the Secretariat after the January 2009 Russia-Ukraine gas crisis—which spread to include the whole Treaty and the Energy Charter Process. The long-term lack of formal internal organization and coordination between Russian State agencies in relation to participation in the Energy Charter Process has also proved problematic. The fact that Russia is not a member of the ECT but only a signatory is not a reason for non-participation in the process (or a reason not to send a negotiation team to the meetings!). Just look at Norway, which is a signatory of the ECT but not a Member State: Norway actively pursues and defends its interests. This is not always the case with Russia. In a situation where Russia is not present, why would the REIO clause be discussed at all?

It seems that the focus is on the Russian attitude to the ECT. In addition to and not instead of this, a more balanced approach reflecting the political and practical realities should be adopted. This would include a discussion of the EU's attitude towards the ECT. Only if this is done, can we move towards a lasting solution.

6.5.1.9 *The Growing Gap between the ECT and the EU Energy Acquis*

When the ECT was first negotiated in the early 1990s, it was largely based on the approach taken in the first EU energy market directives. There was a clear correlation between the two. Then the second energy market package emerged in 2003 and the level of liberalization between the ECT and the EU energy *acquis* started to diverge. The new unbundling and third party access rules moved EU energy regulation to a deeper and more intrusive level. The third party access provisions under various directives provide an example of this. Regulated third party access is not required by the ECT. Nor was it required under the first energy market directives, which included a choice between regulated and negotiated third party access. This freedom of choice was eliminated from the subsequent directives (in 2003 and 2009). This growing gap in the levels of liberalization between ECT and EU is the first dimension of the problem.

At the same time, the enlargement of the EU in an eastward direction took place, increasing the number of Member States, at first from 15 to 25 and then to 27. In this regard it should also be noted that the EFTA countries also implement most of the EU energy *acquis*, bringing the number of countries applying EU energy laws to 30. In addition, Energy Community Treaty Member States also apply the first and second energy market packages. The potential for conflict between the more liberalized EU energy *acquis* and the ECT as the minimum standard for its Member States (those not members of the EU or the Energy Community Treaty) grows in tandem with the number of Member States in each of the legal systems.

The European Commission's approach seems to be that the EU energy *acquis* is the dominant legal framework and that international law will have to adapt in order to correlate with EU energy law. In line with this, it seems that in the mind of the Commission, any and all conflicts fall under the competence of the ECJ (and not international arbitration). An interesting situation might have arisen had the proposal for mandatory ownership unbundling as a part of the third energy market package in 2009 been accepted by the European Parliament and the Council. In this situation, companies would have been able to initiate arbitral proceedings (under Article 30) against the EU under the ECT (claiming expropriation). Here, the increasing gap between the two legal systems creates a situation where the ECT can provide international law protection against excessive liberalization in the EU.

Interestingly, the relationship between the EU energy *acquis* and the ECT was one of the issues at stake in Case C-264/09, *Commission v Slovak Republic*. In this case, AG Jääskinen was of the opinion that the detailed provisions contained in Directive 2003/54 could not be overridden by the more general provisions contained in the Energy Charter Treaty.[100] He also took the view that EU energy law as it stands under Directive 2003/54 and Regulation No 1228/2003 cannot be considered as failing to achieve the standards required by the Energy Charter Treaty insofar as investments falling within the *ratione temporis* of those legislative acts are

---

[100] Case C-264/09, *Commission v Slovak Republic*, judgment of 15 September 2011 (not reported at time of writing), para. 61.

concerned. Moreover, with respect to the enjoyment and protection of investments, the general level of protection of fundamental rights provided by EU law affords protection to investors, which fulfils the obligations resulting from Articles 10(1) and 13(1) of the Energy Charter Treaty. Interestingly, the AG adopted the interpretation familiar from the *Kadi*[101] and *Al Barakaat*[102] cases heard in the Court of First Instance (now the General Court)[103] and noted that the capacity reservation contract at stake in that case was protected by Article 307(1) EC (now 351(1) TFEU), instead of the applicable international law instruments (the ECT and a BIT between Slovakia and Switzerland).

6.6 The Exportation of the EU Energy *Acquis*: From the ECT to the Energy Community Treaty

The EU clearly regards the exportation of its energy legislation to third countries as its preferred *modus operandi*. The EU attempts to expand the geographical area of implementation of the energy *acquis* in different ways, using different methods (formal legal methods and softer methods). Harder and more formal methods include the enlargement process and integration of new countries into the EU, the creation of the Energy Community Treaty bringing South East Europe under the umbrella of the EU energy *acquis* and expanding membership of this organization further east (Ukraine, Moldova, and so on). The softer methods include EU neighbourhood policies with North African or CIS countries and various memoranda of understanding with the CIS and Caspian countries. There was an attempt to adopt a similar approach with Russia, but this was abandoned for political reasons. In a similar way, various partnerships have been entered into as a softer method of gradually expanding the geographical scope of the EU *acquis*, including in the energy field.

6.6.1 The Energy Community Treaty

While the ECT was clearly inspired by the approach of the first EU energy market package, further integration and regulation of the markets through the ECT mechanism became—understandably—difficult. The reason for this was that Russia and other resource-rich and powerful nations would not compromise their approach to energy markets. The Energy Community Treaty was the next step in exporting the EU energy *acquis*. Based on various memoranda of understanding from 2002 and 2003, the Energy Community Treaty was signed on 25 October 2005 by the EU and the (nine, at time of wiritng) Member States of the Energy Community.[104]

---

[101] Case T-315/01, *Kadi* [2005] ECR II-03649.
[102] Case T-306/01, *Yusuf and Al Barakaat* [2005] ECR II-03533.
[103] G. De Burca, 'The EU, the European Court of Justice and the International Legal Order after Kadi', 1(51) *Harvard International Law Journal* (2009).
[104] At the time of writing the members are Albania, Bosnia and Herzegovina, Croatia, the former Yugoslav Republic of Macedonia, Moldova, Montenegro Serbia, Ukraine, and UNMIK. In addition,

In addition to the substantive provisions, the Treaty formalizes the institutional set up created though the above-mentioned memoranda of understanding and the Tirana Declaration. These institutions mirror those of the EU: there is a Ministerial Council (the role of which is similar to the EU Council), a Permanent High Level Group (much like the European Commission, it prepares Council decisions and ensures follow-up), a regulatory board, gas and electricity fora (which have a similar role to the Florence and Madrid fora), and a Secretariat.[105] The Secretariat reviews the proper implementation of the obligations contained in the Treaty by the Member States and submits an annual progress report to the Ministerial Council. As such, the Secretariat also acts as a 'guardian of the Energy Community Treaty'.[106]

The objectives of the Energy Community Treaty were described by the Commission in the following passage:

'Energy Community is about investments, economic development, security of energy supply and social stability; but—more than this—the Energy Community is also about solidarity, mutual trust and peace. The very existence of the Energy Community, only ten years after the end of the Balkan conflict, is a success in itself, as it stands as the first common institutional project undertaken by the non-European Union countries of South East Europe.'[107]

Regardless of its positive impact on trust and peace, it seems that the Energy Community Treaty is essentially inspired by two somewhat related objectives: EU energy security and the strong commitment to the export of the EU energy *acquis* to the neighbouring region. While an analogy can be drawn with the creation of the European Steel and Coal Community, which was the genesis of the EU,[108] it seems that the current focus of the Treaty framework is rather on EU energy security and the export of EU energy laws.[109] This type of approach is also visible on the website of the Treaty Secretariat: 'As of February 2011 [accession of Moldova and Ukraine], the Treaty rather aims at implementing EU energy policy in non-EU countries.'

The substantive provisions of the Energy Community Treaty identify certain EU law instruments which the Member States have to implement. The Treaty refers to the Second Internal Energy Market Package for electricity and gas from 2003.

---

14 EU Member States are 'participants' in the process (Austria, Bulgaria, Cyprus, the Czech Republic, France, Germany, Greece, Hungary, Italy, the Netherlands, Romania, Slovakia, Slovenia, and the UK) and Georgia, Norway, and Turkey have the status of Observers.

[105] M. Hunt and R. Karova, 'The Energy *Acquis* Under the Energy Community Treaty and the Integration of South East European Electricity Markets: An Uneasy Relationship?', in B. Delvaux, M. Hunt, and K. Talus (eds), *EU Energy Law and Policy Issues* (Brussels: Euroconfidentiel 2010), pp. 51–86.

[106] Report from the Commission to the European Parliament and the Council under Article 7 of Decision 2006/500/EC (COM(2011) 105 final) 10.3.2011.

[107] Report from the Commission to the European Parliament and the Council under Article 7 of Decision 2006/500/EC (COM(2011) 105 final) 10.3.2011.

[108] Press Release, 'The EU and South East Europe sign a historic treaty to boost energy integration', IP/05/1346, 25.10.2005. Clearly, the Balkan region had come from a period of war and conflict prior to the Energy Community Treaty. However, the focus has now moved beyond that region (with accession of Moldova and Ukraine).

[109] This was also underlined in K. Yafimava, *The Transit Dimension of EU Energy Security: Russian Gas Transit Across Ukraine, Belarus and Moldova* (Oxford: OUP 2011), p. 50.

In addition to this, certain directives on environmental protection and the promotion of renewable energy, and the main antitrust and state aid rules, had to be implemented. The subsequent additions and modifications to the EU energy *acquis* were made on the basis of decisions of the Ministerial Council. The directives on security of electricity and gas supply were added in 2007, while those on the energy performance of buildings, energy labelling, and energy end-use efficiency, and energy services were added in 2012.[110] In 2011, the Third Energy Package was added to the list of EU law that the Energy Community Member States had to implement (by January 2015). The contracting parties have moreover agreed to start implementing parts of Directive 2009/28/EC on the promotion of renewable energy and the 'Third Package' on the internal market in electricity and gas on a voluntary basis, as a first step, following recommendations issued by the Ministerial Council.[111]

Coming back to the two objectives (in practice, regardless of references to other objectives contained in the legal instruments) of security and the export of EU law, the accession of Moldova and Ukraine clearly reflect the first objective. By including transit countries within the ambit of EU law (and the EU institutions, since these, the European Commission in particular, have a significant role in the Energy Community[112]) the EU's control over flows of gas is greatly increased.[113] Considering the conflicts between Russia and Ukraine in this respect, it is hardly a surprise that the EU would like to play a stronger role in this country and in its gas trade with Russia. As noted by Yafimava, while there are clear benefits for the EU in the accession of Ukraine and Moldova, the benefits for these two countries from such accession (given the limitation on sovereignty involved) are much less obvious. She suggests that their willingness to sign up may be attributed to their aspirations to join the EU, which they are keen to avoid compromising by stalling on Energy Community membership.[114] In this regard, Hunt and Karova have referred to the 'EU membership carrot'.[115]

As far as export of the EU energy *acquis* is concerned, the first obvious question to be asked is how a legal regime incapable of achieving its intended objective can be exported. The Energy Community was initially based on the 2003 Energy Law Package, which at the time of implementation in the Energy Community countries

---

[110] Report from the Commission to the European Parliament and the Council under Article 7 of Decision 2006/500/EC (COM(2011) 105 final) 10.3.2011.

[111] Decision on the implementation of Directive 2009/72/EC, Directive 2009/73/EC, Regulation (EC) No 714/2009 and Regulation (EC) No 715/2009 and amending Articles 11 and 59 of the Energy Community Treaty, Ministerial Council Decision D/2011/02/MC-EnC, 5.10.2011.

[112] The EU is not only a party to the Energy Community Treaty but also acts as the the permanent Vice-President of the Energy Community. In addition, it has bilateral relations with the nine Energy Community Member States either in the context of the enlargement process or that of the European Neigbourhood Policy.

[113] K. Yafimava, *The Transit Dimension of EU Energy Security: Russian Gas Transit Across Ukraine, Belarus and Moldova* (Oxford: OUP 2011), p. 51.

[114] K. Yafimava, *The Transit Dimension of EU Energy Security: Russian Gas Transit Across Ukraine, Belarus and Moldova* (Oxford: OUP 2011), p. 51.

[115] M. Hunt and R. Karova, 'The Energy Acquis Under the Energy Community Treaty and the Integration of South East European Electricity Markets: An Uneasy Relationship?' in B. Delvaux, M. Hunt, and K. Talus (eds), *EU Energy Law and Policy Issues* (Brussels: Euroconfidentiel 2010), p. 59.

was already regarded as insufficient to create a properly functioning competitive market. The impact of the third package is still unclear and its ability to establish security of supply will only be seen over the coming years. However, given the shift from the more market-based philosophy of the first and second energy law packages towards more state and public sector control in the second energy law review and the subsequent legal and policy instruments, the export of the second and even the third package seems premature.[116]

One of the problems with the Energy Community Treaty is its actual implementation. This was specifically noted in the Commission report on the Energy Community Treaty: 'Bridging the existing gap between theory (political commitments) and practice (full implementation of the Energy Community *acquis* and enforcement of the rules adopted) remains the main challenge, and the key question is how to prompt Contracting Parties in the region to apply and enforce the rules.'[117]

It is hardly a surprise that a simple export of the EU model, embodied in the energy directives, would not work as envisaged. Liberalization and full competition are often not conducive to building modern new energy facilities, in particular when cross-border competition operates under more favourable conditions. These issues have not been fully appreciated as yet. They may in fact also delay the establishment of an efficient energy industry when full competition meets obsolete and unsatisfactory energy infrastructure. The solution here should be to identify where liberalization and competition will bring benefits, and where time-limited special regimes are necessary to encourage large-scale and long-term energy plant investment, instead of simply importing the EU model wholesale. It needs to be remembered that the implementation of the second package was highly problematic even within the EU. Furthermore, too much attention may have been paid to competitive markets, and not enough to the conditions for investment, including direct financial support, risk guarantees, and viable long-term contracts.

With the gradual expansion of the Energy Community, it must be noted that the South East European countries are, with respect to energy, in a very different situation from the Central Asian, Caucasus, and Caspian states. While the EU, before embarking on a process of liberalization, had an efficient and reliable energy infrastructure in place, this is not the case for Eastern Europe or the Central Asia, Caucasus, and Caspian region. Azerbaijan, Kazakhstan, Turkmenistan, and Uzbekistan hold significant oil and gas reserves. Their problem was, and to an extent still is, internal political stability and internal as well as external security. They have been used as chess pieces in the post-Cold War rivalry between Russia and the US. Their interest is in depoliticizing energy relations and developing (and to some extent sharing with Russia) oil-based prosperity through investment, transit, and trade. The role of the EU and the TACIS programme in this area should have been to help to create an internal culture of law and order, to facilitate depoliticized and more commercially-oriented neighbourly relationships, and to help create transit

---

[116] This shift is examined in Chapter 7.
[117] Report from the Commission to the European Parliament and the Council under Article 7 of Decision 2006/500/EC (COM(2011) 105 final) 10.3.2011.

corridors through which to bring oil and gas to the markets, in particular Turkey and South East and East Europe. This emerged late, primarily through Nabucco, and was motivated by the aim of reducing dependency on Russian gas. But even here, the Chinese seem to be ahead in the great Caspian game—while Nabucco has remained a paper project with faith in it increasingly unclear,[118] the Chinese are already importing gas from the Caspian region.

There are significant political, geopolitical, geological, and developmental differences between these states and Western Europe, which means that the 'one size fits all' export model will not work. Instead, a more gradual and flexible approach should be adopted. The degree of flexibility offered by Article 24 of the Energy Community Treaty is likely to be insufficient.

6.7 Finally: Who Steers the Boat? Who Represents the EU? The EU Speaking with One Voice

With the slow emergence of certain elements of the EU's common external energy policy, the European Commission has been asking for a more united front and a more coherent approach to the EU's external energy relations. From 'a need for better coordination of EU and Member States' activities with a view to ensuring consistency and coherence ... with key producer, transit and consumer countries'[119] to the demand that EU Member States *speak with one voice*,[120] the Commission has pushed for more competence to act in respect of external energy relations. These efforts have led to two related developments: some elements of a common external energy policy have emerged and the Commission is establishing itself as the leading actor in this area.

In the early part of 2011, the European Council asked the Commission to prepare a communication on security of supply and international cooperation in order to improve the consistency and coherence of the EU's external action in the energy field.[121] It was thought, in particular, that the EU should take initiatives:

'... in line with the Treaties in the relevant international fora and develop mutually beneficial energy partnerships with key players and around strategic corridors, covering a wide range of issues, including regulatory approaches, on all subjects of common interest, such as energy security, safe and sustainable low carbon technologies, energy efficiency, investment environment maintaining and promoting the highest standards for nuclear safety.'[122]

---

[118] In addition to the competition from the South Stream project, it faces competiton from EU projects like ITGI (Interconnector Greece-Turkey-Italy) and TAP (Trans-Adriatic Pipeline).
[119] Commission, 'Green Paper: A European Strategy for Sustainable, Competitive and Secure Energy', COM (2006) 105 final, 8.3.2006, p. 14.
[120] Commission Communication, 'An EU Energy Security and Solidarity Action Plan', COM (2008) 781 final, 13.11.2008, pp. 3 and 17.
[121] European Council, 'Conclusions on Energy', 4 February 2011 (EUCO 2/1/11 Rev 1, 8 March 2011), p. 4.
[122] European Council, 'Conclusions on Energy', 4 February 2011 (EUCO 2/1/11 Rev 1, 8 March 2011), p. 5.

In response to this, the European Commission adopted its Communication on security of energy supply and international cooperation—'The EU Energy Policy: Engaging with Partners beyond Our Borders'—on 7 September 2011. As part of the package adopted that day, the Commission proposed that the Parliament and the Council take a decision setting up an information exchange mechanism with regard to intergovernmental agreements between Member States and third countries in the energy field. The proposal urged that Member States be required to advise the Commission of all new and existing bilateral energy agreements with third countries.[123] (This also relates to the Council meeting in February 2011 which, in addition to this notification and other requirements, also invited the High Representative to take full account of the energy security dimension in her work.[124]) In addition to this notification requirement (increasing transparency), the proposal aims at strengthening coordination when approaching partner countries, adopting a common position in international organizations and developing comprehensive energy partnerships with key partner countries.[125] The stated objective of the proposed mechanism is to 'strengthen the negotiating position of Member States *vis-à-vis* third countries, while ensuring security of supply, proper functioning of the internal market and creating legal certainty for investment'. However, this is hardly the case in practice. In this regard, the second development is clearly visible: strengthening the role of the European Commission. The trend here seems to be in the direction of a more European-style foreign energy policy.[126] In addition to the information required by the Commission, a Member State 'may' request the assistance of the Commission in negotiations with a third country when entering into such negotiations in order to amend an existing intergovernmental agreement or to conclude a new intergovernmental agreement. But there is more: the Commission will also have *ex ante* control over intergovernmental agreements. The Commission may on its own initiative assess the compatibility of the negotiated agreement with EU law before the agreement has been signed. If there is concern over the issue of compatibility, the negotiated but not yet signed draft intergovernmental agreement will be submitted to the Commission for examination. The Member State concerned has to refrain from signing the agreement for a period of four months following the submission of the draft intergovernmental agreement. Finally, the Commission grants itself the right to 'negotiate EU level

[123] Proposal for a Decision setting up an information exchange mechanism with regard to intergovernmental agreements between Member States and third countries in the field of energy, COM(2011)540, 7.9.2011, Article 3.

[124] European Council, 'Conclusions on Energy', 4 February 2011 (EUCO 2/1/11 Rev 1, 8 March 2011), p. 4.

[125] Proposal for a Decision setting up an information exchange mechanism with regard to intergovernmental agreements between Member States and third countries in the field of energy, COM(2011)540, 7.9.2011. See also Commission, Speaking with one voice—the key to securing our energy interests abroad, Press Release IP/11/1005, 7.9.2011.

[126] See the discussion in J.-P. Pielow and B. J. Lewendel, 'Beyond "Lisbon": EU Competences in the Field of Energy Policy', in B. Delvaux, M. Hunt, and K. Talus (eds), *EU Energy Law and Policy Issues* (Cambridge: Intersentia 2011).

agreements with third countries where necessary to achieve the EU core objectives, for example to facilitate large-scale infrastructure projects'.[127]

This is not a merely theoretical possibility, as the Trans-Caspian Pipeline System case shows. Here, the EU mandated the European Commission to negotiate a legally binding treaty between the EU, Azerbaijan, and Turkmenistan to build a Trans-Caspian Pipeline System on behalf of all 27 EU Member States. Related to the EU-backed Nabucco project, this is the 'first operational decision as part of a co-ordinated and united external energy strategy', as proposed in the European Commission's Communication on security of energy supply and international cooperation—'The EU Energy Policy: Engaging with Partners beyond Our Borders'. Commenting on this development, Energy Commissioner Oettinger stated that 'Europe is now speaking with one voice',[128] at least in this particular case.

6.8 The EU and International Energy Trade: Governance, Sanctions, and Ethics

As energy markets internationalize and become part of the global economy, politicization follows. Political conflicts once arose from action taken by national governments, but in the global economy the influence of governments is diluted and that of markets increases. This does not mean that political issues fade away, but rather that political focus moves away from an exclusive focus on governmental action to the action of the actors visible in the global economy—mainly multinational companies, international agencies, and non-state actors such as NGOs and business organizations.[129] As political parties engage mainly in the competition for votes in formal elections, NGOs have taken over a substantial role in politicizing international relations, in particular by focusing on specific situations and value clusters (the environment and human rights, wildlife, indigenous people). These, naturally, represent the core contemporary values of the politically dominant middle classes in the prosperous Western societies. With the collapse of communism and the Cold War, NGOs and 'civil society'—a term encompassing the self-appointed guardians of high moral values of the West—have become the main voice of opposition and criticism. The internet has proved an effective tool for bringing together geographically distanced people and groups more rapidly than was previously possible, and for organizing action aimed at capturing public opinion—as demonstrated, for instance, in the unfolding of the 'Arab Spring'.[130] It has thus helped to influence formal political processes resulting in 'law', and has also, for NGOs engaged in

---

[127] Commission, Communication from the Commission to the European Parliament, the Council, the European Economic and Social Committee and the Committee of the Regions on security of energy supply and international cooperation—'The EU Energy Policy: Engaging with Partners beyond Our Borders', Brussels, 7.9.2011, COM (2011) 539 final.

[128] Commission press release, 'EU starts negotiations on Caspian pipeline to bring gas to Europe', IP/11/1023, 12.9.2011.

[129] S. Strange, *The Retreat of the State: The Diffusion of Power in the World Economy* (Cambridge: CUP 1996) and J. Mitchell (ed.), *Companies in a World of Conflict* (London: RIIA 1998).

[130] For the role of internet and modern telecommunications, see P. Stevens, *The Arab Uprisings and the International Oil Markets* (London: Chatham House 2012).

intense competition, served to develop their profiles (i.e. a kind of 'brand value' in the minds of the public), which helps raise funds, drum up support, and coordinate efforts. Political parties, suddenly subject to such competition from outside of the oligopoly of election contests, are compelled to pay attention to and follow NGO campaigns which are proving adept at grabbing public attention. But what does all of this have to do with the external dimension of EU energy law?

The EU institutions, in particular the Commission, have very little political legitimacy, and must therefore take care to be seen to respond to demands from 'civil society' in order not to alienate their supporters. The OECD, for the public a largely faceless talking shop for bureaucrats, has learned through the failure of the Multilateral Agreement of Investments (MAI)[131] that an international organization now has to develop the capability to engage meaningfully with 'civil society',[132] a point which has been taken up with much more vigour by the World Bank and the WTO.[133] NGO pressure therefore works directly on the Commission, but also through the European Parliament (EP), since this institution also, and perhaps to an even greater extent, needs to develop a level of political acceptance that more closely reflects its formal political legitimacy (which is itself in heavy deficit). As energy markets internationalize, political attention, now largely activated by NGOs in conjunction with the educated media,[134] focuses on what international agencies and multinational companies do. As NGOs, in combination with the media, do not make a living out of positive news or support, but rather out of focusing on and highlighting 'scandal', accompanied by outrage, their influence is both negative (i.e. making existing activities more difficult) and positive (i.e. pushing international agencies, in particular, in the desired direction).

The confrontation between NGOs/'civil society' and international energy companies is typically focused on a particular situation. It may also be characterized by fractious relations between federal governments and several, competing local populations, possibly involving breaches of rules of criminal procedure regarded as fundamentally important in Western countries (e.g. the Ogoniland trial and the execution of Ken Saro-Wiwa).[135] Examples of typical cases include the (legal and approved) abandonment of an offshore platform, in the Shell—Brent Spar case; the

---

[131] Details are provided at <http://www.oecd.org/investment/investmentpolicy/multilateralagreementoninvestment.htm> (last accessed 6.8.2012).

[132] D. Henderson, *The MAI Affair: A Story and its Lessons* (London: RIIA 1999), J. Huner, 'Lessons from the MAI: A View from the Negotiating Table', in H. Ward and D. Brack (eds), *Trade, Investment and the Environment* (London: Earthscan 2000), p. 242.

[133] H. Bergesen and L. Lunde, *Dinosaurs or Dynamos? The United Nations and the World Bank at the Turn of the Century* (London: Earthscan 1999).

[134] It should not be forgotten that a significant influence even on EU external energy policy comes the discussion and interpretation of events in the *Financial Times, The Economist, Wall Street Journal, Le Monde, New York Times, Frankfurter Allgemeine Zeitung,* and *Neue Zuercher Zeitung.* Political capital dissipated from the MAI negotiations not only because of NGO criticism (as a rule misinformed and emotionally agitated), but because of critical reporting in the *Financial Times* (Guy de Jonquiéres). The Secretary General of the Energy Charter Secretariat was ousted in December 1999 largely because of *Financial Times* criticism.

[135] Shell, Brent Spar case, S. Howarth, *A Century in Oil: The Shell Transport and Trading Company 1897–1997* (London: Weidenfeld 1997), pp. 334–6, 338. See also, <http://www.guardian.co.uk/world/2009/jun/08/nigeria-usa> (last accessed 6.8.2012).

(legal) exploitation of oil in the Nigerian Delta area; exploration for oil in areas populated by indigenous people (Ecuador); the exploitation of minerals in an area characterized by tensions between central government and local people (Ok Tedi and Bougainville, Papua New Guinea); oil development under a (legal) concession from the (legal) government involved in a civil war of secession (Talisman in Sudan); human rights violations by security forces to protect a BP pipeline in Colombia; and the use of forced labour by government services to support infrastructure for an oil pipeline in Burma.[136] In all of these cases, companies were acting legally, in full conformity with national law and with the consent of the national government. The government, however, employed practices regarded as typical of 'underdeveloped' countries (the nineteenth century term was more pejorative: 'uncivilized') in its fraught relations with secessionary movements or local, often indigenous people. NGO campaigns are aimed not only at the companies (where they have an effect), but also at harnessing the regulatory power both of governments and of international organizations such as the EU. The stated aim is to use the financial and political leverage of the EU—as well as that of multinational companies—to improve the 'governance' of the developing countries. Energy—here oil and gas development— is one of the prime targets. The reason for this is that the oil and gas industry seeks to investigate newly discovered geological targets, which tend increasingly to be found in developing countries and remote areas. The EU therefore comes under increasing pressure to take action, or at least to go through the motions of doing so, to combat visible human rights violations and avert environmental disasters in connection with the oil and gas operations of EU-based companies in particular. However, the issue is wider than that. The failure of statist systems in developing countries to supply enough energy for rapidly escalating needs has led to large-scale privatization and opening-up of energy investment opportunities. EU companies—in order not to lose out in global competition (with Chinese and US companies)—have now followed suit and acquired and established power plants, transmission grids, distribution systems, and gas pipelines particularly in resource-rich or energy-hungry large developing countries (Pakistan, India, Indonesia, Argentina, Brazil, and Bolivia). These operations may sometimes have the human rights and environmental implications of the typically more remote-area investment of oil and gas but such investment is principally carried out under conditions of governance which do not correspond to the reality, or ideal, of Western countries. This applies in particular to the widespread corrupt practices required to do business, or at least to the equivalent practice of having to co-opt the local strongman's cronies. As these matters are now common knowledge, pressure is mounting both on companies and on the EU and national governments to introduce national and international regulation to combat such features of bad governance. The new international and national regimes on anti-corruption are just one example of this.[137] The EU is

---

[136] This was suggested in: <http://www.independent.co.uk/news/world/asia/burmese-villagers-forced-to-work-on-total-pipeline-1771876.html> (last accessed 6.8.2012).

[137] For this, see L.A Low, T.K Sprange, and M. Barutciski, 'Global Anti-corruption Standard and Enforcement: Implications for Energy Companies', 3(2) *Journal of World Energy Law and Business* (2010), pp. 166–213.

certainly responding to these pressures. The inclusion of 'good governance' obligations, reflecting NGO and EP pressure, is now a mandatory feature of international agreements. The rapid recent progress on these matters can be observed by comparing the ECT and the Cotonou Agreement. The ECT, negotiated during 1992–94, includes no specific 'governance' provision. The Cotonou Agreement of 2000 is replete with 'civil society' elements. For instance:

- Article 6 specifically mentions 'civil society in all its forms' and NGOs as 'actors of cooperation';
- Article 8 contains an obligation for there to be 'political dialogue' relating to the arms trade, organized crime, ethnic, religious or racial forms of discrimination, but also human rights, democratic principles, the rule of law, and good governance;
- Article 9 covers human rights and sustainable development, the equality of men and women, and transparent and accountable governance;
- Article 10 mentions the need for the greater involvement of civil society and justice;
- Article 10 deals with the protection of the rights of female children;
- Article 31 deals with women's access to economic and other resources; and
- Article 97 covers corruption.

These provisions give the EU a basis on which to exercise leverage, be it through the dialogue envisaged under the agreement, through formal arbitration (Article 98)— and presumably by withdrawal of financial and technical assistance—and/or also through the significant trade concessions provided for the ACP countries under the Treaty ('appropriate measures', Article 96). In essence, the agreement provides a stick of political, financial, and trade character, which the EU can use to sanction ACP countries (i.e. former colonies) that do not mend their ways. The legal reciprocity of this treaty does not obscure the fact that it is in essence an instrument to legitimize the overwhelming leverage available to the EU against misconduct by developing countries which, by definition, have weak governance structures. For the energy sector, this means that projects which are a governance liability— which is to say, virtually any project in any developing country—is now burdened with the risk of NGO campaigning, reverberating with shareholder pressure and sometimes public-opinion-focused litigation,[138] with economic sanctions by the US government, and now also the prospect of the country in question being blacklisted by the EU and having financial assistance and trade concessions withdrawn. It is not that business cannot continue under these conditions, but that it is likely to become 'rogue business' done in the shadows, with large profit margins for adventurous companies and with an entry-point for international crime.[139]

---

[138] H. Hongju Koh, 'Transnational Public Law Litigation', 100(2347) *Yale Law Journal* (1991).
[139] This was discussed in the Bingham report on oil supply against UN sanctions to South Africa: T. Bingham and S. Gray, *Report on the Supply of Petroleum and Petroleum Products to Rhodesia* (London: HMSO 1978).

The implication of this emerging international law of 'good governance'—embodied in treaties such as the Cotonou Agreement, the OECD Anti-Bribery Convention, international human rights treaties, numerous guidelines, codes of conduct serving as aid conditionalities, as well as the emerging civil law on the corporate liability of multinational companies—is, *inter alia*, that companies, international organizations and governments cannot rely on the defence of 'compliance with national law'. The strong emphasis on non-intervention into the domestic affairs of another state, enshrined in the UN Charter and the World Bank Convention, are *de facto* superseded, in the eyes of the 'civil society' movement in Western countries, by good governance considerations. The pendulum—which in the 'New International Economic Order' (NIEO) era emphasized an extreme 'absolute state sovereignty', the Calvo Clause, permanent sovereignty over natural resources and economic activity, the inadmissibility of any foreign intervention into national affairs, and the exclusive jurisdiction of host (developing) states—has swung back 180° to its opposite.[140]

An as yet inchoate principle of the international customary or comparative law of major Western countries may be emerging, according to which multinational companies will bear some responsibility for serious breaches of good governance principles when their investment supports the activities of certain governments.

But these developments are not as 'good' or 'godly' as they may appear to activists at first sight. They place the principal targeted actors on the horns of a series of dilemmas: the EU and its Member States depend, increasingly, on energy imports overwhelmingly from states that could easily become the targets of sanctions. Most of the petroleum producers (notably Saudi Arabia) have not acceded to the major human rights conventions; Russian and Chinese practices against secessionist movements are not that different from those practised by Sudan. The *raison d'être* of oil companies is to go out and get the oil where it is located—if this was forbidden, they would go out of business, and Western societies would slip into crisis. The idea that benevolent intervention from outside will solve deep-rooted domestic problems has as a rule not worked in practice. Financial and technical assistance, and trade, are ways to make properly functioning economies more prosperous and civilized, but cannot contribute greatly to the resolution of deep internal government problems. The past decades of development have not eradicated bad governance or poverty, and there is no indication that changing tack towards imposing Western cultural concepts borne out of specifically Western experience would suddenly prove more successful. The current approach adopted both by governments and by the EU (and its Member States) is to emphasize the human rights element as much as possible for public consumption, but to try to avoid taking treaty language formulated primarily for public relations purposes too seriously. While Sudan and Sierra Leone might be suitable targets for trade sanctions, China, Russia, and Saudi Arabia are not. This pattern replicates the internal EU pattern of political

---

[140] T. Wälde, 'A Requiem for the "New International Economic Order"', in G. Hafner et al. (eds), *Festschrift Ignaz Seidl-Hohenveldern* (The Hague: Kluwer Law International 1998), pp. 771–804.

sanctions—e.g. all well and good against Austria, but not against some other EU countries. A system of partly recognized hypocrisy is of doubtful value, as it down-grades the moral legitimacy both of the values that are pursued hypocritically and of the institutions involved in such pursuit.

There is more to the issue of the pursuit of good governance through treaties. The imposition of Western values via treaties, money, aid, and trade with former colonies may seem workable now. It did not work in the period when there was a balance of power between East and West: developing countries, newly decolonized, then had much more breathing space in which to indulge in exaggerated notions of absolute sovereignty. With the rise of the Asian economies (China in particular) our current good governance mode of relations with the developing countries might at some point be put under pressure. It is hard to deny that the modern-day 'civil society' use of EU, governmental, and market powers to impose values on the weaker countries, albeit intended to be for 'their' benefit, has a heady whiff of the nineteenth century. Then, as now, missionary societies went out, privately funded, but with government support, to civilize the savages. Trade, aid, and missionaries went hand in glove. The essential precondition for this state of affairs was a strong imbalance of power and the absence of an effective opposing force—the colonizing countries may have competed with one another in their carving-up of the globe, but there was no fundamental dissent in the 'concert of the great powers' over the mis-sionary mandate of the colonial powers. Perhaps such a revival of a neo-colonialism which accepts the formal trappings of statehood acquired in the decolonization process, but not the rule of non-intervention, is an inevitable consequence of our era's highly unequal relationships of economic, technological, cultural, political, and military power. But it is not guaranteed to last.

As to the future influence of good governance principles on the EU's external energy policy and law, mainly through treaties based on the EU's economic leverage, these may work better with weaker countries (i.e. not Russia, India, and China), and in countries with no large—and therefore crucial—petroleum potential, than with major oil and gas producers (e.g. Saudi Arabia). In addition, it remains to be seen whether the leverage potential in agreements such as the Cotonou Agreement can realistically be activated. Any imposition from abroad is bound to lead to resist-ance, as colonial and post-colonial history shows.

Economic sanctions are one of the principal instruments of international coercion, and have been a particular problem for the energy sector, given its need to go into problem countries where energy resources are often to be found. Just con-sider the current situation with Iran, a country with major oil and gas resources. At an international level, UN sanctions against Iran currently comprise four Security Council resolutions imposing arms embargoes, travel bans on individuals associ-ated with the regime and the freezing of those individuals' assets located in foreign bank accounts.[141] At national or regional level, EU Council Decision 2012/35/

---

[141] UN Security Council Resolutions 1737 (23 December 2006); 1747 (24 March 2007); 1803 (3 March 2008); and 1929 (9 June 2010). UN Security Council Resolution 1835 (27 September 2008) reaffirms 1737, 1747 and 1803, but does not impose further sanctions. For details see M. Parish and T. Fresquet, 'International Sanctions and How to Evade Them', 3 *OGEL* (2012), <http://www.ogel.org>.

CFSP bans the sale of equipment related to the petroleum industry to Iranian entities or entities controlled by Iranian citizens.[142] Similarly, the United States has added Iranian entities to the list of entities with which US persons and entities are prohibited from dealing.[143] The UK maintains a similar list.[144] As a result, the Chinese companies are moving in and securing large contracts with Iranian companies.

These sanctions bring an additional politicization to commercial relationships which are made more difficult in the first place by internal politics in the host state, the home state, often also in transit states, as well as by international politics in general.[145] Corporate management now faces not only the challenge of managing very complex political risks in the oil and gas rich states, but the new and additional risk of international sanctions, as well as the new type of public relations and market-based sanctions engineered by NGOs. They are still expected to bring the petroleum to market, but are now also held liable for the actions of 'uncivilized' governments, over which companies have little, if any, influence. As part of external EU energy-related law, sanctions have two sides. First, as a sender organization, the EU imposes sanctions.[146] Secondly, the EU itself has not been subject to political sanctions,[147] but oil companies domiciled within its Member States have been subject to US economic sanctions for investment in Cuba, Libya, and Iran: in this regard, the EU is not an imposer of sanctions, but a defender of its own companies against US sanctions. Both sides should be examined more closely.

As an imposer of sanctions (the prohibition of trade and the interruption of services), the EU as a rule participates in sanctions decided by the UN Security Council and binding on Member States under Article 25 of the UN Charter. In addition to the Iran sanctions noted, pertinent sanctions were imposed on Iraq, following the invasion of Kuwait, pursuant to UN Security Council Resolution 661 (1990), which forbade all commercial transactions promoting, *inter alia*, the export of oil or oil products from Iraq.[148] Sanctions were also imposed by dint of

---

[142] Council Decision 2012/35/CFSP of 23 January 2012 amending Decision 2010/413/CFSP concerning restrictive measures against Iran, Article 4a.

[143] Iranian Transaction Regulations 31 C.F.R. § 560, administered by the U.S. Treasury Department's Office of Foreign Assets Control (OFAC).

[144] Details available at <http://www.hm-treasury.gov.uk/fin_sanctions_index.htm>. For details see M. Parish and T. Fresquet, 'International Sanctions and How to Evade Them', 3 *OGEL* (2012), <http://www.ogel.org>.

[145] On sanctions in oil and gas: T. Wälde, 'Managing the Risk of Sanctions in the Global Oil and Gas Industry', 36 *Texas International Law Journal* (2001), pp. 184–230 and B. Cova, 'The European Response to US Extraterritorial Legislation', 15 *OGTLR* (1997), p. 353.

[146] Like Council Decision 2012/35/CFSP of 23 January 2012 amending Decision 2010/413/CFSP concerning restrictive measures against Iran.

[147] With the exception, naturally, of WTO-based trade sanctions, mainly by the US (i.e. higher tariffs, import restrictions and quota, and anti-dumping measures). EU companies will have been subject to sanctions for dealing with Israel (anti-Israel boycott blacklist by Arab League).

[148] As is generally the case, these sanctions could be circumvented. See M. Parish and T. Fresquet, 'International Sanctions and How to Evade Them', 3 *OGEL* (2012), <http://www.ogel.org>. As noted by the authors: 'The legacy of Iraqi sanctions will forever be associated with the corruption in the 'Oil for Food' Programme, a UN-approved exception to the sanctions regime (The 'Oil-For-Food Programme' was established by UN Security Council Resolution 986, 14 April 1995) in which Iraq would be permitted to sell oil, the purchase price for which would be paid into an escrow account and subsequently released to the Iraqi government to purchase essential approved items for civilian use.

Resolution 748 (1992) against Libya, following the Lockerbie bombing. These were more limited in scope, involving a prohibition against trade in goods and services. A contractor from a sanctioned country who suffers commercial losses is not entitled to compensation.[149] The problem of economic sanctions is that they provide a competitive advantage to companies not subject to sanctions, whether by law or through non-enforcement in their home state. Economic sanctions typically engender a grey and black market for sanction-breakers[150]—such as the subsidiaries of respected international oil companies in the 1970s sanctions against Rhodesia. In most cases, the effective imposition of sanctions requires a multilateral regime, normally initiated by a UN Security Council Resolution, followed by serious enforcement by all UN member countries, and even then sanctions are not full-proof. The closer to being unilateral a sanction is, the less prospect it has of being effective. Conversely, the more multilateral it is, the more universally and more effectively enforced, and the more embedded in public opinion, NGO attention, and corporate management, the better it usually works. Large EU energy companies usually—which was not necessarily the case in the 1970s—comply with sanctions. They are also less likely to participate in the grey and black market of sanction-breaking where the profits to be made usually reflect the level of risk involved—the better the enforcement, the higher the profit premium and the greater the sanction-breaking incentive for risk-taking commercial and criminal operators. One of the consequences that arises when sanctions are inadequately enforced is that the sanctioned country indirectly bears the sanction-breakers' risk premium. There is usually also a quiet race among oil companies to occupy positions within the sanctioned country (e.g. Iraq, Libya, and Iran), thus putting themselves in pole position rapidly to edge out more compliant competitors as far as exploration, production, and exportation are concerned once sanctions are lifted. The oil trade, being much less visible and notoriously difficult to control, is likely to involve many more oil trading firms than the much more visible investment. While sanctions may not achieve their intended objective, they may be more important as a political signal made by the sender countries (e.g. the EU) both to the target state and its allies, and as a symbol of a proper response (even if ineffectual) to domestic political pressures.

The other side of the EU coin on sanctions is where EU companies are penalized by US sanctions affecting non-US citizens and activities in EU territory ('extraterritorial sanctions'). Energy, again, is a primary area of application for such sanctions. The US is the most active imposer of economic sanctions, which largely appear to exist in order to appease its large number of émigré communities harbouring a particular grudge and, more recently, the NGO movement.[151] The problem is that sanctions

Part of the escrowed funds would be withheld to pay Kuwait war reparations and for UN operating costs. It subsequently emerged that skim payments were being withdrawn from the fund and paid to Iraqi and UN officials.'

[149] Case C-237/98 P, *Dorsch Consult v Council and Commission* [2000] ECR I-4549.

[150] On the ways to effectively circumvent the sanctions, see M. Parish and T. Fresquet, 'International Sanctions and How to Evade Them', 3 *OGEL* (2012), <http://www.ogel.org>.

[151] Section 232(b) of the Trade Expansion Act of 1962 (19 USCA § 1862) as amended, has been used to ban importation of oil products from certain embargoed countries, such as Libya in 1982 (47 Fed.

in which the major economic actors do not participate tend to achieve nothing but confer a competitive advantage on companies from countries outside the US. To issue sanctions and then see economic competitors benefit from such action, with little damage to the target, is clearly not very satisfactory in the US political process. Therefore, and also through the tradition of missionary politics[152] and US hegemony,[153] the US has on several occasions over the last 50 years designed sanctions which were applicable to subsidiaries of US companies incorporated abroad (e.g. the *Fruehauf* case), to European companies involved in the purchase of Russian gas and construction of pipelines in the early 1980s, to non-US companies investing in the oil and gas sector in Libya and Iran, and to non-US companies conducting any business in Cuba.[154] The EU considers the extraterritorial reach of such sanctions to be a contravention of international law. However, international law does not condemn extraterritorial regulation per se, since there are several recognized exceptions; in addition, a multilateral, UN-covered sanction regime can probably legitimately affect persons and activities outside the territorial jurisdiction of the sanctioning state. But US sanctions—mainly the imposition of specific sanctions relating to access to the US capital markets for non-US companies—which are unilateral, not covered by a formalized international consensus, and represent a response to actions that do not directly affect US rights, are regarded as incompatible with the international law principle of territorial sovereignty. This view is held almost universally, and even to a large extent within the US international law community. The EU, and various states, have reacted with 'blocking statutes'[155] which forbid compliance with US sanctions and contain certain counter-sanctions applicable to US legal or natural persons trying to enforce, in particular, the Helms-Burton Act rights against non-US citizens conducting business in Cuba. The EU has also initiated proceedings through the WTO dispute settlement system asserting breach of a number of WTO disciplines.

It is difficult to reach a conclusive judgement on the EU's recent opening up to 'civil society' as this is a matter very much in flux. It is hard to distinguish between what is the current fashion of political correctness, and what is a longer-lasting trend towards the application of Western cultural ideas about good governance to non-Western societies, at the instigation of and under pressure from NGOs, which

---

Reg. 10507 (1982)) and Iran in1979 (44 Fed. Reg. 65581 (1979)). For this, see K. Talus and M.A. Nunes, 'Regulation of Oil Imports in the United States and the European Union', 2 *OGEL* (2011), <http://www.ogel.org>. Extensive literature: T. Wälde. 'Managing the Risk of Sanctions in the Global Oil and Gas Industry', 36 *Texas International Law Journal* (2001), pp. 184–230.

[152] H. Kissinger, *Diplomacy* (New York: Simon & Schuster 1994).

[153] L. Brilmayer, *American Hegemony, Political Morality in a One-superpower World* (New Haven: Yale University Press 1994).

[154] For a pro commentary: A. Lowenfeld, 'Congress and Cuba: The Helms-Burton Act', 90(419) *AJIL* (1996) considering the US legislation illicit; see, contra commentary, B. Clagett, 'Title III of the Helms-Burton Act is Consistent with International Law', 90(434) *AJIL* (1996).

[155] EU Council Regulation No. 2271/96 of 22 November 1996—published with the similar Canadian Foreign Extraterritorial Measures Act and the Mexican Act to Protect Trade and Investment from Foreign Norms that contravene international law are all published with notes in: 36 ILM 125 (1997), 36 ILM 111 (1997), and 36 ILM 133 (1997).

are mainly self-appointed, but which as a conduit for public opinion are often—though not consistently—influential guardians of such values. There are elements of hypocrisy, of missionary proselytizing for values against societies who may not want such values, but are too weak to fight back. There may also be elements which help to make international relations more civilized and indirectly prosperous by providing a social dimension to the otherwise purely economic impact of globalization. It is likely that we will see, on the one hand, minimum rules of civilized governance, and on the other an increasing contradiction between values promoted by quite different interest and quasi-religious value groups. The EU would do well to take a very cautious line. If it embraces the 'civil society' with excessive enthusiasm, it also risks the possibility that its growing legitimacy becomes undermined by the inevitable contradictions between solid interests (e.g. in energy supply and prosperous commercial relationships under a commonly agreed legal order) and the much fuzzier and volatile ideologies of the day. There is an argument for helping societies move to more law, order, and security if they are on that road already and if there are vigorous domestic forces in that direction; but there is little practical argument in favour of trying to foist European values and system on societies which are not prepared, not interested, and which perhaps are even, surprising as this may seem to neo-missionaries, attached to their own, distinct system of values. A safe and civilized international intercourse may be a more reasonable and realistic goal than taking up the 'white person's burden' to better the modern-day 'sullen people'.

Section 6.9 deals with a different but related issue: the impact of international law on trade in energy. The discussion of this topic focuses on environmentally-motivated import restrictions and WTO law.

6.9 The Impact of International Law: Trade in Energy Goods and Services and Environmental Protection

In the 'good old' energy monopoly days, energy trade was not an issue. State-owned or protected monopolies 'exchanged' electricity at times, but only if both they and the states involved wanted to do so—there was no need to rely on international trade law to obtain access, reduce tariffs, eliminate non-tariff trade barriers, combat state aid, and participate in the procurement of energy by public agencies. The oil trade was liberalized in developed countries in the 1980s; since the consuming countries are mostly dependent on oil, there were no tariffs on imported oil (excepting some protectionist measures put in place in the US before the first oil price hike in 1972).[156] Nor were they any significant non-tariff barriers (e.g. regulation, standards, import licensing practices).[157] As first oil, electricity, and then increasingly gas (by

---

[156] See K. Talus and T. Nunes, 'Regulation of Oil Importation to United States and European Union', *OGEL* (2011).
[157] See K. Talus and T. Nunes, 'Regulation of Oil Importation to United States and European Union', *OGEL* (2011).

pipeline and LNG) started being traded across borders, into increasingly competitive markets, issues relating to tariff and non-tariff barriers inevitably began to arise. First, protectionist sentiments, translating into trade restrictions against imports of primary energy sources, sometimes appeared. This is rare, but has been an issue twice in periods of low oil prices imposed by high-cost US producers against oil imports— arguing that lower oil prices prevailing in the producer countries (Venezuela, Mexico) plus the predominant role of the state with no clear distinction between government and state enterprise budgets indicated either dumping or export subsidies—to be countered by US anti-dumping duties or other import restrictions. The German coal subsidy scheme (including direct subsidies and domestic minimum purchase obligations) can be seen in a similar light as representing protection for German coal against more competitive energy sources and against coal imports.

Trade restrictions typically come into play as more value is added by the producer (thus threatening importer state refining and petrochemical industries), but also as different regulatory and tax regimes change the elusive 'level playing field' to which all theorists aspire. Under GATT, a US import restriction on Venezuelan and Brazilian gasoline was held to be discriminatory. While there was a worthwhile environmental rationale for this, its application was discriminatory and favoured US competitors.[158] Under Chapter XI of NAFTA, trade restrictions on certain chemicals and hazardous waste may have been, according to the plaintiff and at least one arbitral tribunal, an environmental cover for what was in effect protectionist discrimination.[159] These cases illustrate the growing importance of real— and fake—environmental policies used to justify trade restrictions.[160]

Within the EU, the modified EU ETS Directive under Directive 2009/20/ EC[161] refers to import restrictions relating to differences in requirements in the EU and other countries:

'Energy-intensive industries which are determined to be exposed to a significant risk of carbon leakage could receive a higher amount of free allocation or an effective carbon equalisation system could be introduced with a view to putting installations from the Community which are at significant risk of carbon leakage and those from third countries on a comparable footing. Such a system could apply requirements to importers that would be no less favourable than those applicable to installations within the Community...'

---

[158] WTO Appellate Body: Report of Appellate Body in US—Standards for Reformulated and Conventional Gasoline, 35 ILM 603 (1996).
[159] *Myers* case, export restriction on hazardous waste to favour a Canadian competitor; *Ethyl* case, trade restriction on hazardous chemical, but without a similar impact on Canadian competitors; *Ethyl Corp v Government of Canada*, 38 ILM 700 (1999) (settled in favour of plaintiff before final award); *Myers v Canada*, <http://www.naftaclaims.com>.
[160] S. Moreno, J. Rubin et al., 'Free Trade and the Environment: The NAFTA, the NAAEC', 12 *Tulane International Law Journal* (1999), pp. 405–58, P. Mavroides, 'Trade and Environment after the Shrimps-turtles Litigation', 34 *Journal of World Trade* (2000), pp. 73–88.
[161] Directive 2009/29/EC of the European Parliament and of the Council of 23 April 2009 amending Directive 2003/87/EC so as to improve and extend the greenhouse gas emission allowance trading scheme of the Community, OJ L 140, 5.6.2009, pp. 63–87.

The obvious question is, of course, whether this type of scheme is in line with the WTO rules.

Over ten years ago, the Commission raised the issue of 'unfair competition' in relation to power plants not subject to strict EU environmental standards and in relation to 'unsafe' export of nuclear plants into the EU. It argued that unlimited access would undermine the basis of the EU energy liberalization process, which requires a 'level playing field'. It also referred in this context to the need for political and environmental acceptance if the view were that such imports would facilitate the continuation of unsafe operations.[162]

What is environmentally beneficial or needed in the name of the environment in practice is, of course, a different question from what appears in legislation on the subject. It is usually quite easy to assert from a self-centred national perspective that the environmental regulation in one's own country is superior to others, but more difficult to sustain this assertion once an objective and balanced assessment has been made. For example, the oft-cited higher quality of German environmental legislation relating to energy must be set against the fact that Germany has by far the highest CO_2 emissions in the EU, and against the fact that for decades it actively subsidized—and fought for EU state aid exemption for—its environmentally extremely damaging coal production, and the mandatory use of this coal for domestic energy purposes. Arguments against 'dirty' foreign energy—such as that produced by East European nuclear plants, for example—do not look at all credible when assessed from a climate change perspective.

Clearly, high environmental standards can be used as protectionist measures ('green protectionism'). Such measures can stop exports from other countries with less developed systems which might simply be unable to meet certain requirements.[163] In this respect, it is worth noting that the 2010 revision of the Cotonou Agreement led to the inclusion of text stating that the parties 'agree that environmental measures should not be used for protectionist purposes'.[164]

The common presumption that energy imports from less regulated countries are by force of necessity more competitive and that 'dirty' energy will thus crowd out 'clean energy', a concept much relied upon in environmentalist argument about 'races to the bottom', is far from proven.[165]

Economists argue that good environmental taxes need to be imposed globally, since otherwise competition will handicap companies subject to such environmentally acceptable fiscal and regulatory regimes.[166] But it is far from proven or universally

---

[162] Commission working paper, 'Completing the internal energy market' (SEC (2001) 438) March 2001.
[163] For more, see G. Marin Duran and E. Morgera, *Environmental Integration in the EU's External Relations: Beyond Multilateral Dimensions* (Oxford: Hart Publishing 2012), p. 49.
[164] Article 49(3) of the revised Cotonou Agreement.
[165] Even if we accept that unevenly imposed or enforced environmental standards can create a 'race to the bottom', this concern should not be over-exaggerated. In addition to the economic value that this would create, there are also image and reputational questions that have their impact.
[166] Also M. Radetzki, 'Taxation of Energy in an Increasingly Interdependent World: An Introduction', 17(7) *International Journal of Global Energy Issues* (1999).

accepted that higher standards of required quality are undermined by lower standards.[167] Higher standards can encourage technological innovation, lead to better cost control and easier acceptance of products by the markets. Lower standards may often reflect the level of development of an economy: i.e. be appropriate for the particular country. They allow countries with a lower level of general prosperity (e.g. transition or developing countries) to secure market share and move upwards in terms of development and, in tandem with development, quality standards; while higher standards tend to act as a barrier to market access by competitors from less developed societies. There is therefore an element of abuse of market power and economic dominance if higher-standard societies try to impose their standards against competition from other countries. It is also far from certain that purchasing from power plants subject to a different regulatory regime (sometimes lower level, but sometimes only different) helps lower standard operations to survive. Buying from power plants in the CIS countries, for example, may generate cash flow for modernization and upgrading, while denying such income may cause the owners of such power plants to focus on poorer markets, thus contributing to low levels of safety.

A formally level playing field is not always necessary, and sometimes a playing field is level when some of the cards are stacked in favour of the weaker players. Much of the intensity of feeling lies in the convenient combination of both a sentiment of moral superiority combined with a form of protectionism which safeguards not only better environmental standards, but a comfortable way of living. For these reasons, a proper legal assessment of import restrictions under established principles of international trade—mainly WTO law—is both necessary and, in practical terms, justified. This is quite clear in the EU papers where the doubtful legality of import restrictions is implicitly acknowledged and where suggestions are made to bypass WTO law as it stands by means of bilateral agreements—i.e. agreements where the dominance of the EU can be better utilized than on the more level playing field of WTO dispute settlement. WTO rules are not only applicable between EU Member States and non-EU WTO members, but also by way of the reference in the Energy Charter Treaty to WTO rules for relations between EU Member States and states which are not members of the WTO but are members of the Energy Charter Treaty (Article 29). The EU has a difficult task in seeking to justify energy protectionism against poorer countries in the CIS. An analysis of the applicable WTO rules makes this clear. While anti-dumping and safeguard measures may be allowed, the sale of energy produced under a regulatory regime different from the environmentally stricter EU regime does not constitute dumping. On the contrary, it is quite likely that the electricity is exported at a higher price than the domestic price: i.e. rather the opposite of dumping. 'Eco-dumping' is not currently a legal concept under WTO law. There is very little by way of precedent dealing specifically with electricity under the GATT/WTO system, as electricity was not competitively traded across borders until more recently. In this

---

[167] For a review of the discussion: R. Stewart, 'Environmental Regulation and International Competitiveness', 102(2039) *Yale Law Journal* (1993).

regard, recent disputes on the requirement to use local/domestic products in order to qualify for a green energy subsidy are of interest. The Canadian scheme—the Ontario Green Energy and Economy Act—accepts solar projects only if at least 40 per cent of their initial development is made up of Ontario products and services.[168] These types of measures can be seen as prohibited subsidies under Article 3(1)(b) of the WTO Agreement on Subsidies and Countervailing Measures, which rules out subsidies 'contingent, whether solely or as one of several other conditions, upon the use of domestic over imported goods'. They also raise questions regarding possible less favourable treatment in the sense of Article III:4 of GATT 1994, investment-related measures (TRIMs), and the WTO Plurilateral Agreement on Government Procurement. The energy trade receives no specific special treatment under the WTO: energy goods, including electricity, are treated in the same way as any other goods.[169] The EU does not apply any duty with regard to electricity imports, although some Member States may.[170] The national treatment rule contained in GATT (Article III:4) means that once it has entered the EU, it must be treated as electricity produced in the EU.[171]

Import restrictions are forbidden under GATT Article XI as a 'quantitative restriction'. There is no doubt that electricity has to be considered as a 'good' under WTO law.[172] The relevant question is that of whether the exceptions contained in Article XX, in particular section (b)—'necessary to protect human... life or health'—apply. Reports from the GATT and WTO panels and the WTO Appeal Body[173] seem to establish the following sequence of tests for Article XX: import restrictions must be based on legitimate environmental objectives, without discrimination, and selecting the least restrictive measure. The measure must primarily be based on environmental harm coming from the product itself—not the

---

[168] See the WTO case J. von Reppert-Bismarck, 'EU challenges Canadian green power rules at WTO' (Reuters, 11 August 2011), available at <http://www.reuters.com/article/2011/08/11/us-eu-canada-trade-idUSTRE77A2WU20110811>.

[169] There is however still an ongoing discussion on whether electricity is to be considered as a good under the WTO regime. The recent cases on green energy subsidies suggest that it is. This is also the approach under EU law.

[170] Case C-213/96, *Outokumpu* [1998] ECR I-1777.

[171] Commission working paper, 'Completing the Internal energy market' (SEC (2001) 438) March 2001, p. 67

[172] UNCTAD, 'Energy Services', p. 7; WTO, 'Energy Services, Background Notice by the Secretariat', S/C/W/59 of 9 September 1998.

[173] GATT Panel Report, United States—Restrictions on Imports of Tuna, 3 September 1991 and GATT Panel Report, United States—Restrictions on Imports of Tuna, 16 June 1994, WTO Appellate Body Report, United States—Import Prohibition of certain Shrimp and Shrimp Products (DS 58) ('US–Shrimp'), 12 October 1998, WTO Appellate Body Report, Korea—Measures Affecting Imports of Fresh, Chilled and Frozen Beef (DS 161/DS 169) ('Korea–Beef'), 11 December 2000 and WTO Appellate Body Report, Brazil—Measures affecting imports of retreaded tyres (DS 332) ('Brazil–Tyres'), 3 December 2007. For detailed discussion: J. Cameron and K. Gray, 'Principles of International Law in the WTO Dispute Settlement Body', 50(248) *ICLQ* (2001), pp. 264–8 and G. Marceau and J. Wyatt, 'Trade and the Environment: The WTO's Efforts to Balance Economic and Sustainable Development', in R. Trigo Trindade, H. Peter, and C. Bovet (eds), *Liber Amicorum Anne Petitpierre-Sauvain: Economie Environnement Ethique de la Responsabilité Sociale et Sociétale* (Zurich: Schulthess Editions Romandes 2009), pp. 225–35.

production process. Electricity is not in itself environmentally harmful, so there is no product-based justification for import restriction. Article III GATT makes it clear that allowing the import of electricity from, say, France or Poland, but then excluding electricity produced by nuclear plants from the CIS would constitute discrimination.[174] The issue to be settled here is whether such restrictions can be based on the fact that the 'production process' occurs abroad. If countries were allowed to use trade sanctions based on production processes occurring abroad, they would in essence acquire a trade sanction based on extraterritorial regulatory power over conduct in foreign countries. This would mean that strong economies would be able to impose their standards on weaker ones dependent on access. That seems in principle prohibited, except for narrow exceptions, under general international law.[175] WTO law is based on 'regulatory competition' and *de facto* on mutual recognition of standards.[176] A country cannot, under WTO law, impose its standards by extraterritorial reach outside its own territory. But both the *Tuna-Dolphin* panel reports and the *Shrimp-Tuna* Appellate Body decision have left an opening: if there is a tangible impact on the importing state, then import restrictions could be justified if there is a good environmental reason, sound scientific evidence, and reasonable prior efforts to reach a bilateral or multilateral agreement and if the least restrictive measure necessary for the purpose is chosen.[177] It makes sense to leave decisions on environmental policies to the exporting state if there are no cross-border externalities—while careful regulation of the role of the importing state by reference to procedural and substantive rules makes more sense if the production process has extraterritorial effects.[178] Unilateralism combined with an extraterritorial reach for such trade sanctions tends to indicate incompatibility with Article XX GATT; while the existence of recognized international standards (best in an environmental treaty to which both countries are parties), together with a serious effort to find a consensus-based solution, tends to indicate compatibility. This WTO-specific formulation is not that far from the 'protective' principle which is often used in general international law to justify extraterritorial regulation. Furthermore, reliance on and conformity with relevant environmental agreements—i.e. those effective between the parties—or with universally accepted multilateral guidelines can justify such trade sanctions, again provided that there is no protectionist intention and effect,

---

[174] See here also the detailed discussion of the problems the EU had in making its import restriction against furs from animals caught by leghold traps GATT-compatible: J. Scott, *EU Environmental Law* (London: Longman 1998), pp. 95–6. The internal conclusion was that short of a multilateral agreement or recognized guideline to rely on, such import restrictions based on the production process rather than on the product itself were infringing the GATT obligations of the EU and its member states.

[175] T. Wälde. 'Managing the Risk of Sanctions in the Global Oil and Gas Industry', 36 *Texas International Law Journal* (2001).

[176] J. Weiler, 'Epilogue: Towards a Common Law of International Trade', in J. Weiler (ed.), *The EU, the WTO and the NAFTA* (Oxford: OUP 2000), pp. 201, 230, 231.

[177] The first Tuna/Dolphin report considered it relevant that the US had 'not demonstrated that it had exhausted all options reasonably available to it to pursue its dolphin protection objectives, in particular through the negotiations of international cooperative arrangements'. The report is available at: <http://www.worldtradelaw.net/reports/gattpanels/tunadolphinI.pdf> (accessed 9.8.2012).

[178] See H. Ward and D. Brack (eds), *Trade, Investment and the Environment* (London: RIIA 2001).

no discrimination and the least restrictive method necessary for the purpose is chosen.[179] One can perhaps infer from the sequence of WTO decisions that, once a country uses trade sanctions to impose its standards on others, it bears a heavy burden of proof as to legitimacy of principle, solid scientific evidence of risk, conformity with accepted international guidelines or environmental agreements effective between both states, and evidence of serious efforts to reach an agreed solution. This set of tests requires some reasonable assessment of the likely impact of the measure proposed (and the proposal of alternative and less restrictive measures commensurate with the risk) for the objective. These standards are very reasonable: they take into account that each country (or the EU) will find its own standards superior to others, represent rather the morally superior environmental intention then the more basic protectionist effect and are blind towards environmental damage caused within the country while being extra sharp-eyed as regards the eco-faults of the other country.

In short, the WTO standards act as a countervailing force to the arrogance of economic power blinded by an ideology of self-superiority. One needs to realize, though, that while the WTO standards may afford legal protection to weaker countries against the leverage exercised by stronger economies, the economic pull of standards in a powerful market will, whatever the legal situation, exercise strong pressure on the importing country producers to conform. The instruments of pressure are consumer expectations, increasingly formalized in labelling and other forms of mandatory or voluntary information, importer specifications and many other forms of pressure and types of conditionality. But that should not lead to the imposition of globally harmonized standards at the level of the most powerful import market, as such harmonization would deny the weaker economies the chance to exploit the few comparative advantages left open to them.

The EU's legitimate environmental objective cannot be to compel non-EU countries to adopt their own, better standards in order to create a level playing field. It must be that import restriction is the only way to prevent serious environmental harm to the EU—and in this case, given the extraterritorial reach undermining the sovereignty of the export state, serious efforts at reaching a cooperative agreement must have been tried and reliance on accepted guidelines must have been sought. Lower environmental standards in power production may, for example, have an effect through the emission of noxious (SO_2) gases migrating westwards, basically through low-standard burning of coal and fuel oil. A low-standard nuclear plant may constitute a risk of accident with serious implications (like Chernobyl in 1986) for an EU country. The question then is whether import restriction is necessary to manage that risk, and whether it is the least restrictive method available. But it is likely that under the impact of an import restriction the electricity would instead

---

[179] This is a very short summary of a much more complex and much discussed issue. See F. Weiss, 'The Second Tuna Gatt Panel Report', 8(1) *Leiden Journal of International Law* (1995), pp. 135–50 and F. Abott, 'The North American Integration Regime', in J. Weiler (ed.), *The EU, the WTO and the NAFTA* (Oxford: OUP 2000), pp. 189 and 200. Both the second Tuna-Dolphin panel and the AB in the Shrimp-Turtle case were ready to interpret Article XX GATT in light of environmental agreements.

be sold to lower-tariff-paying customers in East Europe. That would not reduce the environmental risk for the EU, but possibly even increase it—as less revenue would be available for upgrading. The same applies to the nuclear power plant. Shutting nuclear power producers out from a wealthy export market is unlikely to lead to closure, but rather to further deterioration. The Chernobyl accident did not happen because the Soviet plant could export to the EU, but perhaps rather because it could not, and was therefore not connected to the safety culture (resources) of prosperous energy export markets. The right solution, rather than extraterritorial compulsion by the economically and politically stronger country, would be to seek to develop or rely on common guidelines (for nuclear safety and the filtering of coal-based electricity production) which do not have to be those of the EU, but may be drawn from a more neutral source; and also to seek either to provide finance, or to maximize electricity imports to raise finance for such upgrading to better environmental quality and nuclear safety. Protection of the global climate against CO_2 emissions might also be a reasonable environmental justification, based on the Kyoto Protocol. However, an importing country such as Germany cannot rely on climate change considerations when its own policies and industry are much more damaging to the global environment than, for example, nuclear electricity imports, which in fact substantially reduces German coal- or oil-based emissions.[180]

A simple import restriction would be likely to contravene GATT and cannot be justified under its Article XX. Such contravention would also arise if WTO rules were to be applied via Article 29 of the ECT (e.g. to Ukrainian or Russian electricity). Energy investors from ECT member countries operating in the import-restricting country would also be able to invoke Article 26 ECT on investment arbitration if the import restriction could be seen as protectionist discrimination—i.e. if domestic companies could import electricity from their established sources, but the foreign investor could not. It would make a difference if the trade sanction were primarily used to enforce a multilateral agreement (to which both countries must be parties). Such agreements (ratified, effective) with both the EU and the CEEC countries (plus Russia and Ukraine) which impose minimum safety standards on nuclear plants or minimum environmental standards on power plants do not currently exist.

---

[180] There is another parallel to the Tuna-Dolphin, Shrimp-Turtle cases: while the US imposed its standards of proper production on other countries, it was of the five countries involved in the shrimp dispute the one with the lowest record of ratification of multilateral environmental treaties, reference by Arden-Clarke in H. Ward and D. Brack (eds), *Trade, Investment and the Environment* (London: RIIA 2001), p. 184.

6.10 Concluding Thoughts: The Emergence of the EU as an International Player

Given the challenges of the integration process, and in particular the delayed, much-resisted, and technically difficult integration of EU energy markets, it is perhaps not surprising that the external dimension of EU energy law started to emerge relatively late, and is still largely absent. But the EU's energy supply is more dependent than most other areas on the smooth functioning of international trade—and the energy trade is as a rule conducted with volatile, high-risk and, from a governance perspective, problematic countries close to the eastern and southern fringes of the EU. This dependency should be reflected in its approach to its partners. The current approach is too EU centered and should be replaced by a more balanced one where the interests of the producing countries is genouinly taken into consideration when making decisions impact the trading partners. This is particularly so with gas markets.

Energy is affected by most of the EU's economic cooperation treaties. In most cases, the move towards customs union, the principles of investment promotion, sustainability, and environmental attention include the energy sector. But these references and instruments have something intangible about them. There are replete with high-sounding intentions and objectives, but, apart perhaps from trade, short on tangible and specific mechanisms. The EU has not, so far, and apart from the ECT, achieved a tangible, creative mechanism which goes beyond marginal and moral support to facilitation of trade and investment. There is no innovative institution, no working mechanism, to bring Russian and Central Asian gas to Europe (clearly, the EU-Russia Energy Dialogue is not a valid example here), no clear-cut result in making former Soviet nuclear reactors safe, no deal with OPEC involving prices, taxes, production, and climate change (though this is now becoming more feasible), but rather a lot of words, good intentions, and aid funds disbursed by a directorate general without a clear (energy) focus. Why is that so? Perhaps it reflects the fact that the EU has not yet fully grasped the fact that many of the challenges of energy supply are in building solid structures with the supplier countries, and that one has to look not only at one's own interests and constraints (of which there are many) but also at the interests and constraints of the supplier countries to find workable deals. That requires a dramatic change in mental outlook—from the inside to the outside—which may be hard for an organization such as the EU and its services to make. One might also point to a leadership vacuum, reflecting the general difficulty of conducting foreign policy in an inchoate federal system where national jealousy—emanating in particular from former imperial countries—hinders the exercise of leadership. National power and leadership potential seems to have gone, but rather into a black hole than into the Commission and the other EU structures. That is possibly the price to be paid for having a federation, and not a European 'Super State'. Who can speak with authority and strike a deal? It seems that this is increasingly the task of the European Commission. Here, the 'old world' with strong state involvement in the energy sector seems to be returning, but the role of the state is often taken by the European Commission. This ideological shift, from the state to the markets and back, is the subject of Chapter 7.

7

From State to Market and Back

The Changing Role(s) of Markets and States in the EU

Energy market governance in the EU is undergoing another paradigm shift. While the contemporary ideology behind energy market regulation in most western nations over the last couple of decades has been that the introduction of competition will create well-functioning markets and contribute to security of supply, the current paradigm shift leads us back towards a market model more driven by the state and by the public sector.

The past ideology was based on the idea that energy, like other sectors of the economy, responds to the economic rules of the market, going where the prices are highest, with its use, substitution, and investments responding to prices. As is discussed in more detail in this chapter, recent thinking and empirical evidence in this area indicate that the issue might not be this simple. Drawing on the recent economic literature and the experience in the EU, this chapter discusses this paradigm shift and focuses on the question of whether international competition and free markets can deliver investment and security of supply or whether public intervention and control is necessary.

7.1 The 1980s and the Movement from a State-Driven to a Market-Driven Approach to the Energy Markets

European electricity and gas market liberalization is a relatively recent phenomenon. While application of Treaty law was always possible, it was only in the 1980s that things started to move, but not in a European vacuum. The EU was not alone in its move away from state-driven markets to competition-led markets. Similar examples from around the world might be mentioned and the EU could, and did, look for examples from other countries.

The system of energy monopolies served Europe well in the phase of rebuilding the national economies after World War II. However, this system, driven by a public sector populated by national monopolies, had by the 1980s lost its purpose and political legitimacy. The idea that energy could be run privately in competitive markets was generally speaking unthinkable—except in the minds of economic theoreticians—before the 1980s. With models from the US and UK, the EU Member States saw the opportunity to break out from the old 'conceptual and psychological barrier' of state-centred public services to a new era of 'post-welfare or regulatory state'.[1] As a result, the political credibility of the old world concepts like 'public service' lost persuasiveness, in particular because making a simple comparison with other countries' energy policies demonstrated that a proper and universal energy supply could be had in more market-based regimes. In this situation, the EU aligned itself with the development of innovation in these other (national) markets.[2]

Section 7.2 illustrates this first paradigm shift by examining the transformation of two regulatory energy market concepts over time. The aim here is to distinguish between the guiding concepts of the 'old economy' and those of the 'new economy'. The 'old economy' in this context reflects the energy law and policy discourse of the 'old', state-owned, vertically organized, and monolithic energy industry of the 1950s to 1980s (and in practice beyond); while the 'new economy' reflects the influence of the new paradigms of the global markets— i.e. privatization, and the dominance of the horizontal, contractually-organized processes of competitive markets.

7.2 Old and New Energy Economy Paradigm Concepts: Security of Supply and Public Service

There are two traditional energy concepts, both of which are continuously referred to by all participants in the EU energy law and policy dialogue: security of supply[3] and public service.[4] Both express the major concerns of national economies with fully segregated energy sectors: the external concern about failing to obtain the energy resources on which the economy is dependent, and the internal concern of satisfying the politicized expectation that the state will guarantee the availability of energy on terms acceptable to the prevailing political and social culture— whether it is uniform across the country irrespective of cost and bargaining power, or with differentiations (e.g. consumers and/or with special treatment of socially disadvantaged people, industry, attracting new industries) which are accepted. The typical response to security of supply concerns are: stockpiling (e.g. IEA and EU oil stocks); establishing or maintaining otherwise inefficient industries (e.g. German coal); subsidizing the development of otherwise unattractive foreign supply sources;

---

[1] C. Scott, 'Services of General Interest in EC Law: Matching Values of Regulatory Technique in the Public and Privatized Sectors', 6(4) *European Law Journal* (2000), pp. 310–25.

[2] There are various options on how to deal with public services in competitive markets. The Anglo-Saxon approach is based on using the public service model only to correct market failures, an approach that was largely adopted in the EU, at least in theory. See the discussion in R. Karova, *Liberalisation of Electricty Markets and Public Service Obligations in the Energy Community* (Alphen aan den Rijn: Kluwer Law International 2012), pp. 56 et seq.

[3] For the security of supply concept, see K. Talus, 'Security of Supply—An Increasingly Political Notion', in B. Delvaux, M. Hunt, and K. Talus (eds), *EU Energy Law and Policy Issues* (Brussels: Euroconfidentiel 2008).

[4] For public service concept, see T. Deruytter, W. Geldhof, and F. Vandendriessche, 'Public Service Obligations in the Electricity and Gas Markets', in B. Delvaux, M. Hunt, and K. Talus (eds), *EU Energy Law and Policy Issues* (Cambridge: Intersentia 2011).

and emphasizing the political dimension by means of intergovernmental supply arrangements. The response to public service concerns is the obligation for the licensed and/or state-owned monopolist to provide universal supply at standardized regulated tariffs, minimizing otherwise likely differentiation (e.g. based on cost of supply, in particular location and volume).

Both concepts are linked to, and indeed a reflection of, the traditional organization of energy industries throughout the EU. The main model was full vertical and horizontal integration nationwide. Generation, transportation, and supply to industrial and domestic consumers were generally handled by a government monopoly, organized by means of hierarchical planning and command, sometimes through administrative, inter-agency agreements. Countries such as Germany did not have an all-encompassing state enterprise monopoly structure, but a variety of private actors were involved, although electricity and gas distribution was typically handled by a local or regional monopoly. Other countries, such as the Netherlands and Denmark, had a combination of both approaches, with a state monopoly for generation and transportation and private companies for distribution (but again with a local distribution monopoly).[5] In these situations, the state was held directly responsible by the public for all failings in the energy industries, since it had direct influence on decision-making and had set up and protected the various monopolies in existence. Security of supply and public service are hence the reflection of society's political expectations with regard to the state.

Traditional guiding concepts of energy law weighed much less heavily in the new market economy approach which dominated policy choices in the 1990s and beyond. The new market paradigm was that in a functioning market economy, security of supply is ensured by the politically unrestricted operations of market operators. If shortages develop, these will be managed mainly by price signals—higher prices for scarcer commodities will restrict demand and increase output. It was, of course, admitted that there could be some delay in adaptation as energy demand often only responds slowly to small price changes. The thought was nevertheless that inefficient state intervention in markets would be the primary security risk. In a similar way, notions about public services underwent change. It was no longer expected that all consumers, household or industry, would pay the same. Competition and variety of situations generate extensive consumer choice, which again, it was thought, would be reflected in different price patterns. The approach was essentially that, in a proper market economy, one could not expect commercial operators to be responsible for welfare functions—e.g. subsidies to ensure energy access for the poor or for remote regions—but that these could be handled by direct government subsidies or through the use of conditions attached to energy licences in a way that did not provide a competitive advantage to one particular operator.

---

[5] These pre-liberalization schemes and the development towards the more liberalized system are discussed in Chapter 2.

This does not mean that these stalwarts of the past had lost all credibility. They were simply understood in a different way from before. The public still expects the state, as the controller of last resort, to ensure that energy is available under non-abusive conditions, even though public expectations always tend to be greater than the reasonable ability of the government to deliver. But there is one significant difference to the old concept: the introduction of the efficiency considerations to this area of energy policy, well in line with the general drivers of the liberalization of EU energy markets. This search for balance between markets and efficiency and the public services was visible from the Commission's first communications in this area: the 1996 Communication on public services[6] is a good example as it focuses on this interplay between old and new system, and the search for a balance between public services and a market-based method is particularly clear. Here, the Commission noted that the EU's involvement in the area of services of general interest is within the context of an open economy and based on a commitment to solidarity, social cohesion, and market mechanisms.

Now, instead of direct state intervention, the conditions attached to energy operators' licenses tend to ensure that all people have access to energy and that remote areas are not disconnected from the supply. This is done either by means of direct government subsidy, by authorization of otherwise unacceptable cross-subsidization, or by matching some preferences to the (typically) former monopolist against an obligation to act as supplier of last resort: i.e. governmental insurance against the risk of market failure.[7] The same applies to security of supply: the new approach was that it would be very costly for a government to engage directly in intergovernmental deals which then need to be implemented by operators applying commercial criteria. However, the role of the government in this area was not completely abandoned, but rather reduced. There was still a rationale for public encouragement of diversification of supply. But it was thought that such encouragement would be better achieved by facilitating an international environment for peaceful and stable commercial cooperation—i.e. by reducing political risk, minimizing transaction costs, and facilitating large-scale high-risk transactions, rather than by direct intervention. Equally, while the market was expected to balance supply and demand even in times of disruption, there was still scope for public sector encouragement for the establishment of back-up facilities and reserves to avoid localized disruptions.

7.3 The 'Brave New World': Energy Economy Paradigms of the 1980s and 1990s

The new energy economy replaced vertical hierarchical relations with vertical-and-horizontal commercial relations in the form of contracts. In its ideal form,

---

[6] Communication from the Commission, 'Services of General Interest in Europe' (COM(96) 443 final) 11 September 1996.

[7] In the EU, this trade-off and the ultimate distrust to a pure market-based mechanism has translated into the connection between the EU concept of security of supply and public-service obligation.

the functions of generation, transport, and distribution are owned by different, privately-owned companies. Where remnants of monopolies persist—either in the transition from a monopolistic to a market-based system, or in the form of a gradually disappearing 'natural monopoly',[8] with typically over large-capacity, long-distance electricity transmission lines, and gas pipelines[9]—a government agency (a ministry or independent regulator and/or competition authority) will be present. This presence is not maintained in order to instruct companies how to operate, but to monitor monopoly power and to intervene if necessary to counter the effect of dominant market power, most frequently in the form of establishing procedures for access to the natural monopoly facility.[10] The regulator—an absolutely new concept as compared to the traditional 'supervision' exercised by state agencies over state enterprises—is a guarantor of the free play of market forces. If and to the extent that energy markets become competitive, the powers of the regulator have to diminish, until the regulator only retains powers in certain limited spheres and has a general watchdog role. Given that energy supply remains politicized—i.e. the people do continue to expect the government to ensure that supply is not disrupted—the state (the regulator or other entity) also retains a 'last resort' role. That role involves ensuring: the market does not fail to supply energy; coordination if the independent and competing energy companies cannot, through market mechanisms, themselves set up such coordination; and the fulfilment of functions which the markets cannot (or can only at a high transaction

---

See L. Hancher and S. Janssen, 'Shared Competences and Multi-faceted Concepts—European Legal Framework for Security of Supply', in B. Barton, C. Redgwell, A. Rønne, and D. Zillman (eds), *Energy Security: Managing Risk in a Dynamic Legal and Regulatory Environment* (Oxford: OUP 2004), pp. 87–88.

[8] Here, a difference between various countries or regions must be noted. In the US, the more mature market structure allows for a more critical approach to claims of natural monopolies. Just consider gas: the US has several areas with significant natural gas reserves. Geographically, the South Central US, including Arkansas, Kansas, Louisiana, Oklahoma, and Texas, is the key natural gas producing region. While the same region consumes important volumes of natural gas, significant amounts are also transported to other consumption areas such as the North East and Midwest. The distances between the consuming and producing regions are covered by a highly sophisticated pipeline system. Unlike Europe, the pipeline network in the US has mainly been constructed according to economic incentives. Large-scale pipelines transport natural gas from the production areas to the consumption areas. Prices are mainly set in trading hubs, such as the Henry Hub in Louisiana or various Transco zones along the east coast. There are currently thousands of players involved in these markets as producers, pipelines, and purchasers (and a very large number of end-consumers). This different market structure, together with more philosophical factors, has led to a more critical view of natural monopolies and essential facilities. See K. Talus, 'Just What is the Scope of the Essential Facilities Doctrine in the Energy Sector: Third Party Access-friendly Interpretation in the EU v. Contractual Freedom in the US', 48(5) *Common Market Law Review* (2011). For market information, see <http://www.eia.doe.gov>.

[9] Natural monopoly is far from easy to define as it depends on technology, economics, market response, and legal regulation. It used to be assumed that all of the energy industries were natural monopolies. Now it is assumed that only certain elements—typically long-distance transit, where building an alternative is financially prohibitive or prevented by environmental considerations—still form a natural monopoly. It may be that technological change, with due respect to environmental constraints, may also change the natural monopoly character of long-distance electricity transmission.

[10] Through regulation or though strategic application of antitrust rules. On this, see K. Talus, *Vertical Natural Gas Transportation Capacity, Upstream Commodity Contracts and EU Competition Law* (Alphen aan den Rijn: Kluwer Law International 2011).

cost) discharge. These include the initiation and formalization of technical standards, continuing public-purpose functions (the promotion of unconventional and environmentally sound new energy technologies), and the protection of socially disadvantaged people.

The new energy economy paradigm in the EU can therefore be characterized as the juxtaposition of autonomous markets with economic regulation. But the increasing integration of energy industries, first within the EU and then into the global markets, highlights new key concepts. The first is competitiveness. As with the concepts of security of supply and public service discussed, competitiveness is now an ever-present theme in the Commission's official documents.[11] Its new prominence is due to the realization that the EU, and its Member States, as part of an increasingly wide-reaching global economy, are in competition with other economies worldwide and that the EU has been falling behind its main competitors— previously the US and now increasingly China and India. In terms of innovation and innovativeness, the US still seems to be ahead of the game, the 'shale gas revolution' being but one example of the ability of free and competitive markets to deliver new innovations. China's strong economic growth and the state backing given to its companies make it a competitor in a different sense, in terms of inter- national competition for resources.

The presence of a regulatory regime is a significant factor affecting competi- tiveness. A push towards change in the 1980s also came from the realization that price comparisons indicated lower energy prices in large parts of the US and in the competitive energy economies as compared to energy prices in countries where the energy companies were state-owned or organized on corporativist lines—approaches which typically spelled higher production costs (including labour and regulatory compliance costs). This meant that energy-intensive industries in Europe had an additional competitive disadvantage to overcome. Similarly, the utilization and inte- gration of modern technologies, the internationalization of corporate operations and the transformation of energy companies into 'new economy' organizations were more advanced in the US than in Europe, thus giving US energy companies the opportunity to occupy early-starter positions in the new world energy economy, though not always successfully.

In addition to competitiveness, achieving an internal energy market was a second key topic for EU energy policy. While the single market has been an EU objec- tive from the beginning, it evolved only gradually, with great acceleration through the single-market programme of the Delors Presidency in the 1980s. But energy has always been a thing apart. It was disputed for a long time—by the energy

---

[11] For example, Communication from the Commission to the European Parliament, the Council, the European Economic and Social Committee and the Committee of the Regions, 'Second Strategic Energy Review: an EU energy security and solidarity action plan' (COM/2008/0781 final); Green paper, 'A European Strategy for Sustainable, Competitive and Secure Energy?' (COM/2006/105 final), 8 March 2006. See also the Communication from the Commission to the European Parliament and the Council, 'Energy Infrastructure and Security of Supply' (COM/2003/743 final), 10.12.2003, p. 3 and Council Resolution of 23 November 1995 on the Green Paper For a European Union Energy Policy, OJ C 327/3, 07.12.1995, p. 3.

monopolies and affiliated vested interests—whether the energy industries were or should be part of the single market programme, both in policy and legal terms. The internal energy market has only been fully recognized relatively recently as being an accepted EU objective, with grudging acceptance of the consecutive energy directives. It has both an EU-internal dimension—completing economic integration with 'heavy' and very 'national' sectors—and an external dimension, strengthening the competitiveness of the EU in the global economy, although the latter issue seems of less prominence and more important to the liberalizing Member States than to the EU consensus as such. While the European Court in Luxembourg has, as rule, been famous for taking integration-friendly approaches in applying EU law, this has been much less the case with respect to integration of the energy sector. In fact, for a long time, a strong sympathy for the old-economy approach of viewing energy as a thing apart, a strategic asset—thus justifying a much more intensive governmental involvement—could be perceived.[12] It is difficult to explain this relative reversal of a pro-integrationist attitude in energy cases. Probable reasons for it include the Court's reluctance to get involved in an area that seems to require in-depth economic expertise, the risk of being criticized for a questionable assessment of the economic consequences of its decisions, and wariness about intervening in what may have appeared to the Court as an area of wide-ranging, complex economic policy-making. The 1997 judgments[13] against the Commission's attempt to obtain a judicial lifting of the energy import/export monopolies may also involve the Court's tacit desire not to get involved in or disrupt the complex intergovernmental negotiations over the then pending energy directives. The Court may also have been ready to defer more in the case of energy than in other, 'light' industry cases, to claims that opening up national energy sectors may affect the public service obligation perceived and strongly advocated, especially in France, as an essential element of national identity. This approach, however, has seemingly changed in the new millennium with the judgments in cases like C-17/03, *VEMW and others*[14] or C-439/06, *Citiworks*.[15] The first-mentioned case led to major changes in the way in which EU cross-border trade is managed. The second, underlining the central position of third party access in the EU energy *acquis*, required the legislator to provide for more explicit exemptions from third party access.

---

[12] Case C-72/83, *Campus Oil Ltd v Minister of Industry and Energy* [1984] ECR 2727 or the 1997 cases: Case C-159/94, *Commission v France* [1997] ECR I-5815; Case C-158/94, *Commission v Italy* [1997] ECR I-5789; Case C-157/94, *Commission v Netherlands* [1997] ECR I-5699; and C-160/97, *Commission v Spain* [1997] ECR I-5851.

[13] Case C-159/94, *Commission v France* [1997] ECR I-5815; Case C-158/94, *Commission v Italy* [1997] ECR I-5789; Case C-157/94, *Commission v Netherlands* [1997] ECR I-5699; and C-160/97, *Commission v Spain* [1997] ECR I-5851.

[14] C-17/03, *VEMW and others* [2005] ECR I-4983.

[15] C-439/06, *Citiworks AG Flughafen Leipzig v Halle GmbH, Bundesnetzagentur* [2008] ECR I-3913.

7.4 'Back to the Future': A (Partial) Return to the Old Days of State Intervention

As experiences with liberalization in the EU and elsewhere have started to accumulate, the results are mixed. In essence, it seems that privately-run industry acting in a liberalized environment is very good at creating efficiency, since its ability to create value for each monetary unit spent is far greater than that of state-run monopolistic companies. Similarly, its ability to create efficiency from the existing infrastructure is clearly superior to state-run systems. However, its ability to invest in and create new infrastructure is less clear. This does not mean that the end-customer price would be substantially lower post-liberalization or post-privatization. On the contrary, Pollitt shows how privatization in the South East European context improved efficiency where accompanied by independent regulation. However, he also shows that privatization and independent regulation have no clear or significant effect on prices.[16] In a somewhat similar fashion, another study on gas markets in the EU 15 concludes that '[p]rivatization *per se* does not lead to lower prices for consumers'.[17] Of course, privatization is not liberalization, although in many cases these concepts are introduced in tandem or during the same period. Furthermore, liberalization does have an impact on public ownership and public sector control of the energy companies and energy markets. Some degree of unbundling usually forms part of the process of liberalization. Similarly, potential access and new competitive pressure have an impact.[18] Current international experiences with liberalization and privatization are well summarized by Michael Pollitt:

'Liberalisation seems to be associated with improved efficiency, greater investment and access to services, but higher prices for at least some customer groups. However the net gains are small, of the order of 5% of costs. Thus price rebalancing and the raising of utility rates of return can easily leave some customers substantially worse off. This would be especially true if poor consumers (who could be most of the customers in a developing country) were getting heavily subsidised (or even free) electricity. There have also been some very well publicised failed reforms such as in the Ukraine or California. Arguably these are failures to fully implement an appropriate reform model, but undoubtedly the California case highlighted how difficult it was even for a developed country to get the appropriate package of reforms right.' [References omitted.]

7.5 Problems with a Market-Based Approach in the EU

There are two significant and clearly visible caveats to the market-based approach in the EU energy markets. First, real world distortions work against the price

---

[16] M. Pollitt, 'Evaluating the Evidence on Electricity Reform: Lessons for the South East Europe (SEE) Market', 17(19) *Utilities Policy* (2009), pp.13–23.

[17] R. Brau, R. Doronzo, C.V. Fiorio, and M. Florio, 'EU Gas Reforms and Consumers' Prices', 31(4) *The Energy Journal* (2010), pp. 167–82.

[18] M. Pollitt, *The Role of Policy in Energy Transitions: Lessons from the Energy Liberalisation Era* (Cambridge Working Paper in Economics 1216).

responsiveness of energy investments. In the EU, these distortions have been underestimated. The *Italian ENI/Trans Tunisian Pipeline* case[19] offers an example of market distortions or failures. In this case, the leading Italian gas wholesale company, ENI, had blocked a pre-agreed expansion of a pipeline between Italy and Algeria. ENI decided to discontinue the project only after several independent shippers had concluded agreements with suppliers and declared their intention to use the pipeline to penetrate the Italian market.[20] Invoking the potential risk to its supply interests through an increase in gas imports to Italy, ENI blocked the expansion. The Italian antitrust authority concluded that ENI had abused its dominant position on the Italian markets. The European Commission has also investigated similar practices by many major EU companies such as GDF Suez,[21] E.ON,[22] and ENI.[23]

Secondly, while investments may respond to demand in the long term, they do not seem to do so in the short term. It seems that the suggestion that energy will respond to the economic rules of the markets can be considered in long-term scenarios, but is not necessarily the case in the short term, especially for network-bound sectors like natural gas or electricity. Energy investments with long lead-times cannot respond quickly to short-term market signals. In addition, while there might be demand in a given area, this demand might not be important enough to sustain a commercial project. The IKL oil pipeline is an example of this kind of problem, where the markets failed to deliver investment for security of supply. While the markets did not see the need for this alternative supply source for the Czech Republic, it proved to be necessary from a security of supply perspective when the companies supplying Russian crude oil unexpectedly reduced their supplies to the Czech Republic in July 2008.[24]

Because of the difficulties in the EU as explained throughout this book, the previous market-based approach has started to change. This change will now be illustrated on two levels: the level of Treaty law, through the introduction of solidarity as a corrective measure to market failures; and on a practical level, though the Nabucco pipeline project and some of the changes introduced in the third legislative package that entered into force in March 2011.

---

[19] Case A 358, decision by the Italian Autorità Garante della Concorrenza e del Mercato of 15.2.2004.

[20] The DG Competition Report on the energy sector inquiry (SEC(2006)1724) 10.1.2007, p. 59.

[21] Case COMP/B-1/39.316—Gaz de France (gas market foreclosure).

[22] COMP/39.317—E.On gas foreclosure.

[23] COMP/39.315—ENI. For the other recent cases, see COMP/39.316—GDF foreclosure or COMP/39.317—E.ON gas foreclosure. For a more detailed analysis of how interconnectors can be used to prevent competition see K. Talus, *Vertical Natural Gas Transportation Capacity, Upstream Commodity Contracts and EU Competition Law* (Alphen aan den Rijn: Kluwer Law International 2011) (for gas) or K. Talus and T. Wälde, 'Electricity Interconnectors—a Serious Challenge for EC Competition Law', 3 *Competition and Regulation in Network Industries* (2006), pp. 355–90 (for electricity). See also the OGEL database for similar papers (<http://www.ogel.org>).

[24] Commission Green Paper, 'Towards a secure, sustainable and competitive European energy network' (COM/2008/782 final).

7.6 'All for One and One for All': Economic Solidarity after the Lisbon Treaty

7.6.1 Introduction

The references to the EU solidarity in the TFEU seem to relate to two very different notions of solidarity. First, solidarity seems to relate to the social bond between the peoples of Europe (but not people of Europe). This type of the solidarity can be seen as inherent in the idea of a social Europe. The second type of solidarity notion is that of a risk pool: i.e. an agreement between states to intervene on a reciprocal basis if one encounters unforeseen difficulties—one for all and all for one. Energy solidarity is an illustration of this type of solidarity approach in the EU.

While not a new concept in EU discourse, the question of 'solidarity' has recently gained in importance. With the current debt crisis and the situation in Greece and other mainly—but not only—southern European countries, the question of solidarity has been reflected on and debated in great detail in many Member States. On many occasions, the political opposition—riding on the Euro-skeptic sentiments of the populations in many Member States—has grown in popularity.

But the debt crisis is not the only context where solidarity plays a role. Solidarity between the peoples of different countries has been highlighted with the growing significance of the social aspects of EU policy.[25] In this context, AG Kokott has referred to the principle of financial solidarity.[26] This type of solidarity seems to have dominated the EC Treaty, Article 2 of which made reference to the promotion of economic and social cohesion and solidarity among Member States.[27] Similarly, the inclusion of asylum and immigration in the EU *acquis* has been connected to the idea of solidarity. These readings of solidarity have both economic and non-economic aspects. Like AG Kokott, it refers to the sharing of the financial burden that free movement of people and the right to reside in a member state necessarily causes. But on a more abstract level, it also refers to a *de facto* solidarity inherent in the very agreement to create common mechanisms and shared spaces. This type of general solidarity seems to be behind the idea of EU solidarity in the 1992 Maastricht Treaty. Its Article A stated: 'the Union shall be founded on the European Communities, supplemented by the policies and forms of cooperation established by this Treaty. Its task shall be to organize, in a manner demonstrating consistency and solidarity, relations between the Member States and between their peoples.' Furthermore, in the area of common foreign and security policy, Article 11(2) of the Maastricht Treaty stated that the 'Member States shall support the Union's

---

[25] In a somewhat similar but more detailed fashion, the TFEU also refers to solidarity in the area of asylum, immigration, and external border control (Article 67 TFEU). Under Article 80 TFEU, reference is also made to the financial implications of sharing responsibility in this area.

[26] Opinion of AG Kokott in Case C-480/08, *Maria Teixeira v London Borough of Lambeth and Secretary of State for the Home Department* delivered on 20 October 2009, paras. 82–85. The idea of solidarity has also been behind other cases like Case C-456/02, *Trojani* [2004] ECR I-7573.

[27] This was also noted, with references to Article 2 EC, in Protocol (No 28) on economic and social cohesion (1992).

external and security policy actively and unreservedly in a spirit of loyalty and mutual solidarity'. Arguably, all of these references to solidarity will have financial aspects, but it also seems that the primary objective is not a reference to financial solidarity but rather a *de facto* solidarity between the peoples of Europe.

Similarly, the principle of solidarity under Article 80 TFEU refers to both financial and other implications of the common policies on border checks, asylum, and immigration. The implementation of these policies is governed by the principle of solidarity and the fair sharing of responsibility, including its financial implications, between the Member States. Whenever necessary, EU acts adopted under the chapter on border checks, asylum and immigration should contain appropriate measures to give effect to this principle.

In addition to these embodiments of solidarity, energy solidarity appears prominently in the language of the Lisbon Treaty. This is the case with the new energy specific Article 194 TFEU as well as the more general Article 122 TFEU. In this second example, the notion of solidarity was added with the Lisbon Treaty. The provision that existed prior to Lisbon Treaty was Article 100 EC, which read: 'without prejudice to any other procedures provided for in this Treaty, the Council may, acting unanimously on a proposal from the Commission, decide upon the measures appropriate to the economic situation, in particular if severe difficulties arise in the supply of certain products.' But here, though the idea of solidarity can perhaps be read into the text, no actual references to 'solidarity' can be found, nor were there references to 'energy'. This changed with the Lisbon Treaty. Article 122 TFEU notes that such measures may be decided 'in a spirit of solidarity between Member States' and that these difficulties in supply may be experienced, 'notably in the area of energy'.

Similarly to Article 122 TFEU, the new Article 194 (under TITLE XXI (ENERGY)) provides references to energy solidarity:

'1. In the context of the establishment and functioning of the internal market and with regard for the need to preserve and improve the environment, Union policy on energy shall aim, in a spirit of solidarity between Member States, to:
   (a) ensure the functioning of the energy market;
   (b) ensure security of energy supply in the Union;
   (c) promote energy efficiency and energy saving and the development of new and renewable forms of energy; and
   (d) promote the interconnection of energy networks.'

A specific solidarity clause was also added under Title VII in Article 222 TFEU. This provision mainly relates to the mobilization of State instruments, the military in particular, to respond to natural or man-made disasters and terrorist attacks. The details and arrangements for the implementation of this solidarity principle are to be provided by a decision adopted by the Council acting on a joint proposal by the Commission and the High Representative of the Union for Foreign Affairs and Security Policy.[28]

---

[28] In the context of natural disasters, see also Council Regulation (EC) No 2012/2002 of 11 November 2002 establishing the European Union Solidarity Fund, (OJ L 311, 14.11.2002, pp. 3–8). One of the objectives is immediate restoration to working order of infrastructure and plant in the fields of energy (Article 3(a)).

In addition to internal solidarity, which in essence seems to relate to response to certain events, there is also an external element to solidarity. It seems rather obvious that Article 194 TFEU is applicable to external as well as internal relations. In addition to this, solidarity is also mentioned in Article 11(2) TFEU which notes: 'The Member States shall support the Union's external and security policy actively and unreservedly in a spirit of loyalty and mutual solidarity. The Member States shall work together to enhance and develop their mutual political solidarity.'[29]

The relevant question is of course the impact of these references to solidarity on political, judicial, or legislative developments. A first distinction must be made between the provisions referring to the 'principle of solidarity' and the references to 'the spirit of solidarity'. Presumably, the drafters of the Lisbon Treaty made this distinction intentionally. This might suggest that the principle is intended to have a more significant impact than the mere requirements that something be done in the spirit of solidarity.

It has been suggested that it is possible 'to assume that the "solidarity" clause will be applied in the future also in the spirit and purpose of the law and in line with the *effet utile* principle of the ECJ jurisdiction'.[30] This is arguably possible, but the counter-argument would be that the general and open-ended and primarily political nature of the references to solidarity in the TFEU suggests that this addition will have limited judicial impact. Its role would be primarily in policy-making and it would affect political negotiations rather than judicial proceedings. In many ways, its impact could be close to the application of the subsidiarity principle.

7.6.2 Solidarity and Market Failure

The ideology behind the EU's energy market liberalization programme was to maximize efficiency. This was to be done through the introduction of competition. At the height of the market-based approach, the thought was that the introduction of competition would contribute to security of supply. Energy would respond to the economic rules of the market, going where the prices are highest: its use, substitution, and investments would respond to prices. This did not happen and over the last few years, energy security has become 'the big issue', at times challenging climate change as the most urgent concern for EU energy policy.

---

[29] This external element of solidarity was one of the key messages in the 2008 Second Strategic Energy Review: ' ... while each Member State is responsible for its own security, solidarity between Member States is a basic feature of EU membership. With the internal market for energy, specific national solutions are often insufficient. Strategies to share and spread risk, and to make the best use of the combined weight of the EU in world affairs can be more effective than dispersed national actions. For these reasons, energy security is an issue of common EU concern' (Communication from the Commission to the European Parliament, the Council, the European Economic and Social Committee and the Committee of the Regions—Second Strategic Energy Review: an EU energy security and solidarity action plan (SEC(2008) 2870) (SEC(2008) 2871) (SEC(2008) 2872) (COM/2008/0781 final)).

[30] J.-P. Pielow and B. J. Lewendel, 'Beyond "Lisbon": EU Competences in the Field of Energy Policy', in B. Delvaux, M. Hunt, and K. Talus (eds), *EU Energy Law and Policy Issues* (Cambridge: Intersentia 2011), p. 300.

One way of approaching solidarity in the TFEU is to see the introduction of solidarity references as an attempt to create a corrective mechanism to the failure of the markets to achieve security of supply. The notion of solidarity was only introduced after it became increasingly clear that the markets had failed to create security of supply. A market-based security of supply scheme of the 1980s and 1990s was replaced or complemented by a public-sector-based solidarity scheme. Supply disruptions, like those that occurred in the flow of natural gas from Russia through Ukraine, were not sufficiently addressed by market forces. As such, a public-sector-driven response mechanism was necessary: enter solidarity.[31] It has specifically been argued that the reference to the solidarity principle in Article 194 TFEU was introduced in response to requests made by the Polish Government and relate primarily to concerns over the security of gas supply from Russia (illustrated in the Russian-Ukrainian/Georgian gas disputes).[32]

7.6.3 Economic Crises and Solidarity

Similarly to Article 194 TFEU, Article 122 TFEU also referred to both solidarity and energy. It also refers specifically to sudden crises like a supply interruption of an energy source. Compared to the energy-specific Article 194, however, Article 122(1) TFEU is more general in nature. It is applicable to severe difficulties in the supply of all kinds of products. In a similar fashion, Article 122(2) applies generally to severe difficulties caused by natural disasters or exceptional occurrences beyond the control of a Member State. In this type of situation, Union financial aid can be granted.

The regulation establishing a European financial stabilization mechanism[33] used Article 122(2) TFEU as its legal basis. The approach of the Regulation is that Article 122 provides for the possibility of granting EU financial assistance to a Member State in difficulties or seriously threatened with severe difficulties caused by exceptional occurrences beyond its control. According to this reading, such difficulties may be caused by a serious deterioration in the international economic and financial environment.[34]

---

[31] In line with this, Regulation (EU) No 994/2010 of the European Parliament and of the Council of 20 October 2010 concerning measures to safeguard security of gas supply and repealing Council Directive 2004/67/EC (OJ L 295, 12.11.2010, pp. 1–22.), adopted under Article 194(2) TFEU, builds heavily on the solidarity approach. It reflects a stronger role for the state and public sector in ensuring security of supply. (See Article 3 (noting that security of gas supply is shared between the state and the markets) and Articles 9–12 (placing the responsibility for security of supply on the state). Also, recital 20 specifically notes that the ultimate responsibility over gas supply security lies within the State.) The Regulation formalizes the response mechanisms at state, regional, and EU level, all in the spirit of solidarity.

[32] J.-P. Pielow and B.J. Lewendel, 'Beyond "Lisbon": EU Competences in the Field of Energy Policy', in B. Delvaux, M. Hunt and K. Talus (eds), *EU Energy Law and Policy Issues* (Cambridge: Intersentia 2011), p. 300. For the reasons and background to these disputes, see J. Stern, 'The Russia-Ukrainian Gas Crisis of January 2006', 4(1) *OGEL* (2006) and S. Pirani, J. Stern, and K. Yafimava, *The Russo-Ukrainian Gas Dispute of January 2009: A Comprehensive Assessment*, NG 27 (Oxford: Oxford Institute for Energy Studies February 2009).

[33] Regulation No. 407/2010 of 11 May 2010 establishing a European financial stabilisation mechanism, OJ L 118, 12.5.2010, p. 1.

[34] A separate issue is of course that the bail-outs probably have little to do with solidarity and much to do with the fear of contamination and spreading the difficulties to other EU Member States.

However, as has been noted, the wording of the provision is that a 'Member State is in difficulties or is seriously threatened with severe difficulties caused by natural disasters or exceptional occurrences beyond its control'. This seems to refer to events where the Member State had no role in the events that were caused by *force majeure*-type circumstances. Arguably, some economic circumstances may qualify as economic *force majeure* events. The location of Article 122 TFEU in the Chapter on economic policy supports this reading.[35] However, in these cases, to qualify for a situation meriting Union financial aid, Member States could not have contributed to these difficulties. Also, a literal reading of the provision suggests that Article 122 seems to have been drafted with oil or natural gas supply cuts, natural disasters, or similar events in mind. A global financial crisis and economic downturn that have exposed national weaknesses in some—though not all—EU countries, do not easily fit this reading of Article 122.

Section 7.7 examines on a more practical level the paradigm shift from market-driven systems back to those driven by the state and public sector.

7.7 Nabucco Pipeline Project

The Nabucco is a natural gas pipeline that should connect the Caspian region and the Middle East via Turkey, Bulgaria, Romania, and Hungary with Austria and then with Central and Western European gas markets. The pipeline will be approximately 3,300 km long and will be able to transport a maximum amount of 31 bcm per year.[36] Much like the BTC pipeline, Nabucco is of geopolitical significance since it will, if ever completed, bypass Russia and offer an alternative supply route coupled with new sources of natural gas. The main problem for the project is to secure sufficient volumes of gas to fill the pipeline. On the other hand, the availability of gas is not an issue for the second ongoing project, the Gazprom-driven South Stream pipeline, which will bring additional volumes of Russian gas into the same market as Nabucco.[37]

While there is a division between the EU Member States supporting these two competing projects, the European Commission strongly supports the Nabucco project. Much like the US government in the BTC project, the Commission has used various methods, ranging from negotiating with the countries in the region

---

[35] See also K. Tuori, 'The European Financial Crisis—Constitutional aspects and implications', EUI Working Papers, Law 2012/28, noting how, at first glance, Article 122(2), with its explicit reference to natural disasters, seems to address other types of 'exceptional occurrences' than economic crises. But, in fact, in drafting and negotiating what became the Maastricht Treaty, the general presumption was that the emergency provision would also allow for financial assistance to a Member State struck by an economic crisis.

[36] See <http://www.nabucco-pipeline.com>. The various aspects of this project, regulatory treatment, risks, role in EU gas supply and so on, are also examined in K. Talus, *Vertical Natural Gas Transportation Capacity, Upstream Commodity Contracts and EU Competition Law* (Alphen aan den Rijn: Kluwer Law International 2011).

[37] For these and other pipeline projects and related legal issues, see the OGEL pipeline specials (<http://www.ogel.org>).

in order to secure gas supplies to ensuring that the key transit country, Turkey, is behind this project. In this regard, the Commission has assumed the traditional role of a state in its support of the project and its energy companies. Because of these aspects, it is therefore difficult to characterize Nabucco as a purely commercial project.

The strong public sector involvement in Nabucco is also visible when considering the appointment of the 'Nabucco Coordinator'[38] under Decision No 1364/2006/EC.[39] Interestingly, the Coordinator has proposed that the Commission take an even stronger role in this area, suggesting that it 'could also standardize the agreements that underpin pipeline development (intergovernmental agreements, host government agreements, mechanisms for the implementation of strategic and project environmental assessment, etc)'. This suggestion seems effectively to mean that the Commission should impose a standard contract on weaker parties. The Coordinator further suggests that the Commission also 'needs to promote priorities; and contrary to what is now the case, we cannot have four or five "equal" priorities'. This can be read as recommending that the Commission should have an even stronger role in deciding which projects go forward. Even at the present time, the public sector, and the Commission in particular, have a significant role in deciding which projects are of key interest and merit EU funding. With the increase in direct EU funding, this role is likely to become all the more decisive.

The Communication on security of energy supply and international cooperation—'The EU Energy Policy: Engaging with Partners beyond Our Borders'—which appeared on 7 September 2011, and related developments, reinforce the trends discussed: the proposed information exchange mechanism with regard to intergovernmental agreements between Member States and third countries in the field of energy;[40] strengthening coordination when approaching partner countries; taking common positions in international organizations and developing comprehensive energy partnerships with key partner countries;[41] the option for Member States to request the assistance of the Commission in negotiations with a third country when entering into such negotiations in order to amend an existing intergovernmental agreement or to conclude a new intergovernmental agreement; the power for the Commission to exercise *ex ante* control over intergovernmental agreements; and the possibility for the Commission to negotiate EU-level agreements with

---

[38] Activity Report September 2007–February 2009 from Jozias Van Aartsen, European Coordinator, Project of European interest n° NG 3 (Brussels, 4 February 2009). Available at: <http://ec.europa.eu/energy/infrastructure/tent_e/doc/axis/2009_axis_linking_activity_report_2007_2009.pdf>.

[39] Decision No 1364/2006/EC of the European Parliament and of the Council of 6 September 2006 laying down guidelines for trans-European energy networks and repealing Decision 96/391/EC and Decision No 1229/2003/EC, OJ L 262, 22.9.2006, pp. 1–23.

[40] Proposal for a Decision setting up an information exchange mechanism with regard to intergovernmental agreements between Member States and third countries in the field of energy (COM (2011)540) 7.9.2011, Article 3.

[41] Proposal for a Decision setting up an information exchange mechanism with regard to intergovernmental agreements between Member States and third countries in the field of energy (COM(2011)540) 7.9.2011. See also Commission, Speaking with one voice—the key to securing our energy interests abroad, press release IP/11/1005, 7.9.2011.

third countries where necessary to achieve the EU core objectives, for example to facilitate large-scale infrastructure projects.[42] The Nabucco-related trans-Caspian pipeline system case is the prime example of this.[43] These developments are discussed in detail in the context of international dimensions of EU energy law and policy in Chapter 6.

7.8 The 2009 Energy Law Package: From Bottom-Up to Top-Down

EU energy law has developed through three legislative packages (1996/1998,[44] 2003,[45] and 2009[46]). While the first package introduced the idea of competition, the second accelerated the move towards a market-based system. Both legislative packages followed a bottom-up approach to markets. Market forces and competition were to drive investments in both electricity and gas infrastructure. However, with growing fears of an investment gap, the 2009 legislative package followed the changes advocated earlier by the Second Strategic Energy Review[47] and marked a departure from a pure market-based mechanism towards a mixed regime where the role of the state and public sector actors is increasingly significant.

In essence, the idea behind the change is that the private sector is unable to deliver the necessary investment in certain sections of the supply chain, and therefore stronger public intervention is necessary. For example, Article 22 of the new Gas

---

[42] Commission, Communication from the Commission to the European Parliament, the Council, the European Economic and Social Committee and the Committee of the Regions on security of energy supply and international cooperation—'The EU Energy Policy: Engaging with Partners beyond Our Borders', Brussels, 7.9.2011, (COM (2011) 539 final).

[43] Commission press release, 'EU starts negotiations on Caspian pipeline to bring gas to Europe', press release IP/11/1023, 12.9.2011.

[44] Directive 98/30/EC of the European Parliament and of the Council of 22 June 1998 concerning common rules for the internal market in natural gas OJ L 204, 21.7.1998, pp. 1–12; Directive 96/92/EC of the European Parliament and of the Council of 19 December 1996 concerning common rules for the internal market in electricity, OJ L 27, 30.1.1997, pp. 20–9.

[45] Directive 2003/55/EC of the European Parliament and of the Council of 26 June 2003 concerning common rules for the internal market in natural gas and repealing Directive 98/30/EC, OJ L 176, 15.7.2003, pp. 57–78; Directive 2003/54/EC of the European Parliament and of the Council of 26 June 2003 concerning common rules for the internal market in electricity and repealing Directive 96/92/EC, OJ L 176, 15.7.2003, pp. 37–56; Regulation (EC) No 1228/2003 of the European Parliament and of the Council of 26 June 2003 on conditions for access to the network for cross-border exchanges in electricity, OJ L 176, 15.7.2003, pp. 1–10.

[46] Regulation (EC) No 713/2009 of the European Parliament and of the Council of 13 July 2009 establishing an Agency for the Cooperation of Energy Regulators, Regulation (EC) No 714/2009 of the European Parliament and of the Council of 13 July 2009 on conditions for access to the network for cross-border exchanges in electricity and repealing Regulation (EC) No 1228/2003; Regulation (EC) No 715/2009 of the European Parliament and of the Council of 13 July 2009 on conditions for access to the natural gas transmission networks and repealing Regulation (EC) No 1775/2005; Directive 2009/72/EC of the European Parliament and of the Council of 13 July 2009 concerning common rules for the internal market in electricity and repealing Directive 2003/54/EC; Directive 2009/73/EC of the European Parliament and of the Council of 13 July 2009 concerning common rules for the internal market in natural gas and repealing Directive 2003/55/EC.

[47] See Commission, 'EU Energy Security and Solidarity Action Plan: 2nd Strategic Energy Review' (MEMO/08/703, 13 November 2008).

Market Directive—granting the public authorities a significant role in accepting and modifying the annual 'ten year investment plans' submitted by transmission system operators and monitoring that these plans are also followed in practice— marks a significant change from the approach of the previous regimes. Of course, the new scheme is not an exact copy of the old planning regimes inspired by socialistic views of a public economy.[48] Here, the new planning system has been described as 'regulation of self-regulation'.[49] While it seems that this description takes a somewhat positive view of the system and the role of the private sector (or the marginality of the public sector intervention), this is undoubtedly correct. While the EU is moving back towards more state intervention, it's not a return to old days of state and public sector planning. It is a 'partial return to the past', a corrective measure after a period of market hype.

This approach was also reinforced in the Commission policy document, 'Energy 2020: A strategy for competitive, sustainable and secure energy'.[50] This document indicates a need to secure investment on the scale of EUR 1 trillion by 2020. In doing so, it specifically notes that, 'given the scale of such investments, their nature and their strategic character, it cannot be assumed that all the necessary investments will be delivered by the market alone'. Public intervention is therefore necessary.

7.9 Concluding Thoughts: The EU in Search of the Balance

EU energy policy is currently searching for the optimal regulatory framework. The previous overly market-based ideology is rapidly changing to a more interventionist policy based on public intervention for security of supply and, increasingly, environmental purposes. The market-based method is being (partially) replaced by stronger public sector involvement and solidarity between Member States. Since markets fail to deliver security, despite economic theory suggesting that they could, states and the EU step in to fashion state responses to threats to security. Such action represents the essential role of the solidarity principle in the energy context.

But the change is not a complete return to the old days. As noted elsewhere, while the old planning system was built on 'requirements', 'decisions', and 'hierarchy', the new planning scheme is marked by 'cooperation', 'recommendations', or 'consultations' between not only the state and the national company, but numerous stake holders within and beyond the immediate home-state of the TSO. Clearly, this is one of the differences between the old days of state planning and the new

---

[48] I. del Guayo and J.-C. Pielow, 'Electricity and Gas Infrastructure Planning in the European Union', in M. Roggenkamp, L. Barrera-Hernandez, D. Zillman, and I. Guayo (eds), *Energy Networks and the Law: Innovative Solutions in Changing Markets* (Oxford: OUP 2012), pp. 358–9.

[49] I. del Guayo and J.-C. Pielow, 'Electricity and Gas Infrastructure Planning in the European Union', in M. Roggenkamp, L. Barrera-Hernandez, D. Zillman, and I. Guayo (eds), *Energy Networks and the Law: Innovative Solutions in Changing Markets* (Oxford: OUP 2012), pp. 363–4.

[50] 'Energy 2020: A strategy for competitive, sustainable and secure energy' (COM/2010/0639 final).

days of public sector control.[51] But there is one significant change from the old days: while the pre-liberalization markets were driven by national governments, the new scheme is marked by the central role of the European Commission. Among many other things, it defines key infrastructure projects, and then acts as the promoter of these projects—and it intervenes in the markets by proposing new regulatory measures, and more directly through antitrust and state aid enforcement, and so on.[52] Regardless of the differences from the preliberalization structures, it is clear that in many ways, a (partial) return to the old days is underway.

---

[51] I. del Guayo and J.-C. Pielow, 'Electricity and Gas Infrastructure Planning in the European Union', in M. Roggenkamp, L. Barrera-Hernandez, D. Zillman, and I. Guayo (eds), *Energy Networks and the Law: Innovative Solutions in Changing Markets* (Oxford: OUP 2012).

[52] For criticism, see K. Talus, 'Just What is the Scope of the Essential Facilities Doctrine in the Energy Sector: Third Party Access-friendly Interpretation in the EU v. Contractual Freedom in the US', 48(5) *Common Market Law Review* (2011).

8

Conclusion

European Energy Law Under the Impact of Globalization: From State to Market, from Plan to Contract, from Public Ownership to Economic Regulation and Beyond

Even if the EC Treaty was, in principle, always applicable to the energy sector, it was in practice politically out of reach. The energy sector was considered a strategic sector.[1] As such, it was shielded from the effects of EC law.[2] In addition to being practically excluded from the scope of application of the internal market regulation, including competition laws and other relevant provisions of the EC Treaty, the Treaty itself did not deal directly with the Community's competence in this area. It seems as if some efforts to introduce an energy-specific Article dealing with Community competence were made over the years, but these efforts failed.[3]

While the Single European Act,[4] with its internal market impetus, can be considered as the first step towards a more significant Community-level energy policy, it was not until the Maastricht Treaty[5] that Article 3(u) of the EC Treaty made an explicit reference to energy as an area where Community action was necessary. However, no further guidance on how this should be done was provided and this reference did not lead to much actual legislative or policy action.[6] The same Treaty also introduced Article 154 EC on Trans-European Networks. While

---

[1] Thomas Wälde noted how what is a 'strategic sector' may vary from country to country. Sweden considered the shoe industry to belong to this category while France held yoghurt making as a strategic sector. T. Wälde, 'The Rule of Law and the Resource Industries' Cycles', in P. Andrews-Speed (ed.), *International Competition for Resources: The role of Law, the State and of Markets* (Dundee: Dundee University Press, 2008), p. 145.

[2] This is despite the fact that the energy sector was the subject of two of the three founding Treaties: the ECSC and EURATOM Treaties addressed the specific issue of the energy sector.

[3] K. Inglis, 'Anticipating New Union Competences in Energy', 15(1) *Maastricht Journal of European and Comparative Law* (2008), p. 125.

[4] Single European Act 1987, OJ L 169/1.

[5] Treaty on European Union, OJ C 191, 29 July 1992.

[6] For a more detailed discussion on this point, see S. Haghighi, 'Energy Security and the Division of Competences Between the European Community and its Member States', 14(4) *European Law Journal* (2008), pp. 461–82.

law books often referred to these meagre provisions, it is difficult to see what 'legal' value one can squeeze out of them. The EC Treaty, like the current TFEU, was full of hortatory and programmatic language which primarily served the public relations needs of the time of negotiation.[7] At most, one can use the references to 'open and competitive markets' located in the more recent layers in the geology of the EC/EU Treaties to modernize older, and now obsolete features—such as the now problematic Article 345 TFEU, which under an older reading seemed to make national property regimes untouchable by EU law.[8] While a separate energy chapter may have been morally uplifting for the *amour propre* of the Energy Directorate General and more traditional energy lawyers, none of the advocates of a separate energy chapter were really able to demonstrate what such a chapter would actually do, with legally binding and specific results, apart from adding another list of well meaning programmatic statements.

But the EC Treaty did not need a specific energy chapter to be effective and relevant for the energy industries. The EC Treaty was applicable to all industries and economic activities—including energy—except if the activity was explicitly excluded.[9] The economic law of the Treaty was thereby fully applicable to the energy sector, be the undertakings privately- or publicly-owned and governed. Similarly, it was also recognized that energy is a 'good' in the sense of the Treaty's freedom to trade principles, even though the voices of the European energy monopolies had earlier, in defensive sentiment against the erosion of national energy market segregation of both markets and EC law, argued, logically, for energy to be neither a 'good' nor a 'service'.[10]

The Lisbon Treaty changed things in this respect. The EU now has an energy provision—Article 194 TFEU—that provides for a legal basis for EU action in this area. But what will change? It would seem that the TFEU does not contain elements significantly changing the situation *status quo ex ante*. Looking at the content of the new energy Title and the EU activities in the energy markets prior to its inclusion in the EU energy *acquis*, it can be argued that its impact will be limited.[11] Perhaps the primary effects could be to: (i) give the EU and the European Commission a confident boost to take further and bolder action in the

---

[7] See T. Wälde, 'Sustainable Development and the 1994 Energy Charter Treaty: Between Pseudo-action and the Management of Environmental Investment Risk', in F. Weiss et al. (eds), *International Economic Law with a Human Face* (London: Kluwer Law 1998).

[8] F. Blum and A. Logue, *State Monopolies under EC Law* (Chichester: Wiley 1998), pp. 153–4. For a more recent analysis, see B. Akkermans and E. Ramaekers, 'Article 345 TFEU (ex. 295 EC), Its Meanings and Interpretations' 16(3) *European Law Journal* (2010), pp. 292–314, who conclude that the Article is not an obstacle for creation of an European property law regime.

[9] H. Jarass, *Europaeisches Energierecht* (Berlin: Duncker & Humblot 1996), p. 14, also P.J. Slot, 'Energy and Competition', *CMLR* (1994), p. 512.

[10] Case 6/64, *Costa v ENEL* [1964] ECR 585. This was subsequently confirmed in the *Almelo* case.

[11] Similarly, A. Guimaraes-Purokoski and B. Delvaux, 'Vertical Division of Competences between the European Community and its Member States in the Energy Field—Some Remarks on the Evolution of the Community Energy Law and Policy', in B. Delvaux, M. Hunt, and K. Talus (eds), *EU Energy Law and Policy Issues* (Brussels: Euroconfidentiel 2008) and L. Hancher, 'The New EC Constitution and the European Energy Market', in M. Roggenkamp and U. Hammer (eds), *European Energy Law Report II* (Antwerpen: Intersentia 2005), pp. 3–7.

area of EU energy; and (ii) protect Member States from EU action that would completely prohibit the use of a specific energy source, nuclear energy being the primary example.

EU energy markets are now shaped through primary EU Treaty law, and secondary EU law: the directives, Regulations, and other instruments. The Commission is the key player in both areas. The institutional set-up of the EU provides it with both powers to enforce general competition law and the right to propose new sectoral legislation. The relationship between the relevant primary law of the Treaty (mainly Articles on free movement, monopolies, competition, and state aid) and the secondary law (mainly the various directives and regulations relating to various aspects of energy markets) is far from clear. In a formal sense, the primary law of the Treaty, as a hierarchically superior norm, should control and prevail over secondary law. Secondary law should then be based on the Treaty and only have an effect within the scope authorized by the Treaty. In case of conflict, the Treaty should prevail over directives. But the Treaty cannot be viewed purely from the perspective of legal theory. Much of the single-market impetus contained in the key provisions of the Treaty was for decades simply not ready for application; with the change of paradigm—from state to market, from nationally segregated energy industries towards an internal energy market—applicability in practice came closer, but had—and still has—to overcome serious obstacles. As a result, it is sometimes more realistic to interpret the Treaty's primary law rather in the sense of energy directives, which indicate what is politically feasible at a certain point of time. The negotiation of the energy directives itself was facilitated by the prospect of a 'real' application of the legal potential inherent in the Treaty. Similarly, as the directives get implemented, the farther-reaching potential of the Treaty can again be looked upon to try to 'test the waters' in terms of moving the Treaty in its contemporary construction beyond the confines of the directives. A feed-back –style, interactive relationship between the Treaty—in its open-ended, dynamic form—and the directives—identifying what is politically feasible at a given point in time—is perhaps the right way to understand the relationship between these sources of EU energy law.

Finally, one needs to bear in mind that the EU Treaties are very much about placing international controls on the national process of economic regulation. While more 'supranational', intensive, evolutionary, and constitutional than other multilateral treaties, they are not essentially different in this quality—and they are therefore bound to be resented in the national political process as an outside interference from an institution which does not carry the same legitimacy as the domestic political process. It is necessary to place such controls on national regulation by multilateral treaty because otherwise it is not possible to develop the full benefit of prosperity that comes from economic integration greater than merely in a single nation state. It is also important to counteract the natural forces of a national community that will tend to protect domestic interests rather than the much more abstract objective of a level playing field in a supranational economic community with overtones of political integration. The EU Treaties, with their logic of controlling national regulatory practices, are therefore a microcosm of the global economy where less intensive and interventionist treaties—such as the WTO, NAFTA, the Energy Charter Treaty, and similar multilateral economic treaties—generate similar resentment and opposition, although their supra-regulatory impact is more modest.

The core of the economic law of the Treaty is the freedom of movement, goods, and services. These freedoms can only be limited in a non-discriminatory way and to achieve—reasonably and proportionately—purposes which are legitimate in the eyes of the Treaty. This is the essence of Articles 34, 36, 56, 57, and 106(2) TFEU. The issue of government-sponsored monopolies is a contradiction to these essential economic freedoms which are the cornerstones of an internal European market. The Court, the Commission and academic commentators have struggled for decades to come to grips with these issues, in particular in the area of traditional, well-established utility monopolies (telecommunications, energy, transport, post). The problem from a lawyer's perspective is that the Treaty clearly establishes the economic freedoms, but also recognizes the legitimate existence of monopolies. Its way out was to oblige governments to 'adjust' monopolies so they would not harm the objective of an internal market. Monopolies are inherently in contradiction with competitive markets: they prevent competitors from entering a market. They undermine the free play of competition based on performance, rather than on legal or economic monopoly. They cannot generate efficiency as competitive markets can. If monopolies stretch over a whole country in an important sector such as energy, they effectively separate this industry from the rest of the internal market. The original drafters of the Treaty had to tolerate monopolies because they were then prevalent. Article 345 TFEU seems to have been formulated to keep the EU institutions out of questions of public ownership and respond to concerns over interference with nationalization of certain industries, like electricity in Italy and France.[12] They may have hoped that the strategic industries like energy monopolies might have collaborated in creating an internal, though not competitive market. But such an expectation (if it ever existed) did not materialize. They left it, rightly and wisely, to the future to try to solve these inherent contradictions of the Treaty with the insufficient instrument of monopoly control as found in various Treaty provisions.

It is very logical that neither Commission nor Court tackled the 'heavy' monopolies first. These have considerable political leverage, are closely intertwined with the economic fabric of a country and society, and change imposed from 'Europe' would not have worked and would probably have discredited the EU process without great chance of success. The Commission and the Court, however, shaped and sharpened the legal instruments in less 'heavy' contexts. The change of paradigm—from state to market, from monopoly to competition and from national to international and global—must have prodded both actors, as would have the example of the US abolition of major utility monopolies. The first step was to place increasing controls over monopoly conduct, first in less sensitive industries

---

[12] For a detailed examination of the background of Article 345 TFEU, see B. Akkermans and E. Ramaekers, 'Article 345 TFEU (ex. 295 EC), Its Meanings and Interpretations' 16(3) *European Law Journal* (2010), pp. 292–314.

(telephone equipment), than in the more sensitive energy industries (but with less powerful countries such as Greece (*Greek refineries*)), and first in theory (*Campus Oil*) while not yet with practical effect. This method of judicial development of the law—in particular if now relatively old and in very open-ended language—is well known for its mixture of two (mainly conceptual) steps ahead, with one (mainly practical) step back, to familiarize the Member States with the conceptual law as it is formulated without provoking them too much with the practical implications. The first more radical step was the *Terminal Equipment* case[13] where not just the conduct, but the very existence of a public monopoly was questioned. In the energy field, the Court has been more cautious in interfering in one of the most politicized industries in the major Member States by affirming the principle that monopolies need to be legitimated by a good and recognized reason, but by avoiding a clear pronouncement through playing with the burden of proof and stringency of evidence requirement. Only when the political and legal culture in the EU was well on its way from the post-war monopolies to the competitive markets of the global economy did a change occur. But things only changed gradually.

Behind these difficult decisions was the fundamental tension between the identity of a national society, its economic, but also social fabric and culture, and the pressures for change of these elements emanating from the logic of economic integration. Here, features of a society are being undermined by competition, and the exposure to such competition comes from what is domestically seen as 'abroad'. Arguably, a reluctance to exacerbate such tensions and accelerate a process of change is behind the Court's reluctance to accept that the internal energy market requires a change in such features, and the wish to place the responsibility for such change on other shoulders. This tension is now well known in the often acrimonious, emotional, and not well informed debate about the 'global economy' versus 'national sovereignty and culture'. But one should bear in mind that a change in economic regulation rarely brings about change on its own; where the mood and pressure for change is already inherently present, with regulation only formalizing and triggering the need for and visibility of change, then change may well take place.

For the Treaty's freedom of trade and economic integration rules, the problem in particular, has been the diversity of organizational forms for economic activities in the Member States. The problem has been the existence of state-owned (or state-sponsored) monopolies in several Member States. The Treaty's objective has to bring the EU trade and integration rules to bear irrespective of the form of economic activity, which includes their application to state-sponsored monopolies. Otherwise, states with a mercantilist form of economic organization through state-sponsored monopolies would be largely immune from the Treaty's liberalization trends. States with an open economy would be fully subject to EU free trade and competition rules, but would be disadvantaged in competition with enterprises from the mercantilist states. These could generate monopoly rent in protected territory, and then use such advantage to act as predators in the open economies

---

[13] Case C-202/88, *France v Commission* [1991] ECR I-1223.

of their neighbours. This risk of economic policy imbalance was realized as early as during the drafting of the EEC Treaty—witness what are now Articles 37 and 106 TFEU. It shaped most if not all monopoly cases, acted as the major obstruction to rapid conclusion of the energy directives and was visible in the issue of reciprocal (or non-reciprocal) opening up of the respective national energy markets and the competitive advantage enjoyed by better protected national champions in benefiting from the current restructuring of the European energy industries.[14]

In overall terms, the last 30 years have seen a decline of the acceptability of state monopolies (and related, special and privileged enterprises), with the first strictures placed on the conduct of monopolies, then on their leveraging of monopoly power in adjacent areas to stifle competition and then on the existence of a state-sponsored monopoly per se.[15] This trend is likely to continue. At the same time, attention has partially shifted from controlling the disappearing monopolies to controlling their current replacements: i.e. national champions and national regulatory authorities.

While liberalization may have largely broken up traditional monopolies with exclusive rights and protected markets, it has failed substantially to change the market structures. The former monopolies still retain significant market positions and in some cases have become stronger than before. In some cases, competition is not possible due to exclusive access to low-cost generation capacity, as in France. In other cases, insufficient cross-border interconnection eliminates any and all possibilities to compete through exports and imports. Past mistakes in the liberalization process allowed the emergence of large and powerful companies through mergers and acquisitions, some of which should have been prevented. These companies can directly and, through their home state, effectively, have their say in the integration process and in the progress towards liberalization. The Commission's efforts on the sector-specific regulatory side have been unable to get its most daring (and effective) regulatory proposals through the legislative process. Large Member States, Germany and France (and their energy companies no doubt in the background), have been unwilling to accept the loss of regulatory powers on a national level or the break-up of their national pride: large and powerful energy companies.

In part, former monopolies and legal exclusivities have been replaced by contractual exclusivities. Market-sharing agreements and destination clauses continue to ensure that little cross-border trade takes place. Long-term capacity reservation agreements tend to have a similar effect. Where these contractual mechanisms have been exposed and the companies required to eliminate them, these clauses and arrangements tend to continue to exist outside of the explicit contractual frameworks. They move from contracts to gentlemen's agreements and are much more difficult, though not impossible as has been seen,[16] to detect. The Commission

---

[14] See the discussion in A. Johnston, 'Maintaining the Balance of Power: Liberalisation, Reciprocity and Electricity in the European Community', 17 *Journal of Energy and Natural Resources Law* (1999).

[15] M. Cini and L. McGowan, *EC Competition Policy* (London: Macmillan 1998), pp. 166, 167–9 for telecommunications, pp. 169–72 for energy; L. Hancher and P. Trepte, 'Competition and the Internal Energy Market', 4(149) *ECLR* (1992).

[16] See the E.ON/GDF Megal pipeline case (Case COMP/39.401—E.ON/GDF) and the Gazprom case (Case 39816 – Upstream gas supplies in Central and Eastern Europe).

has been fighting these arrangements through both sector-specific regulation and through the use of general competition law. The institutional set-up of the EU places the Commission in a key position: it can propose new sector-specific regulation to create a legislative framework that is capable of creating competitive conditions conducive to competition. It can also apply the general competition law and use this power either to support the objectives of the existing sector-specific framework or to push the markets further towards competition. Following the 2007 sector-specific inquiry,[17] the Commission has initiated a focused competition law enforcement campaign to improve market conditions though its antitrust powers and, in essence, to re-design the pre-existing energy market structure. The Commission, and in particular its DG COMP, now boasts that the nine current energy-market-related cases are changing the landscape of the energy sector. Many of these cases included suspected anticompetitive behaviour that falls under the scope of Article 102 TFEU, ranging from strategic under-investment to the anti-competitive use of long-term electricity or natural gas contracts and corresponding capacity reservations. While these cases will undoubtedly move the markets towards more competition, the administratively-designed markets mean effectively that the regulator is making certain assumptions about the most effective market design. In the EU electricity and natural gas markets, this has meant the clear separation of commodity and capacity contracts, an ever-shortening duration for capacity reservations, significant limits to commodity contracts in terms of volumes and duration, and limits on companies responding to market failures where the national action would contradict EU energy market policies. Some of these trends might not be the correct way to proceed. Competition cannot be pushed by any means and to any extent. For natural gas markets, the limits of competition can follow from the structure of upstream supply markets. Creating a truly functioning and secure downstream market can be difficult when the supply market does not follow the same logic. Even if competitive markets would emerge under these conditions, does this really benefit the customer? Competition should not be pushed just for the sake of competition. Competition is only an instrument to create additional value for final customers and society as whole. In the heat of the moment, this can be forgotten.

The impact of sector-specific regulation and the enforcement of EU competition law has been profound: the market structures are moving from a secure energy system providing long-term predictability for all parties involved in the energy chain (from producers to end-customers) to a more volatile and shorter-term-focused energy business. In part, this trend has been countered by the creation of national champions (and national support of these national champions on their way to being European champions); but even in these cases, the trend is that the regulatory changes have pushed the industry towards shorter-term focus. Here, the relevant question is customer preferences: does the end-customer prefer predictability with a higher cost, or volatility and unpredictability with a (slightly) lower cost? Where

---

[17] Inquiry pursuant to Article 17 of Regulation (EC) No. 1/2003 into the European gas and electricity sectors (Final Report) (COM/2006/851 final), 10 January 2007.

the sector-specific regulation has failed to create the change, the Commission has used general EU competition law to push the markets and the industry in the 'right' direction. Sometimes this can have unintended consequences, like the asset divestiture of EON's grid. Here, there is a growing concern over the ability, or willingness, of the buyer, Tennet, to invest in the German grid which it acquired as a result of the EON commitments.[18] This will have a direct impact on the plans for offshore wind power, among other things.

The liberalization of EU energy markets is not only an internal EU question. The liberalization within EU has its impact on the entire energy value chain. This means that companies abroad have to take the changing regulatory framework into account when devising company policies. Similarly, the changing regulatory framework for EU energy will affect the energy policies of its supplying countries. These countries are not EU Member States and in most cases will never be. Despite this, they feel the impact of changes in the EU energy markets and their regulation. And there is more: in addition to the EU, the countries of the EEA agreement also apply most of the EU's energy law. The EU is also actively exporting its energy laws and policies. This happens both formally and informally: countries of the Energy Charter Treaty have commited themselves to certain principles which in many ways reflect the early days of EU energy law. The next step has been the Energy Community Treaty, where the Member States thereof have an obligation to implement large parts of the EU energy *acquis*. Informally, the EU has in the past used various technical assistance programs like TACIS, PHARE, SYNERGY, ALTENER, SAVE, or INOGATE. They are intended to help the recipients to get expertise they do not have and cannot, pay for themselves. However, they are also a way to influence the partner countries' energy policies in the EU direction. And this process is in many cases driven and controlled by the EU.

In addition to being an example of a region with international energy regulation being adopted by the Member States and supranational institutions being given the power to interpret and enforce these common legal instruments, the EU also actively exports its energy *acquis* and therefore enlarges the area where this body of law is applied. But EU is not only an exporter of energy law and policy; it is also influenced by international trends in this area. The obvious examples include the international climate change instruments which the EU adopts and further develops, then exporting the end-result, taking the development in this area further again. This process of internationalization of EU energy law takes place at various levels and through various mechanisms: money and treaties being the primary drivers.

EU energy policy is not only about liberalization and competition. It is also about sustainability and security of supply. The latter concept is very much linked to liberalization and subject to an intense debate. The EU has moved from a system where state and public sector provided security to a system where markets should

---

[18] See the German press release about the government discussion on replacing Tennet because of lack of investment: <http://www.handelsblatt.com/politik/deutschland/niederlaendisches-staatsunter nehmen-tennet-wird-zum-aussenpolitischen-problemfall/6993482.html>.

deliver investments and security. This, however, does not seem to be happening, at least to an extent where the system would be regarded as 'working'. One problem is, of course, that the markets which should deliver do not exist. Now, the emerging question is whether this market will ever exist. Perhaps public sector intervention is necessary, and even more than what is the current *status quo*.

Clearly, the push for a market-driven energy policy has its limits: this is becoming increasingly apparent. The significant investments required in the near future are not going to be delivered by the markets, at least not alone and not in a world of constantly changing policies and ever-increasing regulation. The role of public sector intervention is particularly apparent in the renewable energy sector. Here, little or no investment would take place without government subsidies. This is a rapidly developing and growing market. However, the current growth figures would not be possible without government intervention. In addition to effectively eliminating the market-based methods in this area, it also means that the governments are picking the winners.[19] The technologies that are promoted through subsidy schemes continue to grow and develop, while those that fall outside government support schemes will slowly die. Voluntary schemes based on informing the customers have not worked: the failure of the energy efficiency instruments is a blatant reminder of this. The EU citizen is ready to save energy, as long as s(he) can still enjoy the luxuries of a western lifestyle and drive the SUV. Similarly, voluntary agreements with the industry have failed. In this area, the EU has not been able to create a clear policy: is it going to trust the markets, like the EU ETS, or will the public sector intervene (as in energy taxes); will it negotiate voluntary agreements or will it impose energy saving targets? This is an area where regulatory uncertainty reduces the chances of success.

This book has made an attempt to picture EU energy law and policy in its actual context. It has not intended to paraphrase the existing energy law *acquis* or immerse itself in the complexities of EU energy regulation. Instead, it has provided an overview of EU energy law and policy as a whole and offered the reader enough context and background to understand why policy and legislative choices have been made and why certain areas continue to be difficult. In this contextual approach, EU energy policy does not emerge as a technical regulatory framework that regulates internal and external EU energy markets or energy market actors. Instead, EU energy law and policy appear as a dynamic and constantly moving target. The application of Treaty provisions changes over time, depending on outside forces, external to the energy sector, energy market actors and even from beyond outside the EU. The contemporary energy market ideology is also subject to constant changes. These changes do not take place in a vacuum. They are affected by international trends and they, in turn, have an impact on international trends.

---

[19] See also A. Johnston, 'The Future Shape of EU Energy Law and Policy' in A. Arnull, C. Barnard, M. Dougan, and E. Spaventa (eds), *A Constitutional Order of States? Essays in EU Law in Honour of Alan Dashwood* (Oxford: Hart Publishing 2011), Ch. 21.

Bibliography

Abott, F., 'The North American Integration Regime', in Weiler, J. (ed.), *The EU, the WTO and the NAFTA* (Oxford: OUP 2000)

Akkermans, B. and Ramaekers, E., 'Article 345 TFEU (ex. 295 EC), Its Meanings and Interpretations', 16(3) *European Law Journal* (2010)

Anderson, D., 'Port States and Environmental Protection', in Boyle A. and Freestone, D., *International Law and Sustainable Development* (Oxford: OUP 1999)

Anderson O. and Lowe, J. (eds), 'Special Issue on Oil Spills', 3 *OGEL* (2010)

Anderson, S., *The Struggle over North Sea Oil and Gas: Government Strategies in Denmark, Britain and Norway* (Oslo: Scandinavian University Press 1993)

Albers, M., 'Competition Law Issues Arising from the Liberalisation Process', in Geradin, D. (ed.), *The Liberalisation of Electricity and Natural Gas in the European Union* (The Hague: Kluwer 2001)

Arai-Takahashi, Y., *The Margin of Appreciation Doctrine and the Principle of Proportionality in the Jurisprudence of the ECHR* (Antwerp: Intersentia 2002)

Arentsen, M. and Künneke, R., '*Economic Organization and Liberalization of the Electricity Industry*', 24(6) Energy Policy (1996)

Armstrong, J., 'The EC Remedies Directive', in MacDougall, D. and Wälde, T. (eds), *European Community Energy Law* (London: Kluwer 1994)

Arrowsmith, S., *The Law of Public and Utilities Procurement* (London: Sweet &Maxwell 2005)

Ayral, M., *Droit Communautaire de l'Energie* (Paris: Joly Editions 1997)

Bamberger, C. and Wälde, T., 'The Energy Charter Treaty', in Roggenkamp, M. et al. (eds), *Energy Law in Europe* (Oxford: OUP 2008)

Barnard, C., *The Substantive Law of the EU—The Four Freedoms* (Oxford: OUP 2004)

Barton, B. et al., 'Introduction', in Barton, B., Redgwell, C., Rønne A., and Zillman, D. (eds), *Energy Security: Managing Risk in a Dynamic Legal and Regulatory Environment* (Oxford: OUP 2004)

Baquero Cruz, J. and Castillo de la Torre, F., 'A Note on PreussenElektra', 26 *ELRev* (2001)

Behn, D., 'Methods for Allocating Allowances Under the EU Emissions Trading Scheme: Assessing its Interaction with the EU State Aid Rules', in Delvaux, B., Hunt, M., and Talus, K. (eds), *EU Energy Law and Policy Issues* (Cambridge: Intersentia 2011)

Bellis, J., 'Liberalisation and the Creation of Strategic Alliances', in Geradin, D. (ed.), *The Liberalisation of State Monopolies in the European Union and Beyond* (The Hague: Kluwer Law International 2000)

Belyi, A., 'Institutional Weaknesses of Intra-FSU Gas Trade', 4(4) *OGEL* (2006)

Belyi, A. and Petrichenko, K.V., 'Energy Efficiency Policy in Russia', 1 *OGEL* (2011)

Bergesen, H. and Lunde, L., *Dinosaurs or Dynamos? The United Nations and the World Bank at the Turn of the Century* (London: Earthscan 1999)

Biava, A., 'L'action de L'Union Européenne Face au Défi de la Sécurisation de son Approvisionnement Energétique', 22 *Politique Européenne* (2007)

Bickler, C. and Renger, M., 'European Union', in Tudway, R., *Energy Law and the Regulation in Europe* (London: Sweet and Maxwell 1999)

Bingham, T. and Gray, S., *Report on the Supply of Petroleum and Petroleum Products to Rhodesia* (London: HMSO 1978)

Bjornebye, H., *Investing in EU Energy Security: Exploring the Regulatory Approach to Tomorrow's Electricity Production* (Alphen aan den Rijn: Kluwer Law International 2010)

Blum, F. and Logue, A., *State Monopolies under EC Law* (Chichester: Wiley 1998)

Bolze, R., Peirce, S. and Walsh, J., 'Antitrust Regulation: A New Focus for a Competitive Energy Industry', 21 *Energy Law Journal* (2000)

Bosselman, F., Rossi J., and Weaver, J., *Energy, Economics and the Environment, Cases and Materials* (New York: Foundation Press 2010)

Bovis, C., *EC Public Procurement: Case Law and Regulation* (Oxford: OUP 2006)

—— 'The New Public Procurement Regime: A Different Perspective on the Integration of Public Market on the European Union', 12 *European Public Law* (2006)

—— *EU Public Procurement Law* (Cheltenham: Edward Elgar 2007)

Brau, R., Doronzo, R., Fiorio, C.V., and Florio, M., 'EU Gas Reforms and Consumers' Prices', 31(4) *The Energy Journal* (2010)

Brilmayer, L., *American Hegemony, Political Morality in a One-superpower World* (New Haven: Yale University Press 1994)

Broberg, M., 'The European Commission's Extraterritorial Powers in Merger Control: the Court of First Instance's Judgment in Gencor v. Commission', 49 *ICLQ* (2000)

Buendia-Sierra, J., *Exclusive Rights and State Monopolies under EC Law* (Oxford: OUP 1999)

Burchard, F., and Eckert, L., *Natural Gas and EU Energy Law* (Baden-Baden: Nomos 1995)

Caillard, A., 'EU: US Extraterritorial jurisdiction—EU/US Agreement', 4(4) *International Trade Law & Regulation* (1998)

Campbell-White, F., 'Property Rights: A Forgotten Issue Under the Union' in Neuwhal, N.A. and Rosas, A. (eds), *The European Union and Human Rights* (The Hague: M Nijhoff 1995)

Cameron, J. and Gray, K., 'Principles of International Law in the WTO Dispute Settlement Body', 50(248) *ICLQ* (2001)

Cameron, P., *Gas Regulation in Europe* (London: FT Reports 1996)

—— *Competition in Energy Markets: Law and Regulation in the European Union* (Oxford: OUP 2001)

—— *Legal Aspects of Energy Regulation: Implementing the New Directives of Electricity and Gas Across Europe* (Oxford: OUP 2005)

—— *Competition in Energy Markets: Law and Regulation in the European Union* (Oxford: OUP 2002 and 2007)

Cardoso e Cunha, A., 'The Internal Energy Market', 9(290) *Journal of Energy and Natural Resources Law* (1991)

Chalmers, D., Davies, G., and Monti, G., *European Union Law* (Cambridge: CUP 2010)

Cini, M. and McGowan, L., *EC Competition Policy* (London: Macmillan 1998)

Conte, G., Loriot, G., Rouxel, F., and Tretton, W., 'EDP/ENI/GDP: The Commission Prohibits a Merger Between Gas and Electricity National Incumbents', 1 *Competition Policy Newsletter* (2005)

Cova, B., 'The European Response to US Extraterritorial Legislation', 15 *OGTLR* (1997)

Cross, E., *Electric Utility Regulation in the European Union: A Country by Country Guide* (Chichester: Wiley 1996)

Cross, E., Hancher, L., and Slot, P., 'EC Energy Law', in Roggenkamp, M. et al. (eds) *Energy Law in Europe* (Oxford: OUP 2001)

Cudahy, R., 'PURPA: The Intersection of Competition and Regulatory Policy' 16 (2) *Energy Law Journal* (1995)

Cultrera, C., 'Les Décisions GDF, La Commission est Formelle: Les Clauses de Restriction Territoriale dans les Contrats de Gaz Violent L'Article 81', 1 *Competition Policy Newsletter* (2005)

Dabbah, M., *EC and UK Competition Law—Commentary, Cases and Materials* (Cambridge: CUP 2004)

Daintith, T. and Hancher, L., *Energy Strategy in Europe: the Legal Framework* (Berlin: Walter de Gruyter & Co. 1986)

—— 'The Management of Diversity: Community Law as an Instrument of Energy and Other Sectorial Policies', 4(1) *Yearbook of European Law* (1984)

Daintith, T. and Williams, S., 'The Legal Integration of Energy Markets', in Cappelletti, M., Seccombe, M., and Weiler, J. (eds), *Integration Through Law: Europe and the American Federal Experience* (European University Institute—Series A 2/5, 1987)

Daintith, T. and Willoughby, A., *UK Oil & Gas Law* (London: Sweet and Maxwell 1997)

de Bruijne, B. and Vedder, H.H.B., 'The Interface between EU Energy, Environmental and Competition Law in the Netherlands', 4 *OGEL* (2012)

De Burca, G., 'The EU, the European Court of Justice and the International Legal Order after Kadi', 1(51) *Harvard International Law Journal* (2009)

de Hauteclocque, A., *Market Building Through Antitrust: Long-term Contract Regulation in EU Electricity Markets* (Cheltenham: Edward Elgar 2012)

—— *Long-term Supply Contracts in European Decentralized Electricity Markets: An Antitrust Perspective* (2009) PhD Thesis, University of Manchester School of Law

de Hauteclocque, A., Marty, F., and Pillot, J., 'The Essential Facilities Doctrine in European Competition Policy: The Case of the Energy Markets', in Glachant, J.M., Finon, J., and Hauteclocque, A. (eds), *Competition, Contracts and Electricity Markets: A New Perspective* (Cheltenham: Edward Elgar 2011)

de Hauteclocque, A. and Talus, K., 'Capacity to Compete: Recent Trends in Access Regimes in Electricity and Natural Gas Networks', in Delvaux, B., Hunt, M., and Talus, K. (eds), *EU Energy Law and Policy Issues* (Cambridge: Intersentia 2011)

Defeuilley, C. and de Hauteclocque, A., 'La Production d'Electricité est-elle une Facilité Essentielle?', LARSEN Working Paper 2010

del Guayo, I. and Pielow, J.-C., 'Electricity and Gas Infrastructure Planning in the European Union', in Roggenkamp, M., Barrera-Hernandez, L., Zillman, D., and Guayo, I. (eds), *Energy Networks and the Law: Innovative Solutions in Changing Markets* (Oxford: OUP 2012)

Delvaux, B., *EU Law and the Development of a Sustainable, Competitive and Secure Energy Policy: Opportunities and Shortcomings* (Cambridge: Intersentia 2012)

Delvaux, B., Hunt, M., and Talus, K. (eds), *EU Energy Law and Policy Issues* (Cambridge: Intersentia 2011)

Deruytter, T., Geldhof, W., and Vandendriessche, F., 'Public Service Obligations in the Electricity and Gas Markets' in Delvaux, B., Hunt, M., and Talus, K. (eds), *EU Energy Law and Policy Issues* (Cambridge: Intersentia 2011)

Devlin, B. and Levasseur, C., 'Energy', in Faull, J. and Nikpay, A. (eds), *The EC Law of Competition* (Oxford: OUP 1999)

Devine-Wright, P., 'Beyond NIMBYism: Towards an Integrated Framework for Understanding Public Perceptions of Wind Energy', 8 *Wind Energy* (2005)

Dundas, H., 'The Impact of EC Law on the UK Oil and Gas Industry: Directives on Services and Licensing', in MacDougall, D. and Wälde, T. (eds), *European Community Energy Law* (London: Kluwer 1994)

Doeh, D., Popov, A., and Nappert, S., 'Russia and the Energy Charter Treaty: Common Interests or Irreconcilable Differences?', 5(2) *OGEL* (2007)

Dore, J. and Wälde, T. in Wälde, T. (ed.), *The Energy Charter Treaty* (London: Kluwer 1996)

Edward, D. and Hoskins, M., 'Article 90: Deregulation and EC Law', 32(159) *CMLR* (1995)

Evrard, S., 'Essential Facilities in the EU: Bronner and Beyond', 10(491) *Columbia Journal of European Law* (2004)

Ezrachi, A., 'Limitations on the Extraterritorial Reach of the European Merger Regulation', 22(4) *ECLR.* (2001)

Faull, J. and Nikpay, A., *The EC Law of Competition* (Oxford: OUP 1999)

Flynn, J. and Langan, J., 'Procurement Licensing and Utilities in the UK North Sea', 14(60) *OGTLR* (1996)

Footer, M., 'External Aspects of the Community's Public Procurement Policy in the Utilities Sectors', 3 *Public Procurement Law Review* (1994)

—— 'Remedies under the New GATT Agreement on Government Procurement', 4 *Public Procurement Law Review* (1995)

Fox, W., 'The United States and The Energy Charter Treaty: Misgivings and Misperceptions', in Wälde, T., *The Energy Charter Treaty: an East-West Gateway for Investment and Trade* (London: Kluwer 1998)

Garcia, P., '"Nunca Mais!" How Current European Environmental Liability and Compensation Regimes are Addressing the Prestige Oil Spill of 2002', 25 *The University of Pennsylvania Journal of International Law* (2004)

Gentile, G. (ed.), *La Privatissazione nel Settore Elettrico* (Milano: Giuffre 1995)

Geny, F., 'Can Unconventional Gas be a Game Changer in European Gas Markets?', NG 46 *OIES* (2010)

Glachant, J.M., Finon, D., and de Hauteclocque, A. (eds), *Competition, Contracts and Electricity Markets: A New Perspective* (Cheltenham: Edward Elgar 2011)

Guimaraes-Purokoski, A., *Vertikaalinen Toimivallanjako EU-Oikeudessa. Tutkimus Yhteisön Toimivallan Kehittymisestä Energia-alalla Sekä Julkisen Palvelun Velvoitteen ja Yleispalvelun Sääntelystä Sähkön Sisämarkkinoilla* (Vammala: Suomalainen Lakimiesyhdistys 2009)

Haghighi, S.S., 'Establishing an External Policy to Guarantee Energy Security in Europe? A Legal Analysis', in Roggenkamp, M. and Hammer, U., *European Energy Law Report VI* (Antwerp: Intersentia 2009)

—— *Energy Security: The External Legal Relations of the European Union with Major Oil and Gas Supplying Countries* (Oxford: Hart Publishing 2007)

Hallouche, H., *The GECF: Is it Really a Gas-OPEC in the Making?* (Oxford: Oxford Institute for Energy Studies 2006)

Hammer, U., 'The Relationship between Capacity Markets and Spot Market in the Gas Sector', in Roggenkamp, M. and Hammer, U. (eds), *European Energy Law Report II* (Antwerp: Intersentia 2005)

—— 'Introduction', in Roggenkamp, M. and Hammer, U. (eds), *European Energy Law Report I* (Antwerp: Intersentia 2004)

Hancher, L., *EC Electricity Law* (London: Chancery 1992)

—— 'Long-term Contracts and State Aid: A New Application of the EU State Aid Regime or a Special Case?', in Glachant, J.M., Finon, D., and de Hauteclocque, A. (eds), *Competition, Contracts and Electricity Markets: A New Perspective* (Cheltenham: Edward Elgar 2011)

Hancher, L. and Janssen, S., 'Shared Competences and Multi-Faceted Concepts—European Legal Framework for Security of Supply', in Barton, B., Redgwell, C., Ronne A., and Zillman, D.N., *Energy Security—Managing Risk in a Dynamic Legal and Regulatory Environment* (Oxford: OUP 2004)

Hancher, L., Ottervanger, T., and Slot, P., *EC State Aids* (London: Chancery 1993)

Hancher, L. and Salerno, F., 'State Aid in the Energy Sector', in *Research Handbook on European State Aid Law* (Cheltenham: Edward Elgar 2011)

Hancher, L. and Trepte, P., *An Overview of Public Procurement in the EC*, 14 *OGTLR* 4 (1996)

Hankey, S., Westbrook, B., and Warne, P., 'The EU Hydrocarbons Licensing Directive', 12 *Oil & Gas Law & Taxation Review* (1994) 283–6

Helm, D., Kay, J., and Thompson, D., 'Energy Policy and the Role of the State in the Market for Energy', in Stevens, P., *The Economics of Energy Vol. II* (London: Edward Elgar Publishing House 2000)

Henderson, D., *The MAI Affair: A Story and its Lessons* (London: Royal Institute of Int'l Affairs 1999)

Hildebrandt, D., *The Role of Economic Analysis in the EC Competition Rules* (Alphen aan den Rijn: Kluwer Law International 2009)

Hobér, K., 'The Energy Charter Treaty—Recent Developments', 5(2) *OGEL* (2007)

Hongju Koh, H., 'Transnational Public Law Litigation', 100(2347) *Yale Law Journal* (1991)

Howarth, S., *A Century in Oil: The Shell Transport and Trading Company 1897–1997* (London: Weidenfeld 1997)

Hueffer, U., Ipsen, K., and Tettinger, P., *Die Transitrichtlinien für Gas und Elektrizität* (Stuttgart: Boorberg 1991)

Huner, J., 'Lessons from the MAI: A View from the Negotiating Table', in Ward H. and Brack, D. (eds), *Trade, Investment and the Environment* (London: Earthscan 2000)

Hunt, M., 'Ownership Unbundling: the Main Legal Issues in a Controversial Debate', in Delvaux, B., Hunt, M., and Talus, K., (eds), *EU Energy Law and Policy Issues* (Brussels: Euroconfidentiel 2008)

Hunt, M. and Karova, R., 'The Energy Acquis Under the Energy Community Treaty and the Integration of South East European Electricity Markets: An Uneasy Relationship?' in Delvaux, B., Hunt M., and Talus, K. (eds), *EU energy law and policy issues* (Brussels: Euroconfidentiel 2010)

Huntingdon, S., *The Clash of Civilisation and the Remaking of World Order* (New York: Simon & Schuster 1997)

Iglesias, G. R., 'The Court of Justice, Principles of EC Law, Court Reform and Constitutional Adjudication', 15 *European Business Law Review* (2004)

Inglis, K., 'Anticipating New Union Competences in Energy', 15(1) *Maastricht Journal of European and Comparative Law* (2008)

Jarass, H., *Europaeisches Energierecht* (Berlin: Duncker & Humblot 1996)

Johnston, A., 'Take-or-Pay Contracts for Renewables: An Analysis of European Legal Issues', in Delvaux, B., Hunt, M., and Talus, K. (eds), *EU Energy Law and Policy Issues* (Brussels: Euroconfidentiel 2010)

—— 'Maintaining the Balance of Power: Liberalisation, Reciprocity and Electricity in the European Community' 17 *Journal of Energy and Natural Resources Law* (1999)

Johnston, A. et al., 'The Proposed New EU Renewables Directive: Interpretation, Problems and Prospects', 1(3) *European Energy and Environmental Law Review* (2008)

Jones, C., *EU Energy Law, Volume I—The Internal Energy Market* (Leuven: Claeys & Casteels 2004)

—— *EU Energy Law—Volume II—EU Competition Law and Energy Markets* (Leuven: Claeys & Casteels 2005)

—— *EU Energy Law—The Internal Energy Market: The Third Liberalisation Package* (Leuven: Claeys & Casteels 2010)

Karova, R., *Liberalisation of Electricity Markets and Public Service Obligations in the Energy Community* (Alphen aan den Rijn: Kluwer Law International 2012)

Kissinger, H., *Diplomacy* (New York: Simon & Schuster 1994)

Konoplyanik, A., 'A Common Russia EU Energy Space: The New EU Russia Partnership Agreement, Acquis Communautaire, The Energy Charter and the New Russian Initiative', in Talus, K. and Fratini, P., *EU-Russia Energy Relations* (Rixensart: Euroconfidential 2010)

—— 'Russian Gas to Europe: From Long-term Contracts, On-border Trade and Destination Clauses to . . . ?', 23(3) *Journal of Energy & Natural Resources Law* (2005)

—— 'Stiff Competition Ahead—As Russia Moots Ways to Increase Presence on European Gas Market', 2(1) *OGEL* (2004)

Kovacevic, A., *The Impact of the Russia-Ukraine Gas Crisis in South Eastern Europe*, NG 29 (Institute for Energy Studies, March 2009)

Kriegelstein, F., *The Application of EC Competition Rules to Liberalised Electricity Markets* (Baden Baden: Nomos 2000)

Lappalainen, V.A., 'Proposed Finland-Russia Interconnector Rejected', 1 *OGEL* (2007)

Leal-Arcas, R., 'The EU and Russia as Energy Trading Partners: Friends or Foes?', 3(14) *European Foreign Affairs Review* (2009)

Leino, P., 'The Journey Towards all that is Good And Beautiful: Human Rights and "Common Values" as Guiding Principles of EU Foreign Relations Law', in Cremona, M. and De Witte, B. (eds), *EU Foreign Relations Law* (Oxford: Hart Publishing 2008)

Lenaerts, K., 'The Principle of Subsidiarity and the Environment in the European Union: Keeping the Balance of Federalism', 17 *Fordham International Law Journal* (1993)

Liesen, R., 'Transit Under the Energy Charter Treaty', 17 *JENRL* (1999)

Lloyd Loftis, J., Tyler, T.J., and Goins, A., 'Arctic Region: Boundaries, Resources and the Promise of Co-operation', 2 *OGEL* (2012)

Looper, S., 'Nopec Goes Bananas: How the Supreme Court Will Thwart Congress's Attempt to Extend U.S. Antitrust Law's Extraterritorial Reach', 1 *OGEL* (2010)

Low, L., Sprange, T., and Barutciski, M., 'Global Anti-corruption Standard and Enforcement: Implications for Energy Companies', 3(2) *Journal of World Energy Law and Business* (2010)

Lukes, R., 'Energierecht', in Dauses, M. (ed.) *Handbuch des EU-Wirtschaftsrechts* (München: CH Beck 1999)

Maedicke, M., 'Competitive-based Contracts for the New Power Business', 17 *Energy Law Journal* (1996)

Maier, M. and Werner, P., 'ECJ, Judgment of 14 April 2005, Joined cases C-128/03 and C-129/03—AEM v. Autorità per l'energia elettrica e per il gas', 4 *European State Aid Law Quarterly* (2005)

Malmendier, B. and Schendel, J., 'Unbundling Germany's Energy Networks', 24(3) *Journal of Energy and Natural Resources law* (2006)

Marceau, G. and Wyatt, J., 'Trade and the Environment: The WTO's Efforts to Balance Economic and Sustainable Development' in Trigo Trindade, R., Peter, H., and Bovet, C.

(eds), *Liber Amicorum Anne Petitpierre-Sauvain: Economie Environnement Ethique de la Responsabilité Sociale et Sociétale* (Schulthess Editions Romandes 2009)

Marin Duran, G. and Morgera, E., *Environmental Integration in the EU's External Relations: Beyond Multilateral Dimensions* (Oxford: Hart Publishing 2012).

Martinez-Lopez, M., 'Horizontal Agreements on Energy Efficiency of Appliances: A Comparison between CECED and CEMEP', EC C.P.N. (2000)

Mavroides, P., 'Trade and Environment after the Shrimps-Turtles Litigation', 34 *Journal of World Trade* (2000)

McLean, B. and Elkind, P., *The Smartest Guys in the Room: The Amazing Rise and Scandalous Fall of Enron* (New York: Penguin 2003)

Mestmaecker, E.J. (ed.), *Natural Gas in the Internal Market* (London: Graham/Nomos 1993)

Ming-Zhi Gao, A., 'The Application of the European SEA Directive to Carbon Capture and Storage Activities: The Issue of Screening', 6(17) *European Energy and Environmental Law Review* (2008)

Mitchell, J. (ed.) *Companies in a World of Conflict* (London: RIIA 1998)

Moen, K.B. and Dyrland, S., *EUs Gassmarkedsdirektiv* (Oslo: Fagbokforlaget Vigmostad & Bjorke AS 2002)

Moreno, S., Rubin, M. et al., 'Free Trade and the Environment: The NAFTA, the NAAEC', 12 *Tulane International Law Journal* (1999)

Mortensen, B., 'The European Court of Justice Decision in Case C-206/06', Essent Netwerk Noord BV, 17(6) *EEELR* (2008)

Motta, M., *Competition Policy, Theory and Practice* (Cambridge: CUP 2004)

Nyssens, H., Cultera, C. and Schnichels, D., 'The Territorial Restrictions in the Gas Sector: A State of Play', 1 *Competition Policy Newsletter* (2004)

O'Donoghue, R. and Padilla, A.J., *The Law and Economics of Article 82 EC* (Oxford: Hart Publishing 2007)

Olson, M., *Power and Prosperity* (New York: Basic Books 2000)

Oliver, P., *Free Movement of Goods in the European Community* (London: Sweet and Maxwell 1996)

Oystein, N., *Oil and Islam: Social and Economic Issues* (Research Council of Norway: J. Wiley & Sons 1997)

Papier, H., *Durchleitungen und Eigentum* (BB 1997)

Parish M. and Fresquet, T., 'International Sanctions and How to Evade Them', 3 *OGEL* (2012)

Patterson, W., *Transforming Electricity* (London: Earthscan 1999)

Pecho, P., 'Good-Bye-Keck? A Comment on the Remarkable Judgment in Commission v Italy C-110/05', 3(36) *Legal Issues in Economic Integration* (2009)

Petit, N., 'Circumscribing the Scope of EC Competition Law in Network Industries? A Comparative Approach to the US Supreme Court Ruling in the Trinko Case', 13(6) *Utilities Law Review* (2004)

Pielow, J.C., Brunekreeft, G., and Ehlers, E. 'Legal and Economic Aspects of Ownership Unbundling in the EU', 2 *Journal of World Energy Law and Business* (2009)

Pielow, J.P. and Lewendel, B.J., 'Beyond "Lisbon": EU Competences in the Field of Energy Policy', in Delvaux, B., Hunt M., and Talus, K. (eds), *EU Energy Law and Policy Issues* (Cambridge: Intersentia 2011)

Pierce Jr, R., 'Antitrust Policy in the New Electricity Industry', *Energy Law Journal* 17 (1996)

Pirani, S., Stern, J. and Yafimava K., 'The Russo-Ukrainian Gas Dispute of January 2009: A Comprehensive Assessment', NG 27 (Oxford: Oxford Institute for Energy Studies February 2009)

Pirani, S., Stern, J., Yafimava K., and Kovacevis, A., 'The Impact of the Russia-Ukraine Gas Crisis in South Eastern Europe', NG 29 (Oxford: Oxford Institute for Energy Studies March 2009)

Pollitt, M., 'Evaluating the Evidence on Electricity Reform: Lessons for the South East Europe (SEE) Market', 17(1) *Utilities Policy* (2009)

—— *The Role of Policy in Energy Transitions: Lessons from the Energy Liberalisation Era* (Cambridge Working Paper in Economics 1216)

Porch, D., *The French Secret Services* (Oxford: OUP 1997)

Praduroux, S. and Talus, K., 'The Third Legislative Package and Ownership Unbundling in the Light of the European Fundamental Rights Discourse', 9(3) *CNRI* (2008)

Pritzsche, K.U. and Meier, A., 'Third Party Access in Germany after the VNC Decision', 13(307) *OGTLR* (1995)

Putnam, R., 'Diplomacy and Domestic Politics: The Logic of Two-level Games', 42 *International Organization* (1988)

Radetzki, M., 'Taxation of Energy in an Increasingly Interdependent World: An Introduction', 17(7) *International Journal of Global Energy Issues* (1999)

Rodriguez, J., 'The Growing Impact on EC Competition Law on Gas Sale and Transportation Agreements', 33 *LNG Journal* (2005)

Roggenkamp, M., 'Full Transparency Through Ownership Unbundling: Ownership Unbundling of Transmission and Distribution Grids in the Netherlands', in Roggenkamp, M. and Hammer, U., *European Energy Law Report VI* (Antwerp: Intersentia 2009)

Roggenkamp, M. et al. (eds), *Energy Law in Europe* (Oxford: OUP 2001)

Roggenkamp, M. et al. (eds), *Energy Law in Europe* (Oxford: OUP 2008)

Rossi, J., 'Public Choice Theory and the Fragmented Web of the Contemporary Administrative State', 96 *Michigan Law Review* (1998)

Roth, P. (ed.), *Bellamy and Child, Community Law of Competition* (London: Sweet and Maxwell 2001)

Salter, J.R., 'Third Party Access to Gas and Electricity Transmission Systems in the Community: Third Party Access—Your Flexible Friend?', in MacDougall, D. and Wälde, T. (eds), *European Community Energy Law—Selected Topics* (London: Graham & Trotman/M. Nijhoff 1994)

Schaub, A., *Europäische Energiebinnenmarktpolitik und Umweltpolitik* (Baden Baden: Nomos 1996)

Schneider, J., *Liberalisierung der Stromwirtschaft durch Regulative Marktorganisation* (Baden-Baden: Nomos 1999)

Schneider, J. and Theobald, C., (eds), *Handbuch zum Recht der Energiewirtschaft* (München: Beck 2003)

Scott, C., 'Services of General Interest in EC Law: Matching Values of Regulatory Technique in the Public and Privatized Sectrors', 6(4) *European Law Journal* (2000)

Scott, J., *EU Environmental Law* (London: Longman 1998)

Schwarze, 'European Energy Policy in Community Law', in Mestmäcker, E. (ed.), *Natural Gas in the Internal Market* (London: Graham & Trotman 1994)

Shu Yu, Z., 'The Proposed EU Energy Security Package vis-à-vis EU Law', 13(6) *European Environmental Law Review* (2004)

Siddiky, C.I.A, *Cross Border Pipeline Arrangement: What Would A Single Regulatory Framework Look Like?* (London: Kluwer Law International 2011)

Slot, P.J., 'Energy and Competition', 31 *CMLR* (1994)

Smith, E. and Cluchey, D., 'GATT, NAFTA and the Trade in Energy', 12(27) *Journal of Energy & Natural Resources Law* (1994)

Smith, E., Dzienkowski, J., Anderson, O., Lowe, J., Kramer, B., and Weaver, J., *International Petroleum Transactions* (Colorado: Rocky Mountain Mineral Law Foundation 2010)

Steen, N. (ed.), *Sustainable Development and the Energy Industries* (London: RIIA 1994)

Stern, J., *Competition and Liberalization of European Gas Markets RIIA* (London: RIIA 1998)

—— 'The Prospects for Third Party Access in European Gas Markets', in Mestmäcker, E. (ed.), *Natural Gas in the Internal Market—A Review of Energy Policy*, (London: Graham & Trotman 1993)

—— *Security of European Natural Gas Supplies: The Impact of Import Dependence and Liberalization* (London: RIIA 2002)

—— 'The Russia-Ukrainian Gas Crisis of January 2006', 4(1) *OGEL* (2006)

Stewart, R., 'Environmental Regulation and International Competitiveness', 102(2039) *Yale Law Journal* (1993)

Stevens, P., 'Oil Wars: Resource Nationalism and the Middle East', in Andrews-Speed, P. (ed.), *International Competition for Resources: The Role of Law, the State and of Markets* (Dundee: Dundee University Press 2008)

—— *The Arab Uprisings and the International Oil Markets* (London: Chatham House 2012)

Strange, S., *The retreat of the state: the diffusion of power in the world economy* (Cambridge: CUP 1996)

Talus, K., *Vertical Natural Gas Transportation Capacity, Upstream Commodity Contracts and EU Competition Law* (Alphen aan den Rijn: Kluwer Law International 2011)

—— 'Just What is the Scope of the Essential Facilities Doctrine in the Energy Sector: Third Party Access-friendly Interpretation in the EU v. Contractual Freedom in the US', 48(5) *Common Market Law Review* (2011)

—— 'Public-Private Partnerships in Energy—Termination of Public Service Concessions and Administrative Acts in Europe', (2)1 *Journal of World Energy Law and Business* (2009)

—— 'Access to Gas Markets: A Comparative Study on Access to LNG Terminals in the European Union and the United States', 31(2) *Houston Journal of International Law* (2009)

—— 'First Interpretation of Energy Market Directives by European Court of Justice—Case C-17/03, Vereniging voor Energie', 24 *Journal of Energy & Natural Resources Law* (2006)

—— 'Role of the European Court of Justice in the Opening of Energy Markets', 8(3) *ERA FORUM* (2007)

—— 'First Experience under the Exemption Regime of EC Regulation 1228/2003 on Conditions for Access to the Network of Cross-Border Exchanges in Electricity', 23 *Journal of Energy and Natural Resources Law* (2005) 266–81

—— 'Security of Supply—An Increasingly Political Notion', in Delvaux, B., Hunt, M., and Talus, K. (eds), *EU Energy Law and Policy Issues* (Brussels: Euroconfidentiel 2008)

—— 'Winds of Change: Long-term Gas Contracts and Changing Energy Paradigms in the European Union', in Kuzemko, C., Belyi, A., Goldthau, A., and Keating, M.F. (eds), *Dynamics of Energy Governance in Europe and Russia* (Houndmills: Palgrave MacMillan 2012)

—— 'Long-term Natural Gas Contracts and Antitrust Law in the European Union and the United States', 4(3) *Journal of World Energy Law and Business* (2011)

Talus, K. and Kuoppamäki, P., 'Relationship Between General Competition Laws and Sector Specific Energy Regulation', 1 *OGEL* (2010)

Talus, K. et al., *Energy Law of Finland* (Alphen aan den Rijn: Kluwer Law International 2010)

Talus, K. and Nunes, M.A., 'Regulation of Oil Imports in the United States and the European Union', 2 *OGEL* (2011)

Talus, K. and Wälde, T., 'Electricity Interconnectors—a Serious Challenge for EC Competition Law', 3 *Competition and Regulation in Network Industries* (2006)

Tridimas, T., 'Proportionality in Community Law: Searching for the Appropriate Standard of Scrutiny', in Ellis, E. (ed.), *The Principle of Proportionality in the Laws of Europe* (Oxford: Hart Publishing 1999)

Tscherning, R., 'The EU ETS Rules on Carbon Leakage and Energy Intensive Industry in the Federal Republic of Germany', 20 *European Energy and Environmental Law Review* (2011)

Tudway, R. (ed.), *Energy Law and Regulation in the EU* (London: Sweet & Maxwell 1999)

Tuori, K., 'The European Financial Crisis—Constitutional aspects and implications', *EUI Working Papers*, Law 2012/28

Udin, A., 'Slaying Goliath: The Extraterritorial Application of US Antitrust Law to OPEC', 50 *American University Law Review* (2001)

Ullrich, H., *The Evolution of European Competition Law—Whose Regulation, Which Competition?* (Cheltenham: Edward Elgar 2006)

Usher, J., *General Principles of EC Law* (London: Longman 1998)

Van Der Elst, R., 'Les Defis de la Nouvelle Directive sur les Energies Renouvelables', in Hirsbrunner, S., Buschle D., and Kaddous, C. (eds) *European Energy Law/Droit Européen de l'Energie* (Brussels: Bruylant 2011)

Van Der Vijver, T., 'Exemptions to Third Party Access for New Infrastructures in European Community Gas Sector—The Exception that Defies the Rule?', 29 *European Competition Law Review* (2008)

—— 'Commission Policy on Third-Party Access Exemption Requests for New Gas Infrastructure', in Roggenkamp, M. and Hammer, U., *European Energy Law Report VI* (Antwerp: Intersentia 2009)

Van der Vlies, R., 'The European Court's PreussenElektra Judgment: Tensions Between EU Principles and National Renewable Energy Initiatives', 22(10) *European Competition Law Review* (2001)

Van Hoorn, V., '"Unbundling", "Reciprocity" and the European Internal Energy Markets: WTO Consistency and Broader Implications for Europe', 18 *European Energy and Environmental Law Review* (2009)

Ward, H. and Brack, D. (eds), *Trade, Investment and the Environment* (London: RIIA 2001)

Vedder, H.H.B., 'The Climate Challenge to Competition', in Roggenkamp, M. and Hammer, U. (eds), *European Energy Law Report VII* (Antwerp: Intersentia 2011)

Weiler, J., 'Epilogue: Towards a Common Law of International Trade', in Weiler, J. (ed.), *The EU, the WTO and the NAFTA* (Oxford: OUP 2000)

Weiss, F., 'The Second Tuna Gatt Panel Report', 8(1) *Leiden Journal of International Law* (1995)

Westerhof, J.G., 'The Third Internal Market Package', in Roggenkamp, M. and Hammer, U., *European Energy Law Report VI*, (Antwerp: Intersentia 2009)

Weisser, H., 'The Security of Gas Supply—A Critical Issue for Europe?', 35(2) *Energy Policy* (2007)

Vermeir, T., 'Electricity Market Liberalisation and Supplier of Last Resort in Belgium', in Roggenkamp, M. and Hammer, U. (eds), *European Energy Law Report I* (Antwerp: Intersentia 2004)

Whish, R., *Competition Law* (Oxford: OUP 2009)

White, M., 'Carbon Capture and Storage: Becoming a Regulatory Reality in Europe', in Delvaux, B., Hunt, M., and Talus, K. (eds), *EU Energy Law and Policy Issues* (Brussels: Euroconfidentiel 2008)

Willems, A., Sul, J. and Benizri, Y., 'Unbundling as a Defence Mechanism against Russia: Is the EU Missing the Point?', in Talus, K. and Fratini, P., *EU-Russia Energy Relations* (Brussels: Euroconfidential 2010)

von Hirschhausen, C., Beckers T., and Brenck, A., 'Regulation and Long-Term Investment in Infrastructure Provision—Theory and Policy', 12(4) *Utilities Policy* (2004)

von Wilmowsky, P., 'Zugang zu den Boden und Sonstigen Naturschaetzen anderer Mitgliedsstaaten: EWG-Vertrag und US Verfassung im Vergleich', 54 *Rabelz Z* 693–732 (1990)

Wälde, T., 'A Requiem for the "New International Economic Order"', in Hafner, G. et al. (eds), *Festschrift Ignaz Seidl-Hohenveldern* (The Hague: Kluwer Law International 1998)

—— 'Comment on Einar Hope's Chapter with a Critical Review of Legal and Policy Arguments Driving the Discussion on Third Party Access', in Mestmäcker, E. (ed.), *Natural Gas in the Internal Market—A Review of Energy Policy* (London-Dordrecht-Boston: Graham & Trotman 1993)

—— 'Die Regelung der britischen Energiewirtschaft nach der Privatisierung', in Tettinger, P. (ed.), *Strukturen der Versorgungswirtschaft in Europa* (Stuttgart: Boorberg 1996)

—— 'Developing a Framework for Russian Oil & Gas Legislation: Will a Russian Model Emerge?', 3(2) *Butterworths Central & East European Business Law* (1993)

—— 'International Investment under the 1994 Energy Charter Treaty', 29 *Journal of World Trade* (1995)

—— 'Environmental Policies Towards Mining in Developing Countries', 10(4) *Journal of Energy and Natural Resources Law* (1992)

—— (ed.), *European Community Energy Law—Selected Topics* (London: Graham & Trotman/M. Nijhoff 1994)

—— 'International Good Governance and Civilised Conduct among the Caspian Sea States: Oil and Gas Lever for Prosperity of Conflict', in Ascher, W. and Mirovitskaya, N., *The Caspian Sea: A Quest for Environmental Security* (London: Kluwer 2000)

—— 'Managing the Risk of Sanctions in the Global Oil and Gas Industry', 36 *Texas International Law Journal* (2001)

—— 'Sustainable Development and the 1994 Energy Charter Treaty: Between Pseudo-action and the Management of Environmental Investment Risk', in Weiss, F. et al. (eds), *International Economic Law with a Human Face* (London: Kluwer Law 1998)

—— (ed.), *The Energy Charter Treaty: An East-West Gateway for Investment and Trade* (London: Kluwer Law International 1996)

—— 'The Rule of Law and the Resource Industries' Cycles', in Andrews-Speed, P. (ed.), *International Competition for Resources: The Role of Law, the State and of Markets* (Dundee: Dundee University Press 2008)

—— 'The Russian Oil & Gas Industry and Foreign Investment', *Opec-Bulletin*, 25 (July 1994) 16–21 Bulletin, Vol. 3, No.2, March (1993)

Wälde, T. and Gunderson, J., 'Legislative Reform in Transition Economies', 43 *International & Comparative Law Quarterly* (1994)

Wälde, T. and Kolo, A., 'Environmental Regulation, Investment Protection and "Regulatory Taking" in International Law', 50 *ICLQ* (2001)

Wälde, T., and MacDougall, D., *European Community Energy Law* (London: Kluwer 1994)

Wälde, T. and von Hirschhausen, C., 'Legislative Reform in the Energy Industry of Post-Soviet Societies', in Seidman, R., Seidman, A., and Wälde, T., *Making Development Work: Legislative Reform for Good Governance* (London: Kluwer 1999)

Yafimava, K., *The Transit Dimension of EU Energy Security: Russian Gas Transit Across Ukraine, Belarus and Moldova* (Oxford: OUP 2011)

Yergin, D., *The Prize* (New York: Free Press 1991)

Zenke, I., 'The Merger of E.ON and Ruhrgas: A Never-Ending Story?', 1 *OGEL* (2003)

Zimmermann, Z., 'Do Electric Interconnectors Improve Long-Term Security of Electricity Supply?', 5(1) *OGEL* (2007)

Index